Praise for Jan Yager's

CREATIVE TIME MANAGEMENT FOR THE NEW MILLENNIUM

"Without a doubt, this is the best book on time management I have read in a very long time. Dr. Yager's approach to the biggest challenge we all face each day is well organized, direct, and easy to follow...Dr. Yager not only identifies time wasters, but gives you the tools to eliminate them..."

—Debbie Williams, organizer, www.organizedu.com

"In an age when everyone seems to have too much to do and too little time to do it, this thorough, well-written guide will enable you to get more done, and feel better doing it. The last chapter alone ("125 Top Time-Saving Ideas") is worth the price of the whole book."

—Mark Sanborn, CSP, CPAE, author and seminar leader

"To get control of your time, your work, your technical gadgets, and your personal life, read *Creative Time Management for the New Millennium*. The practical hands-on advice will repay you many times over."

—Michael LeBoeuf, Ph.D., author, *Working Smart*

"Here's an excellent super-guide to gaining control over your time and your life."

—Lucy H. Hedrick, author, *Five Days to an Organized Life*

"A pragmatic, easy to digest road map to true understanding of effectively managing your precious resource of time."

—Bob Danzig, former President, Hearst Newspapers

"The ideas and insights in *Creative Time Management for the New Millennium* will transform your hectic life into an organized journey."

—Glenna Salsbury, CSP, CPAE, author and professional speaker

Selected Nonfiction Books by Jan Yager, Ph.D.
(a/k/a J. L. Barkas/Janet Lee Barkas)

Making Your Office Work for You

Business Protocol

How to Write Like a Professional

Friendshifts®: The Power of Friendship and How It Shapes Our Lives

Single in America

The Help Book

Victims

The Vegetable Passion: A History of the Vegetarian State of Mind

CREATIVE TIME MANAGEMENT FOR THE NEW MILLENNIUM

Jan Yager, Ph.D.

Hannacroix Creek Books, Inc.   Stamford, CT

Copyright © 1999 by Jan Yager, Ph.D.

(Please note: Dr. Jan Yager's first time management book, *Creative Time Management*, was published by Prentice Hall, Inc. in 1984 under the author's maiden name, J.L. Barkas. That book went out of print in 1991; all rights reverted to the author. This second time managment book began as a 2nd edition of that first book, completely revised and updated, but it evolved into a new book.)

All rights reserved. This book, or parts thereof, may not be reproduced in any form without permission from the publisher; exceptions are made for brief excerpts used in published reviews.
Author cover photograph by Fred Yager.

Published by Hannacroix Creek Books, Inc.
1127 High Ridge Road, PMB 110
Stamford, CT 06905-1203
Phone (203) 321-8674 Fax (203) 968-0193
E-mail: hannacroix@aol.com Web site: http://www.Hannacroix.com

Cataloging-in-Publication Data *(Provided by Quality Books, Inc.)*
Yager, Jan, 1948-
        Creative time management for the new millennium : become more productive and still have time for fun / Jan Yager.
        p. cm.
        Includes bibliographical references and index.
        ISBN: 1-889262-15-3 (cloth)
        ISBN: 1-889262-20-X (paperback)

        1.   Time management. I. Title
        HD69.T54Y34 1998   640'.43
                         QBI98-1096
Library of Congress Preassigned Catalog Card number: 98-73527

1st and 2nd printings of the paperback printed in Canada.
Beginning with 3rd printing, POD (Print-on-Demand) in the United States.
Hardcover printed in the United States.

This publication is designed to provide accurate and authoritative information with regard to the subject matter covered. It is sold with the understanding that the publisher is not engaged in rendering legal, accounting, or other professional advice. If legal advice or other expert assistance is required, the services of a competent professional person should be sought.
—From a *Declaration of Principles* jointly adopted by a Committee of the American Bar Association and a Committee of Publishers and Associations

Trademarks: All brand names and product names used in this book are trade names, service marks, trademarks, or registered trademarks of their respective owners.

Dedicated to my husband, Fred;
our sons, Scott and Jeffrey;
my mother; my sister, Eileen;
my extended family; my friends;
my colleagues, clients, and readers;
and the memory of
my father and my brother

Author's Note and Disclaimer

I retained from the first book, *Creative Time Management*, whatever classic guidelines are still valid today. However, I also added extensive new information and concepts based on original research I have conducted over the last decade as well as adding more contemporary examples. For example, to bring the basic time management information of *Creative Time Management* into the new millennium, I distributed an extensive work survey completed by 234 working men and women throughout the United States and in more than a dozen countries. (For more details about my credentials, see About the Author on the last page of this book.)

Quotes in this book not attributed to a secondary source are from the original research conducted by the author, in the form of either interviews or questionnaires, and are reprinted verbatim and, if necessary, excerpted. If editing of a quote was required for either sense or clarification, those additions or changes are indicated by brackets.

If anonymity was requested, a fictitious first name has been provided; identifying details have also been changed to maintain that anonymity. However, care has been taken to preserve the integrity of each example.

Secondary sources cited within the text have complete bibliographic entries in the Bibliography.

The purpose of this book is to provide inspiration, information, and opinions on the topics covered. It is sold with the understanding that neither the publisher nor the author are engaged in rendering psychological, medical, sociological, legal, or other professional services.

Typographical or content mistakes may be unwittingly contained in this book. In addition, information may be out of date because it was unavailable until after the date of the book's completion, printing, or distribution.

The author and publisher shall have neither liability nor responsibility to any person or entity with regard to any loss or damage caused, or alleged to be caused, directly or indirectly by the opinions or information contained in this book.

Contents

1 CREATIVE TIME MANAGEMENT: **1**
AN INTRODUCTION
What is Creative Time Management?
What are the Benefits of Creative Time Management?
Could Your Time Management Skills Use Improvement?
Fortunately You *Can* Change How You Manage Your Time
Workaholism
Pacing Yourself
Technology and Time Management

2 THE 7 PRINCIPLES OF CREATIVE TIME   **10**
MANAGEMENT
1 - Be active, not reactive.
2 - Set goals.
3 - Prioritize actions.
4 - Keep your focus.
5 - Create realistic deadlines.
6 - D-O I-T N-O-W.
7 - Balance your life.

3 OVERCOMING 10 KEY OBSTACLES   **14**
TO MANAGING YOUR TIME
Doing Too Much At Once
Inability to Say "No"
Procrastination
Paperwork
The Terrible Twos: Telephone and Television
Failure to Prioritize
Commuting and Travel Time
Complaining
Excuses

4 EMOTIONAL BLOCKS   31
TO TIME MANAGEMENT

Perfectionism
Fear of Failure
Fear of Success
Devaluing (or Overvaluing) of Your Activities
Impatience and Low Frustration Tolerance
Jealousy
The Inability to Take Criticism
Boredom
Guilt
Selflessness
Being in Love, and Other Emotional Issues
Bad Habits
Lateness

5 BECOMING ORGANIZED AND   61
MORE EFFECTIVE

Getting Organized
    Becoming Organized is a Trait You Can Learn
    Distinguishing Daily Priorities from Busywork
    Sharpening Decision-Making Skills
Organizing Tools and Techniques
    "To Do" Lists
    Creating a Personal Planning Calendar
    The Everything Notebook
    File Systems
        The 30-Day File Diet
Organizing Your Office
    Health Considerations
    Organizing Your Desk
    Books, Magazines, and Other Reading Materials
    In the Home Office

6 IMPROVING YOUR TIME AT WORK   85

Understanding Your Work Environment
    Becoming More Efficient
    Correspondence and Paperwork
    Technology and Tools for Effective Time Management

Computers
E-mail and the Internet
The Scanner
The Fax Machine
The Telephone
Dealing With Visitor Interruptions
Time Off (Vacations, Sick Days, Personal Leave)
Efficiency Breaks
Working With Others
Delegating
Working With Superiors
Compulsive Talkers
Working Too Much
Making the Most of Meetings
Improving Communication at Work
Work Goals
Long-range Planning
Progress Reports
Measuring Your Success

7   APPLYING TIME MANAGEMENT   117
The Concept of Time
Making Productive Use of your "Hidden" Time
Using Your Energy Highs and Lows
Structuring Time
For "Nine-to-fivers" or Executive Time
For the Self-employed and Freelancers
For the Creative Person
For Small Business Owners
For Students
For Teachers
For the Job Seeker
Balancing Work and Home Life

**8   IMPROVING YOUR PERSONAL   143
TIME MANAGEMENT**
Exercise
Hobbies
Television

C O N T E N T S

Relationships
  Socializing/Entertaining
  Friendships
  Making Time for Partners and Children
  Time for Yourself
Time Management at Home
  Becoming Organized at Home
  Household Responsibilities
  Household Projects
  Household Maintenance

9   125 TOP TIME-SAVING IDEAS   164
The Top Ten Time-Saving Ideas
 Basic Principles
Goal Setting
Organizing
Overcoming Time Management Obstacles
  (Time Wasters)
Equipment and Technology
Work Time
Delegating
Shopping
Office or Household Maintenance
Holiday Time
Personal Time

SELECTED BIBLIOGRAPHY   175

INDEX   177

ABOUT THE AUTHOR   182

1
Creative Time Management: An Introduction

Lost time is never found again.
    —BENJAMIN FRANKLIN (*Poor Richard's Almanac*)

What is Creative Time Management?

Managing your time well means managing your life well. People who handle their time well do it creatively. They show certain characteristics that separate them from those who are usually in a state of unprepared frenzy. They make short- and long-term plans, set and keep realistic schedules, take efficient and timely breaks, and view tasks to be done as opportunities rather than dreaded obligations. They practice creative time management by taking control of their time and therefore their life.

We are not all endowed with brilliance, good looks, or lots of money, but we each get the same number of hours every day. A great deal may be achieved in those 24 hours, or not much at all. It is up to you to make optimum use of those hours.

What Are the Benefits of Creative Time Management?

The most important benefit of creative time management is

that it enables you to feel in control of your life. Those who feel in control of their lives experience less stress, are more relaxed, productive, self-satisfied, and live longer.

Poor time management causes missed deadlines, unfinished projects, disappointed employers, annoyed clients, cancelled appointments, and unfulfilled career aspirations. It can also lead to heightened tension, anger, embarrassment, low self-esteem, and depression. It can cause problems in marriage or romantic relationships as busy couples find there is never enough time to be intimate or spend quality time together. It can be a factor in children growing up strangers to their parents, or potential friendships that never progress beyond acquaintanceships.

In the years I have been researching time management, I discovered a common time management problem shared by those who are usually busy but rarely able to accomplish as much as they want to or know they are capable of achieving: They are *reactive*, rather than *active*, persons. They react to external demands on them, whether for a report due on Friday or a party they are invited to on Saturday, rather than acting according to long-term goals they have set for themselves within which most short-term decisions are made.

Furthermore, the necessity to prioritize what is important usually becomes clear when they get attacks of "if only" ("I wouldn't have been late if only I hadn't answered the phone on my way out," "If only I hadn't started working on that other assignment before I finished rewriting that report") as well as during those moments of pride when the rewards are most obvious — having work done on time, getting to a meeting on time, getting promoted, finishing an in-depth training program, being asked to make a presentation about what you do, publishing a book, feeling in control and on top of your work or family demands.

Through my interviews, observations, and research, I have discovered that most men and women share the same goal: a full life, not a life that is weighted too heavily toward work, family, or leisure activities. The man who never exercises or does anything for himself (until he has a heart attack) because he is attending only to his job and family is someone in need of creative time management as much as the woman who is juggling all her commitments so vigorously—spouse, job, children—that she lacks a moment to put up her feet and just relax.

Could Your Time Management Skills Use Improvement?

To help you determine just how productive you really are, take this five-question self-evaluation. On a piece of paper, or on your computer, answer each question with a *yes, no,* or *sometimes.*

1. Do you make a conscientious effort to separate urgent matters from other demands?
2. Do you take the time to do enough background research so you can make the best possible decisions?
3. Do you allocate at least one hour each day for uninterrupted time for thinking, reading, planning, or creative work?
4. Do you spend sufficient time developing and maintaining business and personal relationships?
5. Do you work hard to do your best—rather than measuring yourself by a standard equated with unattainable perfection?

If you answered *yes* to all five questions, at least on these five issues your time management skills are excellent.

If you answered *no* or *sometimes* to one or more questions, you will benefit by improving your time management skills.

You may already suspect that how you handle your time could be enhanced since you are probably more stressed than you would like to be, busier than usual though getting less done, or finding yourself saying, more and more often, "I just don't have the time."

Read on. You will find knowledge, skills, and help in the pages that follow to give you the competitive edge, and peace of mind, that creative time management provides.

Fortunately You Can Change How You Manage Your Time

Slogans—"Make every day count," "Live each day as if it were your last," "Life is a process, not an event"—provide overall philosophies. However, those phrases do not tell you *how* to apply those philosophies to daily life.

Creative Time Management for the New Millennium will help you pinpoint how you currently manage your time, how you would like to manage it, what's stopping you, and ways to achieve your "ideal" for work, school, or leisure hours.

There will certainly be times in your life when you feel breathless, frenzied, and driven by how little time you feel you have to do all that you want to do, or to be with the people you want to be with. But if you pause long enough to apply to your day the time management techniques that work – prioritizing, breaking huge tasks into manageable pieces, dealing effectively with telephone calls or E-mail, understanding what is behind a specific time management obstacle that slows you down, such as an inability to say "no", so you can overcome it – you will more quickly gain control of yourself, your demands, and your time.

Less stress is definitely an outcome of better time management; effectively managing your time will certainly help you accomplish more, in less time, at work as well as help you make better decisions about what to do with your time in the first place.

Initially there may be frustrations when you take charge of your life and time, but this is only temporary. Fortunately you will quickly see benefits as well, not to mention the permanent and greater long-term gains. This is not the same thing as becoming so narcissistic that everything and everyone is measured by "What does this time demand mean to me?" Sometimes, for example, it may be in your best interest to put others before yourself, sometimes not. Example: You are working on an important assignment. The phone rings. Your friend is upset and wants to talk for ten minutes. You say you don't have the time. Your friend is disappointed. You have that ten minutes for your work, but in the long run, was working on your report the best use of those ten minutes? A creative way to handle that same situation might be to say to your friend, "I have a deadline so I can't talk now. When could I call you back tonight so we could talk?"

The goal of this book is to help you make those crucial judgments about how you spend your time. As each day is spent more efficiently and creatively, you will achieve more in the short run, as well as attaining more of your long-range work and personal goals. That will all add up to a more fulfilling life.

How one manages one's time will depend on where one is in one's life cycle, which, today, has a wider variation than even, say, twenty years ago. A thirty-two-year old woman gives up her job in Manhattan as a magazine editor to begin medical school in Colorado. A sixty-year-old man gives up smoking and devotes more time to exercise than at any time since high school. A thirty-eight-year-old man, a new father, considers trading his freelance writing career for the steady pay check of a corporate position. A forty-year-old woman, faced with her teenager's imminent departure from home, thinks about what full-time work she now wants to do. A twenty-two-year-old college senior wonders if she should get a public relations job or attend graduate school.

There are practical tips in this book about managing your time that will help you spend your time more productively. Used wisely, the phone can be a terrific time saver; for many of us, it wastes hours of time, interrupting projects and in-person conversations. Doing the paper shuffle can consume valuable time; managing your files well could be a time saver. Getting organized refers to such specific techniques as creating an effective "things to do" list; it also involves learning more basic organizing principles that will help you to organize your life, not just your books and files.

Workaholism

Workaholism is often a symptom of poor time management: an inability to begin, pursue, and complete a project leads the workaholic to focus solely on the project. The squeaky wheel gets all the grease and the other wheels get none; the job becomes all. As one reluctant workaholic somewhat breathlessly put it, "I keep working around the clock because I hope somehow I'll get everything done so someday I won't have to work so hard." Pacing yourself, and gaining control of your time, lets you accomplish what you value at work, in school, or at home, and gives you more time for friends, family, and leisure activities. It also helps avert burnout—total loss of initiative or of the ability to continue work toward accomplishing the task at hand. Poor time management can cause the burnout syndrome; even if some key goals are achieved, it is only at enormous personal and professional cost.

Judy, 44, a working mother of two teenagers, was interviewed while on vacation for a week with several women coworkers and friends: "I work in the hospital's maternity ward as a nurse-midwife six days a week, and at the supermarket Saturdays, and on my day off. My children are in high school now, so they can take care of themselves, and my husband's fairly self-sufficient. I like the work I do and I'm never bored. I'm glad I went back to school at age forty, even though, at the time, everyone thought I was crazy."

Judy initially sounded like an effective and rewarded manager of her time. And while she's at work, she is. But upon further questioning, it appeared that not having a set routine while on vacation disoriented her. She finds waking up at seven every day, and having a set number of tasks to perform, more "relaxing" than the unstructured environment of a week in the sun. Judy may be an achiever, but it appears to have cost her a great deal. She is severely overweight, smokes, and a compulsive talker.

We all know people like Judy, competent in one setting, but tense and insecure in others, and we strive for life management that is effective in a variety of work and leisure settings.

Pacing Yourself

Warren, 32, a health care professional, is able to take off Wednesdays during the week. He also never works weekends, unless there is an emergency. "Taking Wednesdays off gives me the ability, energy, and incentive to do my best when I am at work," he explains. "It makes a difference." Sometimes his friends suggest that he would earn more money by working more days; he feels it might be a short-lived gain, since the quality of his work might suffer, along with his job satisfaction.

A freelance researcher has similarly evolved a professionally and personally satisfying work routine. Because his job is physically and emotionally demanding, requiring intense concentration and long hours in front of his computer, he works in two- to three-hour stretches. He uses rest periods to go running, play tennis, place or return phone calls, do grocery shopping, and similar tasks unrelated to work. In this way, he is able to put in twelve-to-fourteen hour work days in his home-based office with enthusiasm and without physical or mental exhaustion. His pattern is the opposite of those heading toward burnout who work like crazy for days, months, even years, tuning out most other considerations only to find, once the project is finished, or their energy is completely diminished, they need weeks, months, or sometimes years to sort out the resultant mess in their lives (and to their health).

Those who work in outside offices are also trying to pace themselves better. Job sharing or flexible hours is becoming more acceptable with time working at home or time on the road counting as a day's work. Those who work away from an outside office, if they are able to handle the social or business isolation it may cause, often remark how much more productive they are without the constant interruptions that they had to cope with in the office.

Being effective, whether you work in an outside office, travel a great deal for your job, or work in a home office, does not always mean working longer hours, or even harder. It may even mean working fewer hours; it may mean changing where and when you work, or it may mean trying to do something in a different way.

Consider a married woman, 29, who had her first child last year. A child care worker looks after the infant while she and her husband are at their offices. Before the baby was born, she was in her office by eight, and did not leave till 6:30 or 7:00 each evening. Now, because of the baby, she does not arrive till nine, and always leaves by 5:00. "I'm amazed that I don't find that my productivity has suffered," she told me. "A lot of that early and late stuff was for show. The only difference now is that I return more phone calls the next day, rather than right away, but I've found the calls can wait until the next day." Although some managers may disagree about the wisdom of letting calls wait, she feels she has adjusted her time to manage her work- and home-related responsibilities more effectively, even though she now has more demands on her time.

For her, the key to her creative time management was her ability to set – and work toward – clear goals in both her professional and personal life. The other key for her was learning her limitations: the thesis she had been writing to complete her master's degree had to be put aside for a year. "I'll get back to it," she says confidently and convincingly.

Technology and Time Management

Over the last decade, there have been numerous changes in the every day world of work, most notably technological advances, such as the widespread use of personal computers and fax machines, the popular use of the Internet, E-mail, cell (mobile) phones, and beepers. With the Internet, we all now have the ability to communicate instantaneously with others, near or far. But for some, the Internet has actually become their new time problem, as they spend hours each day "on line," neglecting their business priorities or even their family obligations.

Because of technology, more is now expected of us in terms of the quality of our work, how much we can accomplish, as well as the speed with which we can achieve or produce it. But technology can only improve our efficiency so far. Word processors or computers may facilitate the physical act of writing or typing and editing or rewriting, but the creative part, the inspiration, the unique way of expressing thoughts and ideas, is still up to each individual, and it unfolds in as mysterious a way as it did before.

Look at the multitude of ways that technology has made it possible to communicate with each other beyond the traditional telephone. Cell (mobile) phones have brought telephone service to people in remote areas who were cut off from telephone service in the past. Beepers enable sending a message to someone who is on the road or away from a telephone. However, beepers and cell phones have made it easier to be interrupted, 24 hours a day, including weekends and holidays, necessitating even greater control over how you self-manage your time than ever before.

Advertising executive Charles Peebler reminds us all about the human element that is still pivotal despite technology:

> Clearly, technology, from computers to executive "toys," has changed the landscape of communications. And I use most of the available tools. But I remain *insistent* that on key issues--matters of urgency and sensitivity, when nuance and judgment are criticial-- that nothing beats *face-to-face* discussion.

The Internet is a valuable tool to quickly access research and information to augment or replace time-consuming research trips. However, regular library visits are still irreplaceable social, community, and intellectual meeting centers for youth and adults.

There is also an information explosion because of technology—there are just more books being written, more information available that needs to be read and digested.

Word processors and computers have made it mandatory to have "letter-perfect" correspondence but perfection is time consuming, and often with little or no support staff to make those changes. Why not just pick up the phone and call to avoid such formalities? Because writing a formal letter on good quality letterhead may be preferred, not calling or sending a fax or E-mail.

Creative Time Management for the New Millennium will help you to spend each day more efficiently as you achieve more in the short-run and more of your long-range goals. That combination will add up to a more successful career and a more fulfilling and less-stressful life. Since most everyone agrees that "time is money," improving your time management skills is a wise use of your time.

The next chapter is a presentation and discussion of the 7 principles of creative time management.

2

The 7 Principles of Creative Time Management

Here are the fundamental principles of creative time management:

1. Be Active, Not Reactive.

Make *active* decisions about how you spend your time instead of *reacting* to every demand on you, whether it is someone calling you on the phone at that very moment or being asked to become membership chair for your professional association.

You decide what is important to you, and you say "no" to anything that intereferes.

It will be much easier to be active if you also follow principle #2, namely, setting goals.

2. Set Goals.

By setting goals you know where you are going. Goals are necessary, at work, school, or play. Without them you flounder, and react erratically to opportunities and problems, with little perspective on the effects they will have on your personal and professional life.

Do you have a grand scheme? At certain times in life it's easier to realize that you need a master plan—for example, when you're in high school or college and practically everyone is making major life decisions—where to go to school, or what subjects or career to pursue. Once a path is decided upon, law school or acting, for example, and once a career is started, it's easy to get caught up in earning a living, dating or marrying, and raising a family. The time for a "grand scheme" may seem to be behind you.

It's not! No matter what age you are, you can develop daily, weekly, yearly, or longer-range goals to guide you. That does not mean becoming such a future-oriented person that you fail to enjoy the present. What it does mean is that by setting goals you can better manage your time and life today.

3. Prioritize actions.

Once you establish your goals, you need to prioritize your activities to achieve those goals. Prioritizing means creating a plan of action. Keep in mind the principle of nineteenth-century Italian economist and sociologist Vilfredo Pareto, Pareto's 80/20 principle, that 20 percent of what you do will give you 80 percent of your results. The key to prioritizing is carefully identifying the right 20 percent of your activities, and making them priorities.

Prioritizing, creating specific goals for each day or hour, and then accomplishing each task before going on to the next, will also help overcome the "I'm doing too much as once" syndrome.

Keep in mind that prioritizing may be stressful since it means putting some people or things ahead of others to get the priority job done.

4. Keep your focus.

Maximize your productivity by concentrating on one major project at a time. Once you have set your goals and prioritized your actions, stay on track until that project is completed. Whatever it is you're doing, give it your all.

Try to simplify your goals, and set short-range priorities, by dividing your goal into a noun and a verb. Just two words. If it's more than two or three words, you may be the victim of muddy thinking or goal overload — wanting to accomplish too many goals at once, and juggling too many demands on you simultaneously, you are encouraging yourself to fail at any one of them.

Sometimes the verb-noun principle is cloudy; if you are dissatisfied at the office, you have to clarify your verb-noun principle to improve your situation. Is it "get a raise?" "Change departments?" "Work shorter hours?" "Vary duties?"

Once you decide on your verb-noun principle, you can consider the actions you need to do that will aid your achievement of that goal. Whatever you do (how you spend your time) should be in the service of fulfilling your verb-noun goal.

5. Create realistic deadlines.

Deadlines, especially if realistic, help keep you focused on specific long-term goals and especially on short-term priorities. You should not dread a deadline but welcome it. If someone else does not impose a deadline on you and your work, create deadlines for yourself.

It is also useful to create a to-do list of projects or goals, but you also have to estimate how long it will take you to complete each task so you can specify concrete deadlines. If you have done a similar task in the past, consider how long it took you previously. If this project is new, your estimates may be more ideal than real. (If you are like most people, you probably underestimate completion time, especially if it involves research, writing, creativity, or working with others. Add ten to twenty percent to your estimate so you are more likely to come out on time.)

6. D-O I-T N-O-W.

Once you decide on a plan and are focused, just do it *now*.

Here is an easy way to help you remember this principle:

D = Divide and conquer what you have to do.

Break big tasks into little tasks and give each part of that task a realistic deadline.

O = Organize your materials, how you will do it.

I = Ignore interruptions that are annoying distractions.

T = Take the time to learn how to do things yourself.

N = Now, not tomorrow. Don't procrastinate.

O = Opportunity is knocking.Take advantage of opportunities.

W = Watch out for time gobblers. Keep track of, and in control of, how much time you spend on the Internet, reading and sending E-mails, watching TV, or talking on the phone.

7. Balance your life.

The 7th principle means creating time for yourself as well as for those you care about--romantic partner, children, parents, siblings, extended family, friends, neighbors, volunteer groups, colleagues, even pets. While becoming more productive at work is certainly a worthwhile goal, having a fuller, more productive and balanced life is even better. So remember to apply these creative time management principles not only to work, but to relationships and leisure activities as well.

The next chapter will examine ten key obstacles to creative time management and how to overcome them.

3
Overcoming 10 Key Obstacles to Managing Your Time

Procrastination is the thief of time.
    EDWARD YOUNG (*Night Thoughts*)

A common misconception about time is that you can waste it. You can't waste time, but you can mismanage it. This chapter examines 10 ways people mismanage their time, providing possible solutions for overcoming those tendencies.

Doing Too Much At Once

I recently conducted a survey of 234 working men and women to determine how people mismanage their time. I was sure the number one way was going to be procrastination. But that came in a distant second (8%), and virtually tied with the 3rd, 4th, and 5th reasons, namely an inability to say "no," paperwork, and perfectionism.

    The #1 reason given for mismanaging time by the most people was "trying to do too much at once" (33%).

    If you think you have too many things to do, you're probably right.

Of course we all have many things to do. The key is how to get everything you have to do accomplished effectively and efficiently in as systematic a way as possible.

Where most run into trouble is when you try to do everything at once so nothing gets done; then you feel like a miserable failure.

You know your situations, your capacities, and your limitations best. As one working woman put it, "I take on so much that all of a sudden I just feel panicked, and I start screwing everything up."

Take on as many tasks as you can competently handle and still meet your deadlines. For some, it's only one; for others, two or three. You need to critically assess your limits and capabilities.

If you have the tendency to do too many things at once, you will have to recognize it, understand it, and force yourself to finish obligations before you begin new ones.

Here are tips to deal with "doing too much at once":

Solution #1 - Prioritize all you have to do in a list, with the most important thing first.

Solution #2 - Use your list to focus on doing one thing at a time.

Solution #3 - Do not start the next task until you've completed the first one.

Solution #4 - Use selective attention.

If you need variety in what you do, rather than sticking to only one job until it is completed, consider the time effective way that the late Isaac Asimov, author of more than 280 books, coped with that by practicing selective attention. He had four major projects that he worked on "at once," but when he was working on any one of those four projects, that one project—whatever stage it was in— had his full attention. (For some, however, shifting gears and going back and forth among several projects throws them off. In that case, a strict one-project-till-finished rule may be what's needed.)

In summary, to overcome your "doing too much at once" syndrome, prioritize, creating clear, specific goals for each day, and each hour (or period) of the day, accomplishing each goal or task before going on to the next one. Decide which tasks require your exclusive attention and which ones you can do simultaneously. You can listen to the radio while driving your car, but you can't read the newspaper. You can read the newspaper or watch TV while working out on a stationary bicycle, but you probably couldn't read a complicated technical report while exercising.

The Inability to Say "No"

Quite often, behind the "doing too many things at once" syndrome is someone who can't say "no." Saying "yes" when you should say "no" arises from the childish wish to please everyone, and represents a failure to adequately define what's important to you. It's hard to say "no." You may fear an opportunity will never come again, or that saying "no" will hurt someone's feelings forever.

Solution #1 - Simplify your goals.

Saying " no"—gracefully—is a two-step process. You decide what your needs and limits are, and then you say "no" to whatever interferes.

You are saying " no" because whatever is asked of you is not the best use of your time right now.

Solution #2 - Practice saying "no" in a way that is kind, gentle, and positive.

It's not the fact that you're saying "no" that usually alienates someone, but *how* you express yourself. Tell the truth but be diplomatic not cruel, express your gratitude for the invitation and, if appropriate, suggest another time to get together, or when to get back to you when you might say "yes" or at least reconsider your "no."

Solution #3 - Desensitize yourself to the word "no."

What do you do if you just can't say the word "no"? The word just never seems to come out of your mouth (although after you get off the phone, or later on, you wish it had).

Write the word in big letters by your telephone or computer, or on the desk where you answer your mail. Don't be wishy washy and say "maybe" if a tactful and firm "no" is what's needed.

Solution #4 - Be clear you are saying "no" to a request but not rejecting the person making the request.

When you do mean "No, never," you can reject the request without dismissing the person asking it. Too often someone with a problem of saying "no" gracefully turns against the person who makes the demand. (A variation on the "blame the messenger for the bad news" syndrome.)

Solution #5 - Handle it as a "No, not this, but..."

If at all possible, turning a flat "no" into a "No, not this, but" may be a good time saver because it enables you to turn almost any "no" situation into an opportunity. Example: after a job interview, you decide this is not the right position for you. How you handle "No, not this, but" may mean the difference between the interaction between you and the interviewer leading to a dead-end versus turning it into a possible future opportunity. You may want to impress the interviewer so that she might someday consider you for a job that is for you. Or you may want to ensure a positive report about you to the referral or employment agency, which will then try even harder to work on your behalf.

The situations to which "No, not this, but" applies are innumerable. You are being considered for a teaching position but making a commitment to a weekly class is not possible right now because of your other responsibilities. You handle the "no" in such a positive way that a year later, after another networking "hello, this is what I'm up to" phone call, you are invited, for a fee, to teach several classes for just one day.

Creatively handling "No, not this, but" encounters will enable you to turn chances that are less than ideal into options – now or in the future. Most important of all, it will help you overcome your inability to say "no" (which probably gets you into a "doing too much at once" syndrome.)

Procrastination

Procrastination means putting off until tomorrow anything that you are supposed to do today. But the very act of delay may have consequences; if you delay making airline reservations long enough you may be forced to take a 6 a.m. flight because everything else is booked or, worse yet, have to take a train or drive (if that is even feasible) because everything is booked. If you miss the deadline for a conference, the registration fee may be much higher, or registration may be filled and closed out so you are unable to attend at all. If you wait so long before you start a project that you lack adequate time to do a good job on it, you've given yourself a less than optimal chance to succeed.

Here are several solutions for overcoming procrastination:

Solution #1 - Make whatever you are procrastinating about the very first task you do that day.

Force yourself to do what you have to do first thing in the morning, as soon as you wake up, or as your first task at work, before going on to anything else. "Hold all calls" if necessary till you get that project or commitment done.

Solution #2 - Try the reward system.

Make sure the reward that you decide on is something you truly enjoy so you'll have the motivation to keep at your necessary task.

Solution #3 - Try creative procrastination.

Another solution to procrastination is *creative procrastination*. It's creative because it helps you to achieve your overall goal by reordering short-term priorities (or steps) so that energy-sapping "blocks" are avoided. Although you temporarily avoid one unpleasant task by replacing it with a pleasant one, you discipline yourself to choose a pleasant one related to your overall goal. For example, you have to write up a report and you've reached a point where you find yourself putting it off and getting involved in distractions and less important things, like chatting with a co-worker or surfing the Internet. (Unfortunately some other "things," like starting another report, may generate more tasks, and related activities, that get you committed to tasks that you may, again, procrastinate about accomplishing.)

Instead of procrastinating by making a call to a friend—and not really enjoying the conversation because you feel guilty that you are procrastinating— you accomplish tasks related to your number one project. Let's say your report requires a bibliography. Instead of calling your friend when you are blocked on writing the report, you work on the report's bibliography. Another example: you have correspondence to do and you're procrastinating so at least you address the envelopes, or gather the necessary documentation to write the letters, rather than switch to an unrelated task.

Creative procrastination allows you to deviate from your ideal of working sequentially, from task to task, until you're done, but you will probably get the job done in the same, or even less, time. This method requires flexibility in your approach to your tasks (and it may not work in all situations), but for projects comprised of numerous steps it can help you to conquer a seeming insurmountable tendency to delay.

Solution #4 - Allow for delays.

Like all solutions you have to be careful that "allowing" yourself to procrastinate does not get out of hand so that you permanently avoid an unpleasant task. Sometimes just an hour, a day, or a week away from the task you are procrastinating about will provide the necessary energy, and motivation, to go forward with that task. (You may also find that an external motivation occurs to prompt you along: "The moving men are coming in two days" can inspire you to finish the packing you put off for two months.)

Procrastination may be tied to perfectionism in that you want, or need, to perform in a way that conforms to an unrealistic standard of excellence. Giving yourself permission to "goof off" or have a period of controlled procrastination may help you deal with this common problem without guilt or self-downing. "I'll call to cancel my reservation after I read this newspaper article" is more efficient than putting off the phone call, spending more time reminding yourself to do it than the time it will take to actually call.

You reap the benefits of licking procrastination, just as you pay the most for failing to overcome it. In some situations, however, delay is necessary or beneficial—e.g., planning something before doing it, completing your most important goal before your secondary ones. The trick is to know the difference between effective and self-indulgent procrastination.

Solution #5 - Don't let embarrassment exacerbate your procrastination.

The worst thing procrastinators can do is to abandon an important goal, or task, because they feel too embarrassed, discouraged, or guilty to finally tackle (and finish) a long-avoided activity. Usually "better late than never" is the adage to apply.

Paperwork

Anyone who deals with information, whether in an office or a hospital, is going to have paper to go through. Letters, memos, forms, reports, evaluations, meeting notices...the list goes on.

More will be discussed about paperwork in Chapter 6, *Improving Your Time at Work.* Another cause of paperwork that becomes overwhelming and messy clutter is failing to have systems to deal with the paperwork so that each type of incoming item, from letters and magazines to memos or upcoming meeting notices, is dealt with in a consistent way.

Solution #1 - Become ruthless about what you do with the paper in your office.

Make doing something about each piece of paper that comes across your desk a priority concern until you get your paperwork under control. Throw out, file, recycle, pass along, or scan each piece of paper into a master file so everything is in its place. If possible, avoid the temptation, or habit, of creating huge piles of paper (that may conceal the papers that are really important as well as requiring literally hours at a stretch to go through once it accumulates).

Solution #2 - Set aside regular time to sort through your paperwork.

Whether it is once a day, once a week, or even once a month, set aside time when you will sort through your paperwork. Include "paperwork" as part of your work or personal responsibilities, rather than seeing it as an annoyance that somehow you hope to "get through" once and for all.

Solution #3 - Have a system for dealing with each and every aspect of your daily mail and papers.

Promise yourself that you will go through your mail each day, putting the mail and other papers into the system you have created. (If you need help creating a system, see Chapter 6.)

The Terrible Twos: Telephone and Television

More will be said about these two notorious potential time gobblers later—the telephone in Chapter 6, and television in Chapter 8. For now, just start being aware of how much time you spend engaging in either activity, and what you should have—could have—been doing instead. Both are examples of habits which, uncontrolled, can eat up enormous amounts of time. Neither piece of equipment is in and of itself a bad habit; the frequency and duration of use determine its detrimental or beneficial effects.

Solution # 1 — Start a telephone or TV time log.

Begin keeping track of how long you spend engaged in either task, as well as what you are specifically watching or with whom you are speaking.

Start to note when you place calls; what you're doing when you receive calls (and if that effects how you deal with the caller); how long you usually stay on the phone, and who is the first to say "I have to go now."

Take stock of your television viewing as well, noting for starters if you watch specific programs or just have the TV on all the time. (As important as it is to stay abreast of current events, even watching the news all day long, if it is excessive and stopping you from doing your other work at hand, can be a time gobbler.)

Solution #2 — Designate a specific time to place or receive phone calls.

Instead of allowing calls to be put through constantly throughout your work day, pick out blocks of time when you will answer, or place, telephone calls. During the time when you prefer to do quiet creative work, or even have uninterrupted meetings, let your secretary screen calls or allow the voice mail or answering machine to take messages. If you wish to avoid telephone tag, you could also advise callers when to call back when it is more likely you will be there to take their call.

Solution #3 – Watch TV selectively.

Pick specific shows you will watch rather than having the TV on all the time. Excessive TV watching, if it is interfering with accomplishing work or leisure tasks that are more fundamental to your success and happiness, is as much of a bad habit as compulsive Internet use. Take control of the TV by observing just how much TV watching you are doing as well as the specific shows you want to view. (It also makes it easier to set an example for your children, whom you are probably trying to encourage to read, when they see their parents reading at night instead of watching too much TV.)

Solution #4 – Use a VCR to record your TV shows.

By recording your favorite programs using a VCR (video cassette recorder) you will have more control over when you watch TV. If you wish, you can also speed through commercials, spending only about 45 minutes watching an "hour" show.

Failure to prioritize

In addition to the solutions below, for help overcoming a failure to prioritize review the suggestions in the beginning of this chapter about solutions to overcome the "Doing Too Much at Once" syndrome as well as the advice for planning and goal setting in the previous chapter.

Solution # 1 – Be clear about your goals.

Having clear goals will help you prioritize (by saying "no" to anything that is not your #1 priority.)

Solution #2 – Take your time saying "yes."

If you at least take your time deciding to do something, you have a better chance of reminding yourself what your real priority is, and saying "no" to anything that distracts you.

Get comfortable saying these words, "I'll get back to you on that."

Commuting and Travel Time

Whether you spend two hours round trip each day commuting, or you work from home but spend four hours monthly on an airplane or an hour a day driving to work-related appointments, there's a lot of time at stake that is spent commuting daily or traveling for business.

There is a wide range in how this commuting or business travel time is utilized. Some flip through magazines, some read others' newspapers, some chat with a group of commuting friend regulars, some snore, and some stare into space, daydreaming or planning their day's activities.

What are some ways to make the most of travel time?

Solution # 1 – Have a commuting or travel time plan.

To creatively use your commuting or travel time: first, have a plan. Don't commute or travel aimlessly day after day, trip after trip. Based on how you commute, and how long it takes, decide if you will use your commuting time to do your work, for recreational activities, or for some combination of the two.

Solution #2 — Pick work-related tasks you can do while commuting or traveling for business.

If you commute alone by car there are safe, work-related tasks that you might consider, such as listening to work-related tapes or books on tape, known as audiobooks, available for sale or rental through bookstores, libraries, or special audiobook stores. You could also speak into a tape recorder to record your thoughts or letters for transcribing.

There are also numerous commercial and educational companies that sell prerecorded books that are ideal for commuters or travelers. (I often use driving time to listen to the monthly "audiomagazine" provided to busy members by the National Speakers Association, one of the associations I belong to.)

Solution # 2 – Bring along a portable or hand-held computer.

Having a portable computer could be a way for you to make maximum productive use of your commuting time. (Even if you do not have a portable or hand-held computer, you could still do your work the old-fashioned way, by taking along a pad and pencil or pen for writing; or magazines or books for work-related reading.)

Solution #3 – Use car commuting time for recreation and to reduce stress.

Listen to stress reduction music or tapes. But if you have a busy life, you might even find the silence while commuting alone a stress reducer of another sort. "I like the quiet," says a woman who commutes two hours a day alone in her car. "It gives me time to think," she adds, explaining how the rest of her day she's around people and scurrying between activities.

Although a car pool minimizes worrying about safety, it can introduce interruptions by other passengers. One van pool commuter, if she wants to read, and someone else wants to talk, answers whatever question or statement has been put to her, and immediately turns back to her reading, nipping a lengthy conversation before it starts.

Solution #4 – Exercise.

Productive use of commuting time by foot is, of course, the

utilization of that time for physical exercise. Walking to work is a way to combine exercise with your necessary commute.If you live within ten miles of your office, another possible option, if it is safe enough, is biking to work.

Solution #5 – Sleep.

Sometimes getting a nap on the train or plane is enough to replenish you for the workday (or leisure time) ahead. Of course you want to make sure you are awake before you reach your destination; you also want to be sure you keep your belongings safely concealed so nothing is stolen from you as you sleep.

Solution #6 - Socialize.

For some, the time spent in the car, on a train, bus, or plane talking with friends, co-workers, or even strangers adds welcome time for socializing to their workday.

Solution # 7 – Read.

You could use the commuting or business travel time to read for work or whatever you rarely seem to have the time to read — for example, the latest best-selling novel, a literary classic, a magazine about your hobby, poetry, or your child's latest school composition.

Solution # 8 – Daydream.

Not only is daydreaming relaxing, what you dream about just might offer you solutions to work-related problems you are trying to solve.

Solution # 9 - Meditate.

Meditating is known to reduce tension and stress.

Solution # 10 - Reconsider your long-term goals and your plans

to achieve them.

Use this commuting or business travel time to think about, or write about, your long term goals.

Solution # 11 - Take along stationery and catch up on your correspondence, or begin a personal journal.

Even though E-mail is replacing conventional correspondence in many instances, there are still times when an old-fashioned, handwritten note, or letter, is called for. Commuting or business travel time could provide just the opportunity for writing those letters or notes.

Solution #12 - Pick one obstacle to how you manage your time and map out a plan to overcome it.

Your commuting or business travel time could offer you the opportunity to work on your number one time management obstacle.

Solution #13 - Use commuting or business travel time to do errands or chores.

To or from work you could do chores or errands. Business travel time could provide the time and opportunity for buying holiday or birthday presents.

Complaining

How often have you uttered a complaint, and immediately wished you hadn't? Our culture sanctions silent stoicism, with phrases like "stiff upper lip," and "never complain, never explain."Yet, the act of complaining is natural, and quite prevalent. Its legitimacy is judged by: what you gripe about; to whom you bleat; and how often you grumble.

These three criteria interrelate; together, they determine whether a statement is deemed an observation, a self-pitying complaint, or a time waster. For example, getting your gripes off your chest once in a while might help you break through your delaying tactics. Complaining might provide you with information; e.g., you complain to a coworker about the deadline pressures you feel and she tells you the proposal isn't due for another month.

By and large, chronic complaining wastes time that could be spent thinking and doing. Complaints can bring strangers and intimates closer—or send them running for cover. Hilda, 68, a retired librarian, says, "Complaining is probably good for the person who complains, and awful for everyone else around."

Complaining may be a way to gain sympathy or control in a situation. Example: "I worked like a dog today. Stuck in traffic for two hours, trying to fix equipment for five hours, and you think you have problems?" The man who said that to his wife did not want to listen to her. His complaints may be his way of justifying his demand she spend her time catering to his needs.

Solution #1 - Deal with the source of your complaining.

If your complaint is about a specific person—and you can't go forward until your differences are resolved—a face-to-face confrontation might be the most efficient way to handle things. If that is unrealistic, writing a long letter—one that you might ultimately decide would be best not mailed—can "get it all out" and help you go on with the business at hand. (A daily journal serves the same purpose, but on an ongoing basis.)

Solution #2 - Recognize the potential career consequences to complaining.

Complaining not only wastes your own time, but also creates a very poor image of what you're like—people will welcome your sympathy yet will make a mental note that you cannot be relied on for "positive thinking." You may find the label "gloomy" a difficult one to live down.

Solution # 3 —Put things in perspective.

Listen more to what others say and you may realize your complaints are petty. Read some inspirational books, like Harold S. Kushner's *When Bad Things Happen to Good People* or Viktor E. Frankl's *Man's Search for Meaning*, and consider ways other than complaining that you might try to get through life's disappointments. A thirty-year-old bachelor, for example, does volunteer work with terminally ill cancer patients rather than complaining about his own loneliness. Accent the positive in life, and be more realistic in expectations, so you'll have less to complain about. One chronic complainer confesses, "Even if I go beyond my goals I am still not satisfied."

Solution #4 — Find other things to talk about.

Ask yourself: Do I complain because I have nothing else to say? If you answer "yes," read about compulsive talking in this book.

Solution #5 — Find other ways to get attention.

Do you complain to get attention? If so, find more effective attention-getting mechanisms, such as increasing your knowledge in a certain area so you have more to say, or looking more attractive. Plan, and execute, actions that may correct specific complaints that now preoccupy you. Speak your complaints into a tape recorder and force yourself to listen to the tape, as if you were the coworker, friend, or spouse who might have to listen to you. If all else fails, complain to taxi drivers, bartenders, or therapists who expect to hear complaints as part of their job.

Excuses

An occasional excuse, when valid, because a completely unexpected event occurs that necessitates a change in your plans, is simply part of life. For example, you would have gotten to work on time but you had an unexpected car emergency and had to bring your car to the service station on your way to work. But when excuses become chronic, and a too easy way to cover up poor planning, procrastination, or an inability to prioritize, you have to look at the pattern of excuses, and the consequences, and stop yourself from making excuses.

Solution #1 — Keep track of your excuses by writing them down.

You may be unaware of how often you use an excuse to put off doing what you have to do. By writing down your excuses, you will become more aware of this habit, as well as having evidence of exactly what excuses you are using. This could help you see what pattern your excuses fall into, and how to get out of using excuses as a way of sabotaging yourself and stopping yourself from better time management (and greater success).

Solution #2— Try to figure out what is behind each excuse.

Look at the excuses you have written down. Is there a pattern to your excuses? Are you always blaming someone else for your shortcomings? Are you always using something you have no control over, like the weather, to justify your actions (which you do have control over)?

The next chapter will discuss emotional blocks to time management such as fear of failure and fear of success.

4
Emotional Blocks to Time Management

Time is flying, never to return.
> VIRGIL, *Georgics III*

Consider the emotional blocks to time management discussed in this chapter. It will help to recognize, and overcome, each one that might be blocking your effective and creative time management.

Perfectionism

The perfectionist is never pleased and, sometimes without knowing it, belabors assignments beyond what is required for a best effort, and reworks things past deadlines (if they finish at all). Perfectionism is a difficult habit to break because it means rethinking one's entire approach to how one appraises people, things, and events.

We all need ideals to aspire to, but when the ideal becomes a day-to-day unrealistic and unattainable goal, frustration and poor time management may result. Why try at all if your efforts will never satisfy you or anyone else? or so thinks the perfectionist.

The perfectionist never finishes a report, or misses deadline after deadline, because there's always "just one more" reference to read. A new product is revised so often, far beyond what is needed, that the competition is able to launch theirs first, enjoying all the atttention and profits that could have been the perfectionist's.

On a personal level, sometimes those who are overweight are really perfectionists about their appearance. Overweight, they can fantasize about how perfect they'd be if they lost weight. Sometimes those who look for the "perfect" mate fail to find a mate at all.

Perfectionism camouflages fear of failure and of success. Someone is so afraid of failing that he or she set standards inappropriate to the task—for example, spending four days over a one paragraph letter that has to be written, writing and rewriting beyond realistic standards of excellence. Or you are so (unwittingly) afraid of succeeding that you convince yourself your letter is *still* not good enough so you never send it or you send it thinking you could have—should have—done better.

Perfectionists have a low self-image concealed behind their "I know what's right" facade. Perfectionism is a character trait that interferes with effective use of your time. It causes mismanaged time; strive for excellence, not unattainable perfection.

Solution #1 – Recognize that you are a perfectionist.

The first cure for perfectionism is realizing that you even have this problem in the first place. Once you realize you are a perfectionist, you can begin to recognize when you're defeating yourself by setting unrealistic, unattainable goals, which are out of reach. Are you a perfectionist? You may not be a perfectionist about everything, just certain things. You may be a perfectionist about others, always finding fault and wishing they dressed, spoke, acted, or went about their lives in a different ("perfect") way.

Solution #2 — Accept that no one, including you, is perfect, and learn to feel comfortable by praise.

Embrace and accept yourself for what you are, with all your failings and imperfections. Develop more realistic assessments of yourself, others, and situations. (This change in attitude, however, should not become a way of excusing sloppiness or behavior that is unacceptable.)

If your perfectionism is a way of preventing yourself from feeling good about yourself or what you do, learn to feel comfortable being complimented.

Solution #3 – Learn to pursue attainable excellence, rather than unattainable perfectionist standards.

What you want to do, if you have this trait in one or more areas, is to turn your perfectionism into high but more manageable and realistic standards that are *attainable* by you. By becoming more realistic in your expectations, perfectionism can be channeled into high, but attainable, standards.

Solution #4 — Delegate.

Another possible solution for the perfectionist is to delegate authority. By accepting that someone can do certain jobs for you, perhaps not exactly the way you would do it but as well as the task requires—you will free up valuable time and energy for other pursuits. The time you save by having a research assistant find and order the latest books on a topic or having an intern or a secretary screen your telephone calls may help you to devote more time to your priority tasks as well as providing you with more leisure time. By welcoming the help of others – and recognizing that they can assist you in completing some of your tasks and that they can do that work adequately – will help you to overcome the perfectionism that has probably caused you to feel only you can do your work.

Becoming more accepting of the strengths, and weaknesses, of others is the first step toward a more relaxed approach to yourself and to your work.

By delegating to others, you will learn to become more flexible (and less of a perfectionist) by accepting that there are more than two ways to do something (your way, and the wrong way.)

Solution #5 — Be aware of the consequences of perfectionism.

Another solution to perfectionism is to become aware of what you miss out on because of your perfectionism. It may, interestingly, be in only one or a few areas that you, or someone you know, is a perfectionist. Parents may have such unrealistic standards for their children that their offspring can never please them (or themselves). You miss out on enjoying what you or others *are* accomplishing as well as on reality by focusing on perfectionist fantasies.

Fear of Failure

If you don't try, you can't fail, or so thinks the person with a fear of failure. But by working at a level far below your potential, or by never finishing a major project that you could be judged by, you may bring on the very failure you fear since you may not give your all, whether to a project, a relationship, or a job.

Here are some suggestions for overcoming a fear of failure:

Solution #1 – Get adequate training and experience.

Confidence, which reduces a fear of failure, comes from competence and accomplishment. A fear of failure may be reduced or eliminated by doing all that you can to insure your success.

Solution #2 - Change your attitude toward failure.

Another way to conquer your fear of failure is to reevalute how you view it. Making mistakes (failures) has a negative connotation in our culture; we applaud achievement and push thwarted relationships or projects under the rug. Without those "failures," (it's better to call them "efforts"), there could be no successes. Susan, 34, an actress who has had more jobs as a waitress than parts in plays, describes her fear of failing as an actress:

I wonder if all the time that I thought I was good, and thought I was talented, maybe it wasn't really true. That would mean that I would have to change my whole life, change my career. I would have to have a whole new life, and that's very frightening.

Once Susan, and others who fear failure, analyze the situation that they fear, they may open up new options (and opportunities) for success. This is how management consultant Peter F. Drucker views failure. Writing in *The Practice of Management*, he states:

Nobody learns except by making mistakes. The better a man is the more mistakes he will make—for the more new things he will try. I would never promote a man into a top-level job who has not made mistakes, and big ones at that. Otherwise he is sure to be mediocre. Worse still, not having made mistakes he will not have learned how to spot them early and how to correct them.

Failure itself is usually not fatal; fearing it can put a negative spin on all your efforts, even narrowing your initial vision so you stop yourself from striving for the goals you really want to achieve.

Solution #3 — Imagine the worst consequence of what you're doing, and see yourself surviving that situation.

Another way to cope with a fear of failure is to imagine the worst consequences of what you are doing. Take the failure you fear and fantasize it to the extreme. Example: you overcome your fear of failure and give up your middle management job to go back to school and become an accountant. You graduate, become licensed, but cannot get a job. Or you cannot get clients. Or you decide, after all that, that you really liked the job you left better than your new goal. Ask yourself: Can you live with that? Could you still view the years of study as useful even if you return to your old job?

By imagining the worst that might happen, and picturing yourself overcoming that failure, you can go on to try to achieve the goals that you fear.

Solution #4 — View failure as a training ground.

Fear of failure is tied very closely to fear of success. The solution for a fear of failure is similar to the solution for a fear of success: do your best but if you fail, learn what you can from what you did (or did not) do. Each experience increases your ability to withstand further failures (mistakes) and to achieve even more successes.

Solution #5 — Be realistic about the causes of your failure; take responsibility for your part in it.

If you find yourself blaming everyone else or circumstances "beyond your control" each time you fail, your fear of failure may be causing you to mismanage your time by avoiding responsibility. Objective self-evaluation, unlike "if only" fantasies, saves time by using mistakes creatively for self-advancement.

Fear of Success

No one wants to fail, and everyone wants to succeed, right? Wrong. According to psychologist Leon Tec and others, a fear of success is quite common. In *Fear of Success,* Tec writes:

> I believe the fear of success is universal, so widespread that it must be considered normal. It may be severe in some people, less intense in others, but it is always there. Even for those who ostensibly have succeeded and reached the top of their fields, the fear of success may exist and rob them of the enjoyment of their feats.

Here are recommendations for coping with this time waster:

Solution #1 — Fantasize about success and imagine yourself dealing with all the consequences of it.

Take a few moments to fantasize about what would happen if you were successful—really successful—in either your professional or personal life. Would friends or relatives be jealous? What would you do differently? Would you squander your fortune, or become addicted to drugs? Would the old gang feel you're not one of them any more? Would you become depressed because you would have nothing left to strive for? Strange as it sounds, some people grow used to being unhappy—or poor or fat or lonely. Susan, the struggling actress, says, "There's something secure in staying where you are, no matter how bad it is, rather than going into something else, unknown ground."

Try this to face up to your fear of success: imagine the best that could happen—and all the negative consequences that might follow—and see yourself coping with that. Picture yourself coping with the joys success will bring, as well as the disappointments.

Solution #2 — Analyze how realistic you are about what success means.

Ask yourself how realistic your images of success are. Is it all rosy and wonderful? If you fantasize success as only positive you may be afraid to succeed and test out your unrealistic expectations. Consider that success may mean that you, and everyone else, may expect more from you in the future. You may be afraid of the good, and bad, changes that success will necessitate. Is success your "if only. . ." one-note song that camouflages deep-seated insecurity? Are your standards so high, and so unrealistic, that you are successful, and you don't even know it? Thus you may have to become more realistic about what success means—at work and in personal relationships— to discover if you have achieved it and, if not, how to go about getting it.

Devaluing (or Overvaluing) of Your Activities

For some, it's difficult to believe—and live up to the belief—that what you do matters. "In the end it doesn't really matter what you do," says a man with low self-esteem. There are also those who are so self-important that they think their every deed is momentous. ("Look at me," they seem to be saying, as if the whole world is one big parent whose love they are trying to win.) Then there are those who waver back and forth between these two extremes— either what they do is the best or the worst, very important or meaningless.

Dealing with life realistically means operating somewhere in the middle of these extremes. It is a waste of time to be either a minimizer or a maximizer; both are distorted views of events and persons. It's also unrealistic to expect everyone around you to match your own natural intense self-interest.

Solution #1 — Develop standards that are more realistic and objective.

A solution to devaluing, or overvaluing, your work or personal activities is to honestly appraise your past efforts, your current time demands, and your future goals. Are your paintings good enough to show in a gallery? If not, are they still first-rate as a hobby? Is the report you wrote terrific, or just " so-so," and not something you should be bragging about? As a friend used to say, when asked what she thought about a new date, "Good, not great." Most efforts fall into the "good, not great" category. Perceiving everything you do as worthless or, the opposite extreme, brilliant, mismanages your time.

Solution #2 —Work on your self-esteem so you need not be a self-downer nor someone who always has to "one-up" everyone.

When I give writing seminars, my students – the typical eighteen-year-old college student as well as the fifty-year-old full-time employee or the seventy-five-year-old retiree who is looking to writing as a second or fifth career – are comforted when I say "You can still get your writing published even if you are a good but not a great writer. There's still a need for writers who are good but not as brilliant as Hemingway or F. Scott Fitzgerald."

For some, that more realistic self-assessment of their writing helps them to overcome writer's block – or the selling block – that is preventing them from completing their magazine or book projects and finally getting their writing published.

Impatience and Low Frustration Tolerance

Are you impatient? Impatience prevents optimal use of your time. Examples: you're so eager to complete one phone call, and get on to the next, that you fail to be a good listener or to remember much of what was said. You send someone a non-urgent E-mail asking for some information for your own personal use. Instead of waiting for a reply, a few days later you call, further annoying the busy person who had planned, in good time, to respond to you.

Difficulty in handling frustration is related to impatience. That wastes time because your energy is spent fuming at problems— not solving them. Both of these "I want it *now*" personality traits are time wasters in the same way that perfectionism wastes time. Impatience may cause you to give up before you have expended the time and effort needed for the task at hand; perfectionism may cause you to continually redo or prolong a task too long because your standards are too high and unattainable.

Those who are impatient, and have low frustration tolerance, are filled with self-loathing, since they give up too quickly to see the results that they crave. Those who are perfectionists are usually too hard on themselves (and others) and won't give up even when they have done as much as is necessary or feasible.

Impatience and low frustration tolerance is symptomatic of immaturity and a need for immediate gratification. Yet many of the greatest rewards in how we spend our time at work or in our personal lives are for accomplishing little steps and continuing on a path even when frustrated. Curing impatience and low frustration tolerance means becoming process, as well as product, oriented. You may want to appear on national TV hyping your best-selling book, but you first need to find ongoing rewards in the day-to-day efforts necessary to achieve the first step of writing the book.

Solution #1 — Work on this problem, one task at a time.

Like other time wasters, retraining yourself to be more patient, and to have a higher frustration tolerance, in one area of your life may help you to successfully apply it, step by step, to other areas as well.

Pick just one task you have to complete, or just one bad habit that you want to change, and force yourself to stick with your goal in spite of impatience or low frustration tolerance. That specific instance of conquering impatience may help you to generalize your overall approach to your activities and relationships.

Solution #2 — Count to ten.

The next time something happens that demonstrates that you are impatient or that you have a low frustration tolerance—the photocopy machine breaks down and you want to scream at the machine, a secretary, or anyone nearby who will listen— decide that you have the self-control necessary to handle that frustrating situation in a more patient, mature way. Count to ten. Walk away from the situation and come back once you have regained control. Practicing patience is reinforcing.

Solution #3 — Tackle impatience and low frustration tolerance as if it's a phobia you are trying to overcome.

Look at impatience and low frustration tolerance as phobias and cure those tendencies in the way you would treat a phobic response to, let's say, an elevator. In that case, you would get in the elevator and wouldn't close the doors. Mastering that, you would then ride to the fourth floor. In time, you would be able to still feel comfortable riding to the top of the World Trade Center. In a similiar way, gradually increase your tolerance to frustration.

Solution #4 — Become more patient with others or in delays that are unavoidable.

You may have to learn to handle others more patiently if you are to handle your own time (and impatience) more effectively. Even if you think you can do something faster or better, than someone – everyone – else, you need to be patient with the pace that others are able to handle. Sometimes you may need to tolerate that others have a slower pace, even if that is not the pace you comfortably perform at. By accepting the behavior – or pace – of others, you may become more patient in general.

If you believe in the path you have chosen, even if it means being patient about monetary or other gratifications, it may require convincing yourself or those around to be more patient to avoid wasting time focusing on what cannot be rushed.

Jealousy

Jealousy squanders time because it fosters downing others (and yourself) instead of doing whatever it takes to get what you want.

Learn to recognize jealousy in yourself and in others even when it is disguised. "I don't care if she makes seventy-five thousand dollars, she'll still be miserable" or "It's because of sheer luck that he's gotten where he is" are wet-blanket statements that attempt to diminish an accomplishment (and perpetuate the jealousy of the speaker).

You cannot stop others from being jealous of you, although you may wish to reevaluate why you seem to surround yourself with jealous people. You can, however, learn to understand, and minimize, the jealousy that you feel, and that wastes your time.

Solution #1 — Turn jealousy into something useful and positive.

A solution for your own time-sapping jealousy is to turn it into something effective and productive. Jealousy pinpoints what you value, since the rage and envy you feel when someone else achieves something clarifies what you want for yourself. Turn your jealousy into a fact-finding expedition; find out how someone else did what he or she did and try to learn from his or her example how *you* can do it too.

Put your fantasies of "if only" to the test and see if there is information to be gained that would save you time, and help you to achieve what you really want.

Solution #2 — Build your self-esteem.

Become secure enough within yourself that you do not need to diminish others through feeling, or expressing, jealousy. Take the time and energy that you used to spend being jealous and work at achieving what you want, whether that is wealth, fame, popularity, confidence, a nicer disposition, greater productivity, or whatever your goal or pleasure.

The Inability to Take Criticism

The inability to take criticism is an incredible time waster since it may lead to abandoning a project because one small part has to be changed, to counterproductive self-hate, and to poor relationships, since those who are unable to take criticism often blame, and may actually hate, the ones who criticize them. You have to learn how to deal with criticism in an objective way if you are to make better use of your time.

"Sometimes I can feel so devastated by criticism that I feel that I want to give up acting," says Susan, the aspiring actress who also has a fear of failure. Interestingly, Susan is only "devastated" if the criticism is from someone she "respects." "Some people I just don't respect," she says, "so the criticism means absolutely nothing to me, and I think I know better than they do, so I don't listen to it." Your inability to take criticism may be so all pervasive, however, that it devastates you no matter who is doing the criticizing, or what it is about.

Psychologist Lynn Diamond gives this explanation for the inability to take criticism:

Nobody wants to fail. It's rejection. The fear of failure, or the fear of being rejected, is very great in all of us.... [But] it has nothing to do with you and your project. You are not your product. You could be totally acceptable, but I may not like your writing. The whole goal of acceptance is to set a standard for your performance. "This report was good and I'd like you to change x" doesn't mean that you failed. It means you can do things to get better.

Solution #1 – Create conditions that make it easier to accept the criticism.

The following conditions make it easier to take criticism; try to achieve them in your work and personal situations.
- People know your work.
- They already respect your abilities.
- They like you.
- They are trying to help you to improve (yourself or your product).

You have to learn to distinguish whether you are dealing with a knowledgeable, and critical, person who is providing beneficial advice, or with a sadistic and "always right" person who can never be pleased.

Solution #2 — Develop your ability to accept (and give) criticism.

If you are unable to take criticism, and you seek out only those who approve and praise you, in the long run you may waste time since you, and your work, may not improve.

In the business classic, *One Minute Manager,* co-authors Blanchard and Johnson expressed this idea quite simply: the key to success is one minute praisings *and* one minute reprimands.

Usually the person who is unable to take criticism is also uncomfortable being critical. That's the kind of person who says you look great even when you look terrible.

To work on your inability to take criticism, learn how to give it. If you feel secure, you will be able to discriminate about the criticism that is offered, neither blindly accepting nor blindly rejecting it.

Solution #3 — Redefine how you view criticism.

Look at criticism as observations, rather than judgments, and be objective about it. Is the criticism valid? If it is valid, how will you go about improving whatever has been criticized—the report, your appearance, the time you spend on the Internet or the phone, how you handle meetings? If it is invalid, how can you explain to your criticizer that his comment is unwarranted?

Solution #5 — Self-evaluate so outside criticism occurs less often.

Maintain such high standards of self-evaluation that criticism is an infrequent occurrence.

Solution #6 - Stop automatically defending yourself.

If a criticism might have merit, be open to it rather than automatically defending yourself. If you are uncomfortable thanking someone for a criticism, try to at least say, "I'll consider your comments."

Boredom

Call it blahs, ennui, or tedium, boredom is that "ho-hum" feeling when the meeting is dull, or you have to do the same thing too often. There are discernible trends to boredom. For example, some are able to keep themselves interested outside of work, but are bored at their job. Others, who thrive on their work, are bored in their leisure time. Some are chronically bored; others feel boredom only when they are stressed, insecure, or doing a repetitious task.

How does boredom interfere with effective management of your time? Boredom lends to unproductive activities, or shifting gears in the hope of curing boredom; beginnings are often more exciting than middles so it leads to the "doing too many things at once" syndrome. In the end, however, more time is lost since it is usually more efficient to stick with one thing till it is completed before starting on numerous new things.

Solution #1 - Change the task.

If your boredom is caused by doing too much of the same thing, change the task. For example, if you're tired of writing letters, make a phone call to contact someone; if you are bored returning e-mail, write a letter instead.

Solution #2 — Do the same thing, in a different way.

If you need to finish a task, but are bored, try doing the same task differently. For example, if you are bored writing letters on a computer, try writing a few notes in longhand. If you are tired responding to E-mails, try calling someone on the phone or sending him or her a fax. If you are tired writing a report on your computer at your desk, try taking a draft of the report to a nearby conference room or a coffee shop, where you continue to work on it.

Solution #3 — Change the order of the tasks you have to accomplish.

Consider doing something else first, like running, reading the newspaper, or screening a film, before launching into a boring task (or a task that was initially interesting but has become boring).

Solution #4 – Try the reward system (that is also useful in overcoming procrastination).

Promise yourself a reward for completing a necessary, but boring, activity. "If I finish addressing all these envelopes, I will read that article in the trade journal that peaked my interest." "If I return these last two phone calls, I will get back to writing the report and stay off the phone for at least an hour."

Solution #5 — Become more sensitive to your moods.

Another way to offset the inertia when boredom strikes is to become sensitive to your moods, and then use your moods to save time. For example, if you are feeling "up," tackle boring tasks that might take longer if you are feeling tired or depressed. If you are a "morning" person, do your most creative work when you first get to work. Save the correspondence for after lunch, when you are slower anyway, so you will be less resentful of being bored since you already accomplished your priority tasks for the day.

Solution #6 — Look at the causes of your boredom as a source of solutions for overcoming it.

If your boredom is caused by too much work, or poor planning, you can cure it by getting more rest, relaxing, exercising, or saying "No, sorry. Thanks anyway for asking."

Consider if your boredom actually has a more obscure cause: you took on such an overwhelming task that it is a camouflage for the feeling of fatigue or befuddlement.

Reconsider the frequency of a task as a possible reason for boredom: one progress report a month is useful, once a week might be better, but daily reports might become boring and unproductive.

Solution #7 — Recognize that some boredom is beneficial.

Too much boredom certainly wastes time, but some ennui has value. "I keep busy every minute because I never want to be bored," says a married man with a toddler who works two demanding jobs. "There's no monotony in what I do, and every task is different.

Maybe a little boredom might prove restful," he adds, breathlessly.

Solution #8 — On careful analysis, consider boredom a symptom that you should be delegating certain tasks.

Boredom may be a symptom that you are working so far below your potential and capacities that you are dulled. In that case, see boredom as a sign that you should be delegating those tasks to others who either would not be bored or would welcome doing those particular activities for the experience, the pay check, or a distraction from their own work which is either overwhelming or boring them. (For more information on delegating, see the delegating section in Chapter 6, *Improving Your Time at Work.*)

Guilt

Are you the kind of person who feels guilty about what you *are* doing as well as by what you're *not* doing? Do you feel guilty for working late, because you're neglecting your family, and guilty if you leave work on time, since your work is being put aside?

Most people waste time and energy with minor everyday guilts, like not returning a phone call that could certainly wait till tomorrow, postponing a meeting because something else came up that had to be dealt with immediately. (Note: this section is not about major guilts, like criminal behavior or falsifying a resume, actions that *should* cause guilt.)

How does guilt waste time? Because the guilt itself starts to consume time as the guilty person ruminates, time that could be spent more productively on work or leisure pursuits.

If guilt wastes your time, consider its source. "Most of the guilt I feel stems from my parent's voice, which is something I hear in my head," a guilt-ridden college student says.

Solution #1 – Try to recognize the source of your guilt.

Next time you feel guilty, try to recognize the guilt-provoking voice you are hearing. Is it your father? Mother? Teacher? By recalling that voice and thinking "I hear you, but I refuse to feel guilty"— you're on the road toward a less guilty life.

Solution #2 – Clarify your values, priorities, and beliefs.

Guilt stems from trying to please others, rather than yourself. If you establish your own fair guidelines, you won't blow with the breeze of outside (guilt-provoking) pressure from others.

Solution #3 – Allow yourself to make mistakes.

Stop ruminating over past errors. Learn from current or past mistakes and make notes about what happened and why, but stop beating yourself up over it.

Solution #4 – Remind yourself about what you can and cannot control, and recognize the difference.

You are not to blame for your boss's bad mood, or the decision to relocate your firm. You are not responsible for others, only for yourself, although others may choose to behave in a certain way because of your actions.

Solution #5 – Lower your expectations.

If your expectations are completely unattainable, you are setting yourself up to feel guilty if you fail, even if your standard was impractical. If your goals are unrealistic, adjust them. Try for very good, so if you get excellent, you come out ahead.

Selflessness

For most of us, selfishness has a negative connotation. To philosopher and novelist Ayn Rand, author of *The Virtue of Selfishness: A New Concept of Egoism*, it meant, simply "concern for one's own interests."

Using Rand's neutral definition, the inability to be selfish (selflessness) wastes time because you spend too much of your precious time meeting others' demands. Furthermore, selflessness violates a basic time management principle since you cannot prioritize if self-interests are considered last, if at all.

The inability to be selfish is tied to another time waster, the inability to say "no"—you take on too many commitments for fear of alienating someone, or of losing that opportunity forever.

Till recently, selflessness seemed to afflict women more than men. Women, socialized to put others first, became martyrs. Donna Goldfein, President and founder of ESTE (Easy Steps Toward Efficiency) based in San Francisco, conducts seminars for women; she encourages them to find time for their own priorities. "Women, especially women over thirty, still have a guilt about being selfish," Goldfein explains. How does Goldfein help them to change? "They learn not to live vicariously through others, but to do something for themselves."

The inability to be selfish, however, afflicts men as well. "I often assume the title of 'Mr. Nice Guy,'" says a store manager. "Although this is a personality boost for me, once I start helping others, it's expected. As soon as I slack off, I'm labeled a lazy slob."

Although you need not feel guilty about saying "no" when you are selfless—because you are always saying "yes"—it wastes time because your own goals are ignored or postponed. Resentments may build, reaching a point where you explode, flee, or waste more time than if you had appropriately practiced the right amount of selfishness all along.

If selflessness is wasting too much of your time, here are some solutions for overcoming this tendency:

Solution #1 - See selfishness as a positive trait.

Selfishness reaffirms your priorities by forcing you to say, "This is the #1 concern in my life right now. I will attend to this, or to this person, before everything or everyone else."

If being selfish is an uncomfortable concept for you, try substituting the word *self-interested.* Try saying the word without choking up. "I am self-interested and that is good." Those with healthy self-interest get ahead and succeed; those who are overly selfless often become resentful doormats.

Solution #2 – Reevaluate the demands that others are placing on you.

Which ones are reasonable? Which ones are shifting too much of the work unfairly to you? Learn to say "no" to unfair or excessive requests.

Realize that being selfish is not like being self-absorbed or narcissistic. Selfishness means a balanced system of exchange: you neither get, nor give, too much. If your boss gives you ten clients, and your co-workers have only six, unless you're working on commission, you've lightened their load, at your own expense.

Solution #3 – Equate some selfishness with self-actualizing.

To overcome excessive selflessness, see the right amount of self-interest or selfishness as being self-actualizing because, in moderation, that's what it is. Self-actualizing people are better time managers because they value and wisely guard their time.

Being in Love, and Other Emotional Issues

Take the case of one executive, who was taking three-hour lunches since learning his wife was cheating on him. Or the administrative assistant, whose productivity in the last year has been less than half of what it used to be when her romantic relationship was going well. Or the bride and groom who find phone calls about their upcoming wedding as well as shopping trips and fittings are eating into their workday productivity.

Perhaps you've been upset lately but you thought you would

be able to pull yourself together over a three-day weekend or certainly during your annual two weeks off. Yet you are back at work, still preoccupied with your problems.

Here are some symptoms that your personal problems are affecting your work performance:

- Your concentration is poor.
- Your sense of time is distorted; the hours drag on.
- Your personal problems preoccupy you at work.
- You begin to "look" busy while you're working, but you are only shuffling papers and not accomplishing anything.
- You personalize everything that happens. ("He doesn't like my report because he's trying to undermine my success." "She put through that call because she's angry at me today.")

The most typical solution —trying to solve your emotional crises by talking it out at work—is probably the least effective and riskiest to your career. Yet many workers, seeking quick solutions for their problems or needing to share, ask colleagues, employers, or even bosses for sympathy or advice. Yet the competitive world of work is rarely if ever the place to parade your personal problems.

Should you tell your boss the reason your productivity is lower? Use your discretion and instincts to make that decision.

Here are some solutions to consider if being in love or other emotional issues are causing you to mismanage your time:

Solution #1 — Evaluate your work performance: are you coping well on your own?

Evaluate your current productivity and ask yourself if personal, romantic, or familial situations are affecting how you manage your work time. If you are being productive, no one, including you, should have to consider this issue any further. But if being in love or personal or familial problems are preventing you from doing your best, you have some decisions to make.

Your goal is to solve your problems, of course, but, along the way, you have to do well enough at your job that you don't lose it while you put your affairs back in order.

Solution #2 – Realize that most emotional crises will impact on your productivity, so cut yourself some slack.

Certain types of emotional crises, such as dealing with the death of a loved one, being the victim of a major crime, divorce, or coping with a major illness (your own or a family member's), may cause someone to go through one or all of the stages first described by psychiatrist Kubler-Ross from her work with the terminally ill and their immediate families: shock, denial, disbelief, fright and fear, clinging behavior, apathy alternating with anger, and, finally, resolution. (These stages are also described in greater detail as related to crime victims in Martin Symonds's journal article on crime victims as well as in my own book, *Victims.*)

Since your productivity may be impacted by such major emotional crises, lower your expectations for yourself till you are able to get back to your "old self." If possible, revise deadlines that could be adjusted; delegate whatever you can while still maintaining quality control during this adjustment time.

Solution #3 — Consider finding outside assistance to help you cope.

If you are bringing your problems to work, or it is impacting on your productivity, consider getting help from an individual, family, or marital therapist. Consider short- or long-term therapy. Short-term therapy of three to five sessions is usually directed at a specific situation: "Here's what happened to me. Here's what I want to be able to do. Can you help me?" However, it is only upon consultation with a therapist that you will be able to make the determination if short-term, long-term, or even drug-assisted therapy is needed.

Solution #4 — Consider other sources of help as well.

Not everyone needs outside professional help to cope with personal problems. A support network of friends and family members is invaluable in getting you through a crisis without inappropriately relying on coworkers, subordinates, superiors, or clients.

Support groups might be another source of help. If there has been a death in the family, or of a close friend or even a pet, you might want to consider attending a local support group for the bereaved. Today there are support groups – run by the members or run by a professional therapist – for almost every personal, professional, or medical crisis as well as for the family or friends of those going through such crises, such as coping with cancer, job loss, eating disorders, caring for an elderly parent, and so forth. (For an extensive list of self-help groups, see *The Self-Help Sourcebook* compiled by Barbara J. White and Edward J. Madara through the American Self-Help Clearinghouse.)

Solution #5 — Take some time off.

Perhaps for you just getting some time off from work, or taking a vacation, will help you to resolve your emotional conflicts.

Should you tell those you work with the real reason you need time off? Use your judgment although some experts point out that physical complaints ("I'm not feeling well") may be more acceptable, and carry less of a stigma, than tales of emotional duress.

Solution #5 — Get better separating work and personal roles.

Work at keeping your personal life out of the workplace so you can function effectively at work despite your emotional crises. It's easier said than done but sometimes work actually takes your mind off your problems, if you let yourself get absorbed in your work.

Here's another spin on this issue: Your emotional life may be fine but if you chronically bring problems home from the office, you may be creating a different personal problem that needs to be solved. By letting too much of your work concerns spill over into your personal or family time, you may find your dutiful listeners tuning you out, asking you to switch the subject, or being forced to avoid you if the problem becomes serious enough.

Somehow—on your own, with the aid of friends or family, or with the help of a therapist or a support group—you have to find a way to keep work at work so you do not create personal problems (that will, in turn, begin to impact on your work productivity). Apply solutions 1 through 5 to this different spin on the same problem – namely, you are in love with your work and that over-emphasis on work is causing problems in your romantic or family life.

Refer back to the section in Chapter 3 on complaining (pages 27-29), and concentrate your efforts on improving the faulty situation. You could also refer to the sections in this book on workaholism since often this is a symptom of the workaholic, someone whose life has become disproportionately focused on work to the detriment of others.

Bad Habits

Fortunately, with some effort, time-saving habits can replace time-wasting ones. Whether the time-saving techniques that you wish to adopt are major, like becoming organized rather than disorganized, or minor, they will become habits only if they are consistently applied. You may make more money because of these new, positive habits, or get praise from your family or friends, but, even more importantly, your life will be more orderly and relaxed.

If you procrastinate, or do too many things at once, you will have to make an active effort to change if you want to manage your time more effectively. The only way to change is to make a conscious—and daily—effort in that direction. In *How People Change*, psychologist Alan Wheelis points out: "Personality change follows change in behavior. Since we are what we do, if we want to change what we are we must begin by changing what we do, must undertake a new mode of action."

Initially, however, you may not be thrilled by your new, improved habits. Face the fact that for some, in the beginning, even beneficial changes may make you irritable, disagreeable, cranky, and less efficient. As Wheelis notes: "The new mode will be experienced as difficult, unpleasant, forced, unnatural, anxiety provoking. It may be undertaken lightly but can be sustained only by considerable effort of will. Change will occur only if such action is maintained over a long period of time."

Changing—and coping successfully with new situations— necessitates being in touch with who you are, and what you want. To embrace change means to be secure and self-determined. If you are thrown by change—new and unforeseen circumstances— you may also be reluctant to give up changing yourself and your bad habits, however ineffective and self-sabotaging they are.

In *What Life Should Mean to You*, psychologist Alfred Adler writes about change:

> If we see emotions that apparently cause difficulties and run counter to the individual's own welfare, it is completely useless to begin by trying to change these emotions. They are the right expression of the individual's style of life, and they can be uprooted only if he changes his style of life.

There are entire books you can read on how to change bad habits, but here, in a nutshell, are several possible solutions:

Solution #1 — First decide exactly what *you* want to change about yourself.

Do not blindly accept others' pronouncements for you; your procrastination may be a bad habit, or it may be purposeful and time effective. Focusing your attention on a specific bad habit that *you* want to change will augment your motivation to change it.

Solution #2 — Work on changing just one habit at a time.

If you try to change too many habits at once, such as creating a new file system, getting over perfectionism, or minimizing telephone time, you may fail to change any one habit. Apply to changing bad habits the "one thing at a time" approach.

Solution #3 — Devote at least 3 weeks to changing one habit.

Once you decide on a bad habit that you want to tackle—e. g., doing too many things at once, an inability to accept criticism, procrastination, perfectionism— spend at least twenty-one days changing that habit. As Young and Jones point out in *Sidetracked Home Executives*, the 21-day suggestion is based on research conducted by plastic surgeon Maxwell Maltz, author of *Psychocybernetics*. Maltz discovered that it took patients who had had a limb amputated twenty-one days to lose a ghost image of their missing limb.

Solution #4 — Seek out professional help.

Through referrals or recommendations, find a psychotherapist, psychologist, psychiatrist, or social worker with whom you have rapport who is trained to help someone to change bad habits.

Be realistic, however, that there are few "overnight cures." But whether it takes months, or years, to get at the root of the bad habits that sabotage you, you will be making permanent changes to serve you well. Another benefit: if you get to the bottom of your negative habits, you might avoid passing along those same bad habits to your children.

Solution#5 — Try behavior modification techniques.

This type of psychotherapy uses classic learning techniques to modify behavior including aversion therapy, biofeedback, and reinforcement.

Solution #6 — Join a self-help group.

There are self-help groups for practically every concern you might have including Messies Anonymous and Clutterers Anonymous. The web site http:///www.selfgrowth.com lists hundreds of self-help groups.

Solution #7 — Develop a new, positive habit to replace the current bad habit.

Replacing the undesirable habit, such as telephone interruptions, with a new, desirable habit, such as setting aside a specific time for placing, and receiving, calls will help overcome a bad habit.

Lateness

Lateness wastes everyone's time. If you're late, you are probably getting scores of people mad at you on a regular basis. If you have to deal with people who are chronically late, you are probably anywhere from angry to enraged by their behavior.

You can't control someone else's lateness, but you can help the situation by setting an excellent example. So start with yourself and commit to being on time, all the time.

Solution #1 — Determine if there is a pattern to your lateness.

Are you late only now and then or chronically? Perhaps you always arrive late at work or for business lunches across town. Perhaps you tend to be late for meetings you would rather not attend.

Consider your average workday. What time should you arrive at your office? At what time did you arrive this morning? Yesterday? Do you have a pattern of chronic lateness (whereby you were late more than twice in the last week)?

Solution #2 — Once you determine if there is a pattern, figure out what is causing it.

Now that you see the pattern to your lateness, consider any of the following possible causes:

Mechanical reasons:
Alarm clock did not go off or was set for the wrong time

Transportation problems:
Car broke down
Poor driving conditions
Train or subway delay

Behavioral reasons:
Underestimating how long each task takes (e.g. taking a shower)
Waiting for others

Possible psychological reasons:
Need to be yelled at or noticed
Anger at your boss
As a way of procrastinating to avoid something
Worry about home so reluctant to leave for work
Worry about work so you delay leaving for home

Consider whether the reason you were late today, or this week, is likely to reoccur. If the cause of the lateness was a one-time occurrence, such as a flat tire, you will obviously deal with your lateness differently than if it is due to a habit or routine that you may have to break, such as spending too much time over breakfast, which indicates a pattern of lateness that has to be corrected.

Solution #3 — Plan better.

If you have to be somewhere at a certain time, make appointments with yourself to serve as time checks along the way. For example, "At 6:30 I have to be in the shower. At 7:00, I have to be out the door."

Allow yourself extra time for last-minute emergencies, phone calls, or traffic jams.

You may also have to be more realistic about how long it takes, to get someone on the phone or to do something since lateness also applies to projects as well as appointments.

Solution #4 — Affix a time that will get you somewhere on time that works for you.

If you have a chronic problem with lateness, tell yourself you have to get somewhere 15 minutes to half-an-hour earlier, and stick to that earlier arrival time, which, in your case, should get you there *on time*.

Solution #5 — Put your answering machine or voice mail on as you are preparing to leave.

This will help minimize your temptation to take that one last phone call which will probably be the reason you are late. Even if you can get off the phone quickly, you may be ruder than you would otherwise have been if you were not trying to dash out the door.

Solution #6 — To overcome lateness on projects, set realistic mini-deadlines.

You may have a tendency toward lateness on long-term projects because of poor planning or because your expectations about how much you can accomplish within a certain time frame is unrealistic. It will help if you create "mini-deadlines" to keep yourself (and your team) on track, rather than just one "big" deadline a year or more off in the distance.

It will also be helpful to you to develop and maintain a detailed **time log** of how long projects take, including any previous projects similar to this new one. In that way it may be easier to set more realistic time frames and deadlines for each current or future project so you are less likely to finish late.

Solution #7 — If there are psychological reasons to your lateness, get help to overcome them.

If your lateness problem cannot be cured by planning better, or by simply avoiding getting into a long telephone conversation when you are supposed to be walking out the door, you may need outside help to overcome the psychological reasons behind your lateness. By being late, you are causing people to notice you, but in a negative way. Your lateness is making people angry at you, perhaps even yelling at you. You may need help understanding what is behind this self-destructive pattern.

In the next chapter, the fundamentals of getting organized are probed in greater depth.

5
Becoming Organized and More Effective

Organization is not an end in itself but a means to the end.
PETER F. DRUCKER (*The Practice of Management*)

Being organized means that you are able easily to locate one thing out of your many possessions. Your system should be able to handle information, envelopes, keys, stamps, the annual report, computer files, books, subscription magazines, newsletters, E-mails that you print out, last year's tax return, and your passport, for starters.

Remember that you are trying to find a system of organizing your activities and possessions (or tools) that is best for you. We all have thousands of activities or actions we must follow up on—from the publicity campaign for a new product or your best friend's birthday to writing a monthly progress report. What is at issue is: What organizational system will best utilize your time management strengths and help you to organize your activities or things?

The benefits of getting organized are quickly observed. Sam, 34, a disorganized professor, now is on top of things and able to handle more work and personal activities. Sam explains: "The more I manage to organize my time and work settings, the more I find I can get done." Sam accomplished this transformation by organizing his non-teaching work and leisure time into a fixed routine, "setting schedules and deadlines for projects."

There are those who appear to be "born" organizers, and those who seem to be forever misplacing and forgetting things. The economic costs of disorder are dramatically driven home if you cannot find a valuable or one particular crucical document, like a birth certificate. Not as obvious, but costly nonetheless, are the wasted minutes each day—adding up to hours each month—reluctantly spent on treasure hunts, routinely searching for needed materials. Have you ever been locked out because you forgot your keys, or searched for an hour for your eyeglasses, hidden under yesterday's newspaper? Did you forget someone's birthday? How about the meeting you missed because you mislaid the notice? How about those last minute dashes to the liquor or grocery store just before guests arrived? Have you ever had to say, "I would have called sooner but I couldn't find your phone number"?

In my workplace survey of 234 men and women, almost everyone answered "How much time do you spend *each day* searching for something?" by noting that they spend anywhere from 1 minute to 4 hours searching daily, with the majority searching from 1 to 20 minutes. When I added up the total time that all these men and women are spending searching daily for something, it equals nearly 118.5 hours, or almost 3 full work weeks, that is collectively wasted in these searches.

Top five reasons for the search (in descending order)
1. Trying to find *a telephone number on a piece of paper or an address.* (27%)
2. Trying to *find current work-in-progress.* (24%)
3. Searching for *a contact person for follow-up* or *information about an upcoming meeting.* (15%)
4. Trying *to locate a file folder.* (14%)
5. Trying *to locate a file on a computer disk or hard drive.* (10%)*

*These percentages do not add up to 100% because there are additional #1 reasons chosen by the remaining respondents for the search that are not included in these five reasons. Those reasons include: searching for a book, magazine or newspaper clipping; incoming mail; going through a suitcase that was not yet unpacked; and something misfiled.

Thirteen men and women listed their #1 reason for their daily search was their car keys, house keys, or eyeglasses.

These numbers are tangible evidence of just some of the actual time that is being wasted in offices throughout the world because of disorganization. Beyond the time that is wasted in these searches is the anxiety, tension, frustration, and probably more than a few missed deadlines or miffed managers or clients.

Fortunately, there is hope and concrete help for creating more order and organization in your work and life. In this chapter you will find a discussion of basic organizational principles, as well as several suggested systems; but one of your own creation is, if it works, perhaps even better. Follow this basic principle: Never make the system your focus; the system is supposed to make things easier. If you spend too much time creating, and maintaining, your "system," its purpose is lost.

Extreme disorder and extreme order will both prove to be wasteful of time.

You want to learn how to better organize your thoughts and actions as well as your possessions. Those three elements usually go together. There are exceptions, such as when you are working on a project and need to put everything aside, including filing, till you reach a certain point in your work, but often a continually cluttered desk reflects a cluttered mind. Throughout this chapter remember that your goal is becoming organized in what you do and how you do it but in the service of your overall goal of becoming more productive.

GETTING ORGANIZED

Take a few moments to reflect on the time management strengths observed in the offices of effective and organized individuals:

1. Promptness.

2. Scheduling appointments based on accurate estimates of how long tasks (procedures) will take.

3. Notes and reminders written down in one book, or in an electronic organizer, not on pieces of paper that create unmanageable piles.

4. Notes, and appointments, written in pencil to facilitate corrections.

5. Minimal personal phone or in-person interruptions. If such interruptions do occur, they are handled quickly (and in private).

6. Showing interest in work-related relations by: a) listening; b) making interesting small talk; c) keeping personal problems to oneself; and d) giving explanations in clear but not condescending language.

7. Maintaining a daily "things to do" list.

8. Deciding on, and following through on, short term priorities and long term plans.

9. Dealing with coworkers, clients, and employees in a formal but pleasant manner.

10. Scheduling personal time off for vacations.

11. Replacing files or tools in their proper place after each use.

Being Organized is a Trait You Can Learn

Disorganization frustrates the best attempts to effectively use your time. There are some who gain enormous pleasure from cleaning out their closets and ordering their activities or possessions. However, it's a lot easier to entrust organizing your possessions to someone else than it is to revamp *how* you go about your business or leisure activities.

Have a master plan to your activities. If you are in control of what you do, you will be more effective. Being organized is a tool to increasing your effectiveness.

How do you organize your business or personal affairs? Do you feel "in control" of your everyday activities, or as if you are bouncing off this crisis or that demand? What are your time management strengths? Does your present work or home routine take full advantage of those strengths? Perhaps you work best in long stretches, but you currently interrupt yourself for a one hour lunch at the same time each day since that's what's expected of you, or so you think. Could you take a later lunch, or order lunch in and take a break later on in the day, to aid your work productivity?

You may find that you need to try, revise, and disregard certain schedules and procedures in order to become more organized and effective in what you do. As the demands on your time have changed—and as your goals and values have altered—you need to ask yourself whether your time budget reflects those changes.

Organizing your possessions makes possible more effective use of your time at work and home. Your goal is not to look organized, but to *be* organized.We have all heard of that rare individual who, faced with an elbow high stack of papers, can miraculously pull out of it the one scrap of paper that he needs. To everyone but him, that stack is a mess; but that mess is his order.

If you are unlike that fictional character—and most of us are—becoming organized will take some effort. "Right places" for everything have to be created, so you'll know where to look for things later. Apply an organizing principle to your activities, whether that system is chronological, thematic, general to specific, or specific to general. Impose order on your work, or possessions, if they lack a " natural" order. Example: you have a conference to plan and you need an organizing principle for how you go about planning it. Create a principle by deciding tasks to do in the order of their importance, or in chronological order (e.g. picking a date, finding a location, lining up speakers, creating a brochure.)

Here are four simple organizational guidelines:

1. Eliminate Clutter.
2. Everything in its place.
3. Plan what you have to do and make sure you do it.
4. Group and do similar tasks together.

Distinguishing Daily Priorities from Busywork

If at day's end you cannot point to one productive activity, you are allowing busywork, related to work or personal affairs, to interfere with accomplishing your short term priorities "one day at a time" and your long term goals.

Even if your office job has someone else assigning specific work to you, you may be taking longer than you would like to accomplish those projects. Or you may be failing to accomplish job-related goals for your own advancement. For example, if you need to rewrite your resume, or acquire new skills to add to your areas of expertise, the burden will probably be on you to find the time to do it during your non-work hours.

Busywork is another term for low-priority tasks. Having a third cup of coffee as you read the third city newspaper is probably busywork, unless you work for a newspaper clipping service. You may wish you "did more"at work, but because of poor planning, procrastination, or spending too long on low-priority calls to you (rather than placing those high priority calls that can make the difference in your job or business), you are frustrated by your low productivity.

Two of the biggest inhibitors to being organized and effective are **paperwork** and **telephone calls**. Paperwork can generate hours of busywork. A distinction has to be made between high-priority paperwork, discussed in the next chapter under *"Correspondence and Paperwork,"* and doing the paper shuttle, whereby papers (junk mail, low priority pieces of paper, material to be filed or discarded) are moved around, or piled up in a disorganized fashion, consuming time and space.

You've probably already heard lots of advice on paperwork, like "Handle a piece of paper only once" or " Dot a piece of paper each time you handle it until it has the measles and you do something with it." Doing the paper shuffle, described more extensively in the next chapter, can be an enormous time drain. Minimize your chances of falling into the paper busywork trap by eliminating distracting papers as much as possible. File it. Answer it. Throw it out. Put it with other papers of a similar nature and take care of them all at once.

Telephone calls may also consume hours of valuable time. If you personally take each and every call as it comes in, interrupting whatever you are doing at that moment, how do you expect to be organized? Try scheduling a telephone hour for placing calls—you have more control over when you place calls than when they come in—and budget that hour into your daily schedule.

You might also try instituting a period during the morning and the afternoon at the office when you prefer to receive incoming calls. Write lists, for yourself or your secretary, if you have one, of telephone interruptions that are permissible at times other than your designated "incoming-call hours." (The more strictly you adhere to your "no calls now" policy, the more valuable this way of organizing your day will become.) If you use a cell phone, you might consider getting voice mail on your phone so that callers may leave a message for you. In that way, you will be more likely to avoid automatically answering the phone if there is a safety concern, such as when you are driving, or if you are in the midst of a meeting, project, or conversation.

At home, consider that, except for emergencies, telephone calls should not be allowed to interfere with your dinnertime (often the only time some families have to interact with each other). Say to callers: "We're having dinner now. Can I call you back later?" If you're consistent, your friends, relatives, and even business associates will learn to respect your personal time budget.

Sharpening Decision-Making Skills

Becoming more organized and effective means sharpening your decision-making skills. By making clear decisions you will eliminate clutter because you will decide what to do with each and every piece of paper that comes into your office or passes across your desk.

Postponing decisions about what to do with paper, catalogues, reports, or even phone messages on slips of paper will lead to clutter and the companion to clutter, disorganization.

To sharpen your decision-making, develop well-conceived rules upon which you base decisions. In that way, you will avoid the need to ponder every little situation. Ask yourself these questions any time a decision has to be made:

> How important is this to do?
> What are the consequences of doing it? not doing it?
> Why do it now? the consequences of doing it later?
> How does this new idea (situation, request, etc.) fit in with what's important to me now? for the rest of my life?

By applying the rule of "What is my number one priority right now?" you will sharpen your decision-making skills. You will also sharpen your decision-making, and save time, if you focus on learning, not assessing blame. If a new idea or approach is suggested to you, ask yourself: Is it faster (or better)? Is it slower (or less effective)? What makes the difference? Reducing or eliminating the obstacles to effective time management discussed in Chapters 3 and 4, as well as becoming more organized, will also facilitate your decision-making skills.

ORGANIZING TOOLS AND TECHNIQUES

"To Do" Lists

Mental order is even more important than cataloging your possessions. One of the most effective tools in time management is knowing what you have to do. Maintain a "things to do" list, and write it down. Make sure it's readily accessible to you.

There are several approaches to creating "things to do" list. Such a list makes it more likely that you will act on important matters. Time management expert Merrill E. Douglass offers this advice about effective "to do" lists:

> Frankly, the To-Do lists that are kept by most people provide only

marginal benefits. The reason is that most To Do lists are a random collection of activities which have very little, if anything, to do with the purpose for which people work. Furthermore, most people have such a poor grasp of their objectives and priorities that a To Do list can hardly be an improvement. Thirdly, almost no one gives real thought to how long things take. As a consequence, most To Do lists contain far more than could be done in any given day. An excellent To Do list asks a very critical question: "How long is it going to take me to do it?"

Here are some alternative ways for creating effective "to do" lists for your work and personal goals:

(A) Divide your list to reflect how you arrange your day, such as:

1. Before Work
2. During Work
3. After Work

Within each section, fill in the appropriate activities.

(B) Follow a simpler chronological system, listing the key activities you want to accomplish that day, starting with number one. As you finish an activity, check or cross it off, and go on to the next thing you have to do. A sample of this approach follows:

1. Call airline or go on Internet to purchase tickets.
2. Write memo for meeting.
3. Duplicate memo for distribution.

(C) Write items down in order of descending importance, putting the major daily goal as number one (and not going on to number two until number one is done). Obviously, you will have to break down large tasks— writing a term paper, preparing a speech—into smaller steps, or you may take weeks to get to number two. Here's a sample of that approach:

1. Writing memo for meeting.
2. Duplicate memo for distribution.
3. Call airline or go on Internet to order tickets.

(D) Use the verb-noun principle discussed in the 4th principle of creative time management, "Keep your focus," on pages 11-12. That system is especially useful if you have to complete a major project but you find yourself procrastinating or getting distracted by activities of lesser importance.

Create a "things to do" list and check off each item as you complete it. Include all personal and professional tasks. Decide which organizing principle you will follow, and start by attacking whatever "to-do" item is first on your list.

The idea is not to become a list maker, spending more time in creating lists than in completing your priority tasks. List making is merely a way to organize your obligations—and a way to learn to do thoroughly one thing at a time.

Practically everyone I interviewed who finds list making useful preferred writing a "to-do" list for the following day right before going to bed; some said it actually helped them to sleep better. John, 31, a self-employed glass designer, says: "Between midnight and one, I make a list of items to do the next day. Some are important to do that day and I do those first. Others may be done another day, but I write them down when I think of them."

Creating a Personal Planning Calendar

The importance of a personal planning calendar is emphasized when, because of failure to maintain one, appointments are missed, deadlines ignored, or details of upcoming events are confused. Just in the past week, for example, Gloria showed up a week early for a party, Jim and Claudia forgot their daughter's wedding anniversary, and George had to cancel two meetings because he had failed to note that he would be away on jury duty. Alas, creating a personal planning calendar will not prevent others, who lack one, from disappointing you. However, it ensures that you will be more organized and efficient.

Bonnie, 28, vice-president of a bank, credits her organizational savvy to her personal planning calendar. Without fail, she records all work and personal commitments on that calendar. "It helps me to sleep at night," Bonnie explains. In one place she notes birthdays to remember, upcoming meetings, seminars she has to attend, and vacation days.

Your planning calendar can be a wall calendar, a daily appointment book—whether on traditional paper or an electronic version—but the consensus is that all the information should be kept in one place.

Depending on the work or personal demands on your schedule, you might need to have a calendar of the entire year at your fingertips if, let's say, you want to see the date in April you're scheduled to speak in Denver and the date in June you're scheduled to do a seminar in St. Paul.

Try to get into the habit of recording events as well as preparation time. For instance, you have to give a talk on Saturday, May twenty-first, and, of course, that is noted in your daily appointment book or on your wall chart. Have you also noted what hours or days you will be devoting to the preparation of that talk, including research time and practice sessions?

Remember: apply the same organization rules to your activities as you will apply to organizing your possessions. Eliminate clutter, unnecessary time wasters and interruptions, poor planning, and disorder.

Your planning calendar should provide you with an overview of specific commitments for the days, weeks, and months ahead. If possible, use pencil, so corrections are facilitated. Make sure you note personal plans or you might forget to follow up on them. Consider entering "free day" on your planning calendar, or you may never find the time for one.

The Everything Notebook

A variation on the personal planning calendar is the personal notebook. Like the calendar, all notes, incoming and outgoing phone calls, new addresses and phone numbers, ideas, and random thoughts are jotted down in one place as they occur. The notebook, such as a small spiral, looseleaf, or bound notebook, if possible, is carried with you at all times—in your pants or jacket pocket, pocketbook or attaché case. The advantage of using one notebook, what travel writer Theodore Fischer calls his "Everything Notebook," is that you avoid the disorganized mess of lots of little slips of papers that may be lost, misplaced, or in need of being transferred to another source. (You may still decide to transfer some of your notes and memos, but you always have your master chronological source to refer to.) The Everything Notebook is labeled with the current year. If more than one notebook is used during the year, each volume is numbered consecutively. As Fischer explains:

> This way I have only one source to go to; only one thing to grab when the phone rings. Every bit of business goes into the notebook. Each one lasts about two to three months. I'd feel undressed if I didn't have this book with me. One other thing about the notebooks: each time one is full, I have to decide which names, numbers, and addresses to copy into the new book. This provides a valuable opportunity for taking personal, social, and professional stock because you have to determine which names are still important, which are no longer important, which may be potentially important.

If you prefer an electronic or computer version of the Everything Notebook concept, there are numerous products available to you, from hand-held computers or devices that will synchronize with your desktop computer, as well as writing tablets that are linked to your computer.

Be open to these innovative systems as well as the ever-changing new technology becoming available at a faster and faster pace. Go to electronic trade shows, stop in and talk with sales representatives, or ask a colleague or friend who uses a system if he or she will take some time to demonstrate it for you, and see if these electronic notebooks could help you to keep your thoughts and data organized.

File Systems

The main types of materials that will fill your home or office files are:

1. Originals of incoming correspondence and/or interoffice memos.
2. Copies of outgoing correspondence.
3. Important papers, documents, or records for permanent safekeeping.
4. Reference or research materials.
5. Warranties (and any related receipts), and instruction booklets.
6. Announcements about upcoming meetings or events.

How many files you need will depend upon the kind of job you do, and how much information or material you want or need to have available. (The term *file* as it is used throughout this section refers to the conventional beige manila letter-size file folder. File could also mean oversized envelopes, floppy disks, or magnetic diskettes, or index cards.)

Keep active and inactive items separated, so that you can find day-to-day and priority materials quickly.

Once you decide which files you need ready access to, the major battle against disorganization of papers and research materials is won. Once you create a system, based upon inactive and active categories, it will be much easier to find things.

Within your active files, there are several basic organizing principles to follow for sorting your papers and labeling the files:

1.   **Chronologically (by date).** Going from current backwards, or

vice versa.

2. **Numerically.** Give each item listed or displayed in a master file a number and give each file folder a matching number to that item.

3. **Alphabetically.** If files are for individuals, file by last name, followed by first name. For topics or titles, file by the first letter of the first key word (not by an "a" or a "the.") For titles, you might also consider alphabetizing by the author's last, then first name.

4. **By subject or topic category.**

5. **By immediacy or importance (the priority approach).** Ordering based on the immediacy of response required or the urgency of the material in the file.

6. **By color.** Color coding with a master file identifying what each color signifies.

You can arrange research material alphabetically or by subjects (broad or narrow). You can put important documents in a file broadly labeled " important records" or put each record or document in a separate file; those files can then be organized by category, alphabetically, chronologically, by subject, or by color.

The overruling primary concern for an excellent filing system: in a month, a year, or ten years, will I be able to quickly find this material, or file, again or will I be able to easily explain to someone else where this file is located? If your answer is "yes," you are probably using an effective system.

There is one type of written material that must be filed, and it might be helpful to keep that file separate from the day-to-day originals and copies of memos that you also need to file. These crucial documents are the CY ("Cover Yourself") materials. You might also wish to cross-file these key materials: by category or in the regular file and in the CY special file. That way, if a problem does arise an hour, a day, a week, or even a year or two from now, you can show, through your careful records (the CY file), that you were not at fault, because you had touched second base, notified the appropriate governmental agency within the filing deadline, or made the necessary payment.

Try devising a new or improved filing system:

Step 1: Divide a blank sheet of paper into two columns labeled "Active" and "Inactive."

Step 2: Make a list of all the types of materials that you need to file, such as incoming correspondence, canceled checks, and documents, placing each category under the "Active" or "Inactive" heading (duplicating entries under both headings, if appropriate.)

Step 3: Select one type of material to be filed—e.g., incoming correspondence— and decide what filing system you will use.

Step 4: On a blank sheet of paper, work out on paper how you plan to file that one category, noting the organizing principle that you will follow, the system to be used, who will have ready access to these files, and a way in which active material can be rendered inactive.

Step 5: On separate sheets, repeat this paper planning process for your remaining categories.

Step 6: In order of importance, begin to implement your filing systems, purchasing any necessary supplies. Continue until your files are created.

Step 7: Maintain your planning notes, a help to you if at any point you forget any of the details behind your system.

Another filing system that some effective managers find useful is called a "tickler file." The system works like this: A file folder is made for each day of the month so that there are thirty or thirty-one file folders numbered one through thirty-one. There are also twelve files, one for each month. Any follow-up items are placed in the appropriate "to do" month file; as the month becomes current, pieces of paper are moved to the specific date (file) on which the action is to be carried out.

The tickler file requires some time to set up. For it to be effective, you have to maintain, and use it, as consistently as your daily planning calendar. For example, you might buy enough birthday and anniversary cards for the entire year. Address the envelopes and place the blank cards in the appropriate month when you will need one. When the month arrives, you move the card to the file for the date on which you should inscribe and mail that card. If you have season tickets to sports events, concerts, and so forth, you could file the appropriate tickets with the correct month, moving the tickets to the appropriate date as that month becomes current.

If you use a computer or word processor, there is software available that has calendars and reminders that perform a function that is similar to the "tickler" file. Two such software organizing programs are Day-Timer® Organizer 2000 and and OneStep Connect Personal Organizer. But you may still, however, want some kind of filing system for placing the actual correspondence, memos, cards, or tickets that you are following up on.

Types of possible filing systems include: filing cabinets of all sizes and shapes; document folders; magnetic diskettes (for use with computers/word processors); envelopes; boxes (cardboard, metal, or plastic); containers (decorative or plain); looseleaf notebooks; bound or spiral notebooks; garbage can; or bulletin board. You may find that the system that works best for you is just one of these filing options, or a more eclectic system that combines looseleaf notebooks for certain material, like weekly newsletters arranged chronologically, file cabinets with files arranged chronologically or alphabetically, and boxes for keeping all the material (piles) related to a current project before filing in file cabinets once the project is completed.Using a definite filing *system* to keep your work and materials organized frees up your memory for more important storage—the kind that can't be handled by filing.

The 30-Day File Diet

Quick access to the right information is vital today especially as the information explosion has caused a proliferation of data to be stored, and retrieved.

Streamlined and tightly organized files are one way to make sure you stay on top of the growing information, instead of being buried by it. Thinner files will usually help you get your job done better and more efficiently. Since additional file cabinets cost money and occupy costly office space, thin files will also help a company to keep down its costs.

Step # 1 Pick a target date.

By picking a definite date to thin out your files, you will overcome the biggest obstacle to thin files--procrastination. Mini case history: a midwestern data processing technology supplier picked the company's move to new offices as the target date for its first company-wide file purging program. The 350 headquarters employees were instructed to thin out their files since fewer files meant a less expensive move as well as fewer file cabinets-and more space-in the new offices. To boost employee motivation, the company came up with a charity incentive: for every pound of purged paper, the company would donate a pound of food to a local hunger group to feed the needy.

Just how much paper was purged? Thirteen tons of paper were purged or, to put that into more concrete terms, the paper that was thrown out enabled the company to discard 80 two-drawer lateral files. The campaign was so successful that the company made it an annual event.

Step #2 Be prepared for your file purging.

Have on hand a large empty garbage can and a recycling bin to aid your thinning efforts. Have strong string available if you need to tie up discarded catalogs or magazines for recycling or disposal. If practical in your office setting, if music makes the task more pleasant, have on hand a radio, cassette or CD player.

Step #3 Pick the best time to do your purging.

Whether you work in an outside office, or a home-based one, find a time to prune and purge your files that is convenient for you. If it is hard to find time during the workday, you may want to come in earlier, or over a weekend or holiday. Those with a home-based business may prefer to file in the evening, very early in the morning, before the workday begins, or over the weekend.

Having someone help you sort through your files is another tactic to keep you on track. Budget time for file management.

Step #4 Have clear reasons for keeping or purging material.

Grab a file. It could be the first file in your drawer or a specific category that is especially thick. Now ask yourself the following questions that Cecilia McKenzie, records expert and compliance analyst at Champion International, suggests you consider:
1. Is the information of value?
2. Will it add something new to what I have?
3. Can I obtain it elsewhere?
4. Is it significant for the company's purpose?

Answers to those questions will help you decide if you should hold on to a piece of paper, pass it along to someone else, or throw it in the garbage can or recycling bin.

Step # 5 Thin out files according to your particular filing system.

Use this thinning-out task to clarify your filing system or, if you lack one, to implement one. The better your overall file system, the easier it will be to thin out each file. It could be a system that is alphabetical, chronological, geographic, by subject, by color, by urgency, or an eclectic combination of all six. Example: Require that each file contains a key piece of paper, and that the essential item is the *first* piece of paper in the file.

Whatever your system, having one will facilitate thinner files.

Colored hanging files can add to effectiveness. If one drawer only contains files that are paid and they're all in orange file folders, and all the ones with a debit have green file folders in another place, it reduces the likelihood that someone will accidentally put a debit account in a paid account. When you group things that relate to each other in the same place, it means you use less space.

Step #6 Discard multiple copies or outdated materials.

Shred, throw out, or recycle outdated reports or other obsolete materials that are unnecessary for reference.

Step # 7 Know what you should keep, and for how long.

Your company (or your accountant) may have specific guidelines for a retention and purge schedule for certain kinds of documents. Check with the company's records personnel, lawyer, or accountant.

Step #8 Reward yourself for thinner files.

Now that you've thinned out your files, indulge yourself with something you never find time for but like to do.

Step #9 Establish and maintain a regular sift-and-purge schedule.

Keep on top of your files by instituting a regular pruning schedule, such as once a week or monthly. Consider writing the purge date on each file, or noting it through color coding techniques. See filing as a necessary part of being organized, and in control, of your files. A well-maintained file system will enable you to find what you need quickly, and efficiently, thereby contributing to your goal of creative time management.

Organizing Your Office

Out of 113 who completed a survey on the office that I tabulated for my book on the office (*Making Your Office Work For You*), only five noted that if they could change their office they would redecorate it. For everyone else (89 out of 113), an organizational or physical change, such as a better-organized office, more space or privacy, less noise, or improved lighting, were the key concerns.

My four year original research into the office discovered three principles for organizing an office:

1. productivity
2. status or image
3. a combination of #1 and #2

If your work is your calling card, and you rarely have visitors to your office, such as most writers, artists, salespersons who are on the road most of the time, productivity will probably be the key element to how your office is organized.

Offices organized around status or image use the office as a way of indicating a company's status as well as the position someone occupies in a company. The cues to that status are usually the size of the office, its location on a floor in terms of proximity to one's superiors, or on another floor, whether or not there is a window, if it is the coveted corner office, and the quality of the furniture, artifacts, and wall hangings. But even if you work alone in an outside office, or work from home, having an attractive and efficient office may boost your self-esteem and self-worth thereby boosting your productivity and probably your net worth as well.

Look at the office space you have. Are you in an open office setting without any privacy? Is this having a negative impact on your productivity? Is there anyway to achieve privacy, such as turning your chair and back away from others working nearby?

If you have an office with a door, could you rearrange your furniture to maximize your productivity? Is your office organized for peak efficiency? If you find there are too many drop-in visitors sitting and talking, have you considered removing the extra chair in your office, or replacing a thick upholstered chair with an uncomfortable metal or wooden one?

Health Considerations

Here are some of the health-related issues to consider when you organize your office:

- air quality.
- noise levels.
- eyestrain caused by improper lighting or improperly-used equipment, such as photocopy machines.
- backaches due to poorly-designed workstations, desks, chairs, or too much sedentary work.
- back or leg injuries due to poorly-organized offices such as poorly-positioned file cabinets, open drawers, boxes that block aisles, improperly lifting too-heavy objects or cartons.
- minimizing conditions that contribute to stress and fatigue.

Organizing Your Desk

Your primary goal is to avoid unmanageable and disorderly piles of unrelated supplies and materials in or on your desk. You want everything readily accessible, and in a place of its own. Keep extras of all your supplies, in ample quantity, in a supply closet or another storage area. If possible, have a wastebasket within reach.

Organizing the top of your desk is quite an individual matter but if you have a problem concentrating at your desk, try experimenting with adding or removing items—e.g.. family portraits, pencil holders, paper weights, stapler, tape dispenser, or calendars—to see if your work habits improve.

If possible, you should avoid keeping anything other than your current work on top of your desk— too many files or projects can provoke the "doing too much at once" syndrome. Jessica, 60, a middle management executive, has such a cluttered desk (and office) that she has to find a vacant office at her company to meet with clients. "I never get around to cleaning my desk because I always feel I should be doing real work," Jessica explains. Keeping your desk organized is part of every job. Fortunately, once the initial organizational system is implemented, it takes just minutes each day to maintain it.

Here are three useful tips for organizing your office:
1. **Schedule time for organizing, writing it down on your calendar.**
2. **Have a regular "file purging" day for computer and paper files.**
3. **If you need help reorganizing your office, consider hiring a professional to help you set up your initial systems even if you and your staff regularly maintain it.** Contact the National Association of Professional Organizers (NAPO), for referrals. NAPO is at 1033 La Posada Drive, Suite 220, Austin, Texas 78752-3880. For information and referrals: 512-206-0151 or visit their web site: www.napo.net.

Books, Magazines, and Other Reading Materials

Books, magazines, newspapers, journals, pamphlets, and other reading materials pile up quickly, and can become a major obstacle to an organized office or home. One couple has let the problem get so out of hand that whenever they move, their multiple cartons of unsorted reading materials move with them. The thought of going through those boxes, organizing useful materials and discarding the rest, is more awesome than spending the time and money to continually transport those weighty boxes.

Before it gets out of hand, you will find it a great time saver to evolve an orderly system for the accumulation, and disposal, of reading materials. Have a clear notion of whether you will sort or discard on a daily, weekly, monthly, or yearly basis.

There are a variety of temporary storage systems for reading materials— baskets for the floor or your desk, lucite holders, vertical cardboard units, elaborate 48 or 96 compartment literature organizers, etc.—that you can use for sorting and storing reading materials. You might also consider the altruistic and tax benefits of donating reading materials, that you might otherwise throw out, to college or local libraries, or schools.

Bookcases should fit the space available to you and be of the correct size for what you have to shelve. If you don't want to take the time to measure the height needed for each shelf, get adjustable shelves.

Arranging books by category, author, or another system geared to your needs will, in the long run, save you time, but initially you will have to devote some time to completing that task (depending on how many books you have). Remove the books from the shelves and rearrange one section at a time, working in a systematic way from top to bottom or left to right.

Just as you made a list of incoming magazines and other reading materials, now make a list of the categories of books that you have. If you find that your collection is basically just one or two types of books—let's say reference books such as the dictionary, a grammar book, and works of fiction—you might decide that it is more efficient for you to organize within the fiction section, by author or by title, with a second section for reference books, by title.

One way you can save lots of space and time today is by having at least one CD-ROM version of major reference works, usually updated annually. On just one disk, you could have an entire encyclopedia as well as a dictionary. (Recycle or dispose of outdated disks as CD-ROM disks can pile up and create clutter.)

In the Home Office

Two hundred years ago, as a result of the industrial revolution, work and living space separated. Working from home, however, has become increasingly popular in the last few decades. Because of the computer, and the widespread availability of overnight mail, Internet access, E-mail, and fax machines, as well as the time and expense saved by avoiding a daily commute to work, more office workers than ever before are working at home, some or all of the time.

If you work at home, you have more pressure to become, and stay, organized than most other workers since visitors to your home may also have access to your office.

Even if your home office is a completely separate room, with a door that could close it off to wandering eyes or visitors, the more organized and less cluttered you are, the less likely that anyone waltzing through your office, including children, a spouse, or visitors, could ruin or obscure your work.

Obviously your organizational problems will be somewhat different if your home office is a separate room in a spacious home, or in the corner of the living room in a two-bedroom apartment that you share with a spouse and two children. Certain considerations are universal, however: what are the essential supplies and equipment that have to be nearby and what can be stored elsewhere—in closets, other rooms, even other locations?

Here are additional tips to optimize home office productivity:

1. Make the first thing you do when you get into your home office the most important project of the day.
2. Avoid doing household chores or errands during the workday.
3. Keep a regular schedule. Make sure the phones are covered when you are out of the office.
4. Get a separate phone line for your home office and train your children or spouse not to answer it; use voice mail, an answering machine, or an answering service instead.
5. Take time for lunch and efficiency breaks every few hours if you work in long stretches.
6. To offset the potential emotional and professional isolation that working from home could cause, become active in at least one professional association.
7. Try to attend monthly breakfast, luncheon, or after work get togethers or meetings for social reasons and to keep up in your field.
8. Almost all home-based workers, if you have very young children at home, will need additional childcare help if you are to work more than just during your child's naptime or sleeptime hours.
9. Tell your friends not to call you during business hours.
10. Be flexible. If working from home used to be okay but now you need employees or more space, consider an outside office.

The next chapter provides additional suggestions for improved work productivity, whether you work in an outside or home office.

6
Improving Your Time at Work

More men are killed by overwork than the importance of the world justifies.
　　—RUDYARD KIPLING (*The Phantom Rickshaw*)

In some ways, the structure of the traditional work environment aids time management: although there may be autonomy within each task, employers set rules or guidelines about when to arrive, when to leave, what days to take as holidays, and, often, what to wear. However, procedures for evaluating performance and determining a raise are not always as clearly defined.

Within this framework, then, you are to a large extent on your own. You may know that you have to go to a meeting on Wednesday, but no one tells you how to get the most out of it. So don't let the external structure of your job misguide you that if you just show up each day, follow the rules, and do what's asked, you'll be making the best use of your time (and guaranteeing success.) The hard part of your workday is completely up to you. Although following company policy may seem commendable, that's the very least that's expected. Those rules go along with the job: observe them or quit. But what you do with the work that you're given is what will help you stand out from everyone else, sending you up the ladder, or back to the mailroom.

When it comes to work (or school), ask yourself this question: Is my performance judged on the quality of what I do, the volume of work I generate or complete, or whether or not I meet deadlines? Perhaps it's all three or, perhaps, it changes from day to day, month to month, or project to project. But this is a question that you should be continually asking yourself.

To improve your time at work or in business first make sure you know exactly what is expected of you.

First do what's expected; the extras are the gravy. If you're hired for your contract negotiating skills, but you're wheeling and dealing to try to bring in new clients instead, the person who hired you might not be as pleased as you thought she would be.

UNDERSTANDING YOUR WORK ENVIRONMENT

Laura punches in each morning exactly at nine and goes to the three-walled, metal cubicle in a high-rise office building where she will spend the next eight hours, minus one hour for lunch.

On the surface she is an excellent, reliable worker. She does not need to take work home; she seems to accomplish it all within her workday. She takes two weeks off each year for her paid vacation, all the sick days and personal leave that she is allowed, and she seems always to be busy. Underneath the "perfect employee" facade, however, are these realities: at least two hours are spent on the phone with up to 25 personal calls daily; Laura is not given enough to do, so she reads novels and magazines carefully concealed from her boss, whose office is many cubicles away; She spends a lot of time in traveling to and from the bathroom, chatting all the way.

Those who work hard and are surprised by Laura's lackadaisical attitude might believe that management soon "found out" Laura's ways. They didn't! Laura learned how to get management's expectations lowered to her own standard. When Laura left to take a better offer (and more money), she was sent on her way with roses and glowing letters of recommendation.

There are many who would not want to trade places with Laura even if they could. Job satisfaction means accomplishing a job that you value, not just getting paid for sitting at a desk all day, doing as little as you can get away with.

Some office workers say: "I can only get things done before everyone else gets here" (or after everyone else leaves). The result: they work seven to five or nine to seven, but not all that time is spent well. Their work-related time is longer, yet not necessarily more productive.

Take a hard, critical look at your workday. Write down the demands on you. Keep a time log to see where your time goes.

Managing your time better at work may mean redesigning your work space so you have better working conditions. It might mean asking your boss if you can get a door for your cubicle, because socializing with employees has so gotten out of hand that you find you have less and less uninterrupted time.

You might even consider talking to your employer about the possibility of flexible working hours, also known as flextime—an alternative to traditional fixed work schedules that gives you more flexibility to choose the times of your arrival and departure, and sometimes even the days that you work.

It is up to you, as much as possible within managerial or economic restraints, to make your work environment as efficient, pleasant, and functional as possible. Apply the conceptual and practical organizing principles that you learned in the previous chapter: everything in its place; eliminate clutter; and have readily available the tools and supplies you frequently need.

Becoming More Efficient

Correspondence and Paperwork

Practically all office jobs require writing, and answering, letters; even if you delegate the actual writing of your correspondence to a secretary or an assistant, an incoming letter has to be read and a decision made about whether it should be answered, and what form that answer will take.

Correspondence can become so time-consuming that the real work never gets done. It can also be so integral to your work that without it, there will be no real work. It's best to use correspondence as a warm-up up for the more demanding, or creative, parts of your job.

Michael Korda, editor chief at Simon & Schuster publishing company as well as the best selling author of *Power!* and *Success!*, finds that doing his own mail in the morning is a way he uses his "energy potential," as he puts it in *Success!*:

...then I decided that it was important to begin the day by accomplishing something, however trivial. I would spend the first hour of the morning answering mail. I would take no telephone calls, see nobody. I treated the mail as a separate, important but finite block of work. When I had read it, answered it, taken the necessary action where action was called for and gotten rid of it all, I had a cup of coffee, took a walk around the office to see what was happening, then went back to answer telephone calls on a priority basis. It was not very long before I began to look forward to my first hour—it gave me a sense of accomplishment and purpose.

Korda essentially found a way to turn the tedious task of answering correspondence into something motivational.

If you have a tendency to procrastinate about correspondence, address the envelopes and keep them in front of you. It may help to motivate you to write the letters that have to go inside those envelopes.

Dictating correspondence into a tape recorder is useful if you are experiencing "writer's block." However, traditional dictating letters may waste time since you or your assistant will have to first transcribe the tape and then write the letter.Consider voice recognition software which enable you to speak into a computer, even a hand-held one; the computer recognizes your voice and creates a written version for you or your assistant to edit.

You may also save time by having several "types" of letters for you, or your secretary, to adapt according to specific circumstances, such as business letters that say "Thank you," "Sorry, no jobs are currently available," "May I have the following information. . ." and so forth. These samples differ from a form letter in that they are adapted to a specific person and situation. They are not photocopied nor do they resemble a letter done *en masse* on a word processor.

If you do use a computer, and the body of the letter, make your modified "form" letter as short as possible. One-to-two page single-spaced letters are often a "tip off" that they have been done on a computer.

Computer templates are available for correspondence; these samples of letters, both for wording and for style, are a starting point for correspondence that you or your assistant could customize.

Business correspondence, like phone calls, should be responded to as promptly as possible.

To save time, if appropriate, consider sending an E-mail or a brief memo, rather than a more time-consuming formal business letter.

Some time management experts, such as Alan Lakein, advise: "Handle each piece of paper only once." That advice, like all time management advice, has to be tailored to your own needs. If you tend to procrastinate, are unable to discriminate between priority and low-payoff correspondence, or if out-of-sight is out-of-mind, this more conventional time management approach of handling a piece of paper just once may serve you better than filing paper according to a specific category, to be retrieved, and dealt with, at a later date.

As was noted in the previous chapter on becoming organized, the key is to set up a filing system that works for you. It doesn't matter if it's alphabetic, chronological, thematic, by color, coding by number, or whatever. All that counts is that you can find things in a fast and reliable manner.

How you handle copies of materials can be crucial; over time, paper has a way of piling up and becoming unmanageable. A lawyer I know makes two copies of each memo or letter; one is filed by subject; the other is filed chronologically. This way he has two ways of relocating it at some point in the future.

Do you regularly copy all important memos? Do you make notes about telephone conversations and put them into your files? Keeping track of what you accomplish each day is a way of gaining control of your time. But do not make the written record, or copies of that record, as important as the work itself.

Technology and Tools for Effective Time Management

According to my work survey, a majority (52%) of the men and women who answered a question about what technological advance has been their best time-saver over the last decade checked off personal computer (PC). A very distant second was the fax machine (16%) followed by E-mail (12%), which is actually tied to the computer. [Number 4 was the microwave (less than 1%) and number 5 was the cell phone (less than 1%).]

Technology and equipment, whether it is a computer, a photocopying or a fax machine, can save, as well as waste, your time, especially initially, when you have to learn how to operate it. Make sure you build into your work schedule the one day to 2 weeks learning time that you may need to gain mastery over it. At first, it may actually take more—not less—time to complete a task using the new technology, but over time it will probably save you time and even enhance the quality of your work as well.

When photocopying machines became common in office

buildings, for example, the need to make copies increased—and not just copies of documents that would have been carboned previously. New ways to use the copier emerged. Until employees learned the proper use of photocopying, they, or their assistants, were spending more time duplicating than before (even though it was now faster and easier).

But machines do not eliminate the people factor so crucial to success in business today. My research and observations make it clear to me that in business the best way to communicate is first in person, next, by phone, third, by E-mail, and, finally, by mail. Very soon videophones will become standard but, once again, even the ability to see the person you are speaking with on the phone does not replace the need to say hello, shake hands, and have the face-to-face observations technology will never replace.

Computers

If you use a personal computer, because power outages occur, or computers sometimes freeze or files get deleted unintentionally, take the time to back up your work, as you go along. Back up your data in multiple ways. Have a surge protector to reduce surge damage.

What About a Computer?

A best-selling novelist, when asked if he planned to get a computer (he has written on the same manual typewriter from the beginning of his career), replied, "No," he was not going to get one, but he might get one for his secretary. So, if your system is working, don't introduce new technology just because it's available. It just might cost you time.

How do you decide whether or not a computer is worth the money and time (to learn how to use the machine as well as the software) that getting one would mean to you and how you do your work? Here are some tasks that computers accomplish much more effortlessly than humans:

--repetitive typing, such as retyping the same words, paragraphs, or documents again and again.

--editing and revising copy such as rewriting a report or letter until you are pleased with the organization, length, or specific wording.

--creating charts to enhance your documents such as bar or line graphs or drawings.

--communicating with others via E-mail and the Internet.

--doing mathematical calculations or projections and estimates, including financial spreadsheets.

--the necessity of updating the same basic information on a regular basis, such as price lists, sell sheets, resumes, course overviews, bibliographies, or correspondence.

--creating and maintaining a database for reference or for mail merging correspondence to multiple recipients.

--sending fax transmissions from the computer.

--meeting specialized needs with specific software such as composing music, designing a building, doing desktop publishing of newsletters, magazines, or books.

--creating art work that can be stored or transmitted through the computer.

Computers, as everyone knows, are constantly being enhanced, updated, and outdated. Some opt to rent a computer, getting a newer model at the end of the rental agreement. Others prefer to buy, upgrading less frequently. Some companies have trade-in options built into their purchase agreements whereby you can trade in the current computer for a newer model in a certain period of time. Another option today is to have a computer custom built to your specifications for the amount of memory you need as well as whether or not there is a built in back-up system, and other technical considerations.

Certainly the software you use with your computer is as much a consideration for maximizing your efficiency as the computer itself. Not only should you select a software program suited to your individual needs but you need to take the time to master it so you feel confident about its nuances and subtleties. In addition to spending the time to train yourself by reading the manual or calling the help line of the software manufacturer for advice, you could hire a consultant to give you some time-saving tips or take a course.

E-mail and The Internet

E-mail, the ability to send and receive messages electronically through the Internet, as well as the other benefits of the Internet, such as the ability to quickly obtain research or visit the informational sites of magazines, book publishers, organizations, or businesses, are sometimes offset by the vast amounts of time these technological advances could consume if you are not careful.

It is even possible to get addicted to being "on line;" the immediate gratification and the very powerful pull and mesmerizing power of interacting instantly through E-mail could take up minutes or hours of the time you should be spending finishing up a priority project.

Because of the way the Internet ideally interacts in one seamless flow of information through search engines and key words, you could find just about anything. So unless you take control of the Internet, and how you spend your time on it, you could find yourself drifting further and further away from the original reason you went "on line" in the first place.

Similarly with e-mail, there is an expectation that e-mail will be returned instanteously even if you a) did not initiate the communication b) are busy doing other things c) only check your e-mail now and then or d) are inundated with literally 100+ messages daily, the majority unsolicited.

Once again, you have to establish clear guidelines for when, how, and if you will respond to your e-mails; for certain unsolicited e-mails, you might even want to develop an "auto responder" that you could automatically send back explaining why you will not immediately respond to the e-mail. If it is a communication you have not solicited, other instructions for why or how to communicate with you can be forwarded.

Whether it is the Internet in general or e-mail in particular, be aware of how long you are on line at all times. Some Internet providers will tell you, periodically, how long you are on line, but you should be aware of that time on your own as well.

You should also monitor whether you are on line, or sending or answering e-mail, by choice or by compulsion. Are you getting addicted to being on-line or are you carefully using these technological advances in the service of your time and work? (If you are getting addicted to the Internet, refer to the suggestions for conquering bad habits in Chapter 4 to help you overcome this problem.)

The Internet can also save vast amounts of time, however, especially for instant access to research material through such services as www.elibrary.com or daily newspapers or magazines that post articles or whole issues to the web. Through chat groups and special interest web sites, it is also possible to gather research by polling visitors on specific questions or even just reading and considering the concerns and information that they share.

Budget time for a "technology upgrade" hour, day, or week. Take the time to learn about your hardware equipment or software programs, as well as what is new and better that you could use. Go to trade shows, stop in computer stores, take courses, hire a consultant.

The Scanner

A scanner is a piece of equipment which enables you to scan images (art work, photographs, graphic designs) or text, with the addition of Optical Character Recognition (OCR) software. This revolutionary equipment, which is now available for less than $100 and is even part of a printer-fax-scanner combination machine, is definitely something most offices in the new millennium need to have. Scanning software enables you to edit images before you add it to the desktop publishing application of that image. "Hard copy" or text, instead of typing or typesetting it, can now be scanned and in that way put into a computer file for editing. This technology is revolutionizing entire industries, such as printing and graphic design, as well as writing and publishing.

The Fax Machine

This machine sends data over the phone lines and is definitely one of the key technological tools available today for saving time. For urgent communications, the fax machine eliminates the need for overnight delivery services. However, most agree that lengthy documents (more than 10 pages) should probably be sent by overnight mail unless the person receiving the fax has agreed that very long documents are okay to fax. Furthermore, fax transmissions sometimes go astray so you might want to check if your fax has been received. Plain paper fax machines are generally preferred in business because the fax transmissions are easier to read and will not fade in time.

Unsolicited fax transmissions are generally frowned upon in business as is faxing a resume (unless requested to do so.)

The Telephone

The telephone is a tool or a weapon, depending upon how you use it, or let it use you. Using the telephone for a long-distance phone interview may be the most important work-related task you accomplish on a given day; allowing numerous personal or business calls to interrupt you at crucial times when you are working may be frustrating, as well as time wasting.

Some workers allow personal calls at their offices only during a certain hour of the day, and only for a specified length of time. Others make it clear that personal calls, whenever they are received, must be brief and to the point, related to a specific question such as, "When do you expect us over tonight?" rather than just a way of "shooting the breeze."

If you're having trouble figuring out just how your telephone time is spent, or wasted, consider keeping a time log just for outgoing and incoming calls, noting the reason and duration of each call.

If you are prone to talk compulsively, set a time limit for your calls. Even if you're not, try to have a clear idea of what you want to say, and how long you will allow yourself to say it, whenever you initiate a call.

Secretaries, phone machines, and answering services can be helpful in making better use of the telephone, but only if used well. Most phone machines have monitors, so that you can screen calls and decide whether or not to pick up, without callers knowing you are there. Sometimes you may decide it is better to take a call since returning a call can entail even more time.

One of the few negatives related to most voice mail systems, however, is that you cannot monitor who is calling. If you decide you do not want to be interrupted, and the phone rings, once it goes to the voice mail system, you have to allow someone to leave a message in order to find out who is calling and why.

Some people find it useful to have categories of callers, or types of calls; on this list, personal and business contacts are classified into one of the categories—Always Put Through, Never Put Through, Always Take Message and Say I'll Return the Call. This system can be quite effective, since it eliminates that awkward interaction when a secretary says, "I'll check to see if she's in," and although the caller knows that the secretary is querying her boss, the secretary soon returns, saying, "No, I'm afraid she's not in at the moment, but she will return your call."

If you want to use the phone rather than letting it use you, consider memorizing, and using, this useful little phrase: "I can't talk right now." If you want, add "Can I get back to you?" Here are some other phrases to try if you have trouble getting off the phone, or telling the caller that you are unable to start a conversation:

> "I have to go now."
> "I can't talk much longer."
> "I have someone in my office."
> "I was just on my way out the door."
> "I have a staff meeting starting in a minute so we have to wrap this thing up."
> "Can't talk now, I have a roomful of people."

You may even find it necessary to make a list of friends whom you may dearly love but who have a telephone problem. These people engage in monologues, so it's rare that you can get off the phone in less than an hour. If you do want to call those kinds of friends, call them when you know they are unable to talk— just to give them a brief message or to stay in touch—or when you have plenty of time that you want to spend on the phone.

You should also consider some of the telephone devices that facilitate effective time management. For example, cordless phones permit you to walk around as you speak. This can be a great time saver if you find yourself saying "I'll call you back" because you need privacy; a cordless phone permits you to find that privacy all the time. Of course cell phones allow continual access even if on the train or in the car. Observe mobile phone etiquette by turning it off when in movie theatres, live performances, certain meetings or lectures, as well as safety concerns while driving or walking.

Phone machines or voice mail have become realities at work today. Decide if you will leave a message, or not. If you decide to leave one, speak clearly, slowly, and keep it short and to the point. If possible, leave a return phone number as well as the best time to reach you to avoid telephone tag. (Similarly, make the outgoing message on your machine or voice mail as explicit as possible.)

Here are other phone devices or available services or options to consider to increase your efficiency:

--call waiting

--caller ID (that allows you to see who's calling so you can decide if you will take the call or not; if you lose someone's phone number, you could also track it down through stored caller I.D.s, which could store as many as the last 25 names and phone numbers)

--call forwarding

--three-way or conference calling

--missed call (which, for a fee, allows you to put in a code and be connected to the call that you just missed)

--speed dialing

--speakerphone

last number redial (helpful if you keep getting a busy signal)

Use the phone creatively and avoid getting a reputation for only calling if you want to get something from someone. (One man I know is so used to being called for favors that he answers his phone by asking, "What can I do for you?") Once in a while, call business relations just to say hello. Listen to your business relation. You probably won't want to ask in great detail about the golf game last Saturday or the vacation in Spain, and you probably won't want to stay on more than a few minutes, but a sincere goodwill call may be welcome. The goodwill call suggestion, however, should be used with caution; you don't want to get a reputation for being a telephone time waster any more than you want to be known as an opportunist.

To keep track of calls and callers, instead of single slips of phone message sheets, it may be useful to have a central book, such as a spiral-bound one with a copy of each message. You will also be creating a permanent record of incoming callers, a handy record to have if you misplace a phone number a week or several months down the road. You can also take off the top sheet and give the message to someone but still have the permanent copy in the record book.

Dealing With Visitor Interruptions

In-person drop in visitors are as disruptive as telephone visitors who have, in effect, interrupted you with their call. You may be facile at handling both telephone and in-person interruptions but it is usually easier to get off the phone than to turn someone away who is right there in front of you. Without developing the reputation of being cold and aloof, you do want to establish rules for those you work with, namely, that drop-in visits should be avoided if possible. Get your co-workers or employees to develop the habit of calling first. (In some work situations this is impossible since you may work side by side.)

One technique to discourage drop-in visitors at the office, at least temporarily, is to have an established "quiet hour." You might put a sign on your door, "Do not disturb," or just let it be known that you are unavailable for one or more specific hours each day.

If drop-in visitors cannot be handled in other ways, try to deal with the immediate situation and get them out of your office as quickly as possible. Some executives purposely avoid having a chair in their office other than their own; discomfort (and the awkwardness of just standing there) may push visitors out faster than your words. If your drop-in visitor does not get the hint, especially if you have another appointment, come right out and say so. Obviously, if the drop-in visitor is your boss, more tact may be required to get him out, without encouraging his wrath. You might consider going in to see your boss, on a fixed or flexible basis, so drop-in visits to your office are minimized. In that way you might have more control over the situation, especially if you decide in advance what point or priority project you will be discussing.

If your job depends upon the social relations (and subsequent business) that may result from drop-in visits from customers or clients, such interruptions may not be time wasters for your job. If that is the case, you might, for instance, have a hot pot of coffee "on tap" as well as a comfortable sofa for your uninvited guests.

Each type of visitor interruption will be handled differently. Expected visitor interruptions should be planned for in advance with a written agenda for the meeting, any supporting materials that you will need to show or to distribute should be available.

If the visit is unexpected, you have to determine if it is desirable or intrusive. You could be in the midst of preparing a report for later that afternoon, but if the drop-in visitor is the senior vice president, you might want to stop what you're doing.

Time Off (Vacations, Sick Days, Personal Leave)

The right to shorter hours and longer vacations was achieved through the long efforts of laborers and union members. But no one, however, will make you take advantage of this extra time; it's up to you not just to take the time that's coming to you, but to plan the kind of activities that will be personally and professionally rewarding.

You might think you're saving money by puttering around the house, rather than going away, or saving time by not going away at all. Those who are self-employed often find it especially difficult to take a vacation; they are afraid that their business will deteriorate in their absence, or they are working on overlapping assignments and are unable to take time off during a project. If you can manage it, at least two weeks a year—two one-week vacations or one two-week vacation—will do wonders for your work abilities. It will also help you break the routine, focus on your health and emotional well-being, and allow you the time to renew intimate relationships.

If you can't get away for that length of time, consider what one advertising executive does. He divides his vacation time up throughout the year taking three or four-day mini-vacations with his wife, never traveling more than two hours by car from home.

Some workers may incorrectly fear that taking a vacation means possibly losing their job, but by failing to take one may create more stress and anxlety than by taking time off.

Experts agree that some time off from the job is a necessity for an employee's mental health and for family relationships that have so much influence on the worker's health and productivity.

If you get at least two weeks, your first vacation decision is whether you will take it consecutively, or split it up.

What is the best time to take your vacation? Some companies may require taking it when business is slow. Others may shut down and have company-wide vacations, making the decision for you. But if you do have some choice, pick the weeks that are best for you and your family. Since so many schedules at work will have to be coordinated, get your request in quickly to ensure your first or second favored periods.

There is also the "use it or lose it" policy that some companies follow. Some companies require vacation days to be taken within the calendar year, plus the first quarter of the next year. It is your responsibility to talk to a human resource manager or supervisor and find out what are the vacation policies at your company.

Here are some tips for making your vacation from work easier to take and more refreshing without anxiety about what you've left behind:

- Pick up some of the workload of a vacationing coworker or colleague so he or she will reciprocate when you are away.
- Right before your vacation (and afterwards), plan to put in late nights getting ahead (or caught up).
- If you really want to make sure you get away, be careful about new business that is offered to you in the weeks before your vacation if you would have to have it finished before your departure. Unless you are absolutely sure about your ability to meet, or beat, a deadline, try to either get a delayed deadline for this business, or refer it to a worthy colleague who will probably one day return the favor.
- Make sure a superior will know your vacation whereabouts. Designate someone that will call you if something happens at the office while you're away if something occurs that you should know about.
- Tell management what weeks you'd like to take off, but do your actual vacation dreaming or planning away from the job, and watch out for too much "we're going to .... on our vacation" bragging statements, or you may be seen as wasting company time with personal matters as well as being a braggart.
- Put effort into where you and your family would vacation best. Research and plan it, taking into account what you like to do and the cost. Plan something that matches your non-work interests, such as tennis camp, hiking or going on an archaeological dig. Sitting on a beach may help one person to unwind, but another might find it boring. There are many travel sites on the Internet to help you plan your vacation, such as www.Expedia.com.
- Even if money is a concern, take your vacation time anyway, if you need it, even if you don't go away on a trip.

Sick days and personal leave are other potential respites from work that you should use to your best advantage. As you learned in the section on obstacles to effective time management, employers are more sympathetic to absences because of physical ailments than emotional ones. You, however, are the best judge as to whether a day off this week might be to your advantage, and to your employer's.

Efficiency Breaks

Build into your workday the kind of rests that Elton Mayo found improved the efficiency of the workers at the Philadelphia textile mills in the 1920's. As Frances and Milbourn explain in their text, *Human Behavior in the Work Environment*, after efficiency experts and financial incentives for employees failed to reduce a 250 percent worker turnover rate, Mayo was called in for what became known as "The First Inquiry." Mayo discovered that permitting workers who stood all day to take four brief rest periods increased productivity and caused the turnover rate to drop.

As the late psychologist Dr. David Leeds used to say, "Even prizefighters get two minutes off between rounds."

Enhance your own work effectiveness, reduce fatigue, and decrease the possibility of making mistakes because of exhaustion by taking efficiency breaks or rests for five to thirty minutes, or an hour or longer, if necessary. Become atune to the timing and length of an efficiency break that will maximize your own work performance. Become sensitive to your physical or mental signals that it's time to break away. Note: use discretion in some work settings if your coworkers or employer might misinterpret your break as goofing off. Consider an exercise break, running for twenty minutes around lunchtime as one lawyer in Washington, D.C. does, or taking a walk; if necessary, find a way to take a brief nap.

Working With Others

Delegating

Do You Need Help Delegating More Effectively?

To find out if you could use help with delegating, ask yourself the following questions:

1. Are you working much longer hours than everyone around you, especially your subordinates?
2. Are you spending an inordinate amount of time each day on such easily "delegatable" tasks such as routine correspondence, non-priority phone calls, feeling yourself spread too thin?
3. Have you had an ulcer since taking this job, or felt as if you're heading for one?
4. Do you doubt you could select competent people to delegate to?
5. Do you dwell on past delegating disasters?
6. Are you a perfectionist?
7. Has anyone called you a "control freak"?
8. Are you unwilling to delegate the responsibility for the entire job, along with a specific task?
9. Have you ever fantasized that life could be more enjoyable if you could do *everything* yourself?
10. Have you come close to, or been, fired one or more times over the issue of delegating?

If you answer "yes" to one or more of the above questions, you probably need help with delegating.

Even though it may be harder for some to give up total control and delegate than others, the good news is that delegating well is a skill that can be learned. But first you have to recognize if you have a problem with delegating. Sure tip offs? Working excessively long hours. Second, not getting enough of the important stuff done --and you know what that is for your particular job or profession -- the projects, activities, or actions you should be doing. The activities that bring in sales, income, new customers or clients. The thinking stuff or even the client contact, if that's what you should be doing.

Delegating Effectively

Based on research and observations, here are the seven steps to becoming effective at delegating:
1. Decide what you will delegate.
2. Pick the right person to delegate to.

3. Unless proven otherwise, trust those to whom you delegate.
4. Give clear assignments and instructions.
5. Have definite "check points" for completion of a specific task or job and some system of on-going communication with those you delegate to.
6. Give credit to the person to whom you delegated.
7. Delegate responsibility for the job, not just one task.

1. Decide What You Will Delegate.

There are three considerations in deciding what to delegate:
1. Decide what is your priority task and delegate any tasks or jobs that stop you from focusing on that priority task. 2. Delegate what you can't do yourself because you don't have the skills or expertise. 3. Delegating what you won't do yourself because it's too boring, distracting from your priority task, or not the best use of your time. These are tasks that you could do, but you choose not to, because at this point in your career, someone else could do those jobs for you, such as routine correspondence or screening incoming calls.

2. Picking the Right Person to Delegate To.

Learn the traits and values, such as trust, and characteristics of those who will perform well when you delegate to them. A concern is whether or not someone is asking questions at the time a task is assigned. Listen and observe. As a North Carolina sales director notes, "You find out pretty quickly about people who are willing to take responsibility if they're already taking it on their own."

3. Trust Those You Delegate To.

Along with trust, you also have to grant the persons to whom you delegate the chance to do it their way. There is more than one acceptable way to do most tasks, but you do have the right to require that whatever you delegate is done accurately, and well.

4. Give Clear Assignments and Instructions.

Dr. Harry Levinson, chairman of the Levinson Institute in Boston, and a professor emeritus of psychology at Harvard Medical School, says that the fourth delegating step will especially help those managers who are resistant to delegating. Levinson advises:

> Learning to let go a little bit and trusting their people means giving them clear cut assignments with time boundaries, when they expect the assignments to be completed, and criteria for judging the quality of the work. Then reviewing each assignment, as it's completed, to see how well the person has done to help decide when he or she is ready for increased responsibility so that one let's go gradually.

Career consultant Nella Barkley, President of Crystal-Barkley Corporation, points out another pivotal part of giving clear assignments and instructions. As Barkley says:

> Learn how someone best receives information, whether they're your boss or your subordinate. Some receiving information best orally. For example, some CEOs, if you give them a ten page report, they'll never read it. [But] for some people, it's better to put it in writing first and let them think about it. You will generally learn how people receive information best by how they give information to you.

5. Have Definite Task Completion and a Follow-up System

Establish deadlines at the beginning of a specific project including several "mini-deadlines." In this way you may follow-up and check up on the work, especially till you are comfortable with someone's skills level, rather than waiting till the one deadline at the end.

6. Give credit.

You will inspire loyalty and a wish to serve in those you delegate to if you give them credit for their achievements. Too often those with a problem delegating will have someone do a task and then will complete the job themselves, taking all the credit. This strategy eventually backfires, however, since taking all the credit develops a bad feeling among coworkers and subordinates.

7. Delegate Responsbility for the Job, Not Just the Task.

There are three issues at the bottom of a failure to delegate responsibility for the job, not just one task. The first is that you must trust those you delegate to will do a good job. Second, and this is hard for high achievers, the ones most likely to have a problem delegating, to do: you have to be willing to accept the fact that the person you delegate to may do the job worse or, heaven forbid, even better than you. Third, you have to be willing to help them learn from their mistakes, if they make them.

Only by delegating entire jobs, not just tasks, will you avoid the monkey-on-the-back syndrome, first espoused in the classic *Harvard Business Review* article, "Management time: Who's got the monkey?" Co-authors and management consultants William Oncken, Jr. and Donald L. Wass, step by step, show how managers who fail to delegate responsibility as well as tasks will eventually find themselves reporting to their subordinates, and doing some of *their* work, rather than vice versa!

Here are five additional rules for delegating provided by Letitia Baldrige, etiquette expert and former social secretary to the White House during the Kennedy administration:

> 1. I still think the way to get someone to cooperate with you is to be sensitive to his or her time problems:
> First, you say how desperate you are. Second, you ask nicely. Third, you state for exactly how long you're going to need this person and what the duties will be.
> 2. Encourage the person during the operation, particularly if it's more work, and it's taking longer, than you thought.
> 3. Never be so busy and arrogant yourself that you don't take time to praise.
> 4. After you've delegated the authority and the job is done, be sure to go on record giving credit to those who did a

terrific job. That is very important. Then they'll be ready to work for you again... fast.

5. To ensure permanent-delegation, education comes into it. You may have to bring the person up to speed. That may require giving him or her a special book to read, suggesting a six-week course at night, or just getting a subscription to a trade publication that will make him more sophisticated about his job.

Whether you work with others, or alone, delegating can dramatically increase how effectively you manage your time. (If you delegate improperly, it can be an enormous time drain.) Delegating—giving up total control of your work and entrusting certain tasks to others—is hard for some workers, yet the inability to delegate often undermines your own, or your company's, growth and profits.

If you have a problem delegating, try to analyze where it stems from: Do you need to control everything in your work environment? Do you doubt you could hire someone competent? Have you had bad prior experiences with delegating so you are afraid to try it again? Are you fearful someone else can do it better than you?

You can delegate to another worker or to a machine, a robot or a word processor, for example, or to a service, such as a printing firm that will do addressing and envelope stuffing. Delegating is not the same thing as passing the buck. You are paying someone to perform some of your tasks to free yourself to perform others, usually more important and specialized, ones. Company presidents, who started a firm from scratch, may still be fixing machines when their time would be better spent planning and inventing. By contrast, in large bureaucracies, being given the power to delegate is seen as a status symbol; the more people that work for you, the more important you must be. Delegating well can lead to increased efficiency; delegating badly— misusing your power—can lead to poor employee relations. For example, it may be tempting to ask your secretary to play baby-sitter; in the long run, it may be more efficient to line up a student you call on just for that purpose.

Working with Superiors

Being overly familiar, or too close-mouthed, can cause problems in working with superiors. If you over-involve your superiors in what you are doing—at work or in your personal life—you may be wasting valuable time that could be spent actually working, or make your superior feel burdened by your own personal affairs (and wondering if you can take care of things). If, by contrast, you fail to keep your boss informed about your work, she may falsely believe you are unproductive. Moderation is the key; neither "all talk, no action" nor "all action, no talk" are desirable extremes.

Let's say you are in charge of a specialized reference collection maintained in a college library. Although somewhat autonomous, you were hired by the senior librarian, and she wants to be informed of your activities. You could keep her informed by writing a weekly, bi-weekly, or monthly memo. You could decide a more informal approach is what's needed— updating her over coffee or lunch every so often. Unless your superiors issue guidelines on how and when to update them on your work—and often they do not—it is up to you to devise, and follow through on, an effective plan. Even if you decide the more casual approach is what's needed, it should not be casual for you.

What about socializing outside of the office? Use your discretion. You may think it would aid your office relationship to meet outside of the job. You may decide it would be best to let your boss make the first move. A circumstance might arise, such as an extra pair of tickets to a concert or sports event that you know he'd enjoy, that would naturally lend itself to after-work socializing. Timing, and the personalities involved, should be taken into account on a job by job, situation by situation basis.

Compulsive Talkers

Beware the compulsive talker! Compulsive talkers waste their time, and will gladly waste yours, if you let them. Compulsive talkers take energy away from their work and put it into talking about their work.

If you have a compulsive talking problem, consider maintaining a written daily journal as a way of diverting your output away from those around you. (At the least, you will be saving *them* time.) Maybe you will have to talk into a tape recorder just to get over your need to talk compulsively, or seek professional help to find out what motivates the constant chatter.

What's behind compulsive talking? Muriel Schiffman, author of *Self Therapy* and *Gestalt Self Therapy*, describes two types of compulsive talkers, and their motivations:

> 1. This talker has a dark secret. Talking in this instance is a red herring, like the mother bird who distracts you and tries to lead you away from the baby birds.... He is also trying to atone for years of secrecy by "telling all" now (about something else).... This kind of talker is often entertaining if exhausting.
>
> 2. This talker has never had anyone to listen to him at some important period in his life.... Since a neurotic is someone who never got what he needed in the beginning, he never learned how to get it. So this deprived talker sets himself up again and again to be rejected; he is very boring.

Is there a cure? Schiffman, who had this problem herself, stopped talking compulsively. How? "I sublimated my pattern by lecturing three nights a week and sometimes, by special invitation, from ten am. to six p.m.... Eventually, after many, many therapy sessions which uncovered innumerable facets to my unconscious motivations, I lost the desire to lecture at all as well as the craving to talk too much."

Working Too Much

Are you addicted to work? Would you rather work than do anything else? Are you at work early in the morning, into late hours on weekday nights, as well over the weekends, or even on vacations? Do you even allow yourself to take a vacation? Do you have trouble stopping work once you get started?

Workaholics are perfectionists and high energy people; being around them, or working for or with them, places demands on others that they may not meet. Like alcoholism, workaholism is a hard addiction to cure since work has become a way of avoiding other issues. Furthermore, since there is such an emphasis on the work ethic, many may fail to see their excessively-long hours at work as a negative. When does working hard, a positive value, become workaholism, an addiction that can cause stress and burnout?

"I use my work to avoid socializing," says Kathy, 32, an analyst for a stock brokerage firm. Saturday nights, when she might be out on a date, Kathy is home, rereading financial newspapers.

Workaholism is actually a time waster in disguise. The basis of workaholism is the mismanagement of work and personal time. If the workaholic planned his or her time better, he or she might not need to pull as many "all nighters" to get the work done. Too much of anything, including work, is rarely beneficial to a person's overall well-being, physical, mental, intellectual, emotional, and social. Workaholics, oblivious of the schedules that others adhere to, may even be found working on weekends, Christmas Eve, or other holidays —along with their dutiful employees.

For additional discussion about "Types You May Encounter in Work-Related Situations," see Chapter 9 in my book, *Business Protocol*, covering 17 different types including the manipulator, the spy, the braggart, and the hidden agendist.

Making the Most of Meetings

The daily, weekly, or monthly meeting can be a notorious time waster. Yet, if used correctly, it can also be a time saver. For example, you can use meetings to learn about your company, or your project, so you become aware of new trends.

Here are suggested guidelines for conducting meetings:

1. Make sure there is a reason for the meeting and that all those expected to attend have been advised, in writing, of that purpose as well as the time the meeting will start and finish. Make it clear in your advance notices that the meeting will start on time and that it is important to be on time, not late.
2. Stick to the starting time; latecomers will get the point at least for the next meeting and those who are on time will not be kept waiting for the few latecomers.
3. Have a written agenda for the meeting and follow it.
4. Decide in advance if you, or someone you delegate to, will take notes during the meeting. If you decide to tape record the meeting, make provisions for transcribing the tape.
5. Keep discussions to the topic at hand and control questions that get off on a tangent or your meeting (and you) may start to seem unfocused and disorganized.
6. Be certain that, by the end of the meeting, participants have a sense of accomplishment. Summarize what the meeting achieved, if necessary.
7. Decide in advance if you will followup the meeting with a written synopsis of what was accomplished.
8. End on time.
9. Thank participants for attending and advise them if they will receive a written or oral follow up. If there will be another meeting, announce when it will take place.

If you have to attend a meeting, avoid saying anything just because you want to brag about the work you are doing, as a way of gaining recognition. If you have something specific to contribute, or a pertinent question to ask, by all means speak up. Make notes in advance so that whether you make a statement or ask a question, you present your ideas or questions succinctly and tactfully.

If you attend conferences, set yourself clear goals. If someone else is sending you there, you may be required to write a report detailing what you gained from it. If you do write such a report, keep it simple and clear. You may want to go on for fifteen pages, but you may be wasting the time of the person who has to read it, and your time in creating such a detailed report. Even if you are not asked to set goals, or to write a report, do it for yourself. Before attending any meeting or conference, have a clear idea what you want to get out of it.

Exhibiting at a trade show requires far more planning, effort, and resources than most first-timers realize. If you do plan to exhibit at a trade show, try to "walk the show" the year before you plan to exhibit, noting the kinds of displays that are exhibited as well as what the best position is for your table or booth. If you do not have that much advance time available to you, ask to see a floor plan of the exhibit hall. Also request the names of at least three other individuals or companies that are similar to yours that exhibited before whom you might call for information and guidelines.

Exhibitor is a monthly trade publication devoted to the exhibiting field. There are also experts that you might contact who consult just on making the most of a trade show exhibiting experience.

Improving Communication at Work

Communication in work situations may involve two persons (dyadic), three persons (triadic), four or more persons (social network). There are elements that are unique to each type of interaction. A dyad, say you and your boss, has the potential for greater intimacy (and confidentiality). It also is less secure since it depends on both members for its maintenance but only one for its dissolution. A triad is easier to maintain since the third member serves to perpetuate the group. It is, however, less intimate since secrecy is less assured than in a dyad. A network of four or five, such as a typing pool, has the potential for hundreds of interrelationships. Relationships may be more superficial than in a dyad or triad, but easier to maintain.

Communication at work may be improved by understanding the nature of your work relationships (whether they are dyadic, triadic, or networks), basics about communication skills, and certain complexities of social relationships that may inhibit good communication. For example, the self-fulfilling prophesy means that your self-perception, even if negative, you unwittingly make it come true. Thus if you see yourself as competent and able to relate well at the office, it becomes true. Conversely, if you see yourself as someone who has trouble communicating with your superiors or peers and is insecure, that may also become true.

Therefore it is paramount that you have a good self-image and self-esteem; it will enhance your relationships and communication at work. Improve your self-image by creating a positive progressive spiral. In *Dyadic Communication*, Wilmot describes it: "the actions of the individual supply a multiplier effect in reinforcement. The better you do, the more worthwhile you feel; the more worthwhile you feel, the better you do."

Two communication inhibitors that Wilmot cautions against are paradoxes and double binds. A paradox is a contradictory statement such as the following:

Ignore this sign

A double bind is a type of paradox in which a nonverbal message contradicts a verbal one. For example, you come to work looking exhausted. When your boss asks if you've been working too hard, you answer, "No, I've never been more rested." But your appearance contradicts your statement and places your boss in a double bind.

You cannot control how your boss, subordinates, or coworkers talk to you but you can control your own verbal and nonverbal behavior. Since it is a fact of interpersonal relationships that communication is usually reciprocal— people respond to you as you respond to them and vice versa—through your own behavior you do have some control. If you have a good self-image and avoid paradoxes and double binds, you have a better chance of inspiring better communication at work.

Since communication is reciprocal, avoid telling your boss or subordinates information that it would be inappropriate for them to tell you in kind. Take a long view of work relationships rather than trying to come on too strong and too fast.

WORK GOALS
Long-range Planning

People who fail to manage their time efficiently are usually unable to set and maintain long-range goals. They let the daily work ups and downs interfere with accomplishing their primary goals. Consider your long-range career goals. Where do you want to be in five years? Ten years from now?

Starting to think in terms of objectives to accomplish will make it easier for you to prioritize. Some experts feel that few people are able to handle more than three work-related goals simultaneously. (Some people find they can only handle one!) Within each goal, however, there may be dozens or hundreds of small steps that you have to take. (You may wish to refer to pages 10-11, Creative Time Management Principle #2 - Setting Goals.)

Progress Reports

People who mismanage their time usually need help setting *realistic* daily goals. Breaking a large task up into daily tasks is the foundation of good time management. If you feel overwhelmed by how large your goal is—writing a book, getting a degree, giving a speech, completing a study, selling x number of tractors, or designing an employee manual—break it down into daily goals. You may find that by tackling, and achieving, a manageable task— "Today I will call seven sales prospects" or "Today I will read sixty pages"—you will feel a sense of accomplishment.

Reward yourself for achieving each daily goal. Use any remaining time to achieve another goal (or improve what you've done.)

Progress reports may be only for your boss; a personal progress report might give you the daily feedback that you need to manage your time better. Jerry, an aspiring novelist, bought a diary solely to list the activities he accomplished that day, even if it was just

"Spent three hours thinking about the plot of my novel." In that way, he began to see that the time he thought he was wasting—because he didn't have any manuscript pages to show for it— he actually had used wisely. Even though it took him two years to finish the novel, entering into his diary "Wrote twenty pages today" made the task more manageable than focusing on "How am I ever going to write four hundred enthralling pages?"

Consider creating or purchasing daily progress sheets to keep track of your accomplishments (or your time). Here's a sample of an activity sheet with some of the categories filled in:

Work Sheet	Date Tuesday, June 2
Hours	Activity Accomplished
9 am-11 am	Phone calls. Accepted lecture. Returned calls from yesterday.
11am-12	Correspondence Answered 5 letters.
12-1 pm	Lunch Read *Wall Street Journal*
1-3 pm	Staff Meeting
3-5 pm	Dictating notes on meeting.
5-7 pm	Commuting. Reading magazines.

Your activity/accomplishment log need not be divided up by time periods; one man has his day divided up into these four categories: Work; Chores; Exercise; and Relaxation. Within his own categories, he lists what he's accomplishing that day.

It's important not just to do what you have to do right now, but to follow up. Do you check up on projects, memos, or telephone calls that have not been returned? Do you let too much time—or not enough—elapse between starting and completing a job-related function? Are you projecting an image that will further, or hinder, your career?

In *Getting Things Done*, Edwin C. Bliss advises that right after a project has been completed, while the experience is still fresh in your mind, especially if you have been dissatisfied with the outcome, write yourself a brief appraisal. Note what you learned from that project. Date it and keep it for later review.

Measuring Your Success

The Hawthorne Effect, discovered by Elton Mayo when he was conducting an experiment on the effect of levels of illumination on worker productivity at an electric company in the late 1 920's and early 1930's, shows why measuring your success is important. Mayo found that workers in the control group (who did not have any changes made in their lighting) showed increased productivity; at the same time, whether lights were dimmed or brightened, those in the experimental group showed increased productivity. The phenomenon, known as the Hawthorne Effect, meant this: just the act of being studied or measured led to increased productivity.

You can draw your own conclusions as to whether this increase was due to the need to impress the researcher (employed by management) or because of the favorable human response to being noticed and cared about. Generally, you are not evaluated daily by others. Is there a way you can employ the Hawthorne Effect to your advantage? Daily logs will help; no one can observe you more intimately than you, yourself.

Managing your time at work well means figuring out what you have to do, and doing it, as quickly and effectively as possible.

There are many ways of measuring success—in dollars and cents, by promotions, peer approval, or in public recognition. Whatever your measures for success, make them concrete so you'll know when you've achieved them.

In the next chapter we will look at finding "hidden" time as well as how all the concepts discussed in this book thus far can be applied to a variety of work-related situations, such as the "nine-to-fiver" or executive traditional worker, the self-employed or freelancer, small business owners, the creative person, and others.

7
Applying
Creative Time Management

Time is the most valuable thing a man can spend.
THEOPHRASTUS (?-278 B.C.)

The concept of time

Time is a cultural concept. Westerners, for example, think in terms of twenty-four hours in a day, and seven days in a week. However, those divisions are arbirtrary. There is no such thing as "a week;" we have created that concept. Time is an idea that varies greatly from culture to culture, within each culture, and even between individuals. The workday, for example, will differ for an office worker in Manhattan, for whom it may start at nine, and for one in Lima, Peru, for whom it may begin before eight. Teachers and students view time away from classrooms during the summer months far differently than typical workers who are still in their offices, although in some countries, such as France, the entire month of August may be vacation time for workers, or in the United States, for some occupations, such as psychiatrists and psychologists, as well.

MAKING PRODUCTIVE USE OF YOUR "HIDDEN" TIME

"Hidden" time is time that you previously mismanaged, consumed with distractions, or used for other tasks or activities, that you turn into productive time for pursuing your priority tasks. What are your "hidden" times? Think about your average workday, weekday evening, or free day. Is there time you might reorganize into your "hidden" concentrated time? If necessary, create time logs and analyze how you spend your time. Identify any "hidden" times.

Hidden time may be moments or minutes that you turn into productive use just as much as blocks of time you structure in to your day. For example, you might use the five minutes you usually spend waiting for the bus, or the half hour waiting in someone's office, to plan, dictate, read, work on your laptop computer, return or receive calls on your cell phone, or just relax and meditate.

Your hidden time may also change from month to month, or year to year. When my second son was three, since I did not want to hire a daytime sitter, I soon realized unless I found "hidden" time it would be years before I had blocks of work time. I discovered that if I forced myself to wake up by 4 a.m., I could work uninterrupted until at least 7 a.m. Even though my children are much older now so I have schooltime to work uninterrupted, I still enjoy my "hidden" time for concentrated work on a priority project.

Daydreaming represents another potential opportunity for creating additional productive "hidden" time. Tim Walsh, vice president of marketing and product development for Patch Products, began a whole new career because of daydreaming. Says Walsh: "In 1989 I was working at a rehabilitation center for post-operative back patients. They would be on the treadmill or in the whirlpool and I had time to kill." That time provided him with the opportunity to daydream about a game he and his friends at college had thought up. Walsh went on to switch careers to become a game developer producing the game, TriBond® which has sold over 1.5 million units, as well as numerous other products.

USING YOUR ENERGY HIGHS AND LOWS

Another way to improve the way you plan and schedule a day is to become aware of your personal energy highs and lows. No two persons have the same biological rhythms--your neighbor may thrive on five hours of sleep a night but you feel like a zombie unless you get at least eight.

A primary consideration in planning and scheduling your day is, therefore, whether you are a morning, afternoon, or evening type of person (or some combination of the three). Try to plan your time within your own energy cycles. Another concern is how much sleep you really need. You may need ten hours, or only five; there is no absolute rule about needing eight hours a day.*

Another notion that will help you apply creative time management to your work and leisure time is something Flora Davis, author of *Living Alive!*, and others refer to as the postprandial dip---the period, sometime after lunch and in the afternoon, when someone "just runs out of steam," as Davis says. When psychologists have studied this phenomnon, they found that fifty percent of their subjects experienced postprandial dip. The term, however, is deceptive since researchers have found that postprandial dip has nothing to do with when (or if) you have lunch. What is important to know is that one out of two persons seems to experience a postprandial dip. If you are one of them, plan and schedule your day with that afternoon energy low in mind. Davis, for example, since she has a postprandial dip that is quite late-- between four and five in the afternoon, she tries "not to read something heavy and dull because, on the spot, it's going to put me to sleep." A self-employed freelance writer, in the summertime, Davis will go swimming between four and five "because it wakes me up." In the wintertime, she'll use that time to go grocery shopping. If you work in a regular outside office, your postprandial dip might be an excellent time to do filing, return phone calls, or plan an outside meeting so you force yourself to keep moving.

*For an extensive discussion of sleep and sleep-related issues such as sleep need, sleep deprivation, and fatigue, see *The Encyclopedia of Sleep and Sleep Disorders*, by Michael J. Thorpy, M.D. and J. Yager, Ph.D., New York: Facts on File, 1991.

STRUCTURING TIME

Won't it all work out somehow if you can just "muddle through"? Stop and think for a minute. As the demands on your time have changed in your life, have you adjusted your time budget to reflect those changes? Do you even have a time budget? Perhaps you have just had a child, have a vacation coming up in a week, or you're just gotten a promotion. Did you, to accommodate those changes, shift your activities? Maybe it was not so recently that a change occurred--you got promoted, you switched jobs, your friend moved out-of-town--but are you still managing your time the same old way?

Or maybe you're just sick and tired of always being "busy" but rarely accomplishing anything that means that much to you. It may just be that you don't want to have to apologize again for having to cancel a meeting with a friend, or to keep a valued customer waiting.

Changing circumstances dictate altering how you manage your time. Your primary work role may be that of executive, but your family relations and community activities are other roles that demand your time. Few of us play only one role; how best to perform each role is a key theme when planning your time. You may be an accountant, paid by the hour, with numerous outside obligations, or a self-employed researcher, paid by the project, who is active in sports and culture activities.

But time is relative: a 76-year- old retired grandmother may feel she has less time and is more rushed than her 33-year-old married granddaughter, working full-time and taking care of two toddlers, with her multiple obligations.

This chapter deals with structuring time for various roles; read the section that only pertains to you or read each section since you might benefit from applying those suggestions as well.

For "Nine-to-fivers"or Executive Time

Few people today are exactly "nine-to-fivers" since "start-up" time—getting dressed, having breakfast, commuting back and forth—can aid or interfere with actual work time as much as how early you get to the office, how late you stay, and how much "after hours" studying, entertaining, or traveling you are expected to do.

Those in formal settings may benefit even more from stringent self-checks, since much work may be so routinized one could mistakenly believe that providing one's physical presence is equivalent to working. Your boss may tell you to do a report, and then ask you to do six other things. You let the report slide, complete the other things, and when she asks for that report, you say you need a little more time to polish it, and then write it in a hurry.

The telephone may be your biggest help, and your greatest annoyance. As the treasurer of a 550-employee freight company put it: "We have come full circle. Before the phone it was difficult to reach someone. With voice mail, we have the same problem."

To get around this, be as explicit as possible in your voice mail, or with your secretary, as to when and how someone could reach you. A specific time, such as "I'll be back from my meeting by eleven tomorrow morning" or "Call after four p.m." will be more likely to reduce telephone tag than a general greeting without any useful details.

If you work in a structured traditional office setting, try to pinpoint the uninterrupted work periods available to you, e. g., from arrival to lunch or from after lunch till departure. Then, except for necessary interruptions, use those blocks of work time to concentrate and accomplish your short- and long-term goals. Try to reserve fifteen minutes at the end of each day to review that day's "to do" list, noting where you achieved your goals, where you fell short, and setting your priorities for the next day. As we've seen, it may be counterproductive to your job, or to your personal needs, to frequently need to work outside your office. Trains, chaotic family rooms, and rooms where dinner parties are in progress are family rooms, and rooms where dinner parties are in progress are not the most conducive places to work efficiently. Good planning should minimize the frequency with which this occurs.

Remember, unrealistic deadlines should be revised well in advance of any due dates. You have to be as clear as possible about what deadlines you are capable of meeting. But you also do not work in a vacuum. Sometimes it is management, not you, that is guilty of imposing impossible deadlines.

Sometimes the best way to get the most work done at the office is to work around traditional office hours. That's what the 39-year-old vice president at a manufacturing company in Connecticut does: he arrives each day by 8:15, and leaves by 4:30, but since his secretary and everyone else has left by 3:45, he finds his most productive time is after 4 o'clock. "At that time in the afternoon, the phone calls are not that frequent. I'm the last one here and I'm not getting troubleshooting problems so one hundred percent of my concentration is on my own work. Prior to that I have to split my concentration up between my job and things that are going on in the plant."

He also stays productive by avoiding doing too many things at once. Instead, he will do one job for the entire morning, and another job in the afternoon. That way he avoids "trying to do three or four things at once, which can be stressful."

The biggest time waster at his company? "Petty arguments between employees" that require him to take time to be a referee. (They have 75 employees but do not have a personnel director whose job it would be to deal with such disputes.)

For others, especially working mothers with small children, the best way to organize the traditional workday nontraditionally through flexible hours, part-time, or working some hours or days "on site" and others "at home." For 33-year-old Marilyn, the conference coordinator at a New York college, working three days a week has been the best solution since she has two daughters, ages three and five months. She explains why this is the "best set up both personally and professionally" for her: "[Working three days a week] allows me great flexibility and also super time management. I can say honestly that I enjoy my leisure time at home (though raising kids isn't exactly leisurely) and I enjoy the challenges of work."

Although most are concerned that working part-time can derail a career, a two-year study by Purdue University researcher Shelley MacDermid and Mary Dean Lee, of McGill University in Montreal, found that for the 87 corporate professionals and managers that they studied, working less than full-time had not been detrimental to their career advancement. Ninety percent of the women, were reported to be happier with the reduced work load, and three out of four spouses said the arrangement was a success for the family.

But not all jobs lend themselves to reduced work loads, nor could the woman or family absorb the reduction in salary that usually follows. A married mother of three children, ages five months to five years, whose family needs her second income, manages to work fulltime as an advertising executive. How does she do it all? I asked. She replied: "I focus on three things: getting kids fed, in and out of the house, and in and out of bed. Everything else gets forgotten."

Best-selling author Harvey Mackay, who is also the CEO of the $85 million Mackay Envelope Corporation, devotes a short chapter to time management in his latest book, *Pushing the Envelope*. Mackay notes that he first learned the importance of being on time from his father, who was an Associated Press correspondent. His father used to say, "Miss a deadline, miss a headline."

The theme to all of Mackay's time management tips are that to be successful you should take control of your time and not let it slip through your fingers: you don't get sales from other salesmen but from customers; spend your time with them; work twice as hard as everyone else; use whatever technology, such as a car phone, or service, such as a valet service, to save the precious time available to you.

For the Self-Employed and Freelancers

Although being self-employed carries the connotation of working "for yourself," virtually all self-employed workers are dependent upon clients, patients, patrons, and similar fee-generating income sources. Sometimes being self-employed can place greater restrictions on freedom than working for a single employer (whether another individual or a huge conglomerate.) For many self-employed persons, obtaining work can involve as much time and effort as doing it. By contrast, the traditional nine-to-fiver, by the very nature of the work structure, usually has work "handed" to him.

If you are self-employed, you should rate yourself as an employer. Do you have a pension plan, vacation time, sick days, time for personal leave, maternity leave? If someone else employed you, you'd certainly expect some of those benefits. Don't drive yourself into an unpensioned grave for the seeming luxury of self-employment; you might turn out to be the worst employer you've ever had. Self-employment can mean increased freedom in your daily affairs; it can also mean increased pressure, fewer hours with your friends and family, and little financial security. It may be harder for you to find the time to perform your skill, or create your product, if you are unable to delegate the busywork that would fall on someone else's shoulders if you were in a corporate environment with extensive support services.

A consultant, so involved with handling her current clients that she does not spend time adding new clients or keeping up with previous ones, may find her business begins to suffer.

Creative and effective time management may make or break a self-employed person. Bob, 53, a self-employed counselor, says, "I feel more pressure because I know that the temptation to just sit down and watch TV or to lie in bed till ten o'clock in the morning is very great and there's no one there to say, 'Hey, get up and punch a time clock.'"

Adhering to a fixed schedule, with provisions for overtime, seems to be the time management technique of choice for those who are self-employed in creative professions. Jack, 67, a successful self-employed nonfiction writer for over 40 years, writes: "The *only* way to become successful at free-lancing is to run your operation like a business.... Hit your desk at specific hours. Otherwise the tendency to goof off will take over.... Be prepared, too, for overtime work. There will be times when deadlines must be met, and hence night work and weekend work will be necessary."

Factors that affect time management for the self-employed are: where you work (in your home or "outside"); the pattern of work (at a desk or traveling most of the time); and the nature of work (whether a skill or a product). A psychotherapist with an outside office and a secretary, for example, may sit in a room most of the day with patients coming to see her. The therapist will have a structure imposed on her by the presence, and schedule, of her secretary and clients. It will be more difficult for her to "goof off" than it might be for a self-employed artist who works alone at home. An actor who earns his living making TV commercials may spend eight hours "out on call," with four of those hours spent "waiting" for appointments, or between auditions. He may have to be more disciplined during periods when there are no auditions or parts to be had since he probably does not have an outside "office."

Maximizing efficient communication is especially important for the self-employed. Whether or not you even get a job may depend upon promptly receiving, or returning, phone calls. Here is the suggestion from the president and CEO of one-person consulting company for enhancing communication: "Each person should establish a personal communication protocol to optimize contacts and communicate that via each channel. For example, "Please contact me most reliability via e-mail, unless it is urgent, where voice mail should be used. Please confirm transmission success for attachment via e-mail, and use fax to ensure receipt if there is any question or uncertainty."

Self-employed persons who work at home create solutions to the " how to get going in the morning when you don't commute to work" situation. Brian, 59, a self-employed labor mediator who works at home, begins his day by walking his dog, buying the newspaper, and reading it over breakfast. Unless he has an outside appointment, he begins each workday by nine, as if he just arrived at corporate headquarters.

A factor for those who are self-employed to consider is a phenomenon that I call *time lag*. Let's say that right now you've got more work than you can handle. You might feel your problem is not having enough time to do all the work that's coming your way. Think again. " I was right at the end of finishing a book I had worked on for the past two years when a big newspaper called me," said Arlene, a woman in her forties who writes articles and books. "The editor needed an article, and I said I couldn't do it because I was finishing my book. I told her I'd give her a call when I was free." A few months later, when Arlene was free, she called, but the editor wouldn't take her call. Now Arlene had the time, but couldn't find editors who wanted her time—a classic example of time lag.

The reason that the self-employed have the problem of time lag is difficulty in looking past what they are currently doing, and planning ahead so that something is "in the pipeline," and ready to be started when the current work is completed. The worst time to get work—whether it's a job or a new assignment—is when you're not working. Those who are self-employed have to force themselves to devise basic time management principles to fit their specific needs, such as x, y, and z (future objectives) must be pursued while a and b (current objectives) are ongoing.

Avoiding time lag if you are self-employed requires sharp judgment as to how long a given project will actually take—not how long you'd like it to take. That way you can give yourself or your client a realistic deadline (starting *and* ending) for the next project, whether for two weeks or two years.

You might find it useful to create an organized system for keeping track of your assignments, as well as any potential projects that you are currently circulating or proposing. Try using the "ABC" approach of (A) What You Have, (B) What you Want, and (C) Getting What You Want By Using (A) and (B). Using cards or notebooks, apply the "who, what, where, when, how, why" analysis.

Here's one example of the kind of system you might devise:

```
┌─────────────────────────────────────────────────────┐
│ Sample Card for Keeping Track of Assignments         │
│ Project Description:                                  │
│ Client contact information:                           │
│     (Name, title, company, address, phone, fax, E-mail)│
│ Preferred way to contact:                             │
│ Date Assigned:                Due Date:               │
│ Length/Type:                                          │
│ Fee:                                                  │
│ Budget:                                               │
│ Expenses:                                             │
│ Submitted On:                                         │
│ Follow-up:                                            │
│ Outcome:                                              │
└─────────────────────────────────────────────────────┘
```

For the Creative Person

Guard your creativity as you would guard the most precious diamond in the world!

Protect those moments of inspiration with the respect and reverence that each one deserves. There are numerous examples throughout history of just how delicate true creativity can be, as the writer creates an entire novel just from the dream she remembers upon awakening, the artist paints a nightmare, or the poet finds the words "pouring out" and on to the page, words that come as fast and furiously as never before, only to stop coming again for years or ever more after that intense creative moment.

You cannot force creativity but you can, by creating the right conditions for it, help foster it. (By the same token, you can stop it in its tracks by doing the opposite of these suggestions.)

Here, then, are some ways to save time for the creative person by inspiring additional creative output:

- Keep a pad near your bed so if you have a dream or a nightmare, you can quickly write it down before forgetting it.
- Try, as much as possible, to block out concentrated time periods when you work and don't let anything or anyone

mail system take calls. Even shut off the radio if that distracts you.

- Avoid people whose negativity or criticism shuts down your creative juices.
- Don't show what you're working on too soon or to too many people until you are completely finished.
- Clear up enough in your external environment that your inner creativity is not distracted by the clutter.
- Try to focus on only one project at a time, physically removing other creative pulls from your visible environment.
- Trust your instincts and your sensibilities.
- Date and organize your creative projects so you don't get confused as to what versions or drafts you wish to keep and which ones you wish to discard. (When in doubt, hold on to your creative products. Store it in a closet, file it away. You can always throw something out but some creative efforts, once destroyed, can never be redone or restored.)
- Surround yourself with people who respect your creative spirit and process. Train your children, spouse, and friends to understand how interruptions can cause your creative effort – even your words – to vanish.

Those are some suggestions for enhancing the creative process itself. But there is another way most creative persons needs to learn to spend his or her time, however, and that is with the business end of their creative career. Too many creative people fear that being actively involved in doing even some of the numerous business-related concerns and details of running a business will completely obliterate their creative time. Fearing that, they do nothing at all. As a result, the business end of being creative, including marketing, sales, customer relations, and promotion, gets too little of their time, or none at all, so that the creative person's career suffers in the short- or long-run.

Of course having an excellent manager, or delegating certain tasks to a publicist, marketing, selling, or direct mail company, will help, but the creative person will still need to do a part of the business part of being creative.

Perhaps the best solution is to apply the 80/20 rule: spend 80% of your time creating, and 20% of your time doing the business part of your career. If you start focusing only on the business part, not only will you be frustrated but within a short period of time you will no longer have new creative products to sell.

If you focus only on the creative part, not only will your records be in disarray but you will never become, or will cease being, a business. However, for many, perhaps most, creative people, that's okay. They have managers or agents to handle the business concerns.

The key point to share is that creative people truly are in a different category than business owners or executives. Creative people think differently and, therefore, approach getting organized, or staying organized, as well as how they manage their time in a unique way.

Creative people have to walk the fine line among the time pulls of productive work, often done in isolation, which usually enables them to create, doing the business aspect of their career, as well as interacting with others, often difficult during the hours or even the days or months of intense concentration on absorbing creative projects.

Two popular books that deal just with time management and creative people are Lee Silber's *Time Management for the Creative Person* and Dorothy Lehmkuhl and Dolores Lamping's *Organizing for the Creative Person*.

For Small Business Owners

The advice for small business owners is similar to that of the creative person or freelancer but the difference is that the small business owner has to be responsive to every single customer. The creative person or freelancer is usually more concerned with creating product and with the client who hired him or her than with individual customers. The small business owner is running a business or corporation with financial, legal, accounting, and seasonal concerns that have to be deal with the minute someone becomes a business.

I have observed that the biggest time management issues for a small business owner are how to assign time to the tasks that will lead to the development of additional product (or customers or clients) versus keeping up with current or past customers or clients, and still finding the time to perform the tasks associated with running any business, such as invoicing, accounts receivable, inventory, "picking and packing," (if it is a business that involves shipping out goods), creating and maintaining a company web site, business correspondence, incoming telephone inquiries and calls, creating a catalog, handling returns, and on, and on, depending upon the specific type of business you are in.

Of course you could, and probably should, delegate some or all of the clerical tasks to a paid or unpaid (intern) assistant. You have to be careful, however, that you know enough about the way your business works – you have been in business long enough – that you are delegating tasks you have already mastered (so you will know if the person you're delegating to is doing it the right way or in the best interest of your company).

You may want to be in business at least six months to a year, doing almost everything yourself on purpose, before you begin to delegate certain business functions or job tasks. (This is a different approach to seeing the failure to delegate as a sign that you do not have the money to hire assistants.)

Many of the biggest companies started out with one or two persons doing everything out of their garage or the corner of their bedroom. It is only as the company grows to a certain size that administrative assistants, managers, or even outsourcing to mailing companies, begin to handle the time consuming, labor intensive aspects of the business that they had to do.

For Students

How many of the following questions can you answer "yes" to?

On a separate piece of paper, or photocopy this page, and answer the questions below with a *yes, sometimes,* or *no.*

1. I have a regular schedule for studying.
2. I have a specific place I always use to study.
3. I always get the course requirements before the semester begins so I can buy books ahead and plan.
4. My social life is planned around my exam schedule and required papers.
5. I start papers—planning/ researching—as soon as they are assigned.
6. I always have time to do extra readings in the areas I'm interested in.
7. I enjoy school and consider even tests or papers as challenging parts of the learning process.

Devise a plan to turn every *no* or *sometimes* into a *yes.* The information in this section should help you to accomplish that.

Let's look at the basics of time management in a school situation, remembering that the time pressures on someone returning to school later in life differ from those facing the younger student. Too, the student with a part-time or full-time job will conduct himself differently from one who doesn't work.

Each school year comes predefined as a block of time with certain objectives. Unlike a year-in, year-out, job, school is easily divisible into distinct periods with formal beginnings, well-defined endings, and structured checkpoints along the way. Take advantage of those clear divisions; it makes managing your time as a student somewhat easier.

Have an academic planning calendar that matches your schedule for the forthcoming year, and enter all course requirements (assignments, paper due dates, exams) that you know are due in the coming semester or school year onto your master calendar. Now, allocate certain blocks of time based on these commitments. For example, you might wish to reserve the week before midterms for studying so that you will not unnecessarily distract yourself week after final examinations for social and fun activities (and those inescapable duties you've put off while studying).

Some students find the "short shift" system of studying to be most effective. As one third-year law student put it: " I usually work in short shifts, of no longer than an hour, and I give myself incentives to push myself. Like I tell myself if I get through x a mount of work to do in the next hour, then I'll go play basketball for an hour." He's also a crammer, doing a lot of reading on his own, playing sports, and going out with his friends the rest of the time. " Right before finals, for a week or two, I do all the things I've been putting off all semester—most of my reading and studying."

A young woman, now 21, in her junior year of college in Oklahoma, and majoring in business administration, did not find cramming before exams worked for her. Her grades suffered so much because she went to football games rather than studying, that she dropped out of school for two years, and returned home to Florida to work for her father. Two years later, she returned to school, with a renewed commitment to apply herself.

Whether you study in short shifts or in long stretches, whether you study every night or cram right before exams, whether you retain what you learn only until the exam is over, or for the rest of your life, remembering and learning are the keys to success as a student—not how many hours you put in. In their book, *Study Smarts,* co-authors Kesselman-Turkel and Peterson, freelance writers and teachers, provide a summary of Dr. Walter Pauk's OK4R system, one of the many systems devised to help in remembering what you read. (OK4R is an acronym for *Overview, Key ideas, Read, Rite, Relate,* and *Review.)*

To save time learn speedreading and speedwriting.

You might find it helpful to have an orderly system for taking notes on what you're reading. The card that follows is a sample of one that could be adapted to your needs. (This particular one would be useful in doing a research paper, or familiarizing yourself with the literature on a given topic.)

Sample Bibliographic Information Entry

Author(s):
Title:
Place of Publication:
Publisher:
Year of publication:
Library Call # (if library book)
Summary:
Why This Work Is Important:
Compared to Other Works:
Criticism:
Memorable quote(s) (include page # and quote):
1st reading:
2nd reading:

You will also need a place that is conducive to study—as quiet and free of distractions as possible. Some find library cubicles quiet; others can only study alone in an empty room. No one solution will work for everyone: a library may be best for some students, and a time waster for others (who can only study at the kitchen table).

Similarly, you might find, in spite of the costs involved, that purchasing books saves you time. Libraries are marvelous places to do research especially for older or out-of-print books, expensive references or directories, hard-to-find obscure works, and current or back issues of magazines and journals. For very new materials, however, especially paperback books, you may be better off acquiring these books because: (a) you want to own a copy for your professional or personal library; (b) it's so new the library is still awaiting the copies it ordered; (c) someone else has the book out on loan; and (d) you're too busy to get to the library.(Check if your library has a web site or will check availability of a title for you by phone.) However, don't fall into the trap of buying books, or photocopying articles or specific pages, that remain unread.

Now let's look at the time demands on the older student. Taking an occasional course in an adult education program, is one form of continuing or career education; it is relatively inexpensive and not very time-consuming. A commitment to a full-time degree program requires more of a juggling act—job, school, family, and friends—requiring sacrifices from everyone involved (but primarily from the student). At first, everyone may be sympathetic when studies preclude Thanksgiving this year at Cousin Rose's in Pennsylvania, but when you can't get away next year, or the following year, Cousin Rose may be distinctly less understanding.

Whether you are a typical young student or an older one, poor time management during the school term may contribute to test anxiety. A psychotherapist who runs workshops for overcoming test anxiety, says: "Not being adequately prepared, a cause of test anxiety, may be the consequence of procrastination about studying throughout the semester."

Behind procrastination and poor time habits can be fears of success and failure. Procrastination is an ineffective way of dealing with those conflicts.

Another time management consideration unique to students is that some, especially those who also work, may drive themselves at an inhuman pace for several years. Upon finishing school, it may be unrealistic and unhealthy to attempt to perpetuate those high-gear time schedules. Similarly, the other extreme—becoming lazy and without any drive as a reaction to those intense years—is just as ill-advised. Thus, while in the student role, if at all possible, pace yourself and include some socializing and relaxing as a training ground for creative time management in high-pressure situations.

For Teachers

Teachers traditionally are a very organized group. Indeed, the ability to organize a semester, a course, or a year-long plan of study often distinguishes the effective teachers from the breathless, anxious, and unprepared ones.

By having a firm grip on the overall demands for a specific course or class, you can then focus on how you deliver your material, as well as any extras. If you are uncertain about even what you need to present each day, or each week, it will be that much harder to enjoy your students or teaching.

Plan out the class or the year.

Aim for variety in your presentations, assignments, and materials.

Planning will enable you to see how often you are including audio-visual materials, straight lecture, discussion, or other varied techniques, such as role playing, acting out skits, using technology, and field trips.

Have a written record of each assignment as well as a summary of each day's lectures.

Make it clear what is required of your students in terms of classwork, homework, special reports or projects, tests, notetaking, and even opportunities for extra credit.

Build fun and surprises into your teaching.

Research finds that creative and learning are heightened by adding fun and interesting material to your teaching lessons.

Pace yourself.

Teaching can be even more intense over the 8 (for college) or 10 (for nursery through high school) months that you are working than it is for the typical office worker with just 2-3 weeks off a year. Pace yourself as much as possible throughout the year so that you are not so burned out by the end of May or the end of June, whenever the school year is over, that it takes you the entire summer vacation to recover (only to find, before you can even enjoy your time off, that you are right back at the beginning of another school year).

For the Job Seeker

A few years ago when Linda, a business statistics expert, thought she might lose her job because of cutbacks, she engaged in an organized job search. "I had an extensive plan," Linda explains. "I read books on career planning, such as Richard Bolles' *What Color*

Is Your Parachute?, how to write a resume, and how to find a job. I decided on the geographic area I would cover, and what type of job I wanted to explore. I actually made lists of people to contact in terms of networking and had four ways of searching my university alumni newsletter, newspaper advertisements, word-of-mouth, and meeting people who could give me general leads."

Fortunately Linda's search—which did lead to several firm job offers—became unnecessary once she learned she could keep her current job. That search, however, based on the fundamentals of time management, gave her confidence, and expertise, that she can apply if she ever wants to, or needs to, search again.

As Linda's successful job search demonstrates, an effective job search campaign is essentially a time management issue. In contrast to a haphazard approach, by applying the basics of time management—goal setting, planning, getting organized, prioritizing, to do lists, setting deadlines—your job search will be enhanced and facilitated. You will have immediate payoffs, in terms of finding a job, and long-term benefits, by developing an excellent reputation with potential employers for follow-up and efficiency.

As noted in the beginning of this book, there are two basic approaches to the way someone manages his or her time—reactive, whereby you respond to others' demands; and active, whereby you generate your own options. How you manage your time during your job search will be impacted by whether this is a reactive job search, because you have been fired, or have been told to find a new job; or an active one, in that you could stay at your current job, but you want to find another one. Linda's search was an active one.

By contrast, Bill, whose wife has a lucrative job that provides enough income for the two of them, is engaged in an unplanned reactive job search—if someone tells him of a potential job, he sends in a resume and hopes for the best. (After two years, he is still "looking"for a full-time job as a researcher.)

Whether or not you are currently employed will effect how you manage your time during this job search: if employed, you will have to find "hidden" time for your search before, during, or after work and personal obligations are fulfilled; if you are out of work, your biggest time problem may be to discipline yourself, somewhat like a freelance or self-employed professional or entrepreneur, to create a schedule, or structure, from which you will conduct your search.

You need to know where you are going so you know what to strive for and may plan how to get there. It is tempting to be concerned only with "the next job," but a professional five- or ten-year career plan will aid this and every job search. A broad goal, such as "I'd like to be a CEO" or "I'd like to earn over two hundred thousand a year," differs from a well-conceived plan. A plan includes what you want to be doing next year, and in five or ten years, as well as what jobs, or steps, you should take to achieve it.

Take a few minutes to ponder the following questions, writing down your considered answers:

In 15 years, I hope to be:

In 5 years, I hope to be:

In order to achieve those goals, my next job should be:

Now that you have a long-term career plan, and a "next step" short-term plan, you can zero in on your current job search, more confident that there is a focus and active component to your explorations. In this way, you will be less likely to just react to each and every job offer, no matter how at odds it is with your career plan.

Short-term planning will revolve around all the background research, phone calls, and interviews you will have to carry out in order to achieve your short-term goal, namely a new job. Once again, long-term plans aid short-term planning since you will be doing things, if you haven't been doing them all along that will make each search easier. You may decide, for example, that staying in touch with the key headhunters in your field is a time-saver even after you find a new position since your next search might be easier. You may also decide to continually update your resume, instead of reactively revising it because of a job crisis. Networking may become a long-term priority rather than just a short-term necessity.

Disorganization is an incredible time waster when searching for a new job. Develop a simple but effective information storage and retrieval system that works for you to easily keep track of phone numbers, correspondence, updated resumes and supporting materials, and research pertaining to this search, job hunting in general, as well as to specific companies.

Any number of filing systems could be effective for you: you could file alphabetically; have a "tickler file" by day or month; or file in categories. What's most important is not the kind of filing system you follow, but that you have one so you can quickly file, and retrieve, the information and materials that you need.

You may also have to go out "wide" with some job searches, meaning you will have to send a cover letter and resume to 50, 100, or even more potential employers. Especially when dealing in such numbers, time management skills are a definite plus.

A very effective time management tool when it comes to a job search is a written "to do" list. Like your filing system, "to do" lists may be constructed by any number of organizing principles, such as in order of importance (prioritizing), chronologically, or by linking similar tasks together. Whatever system you use, the vital point is to write it down, and do not cross an item off, or ignore it, until each item has been done, even if you carry that item on your revised "to do" list for days or weeks at a time. Learn to make estimates on how long a task will take you so you can get better at estimating when you could possibly finish each "to do" list item.

In addition to a to-do list, you should have a written or electronic planning calendar, preferably one you carry around with you, in which you enter right on the calendar, such as a daily diary large enough to hold this information, follow-up letters to write, or phone calls to initiate.

Remember that this job search may just be your number one priority. Until you achieve your goal of a new job, learn to say "no" to every optional request on your time that interferes. Furthermore, each job search will have priorities unique to that search so clarify what is most important to you, whether that includes rewriting your resume, taking a headhunter out to lunch, or going to a conference to learn about unadvertised job openings.

A key element to an effective job search campaign is follow-up. Follow-up includes everything from sending a thank you note to an interviewer or someone who recommended you for a job interview to following up on want ads, referrals, or requests for information by potential new employers. Definitely try to follow up on anything related to your specific job search immediately.

Balancing Work and Home Life

A magazine editor's husband stays at home and takes care of their two children while she's at the office. A woman with four children under the age of four, whose husband's salary is not enough, wants to take a job to earn some extra money and "just to get out of the house" a few hours a week. Two executives marry, have twins, and both continue working full time; they have fulltime help.

These are just a few examples of the multiplicity of situations, and choices, open to adults, single or coupled, with or without children. A woman's decision to work after marrying or becoming a parent is viewed today as a personal and economic decision; there are fewer rules than twenty-five years ago. Each woman, and couple, decides what's best; those decisions affect how they will spend their time. Time management will be affected by work arrangements, how many children are present, their ages, any available cleaning or child care help, and, in households of two or more, the division of labor agreed upon by the couple. The theme that ran throughout my interviews with homemakers, whether or not they had other jobs, was that parenting obligations are their biggest time demand. (Those who stay home with young children, and do not work chose to be with their children and temporarily traded their own careers and additional income for full-time parenting responsibilities.) Few now look back on the nonparenting years as stressful in terms of time. Jessica, 32, a a full-time homemaker living in a Connecticut suburb, has two children, ages four and six, and is married to a lawyer. In comparing the years of her marriage before and after her children were born, Jessica says: "There was always time then. There's never enough time now." Marie, 31, a full-time homemaker in Queens, New York, is married to a schoolteacher and the mother of a two-year-old daughter. When her daughter was born, Marie quit her lucrative full-time job as production coordinator for a printer. "My husband and I refer to those early years of our marriage as the single years— married before kids," Marie says. Sara, 31, a corporate executive, married and the mother of a two-year-old, works full time, has full-time help at home, and prefers being at the office as much as any other nine-to-fiver. Sara says: "When I got married I told my husband, 'I don't like cleaning or cooking and I'm always going to work." And she has.

"I loved the job," Marie, who was earning over $40,000 a year, says, "but it was very high-powered and it became a bit much." For now, Marie wants to handle all the child-care responsibilities herself. Marie's cleaning chores are the same as before; she kept the cleaning lady that she used when she was working. Child-care demands structure her day but her husband, a school teacher, is home by three-thirty, so her days are short. The only chore Marie would like help with is cooking. "If tomorrow I wake up and I feel unhappy being home, I'll go back to work," Marie concludes, adding that I may have interviewed her on a "good day."

As noted in the next chapter, housekeeping chores are the least desirable aspect of homemaking reported by Oakley's study of London housewives. Hired help may not be feasible for economic reasons; even with help, there are still chores a homemaker may have to attend to. Jessica, the Connecticut housewife with two children, spends 5-1/2 hours each day doing household chores. Jessica explains: "Two hours for dinner. An hour a day for laundry. It takes me an hour to do [clean] the whole upstairs. Half an hour for breakfast and half an hour for lunch. Half an hour to pick them up at school. But I don't think of it that way because it's something I go along and do. And I don't keep a spotless house."

Parenting responsibilities, even if a parent works and has full-time help, usually consume the evenings and weekends. Jessica suggests spending as much time with your children as you enjoy, not more because you "should." "I like kids," Jessica says. "I can spend twenty-four hours a day, seven days a week with kids. Usually I need a break from kids once every three or four months. But it's important that if you don't want to spend a lot of time with your kids, you shouldn't do it, or feel guilty about [not doing] it. If you're happier working, you're going to have a much better relationship with your children, husband, friends [if you work]."

Corporations are recognizing that parenting presents time demands that may create stress for employees of either sex. In response to those pulls, companies are now sponsoring seminars during the workday to help employed parents cope better. A direct reaction to those seminars has been the formation of informal networks of parents within corporations who offer each other support about their mutual time problems.

Women who are full-time homemakers have time problems of a different sort from homemakers who also have outside jobs. Jessica explains: "Women who work don't have all the extracurricular things that the mothers who stay home have to do. They don't have to be the room mothers. They don't have to be the chauffeurs. They don't have to be the ones who get the calls when the kids in the neighborhood are sick. They don't have to allot time for certain things and they set their priorities differently."

Pam Young and Peggy Jones, sisters and mothers who were then fulltime homemakers, lifted themselves "out of the pigpen"— and wrote a bestseller about their program, *Sidetracked Home Executives.* They changed their lives by establishing and adhering to a time management system with just a few basic rules, such as: Wake up half an hour earlier than the rest of the family and get dressed; Make the bed before doing any other chores; Spend one weekday doing what you want to do (free of chores and errands).

"Time for myself" was a theme that homemakers with or without children, with or without outside jobs, stressed in our interviews. Whether it's working out at the gym, taking long walks alone, writing a novel while the baby is napping, or taking up yoga while the children are small, having personal and professional goals of one's own is important. Jessica explains: "I've always taken a day for myself. When my kids were little, one day a week I had a sitter. Now they're both in school so I don't find I [usually] need any more time than that. [But] if I need more time for myself, I'll get up at five in the morning, instead of seven, or I'll go to bed later."

An alternative to a full-time job for homemakers, especially those with small children, is part-time work inside or outside the home. Employment agencies have sprung up that cater to the part-time work needs of homemakers and potential employers.

Ironically, it is men, who are playing a more active parenting role, who are experiencing the family-work conflicts that women have always had. Don, 32, a research scientist, describes the impact his son's birth had on his work: "I found I wasn't going to the lab that much. When I did, I wasn't concentrating. I just wanted to be with my son. To watch him sleeping. To bathe him and feed him. I'm forcing myself to get back into my work now. I have to."

In the next chapter we will look at creative ways of improving your personal time management.

8
Improving Your Personal Time Management

Wherein lies happiness?
JOHN KEATS *(Endymion)*

The ones who find it hardest to improve their personal time are those who ask, "What free time? because they are unaware that most of their life is free time.*

In a society that applauds accomplishment, doing something just for its own sake occupies a low priority. You don't run because you enjoy it, you do it to exercise the cardiovascular system. You don't join civic groups because you like to be around people, but to make contacts that will help your career. You don't sew because it's fun, but to save money. However, if you value yourself, and your own happiness, you'll want to make the most of your personal time. It is sad that for some, personal time—the time we truly do have more control over—can be less satisfying than the time spent working or doing the things that have to get done.

If you are prone to working too much, it may be as hard for you to make time for leisure activities as it is for someone with too

*"Doing too much at once" (20%) is the #1 obstacle to better leisure time management among the 234 men and women that I surveyed. Reasons #2-#5, in descending order of frequency, are: family responsibilities (11%), devaluing leisure activities (10%), an inability to say no (7%), and commuting time (4%).

little work incentive to work harder. If that's true, you might think of whatever you do outside of work as "productive leisure time" activities. James J. Sheeran in his book, *How to Skyrocket Your Income,* offers six productive leisure-time activities: 1) Become an expert (at something) ; 2) Try local politics; 3) Try teaching; 4) Become an omnivorous reader; 5) Increase communicative skills; and 6) Continue formal education.

Ask yourself this question: If I retired tomorrow, what would I want to do with my time? Whatever your answers are, pick one of those choices, and start doing it now.

Traveling is a leisure time activity that can occupy you (and your family) for months. You can read up on the possible places you want to visit, take time to contact friends to see if they know anyone who lives there, and explore ways to make the most of your stay.

One-day trips from your home—with or without a club—can provide memorable leisure-time fun. Weekend overnight trips, if you keep driving time to under two hours, may be time-saving mini-vacations.

Exercise

Exercising takes time. You've got to love it, relish the competition (if applicable), or believe it's so crucial to your health and well being that you'll make the time.

Consider several timesaving exercise suggestions:

1. Make exercise a part of your everyday routine—walk instead of taking the car, ride a bicycle on errands, do isometrics while you're on the phone, put in ten minutes of calisthenics every morning.
2. Keep your weight down so you exercise to stay fit, not principally as a weight-reducing measure.
3. If you absolutely hate exercising, try doing it with someone else, so it's a social as well as a physical activity; misery loves company.

4. Use the reward system discussed earlier "If I exercise this week, I'll . . ." At some point, you may find the exercising has become its own reward.

Decide now to create a regular and realistic exercise regimen, whether walking an extra two miles a day or taking a dance or karate class. Don't overload yourself by registering for nightly exercise classes. That kind of unrealistic over-commitment will probably result in abandoning the effort.

Make a commitment with yourself to begin a regular exercise/ sports regimen, alone, with your spouse, children, or a friend, even if it's only for 10 or 20 minutes every day, or three times a week. (Check with your physician before beginning any exercise program especially if you have been inactive for a long time, if you are overweight, or if you have any health problems that need to be addressed.)

Hobbies

A hobby can be a rewarding way to spend your time, especially since it can provide the "I did it all by myself" feeling.

If you don't have a hobby, think back to your early years. What did you like to do in your spare time then that you don't find time for now? Perhaps you watched the stars, burned designs in wood, or worked with mosaic tiles. Maybe you had a chemistry set or were an amateur photographer. No matter. You can learn a completely new hobby. The key is to become adept enough at your hobby so that it is something that gives you pleasure.

Hobbies are not, however, things you must do anyway. Try, if possible, to pick a hobby that is unrelated to your work. Example: You are a researcher and your profession requires you to read a lot. Reading could be your hobby, but only if you read something outside of your profession, such as short stories, mysteries, novels; poetry, or popular nonfiction.

Remember: you're not engaging in this hobby so you can

compete in a national contest or have a one-person showing of your work. Initially, and perhaps always, like exercise, this one's primarily for you.

Television

Watching television can be a worthwhile and inexpensive form of entertainment. In moderation, and if watched selectively, TV can be relaxing, informative, and stimulating. TV may also be a time-saver—you don't have to dress and travel to experience it. However, if it is your primary leisure-time activity, you will be missing out on a number of ways to creatively use your free time.

There always seem to be those who can do their homework, read a book, or prepare a report, all while watching television. If you are observant, you will find that either they are only watching television or only doing their homework. Their attention may shift back and forth but most of the time the television serves as background noise, or the book serves as facade for the television viewing.

How many hours do you spend watching TV, especially during the hours that are considered prime time (Monday through Saturday, 8:00 p.m. to 11:00 p.m. and Sunday, 7:00 p.m. to 11:00 p.m.)? Do you watch a specific program, or just whatever you happen to flip to? Do you even know your television viewing habits? Keep a TV log for the next week to find out the hours you watch, the programs you watch (and why), with whom you watch, and how much enjoyment you derive from your TV viewing.

Using a video cassette recorder (VCR) may help you diminish the total number of hours you spend watching TV. By fast forwarding through commercials, you can watch a two-hour movie in 90 minutes. A video cassette recorder enables you to tape a specific program and watch it when it is convenient for you. If you are away from home, for example, or doing something else, you need not stop to watch. In that way, your time is structured around your needs rather than the TV station's programming schedule. Add to this the fact that since you can freeze or stop the tape at any point, you can avoid inadvertently missing a major plot development because of other needs.

RELATIONSHIPS
Socializing/Entertaining

If possible, plan to see your friends, and to develop new acquaintances, around the times that are best for you. The holidays are a time for socializing and, generally, a favored time for entertaining—but if you happen to be studying for finals, or you're in a business with lots of year-end paperwork due right before or after the holidays, this may not be your best time.

Socializing, or getting together with friends or associates, takes place outside your home; entertaining is socializing inside your home—or in some other location you have chosen—for which you are responsible for supplying the food and drink or arranging for someone else to provide it.

To socialize, you might make a phone call or two, and decide when, where, and what (coffee at a cafe, movies, dinner, bowling, etc.), but there is very little "how" to be concerned about. The advance planning for socializing is minimal, yet, unless you have a drop-in arrangement with a friend who lives in the neighborhood or a coworker down the hall (potential time wasters, as we've seen), socializing takes some time and effort. Spur of the moment guests take the least amount of effort and preparation, especially if you've stockpiled suitable food and beverages. How often you socialize, and with whom, will depend on what value you place on that relationship as well as your other commitments.

What counts is not how busy you are, or how many people you see, but whether you feel that you are making enough time for socializing. You may find that there is sufficient socializing for you during the day or just after work that not socializing in the evenings and on the weekends is what you want. (You may be so over-socialized that you lack enough time for yourself or for your spouse.) You may want to schedule a night alone, or a night with your spouse, even if that means you simply read a book or watch

TV. Make sure you keep those appointments as surely as you would any other commitment.

Entertaining usually requires more advance planning. As veteran caterer and party-giver Florence Lowell points out in her book, *Be a Guest At Your Own Party*, entertaining is more fun when you're relaxed. Being relaxed, if you're the host or hostess, usually means planning ahead (even if that means merely picking a date, deciding whom to invite, and hiring someone to carry out your plans for you.)

You can make such a big deal about entertaining that you never find the time. If, you usually keep your home reasonably clean, you won't associate entertaining with "cleaning up." The more frequently you entertain, the more comfortable you'll become at doing it. When it comes to entertaining, however, Murphy's Law is in effect more than ever—it almost always takes more time, energy, and money than you thought it would. Keeping this in mind, the simpler you make your entertaining, the more likely you will be to do it again. However, you have to be careful not to offend your guests; if they believe there was no effort involved, they may feel that you don't think they matter very much.

Make a list of your closest friends and relatives. Make a second list of those business associates and casual friends or acquaintances that you'd like to invite over. Now look ahead at the coming year. How frequently do you want to entertain? Are there times that are better for you (or your family) than others?

Look over your list of names. Figure out what forms your entertaining should take to include these varying individuals and groups. You might, for example, have a small birthday party for your father-in-law, or a huge bash for your whole office. Have one friend over for coffee and cake, perhaps in two months, and invite two couples for dinner, three months from now. If one of your goals is to enable all your guests to have a chance to interact with one another, consider entertaining up to eight persons at the same time. Larger groups will result in some of your guests leaving as unfamiliar to others as when they arrived (which is just fine in a large party situation.)

Have you ever considered giving two parties back-to-back? Those you couldn't include in the first party can be served at the second, and since your hall closet is already cleaned out, why not save time and get extra mileage out of your efforts? Have you also considered serving brunch, in lieu of dinner? It usually takes less time to plan, prepare, serve, and clean up.

Friendships

Make time for your friends. Friendships need time to develop and to be maintained. Certainly not as much time as you invest in a spouse, child, or parent, but if you let other commitments come between you and a close or best friend, you may find your friend has replaced you with someone more available. A worthwhile friend is worth that time. (For a detailed exploration of friendship, see J. Yager, *Friendshifts®: The Power of Friendship and How It Shapes Our Lives.)*

Friendship provides benefits that may be lacking in a family. As one 37-year-old single woman told me: "Your family accepts you with all your faults and they love you anyway, but it's not like that with your friends." She was alluding to the fact that your friends choose you. To reinforce their choice of you (and your choice of them) you will need time together, as well as the ability to be open up (self-disclosure), trust each other, and to be vulnerable (able to withstand the possible end of the friendship).

Here are some suggestions for finding time to get together with your friends no matter how busy you are:

- Call each other just to say hello and chat, not just to share the "big" good or bad news.
- Return phone messages promptly; if you cannot, let your friend know why – e.g. you will be away. But grant your friend some slack if he or she does not return your call right away since there might be a reason (being out of town, phone machine failed, a child failed to deliver the message, etc.)
- Make a commitment to get together on a regular basis, depending upon time and distance, on your own or with your spouses or families.
- Plan vacation time together.

- Keep postcards with you so if you have a spare moment while waiting in the doctor's office, sitting around while your child is taking guitar lessons or playing soccer, or while you're on a business trip, you can write to your friends.
- Remember your friends' birthdays by calling, sending a card, or getting together. Birthday presents don't have to cost a lot or could even be something homemade.
- When you do speak or get together, plan another time for your next reunion.
- If your friend is going through changes or has something new demanding more of her or his time, cut her or him some slack if she's or he's not returning phone calls as quickly or at all, and don't stand on ceremony. Call her or him.
- Make a commitment to be there for each other –physically as well in spirit — for all major events in your lives if it is at all possible.
- If you have a conflict, deal with it, or let some time pass till you are able to work things through with your friend to get your relationship back on track.
- Think before you speak.
- Respect your friend's boundaries. Certain topics may be off-limits, such as spouses or childrearing issues, even if gossiping about dates when you were single together was completely acceptable.
- *Celebrate* your friend's triumphs. Though competitive feelings are normal, deal with yours so it does not sabotage your friendship.
- On occasion or regularly, have a "Friends Night Out."
- Volunteer together.

Making Time for Partners and Children

Ironically it can be easier to find time for friends than for mates and children. In an intimate setting, physical presence need not mean that you're giving time. (You could be going your separate ways even under the same roof.) Friendship, since you're generally separated, requires time and effort if contact is to be maintained, whether by phone, letter, or in person. It is usually necessary to make an appointment for meeting, even if it only means calling a few minutes in advance to say, "Can I come over?" Because contact is generally less frequent than with family members, and because the relationship is less intimate, different rules apply.

Friends may even give each other more attention when they do get together than family members regularly get because the family is around all the time. Furthermore, your expectations are lower from a friendship than from a primary intimate relationship. It may be enough for friends to get together once a month to play tennis; few marriages would tolerate that dearth of interaction.

Time for Partners

If you feel you don't have enough time with your spouse, perhaps some of the following suggestions will be useful:

- Realize that perfect relationships exist only between perfect people.
- If possible, spend some time together during the workday, perhaps meeting for lunch on occasion, so you're not just an "after five" couple.
- Don't wait for your annual vacation to get away, plan mini-getaway weekends together to break up your routine.
- If you feel a need to get away alone now and then, do it. It doesn't necessarily mean there's something wrong with your relationship; a little absence does make the heart grow fonder.
- How much do you really know about what your partner does? Take the time to read books, take courses, and talk to others in that line of work (and vice versa) so you can better understand each other's daily experiences.
- Have a leisure activity that you regularly do together.
- Share parenting and household responsibilities by working them out in a way that's best for both of you.
- Especially when your children are younger, get out at least once a week as a couple. Hire a babysitter, ask a trusted relative to help out sitting, or work out an exchange system with a neighbor or friend you have confidence in: you watch my child and I'll watch yours.

What about sexual intimacy? Once again, personal preferences as to frequency, duration, style, and enjoyment are paramount, but if sex is important to you and your partner, make the time for it, no matter how busy you are. Although sexual intimacy is associated with marital bliss, some, such as Herbert G. Zerof in *Finding Intimacy*, say it is being overemphasized today.

If you are giving sex the proper emphasis in your relationship, however, but are failing to find time for it, sex therapist Avodah Offit, in *Night Thoughts*, suggests making the time. Offit advises couples, on a regular basis, to set aside time exclusively devoted to their intimate relationship. If you wait to be spontaneous, it may never happen.

No time at night? Set your alarm an extra half an hour or hour earlier. Other suggestions? Bring your children to the babysitter or relative and spend a few hours at home, alone for a change, or treat yourselves to a few hours at a nearby hotel. You may be able to negotiate a lower rate if you just want the room for a few hours rather than staying overnight. If you feel comfortable leaving your children with a trusted sitter or relatives, consider going away together for a day or two or even a week. If you or your spouse has to go on a business trip, if appropriate, you might consider accompanying him or her.

Time for Children

Consider the quality, and quantity, of time you spend with your children. How much time do you give to them? "It's important to spend time with your children because they need to know they're loved and cared about," says Linda, 31, a full-time college student who is also the mother of three children, ages 13, 11, and 4. "If you don't spend time with them, they won't feel that they're wanted, loved, or needed. They have to be taught. It takes time to teach them the proper things—values, morals, and all those things," Linda adds.

Here are some tips for finding the time for your children, even as they get into the teen years:
- Commit to a nightly family dinner or at least having meals together on the weekends.
- Spend at least some time over the weekend doing a "family

activity," e.g. going to the movies, bike riding, bowling, skating, and doing volunteer work together.
- Have one night a week that is family game night. At every age level, you can play store-bought games as well as original ones.
- No matter how busy you are at work, find a way to take at least a week each year for a family vacation. Even if you lack the funds to go to Europe or a faraway expensive vacation, plan trips and activities to do together as a family.
- Establish traditions that promote making time for each other, such as baking together for holidays, designing and sending out greeting cards together, and celebrating the traditional family-related holidays, such as Mother's Day or Father's Day, together.

Time For Yourself

We all need some time alone in addition to time with others. If one partner is around people all day, and the other is not, he or she may have opposite needs during non-work time. Similarly, children may want their parents' attention and the parent may not have any attention to give just then.

Management consultant Gisele Richardson has noted that people need three types of time for emotional health: diffused time (exposure to people); qualitative time (one-on-one intimate contact); and alone time (private moments to digest the stimuli from the other two types of time.)

If someone needs "alone time" it shouldn't be taken as rejection. You, or others, should use the time that would have been spent with others to your best advantage; you will all appreciate the time together even more when you do have some.

TIME MANAGEMENT AT HOME

Here are some time-effective strategies for necessary chores—food shopping, cleaning, washing clothes, vacuuming—tasks that almost everyone faces. Unless you are that very rare individual who loves housework, doing these jobs faster will be a welcome time saver. Not surprisingly, Ann Oakley, who studied how London housewives behave, reported in *The Sociology of Housework* that housework was the aspect of married life that the women she interviewed liked least. For the 40 women closely studied by Oakley, the housewives had an average workweek of 77 hours (versus the average 40-hour worker's week). As the number of children increased, so did the number of hours at their job. Interestingly, the one woman in her sample with a full-time job outside the home spent only 48 hours doing house-related work. Perhaps housework (including shopping and childrearing activities), like other tasks, will expand to fill the number of available hours— unless you have a plan.

With so many women working and unavailable for fulltime housekeeping chores, including married women with young children, finding ways to speed up household chores is a necessity. Men are pitching in—to be sure, some more than others are—and they also need ways to get the job done as quickly, and as pleasantly, as possible. If you live alone, housekeeping chores are all yours; you'll probably want to do them quickly so you have more time for other things.

The perfectionist may spend waking hours cleaning, puttering, and worrying about every minor detail in the home. Unless you are willing to devote that kind of full-time attention to your home, you might consider modifying your standards of cleanliness and orderliness. If you have been knocking yourself out dusting every other day, you might try doing it once a week and see if it makes a difference to anyone (including you).

Fear of failure or success may also be a factor in taking too long with housework. If a woman is afraid of competing in the job world (and sees it as a man's world), she may stretch out the time housekeeping takes to justify her not getting a job. She may fear competing at an outside job and use housework to keep busy so she doesn't run the risk of any actual or fantasized repercussions.

The inability to say *no* could be another time waster behind inefficient household maintenance. Especially as children mature, housework should be delegated to each person, not just to the mother, or father, who cannot say "no" when asked to do this or that chore.

Housework also provides instant gratification: results of your efforts are clearly visible when a sink full of dishes disappears or a room is transformed by your purchases. Success in a career may not be so readily apparent. At work, responsibilities may be vague; at home, not only are the responsibilities ongoing and consistent—beds always need to be made, towels need to be washed again—but once a homemaker sets up a ritual, all that's required is steady labor.

There is no single time-effective way to do household chores. Some find a fixed schedule best; others prefer to work *ad hoc*. One retired man jogs after he prepares the salad he's made and put in the refrigerator for dinner. By the time he returns, his wife is back from her full-time job, and dinner's ready. What matters is having a system that works for you so that household chores do not consume time that could be spent in a more meaningful way.

BECOMING ORGANIZED AT HOME

Obviously it is easier to organize an apartment or a home if you have just moved in. Everything is still in boxes, you put up those extra shelves in the pantry, you decide what will go where in each of the closets, you categorize your books as you put them back on the shelves, and so forth. Most of us are already living somewhere, however, and we would like to reorganize our living space without having to move out.

You will save time, and enjoy an uncluttered and pleasant environment, if you start organizing your home, one room or one project at a time. Divide your home up in a way that will make organizing or reorganizing it easiest for you. The most obvious ways of approaching this would be—

By project (e.g., closets, drawers, shelves, etc.)
By room (e.g., living room, dining room, kitchen, etc.)

Consider starting from your front door and working your way

through your apartment or home. First, concentrate on what shows as soon as you enter your home. Seeing the results of organizing your living room or guest bathroom will reaffirm your efforts.

Investing time in creating order will save you countless hours of time for a long time to come.

Second, tackle the more challenging "hidden" areas of disorder, like inside the closets and drawers. Only you, and those with whom you live, will benefit from these organizational efforts. The payoff will be even greater than the compliments received from guests who are impressed by your neat living room.

Systematically organizing your home a room, or an area, at a time may work best for you. That approach allows you to fully explore all the needs that you or your family want that area or room to fulfill. Example: Is your living room where you want to have a study corner for handling paperwork or is it just a place to entertain? Your answer to that question will help you to reorganize your space accordingly. Your dresser drawers can have dividers, so that socks, shirts, undergarments, underwear, and other everyday pieces of clothing are easily organized (and located). For women, a lingerie chest, with small, multiple drawers, is a useful way to organize such small items as pocketbooks, gloves, summer tops, and scarves, in addition to lingerie and undergarments.

Consider organizing the kitchen. You want to have most accessible to you those materials that you need and use most frequently. (This is based on the same Active and Inactive organizing principle that you have applied to your files.) Keep in another part of the kitchen, or even in another room, those materials that you do not use regularly. You may decide your kitchen needs a waste can at both ends, to cut down on unnecessary walking.

Proximity, especially in the kitchen, will save you minutes each day, and hours each week in food preparation, serving, clean up, and in general household maintenance.

It is useful in organizing each area in your home to think of each part of the whole as important in and of itself. For example, the way you organize inside the refrigerator and inside the freezer can save you as much time as how you organize your cabinets and drawers. A well-organized closet or garage can also save you and your family member from hours searching for gloves or a helmet.

Keep in mind all the organizing principles that you learned in Chapter 5 including the following timesaving guidelines:

Frequently used items should be kept in accessible places.
Have a specific place for everything.
Any removed item must be returned to its designated place.
Eliminate clutter.
Periodically go through all your possessions and give away, throw out, or rearrange to suit your current needs.
Create and follow to-do lists for your home-related obligations.
Delegate whenever possible.

Household Responsibilities

Even if you hire someone to organize your home, you will probably have to do the day-to-day maintenance. Everyday maintenance, however, like making the beds or preparing and serving dinner, is often easier to find time for than seasonal timely chores like cleaning the windows, washing the car, or planting the flowers and vegetables. Whether you live alone, with a roommate, or with children, consider delegating specific tasks to others. If those you live with will not, or cannot, do these chores, you might, if you can afford it, consider delegating some of them to paid workers, e.g., window washers, cleaning ladies, someone to do the laundry. If you cannot afford to pay someone for doing those heavy household tasks, consider what skills you can offer or barter in exchange for someone else doing the housework you despise.

If you have a roommate of the same sex, dividing up the household chores may be easier than if you are married. (Socialized expectations about the wife's role in housekeeping complicate what a woman or a man " should" do even if both are working full-time.) For same-sex roommates, make a list of housekeeping tasks and simply decide whose job it is— permanently or an alternating basis.

If you are a parent, have you considered what responsibilities your child can handle even at a very young age. In addition to "feeding my doll, playing with my sister, and being a good girl," a four-year-old girl in Massachusetts gave a list of household responsibilities that are hers alone or that she helps with:

clean up my toys
dress myself
feed the fish
rake the leaves
wash the car
make my bed
wash up
let Daddy sleep late on Sunday

Giving children household responsibilities, and increasing those responsibilities as they grow, takes up less of your time than trying to do it all and complaining about your martyrdom.

HOUSEHOLD PROJECTS

Whether you are decorating an apartment or home for the first time, or renovating one or more rooms where you've been living for a while, *decorate for efficiency as well as comfort and appearance.* It's best to take things one step at a time. In a new home, you can do one project at a time (refinishing all the floors, painting, building wall units, for example); if you're renovating, you may more readily do it a room at a time. In both situations, follow the same time management rules that you've been learning: *Set your priorities and then, in an orderly fashion, go about carrying them out.*

How do you proceed? Do you hire a decorator? Do you try to do it yourself? Hiring a decorator may save you time, but it will be more expensive. You may also lose the creative pleasure of carrying your own ideas through to completion. If you select, trust, and hire a decorator, he can supervise the changes, while you do something else. Hiring a decorator is not simply a matter of finding a name in the telephone directory. You'll need to visit homes he's decorated to see if his concepts and yours are compatible; you'll need to talk with him; you'll need to provide ideas, consider his suggestions, and approve a proposed budget and the completed work. You certainly don't want to hand a check to a decorator and thereafter live in his or her concept of "home."

If major purchases are involved, you should have any necessary structural changes (putting up or tearing down walls/windows/doors, sanding and staining floors, painting, scraping old wallpaper and repapering) completed before the new or recovered furniture arrives. Any processes involving caustic chemicals, paints, sanding, or dust can damage furniture, rugs, and even houseplants.

It may be cost-ineffective to do major work yourself, including repairs. Unless you are a professional and know what you're doing, these are complex tasks, both to learn and to carry out properly. In addition, you will have to rent or purchase all the equipment necessary to complete the job. Finally, if you botch the job, you will have to pay for professionals to undo your mess, and then redo things correctly.

HOUSEHOLD MAINTENANCE
Cleaning, Laundry, and Errands

The best overall time saver in your home or apartment is this: *Make it maintenance-free.* Invest the extra time and money to eliminate as many ongoing cleaning demands as you can: tweed rugs camouflage dirt better than solid ones; high-gloss enamel paint in the kitchen or children's rooms easily wipes clean; durable furniture does not readily show or accept stains, and needs only occasional vacuuming; plastic tablecloths are easier to care for than cloth ones; carefully planned storage units ensure that everything has a place, and tidying up is minimized.

In *Is There Life After Housework?* Don Aslett, president of a cleaning business that he founded, gives this advice about making your home or apartment as maintenance-free as possible: "Work can be lessened, and time saved, by good maintenance planning and decorating.... A bathroom is no place for elaborate bookcases, statues, or other unmaintainable furniture and fixtures. Keep in mind the following: 1. Will it clean? 2. Will it last? 3. Is it usable?"

Create a housekeeping time log or inventory, and base it on the time you *think you* spend in performing each of the major household chores. Then, time yourself and write down the *actual* time spent. You won't feel "on top of things" unless you know how much time you really need/spend, and can allot that much, with a little extra for the "anything that can go wrong" syndrome.

Another way to save lots of time is to purchase six months' worth of household items—especially toiletries and nonperishable maintenance supplies—and have them on hand. Shopping in quantity, and in advance, also allows you to get the best prices. For storage, use the active/inactive principle: most frequently used items most accessible, backup items nearby and surplus items still available but not "at hand."

Another time saver is to compile an up-to-date list of those services and professionals that you may need in the course of maintaining a residence.

Some find it faster to do their household chores before leaving for their office; it sets a time limit on a limitless task and also enables them to look forward to chore-less evenings and weekends. Forty-year-old Gloria, uses Saturdays from 9 a.m. to 2 p.m. to do the week's cleaning. Carol, whose four children are grown and on their own, does her cleaning in the evenings, from 9 p.m. to 11 p.m., after she has prepared, served, and cleaned up dinner. She prefers to do cleaning on weekday nights, since she works full-time, so the weekends, her husband's and her only time to socialize, are clear. For many families, Saturday morning is "cleaning day," with everyone pitching in.

Make sure that the appliances you use for cleaning are the best you can afford.

To save time on errands, make use of as many pick-up and

delivery services as you can. If you have to do it in person, try to do several chores at the same time—leaving some days completely errand-free. For example, pick up your shoes, dry cleaning, and the newspaper in just one trip.

Laundry should not be the time-consuming task that some make it out to be. Do multiple loads daily, or every other day, depending upon volume, if you have enough reserve items. At a laundromat, it takes about the same time (if sufficient machines are available) to do five loads as to do two. If you have a machine in your home, let the machine run while you do other things. Clock exactly how long the washing machine and/or dryer take so you can use that time productively doing something else. You might also consider using a laundromat that will do the work for you.

Household Directories/Records

It will save lots of time in the long run if you have an effective record-keeping system, whether for household financial matters (income, expenses, tax deductions, contributions, etc.) or for health matters (names of physicians and past medical problems, name of any medication currently being taken, dates of vaccinations, etc.).

An important consideration is: Enter the information as soon as it is available or it will not be readily available when needed. To keep track of expenses, consider a pocket-sized expense record that you can carry around with you, right in your wallet or pocketbook, so that you can enter information as you go along.

One way to keep track of physician visits is to schedule all semi-annual and annual check-ups during the same two-week period each year, or on or around a memorable date, such as your child's birthday, for his or her annual check-up. Then, when that time of year comes around, it's a reminder that it's time to go for your check-ups.

Create a list of personal records (credit card numbers, driver's license number, etc.), and keep it in a safe place (not your wallet)! Also create a list of key names and phone numbers that is kept up to date to facilitate contacting any of these services or professionals quickly, such as fire and police department, and physicians.

Food: Preparation, Shopping, Storage, and Cleanup

Food is one of the necessities in life and, if you are not organized about it, one of the biggest time-drainers—even several hours a day. If you have been solely responsible for all the meals, you might consider weaning your family away from this dependency with one or both of the following ideas: have a "fend for yourself night," or ask your spouse if just one night a week, dinner could be his or her responsibility.

You might also consider doing all your cooking for the weekend on Fridays—preparing tuna fish, egg salad, shrimp salad, and pot roast, for example—so that you can have a completely non-cooking weekend. If you've been cooking every night, you might try ordering in or eating out once a week, if the budget can bear it. Remember, eating out may not save time—you've got to get to the restaurant, order, eat, and get back—but at least you don't have to think about what you'll prepare, or do the cooking, serving, and cleaning up afterwards.

Saving time in the kitchen requires planning—you need a clear idea of what you're going to do, and what equipment or ingredients you need, as well as directions for carrying out your plan. One married woman of 65 (who worked full-time even while her three children were small) never starts a dish until all the ingredients are on hand and in front of her on the kitchen counter.

Follow the suggestions at the beginning of this chapter for organizing your kitchen. You might also consider having close at hand a chart listing the use for each spice and condiment.

The microwave has revolutionized mealtime preparation; it is now considered an indispensable, time-saving piece of kitchen equipment even if a conventional oven seems favored for preparing some dishes from scratch (or reheating certain foods).

Food processors may save you time mixing dough or grinding large quantities of food. For chopping vegetables, however, the consensus seems to be that a sharp knife and your hands are the fastest method. By contrast, electric mixers and juicers are faster than comparable equipment relying on arm power.

When shopping and storing food, find out, and keep in mind, the storage capacity and shelf life of specific perishables, frozen and canned foods. Consider stocking dehydrated and freeze-dried foods, which will usually last even longer than canned goods. You should also check your pantry, from time to time, making sure you are not keeping (and opening yourself up to the possibility of using) canned or dry goods past their stamped expiration date.

To save time food shopping, keep a pad and pencil in your kitchen to jot down items as you realize you need them. You might also create a master grocery list, and have blank forms on hand, bringing a completed form with you on your trip to the supermarket.

Make a plan—decide on a menu, whether for breakfast, lunch, or dinner—and execute your plan as quickly as possible. The biggest time waster in the kitchen is to select ingredients willy-nilly and try to pull a meal together. Unless you're a "born" cook, try to have at least ten or twenty recipes memorized or nearby that you and your family enjoy. For those nights you just don't want to take the time to cook, ask your partner or, if they are old enough, your children to prepare the meal. Also have a list of restaurants or food services handy that you can call to order in dinner. If it doesn't offend your environmental sympathies, have paper plates and cups on hand for those times when you don't want to take the time to do the dishes.

In the next and last chapter you will find 125 top time-saving ideas in these key areas: the top ten creative time management ideas; basic principles, goal-setting, organizing, overcoming obstacles to time management (time wasters), equipment and technology, work time, delegating, shopping, office or household maintenance, holiday time, and personal time.

9
125 TOP
TIME-SAVING IDEAS

Pythagoras, when he was asked what time was, answered that it was the soul of this world.

   PLUTARCH (*Platonic Questions*)

You now know basic guidelines for creative and effective time management at work and in your leisure hours. Here to reinforce the key concepts and to share some new ideas are 125 useful time-saving ideas.

The top ten time-saving ideas
   1. *Practice the 7 principles of creative time management:*
1. Be active, not reactive; 2. Set short and long-term goals;
3. Prioritize actions; 4. Keep your focus; 5. Create realistic deadlines; 6. D-O I-T N-O-W; and 7. Balance your life.
   2. *D-O I-T N-O-W*
   D – Divide and conquer what you have to do.
   O – Organize your materials, how you will do it.
   I – Ignore interruptions that are annoying distractions.
   T – Take the time to learn how to do things yourself.

N – Now, not tomorrow.

O – Opportunity is knocking.

W– Watch out for how much time is being spent on the Internet, watching TV, or talking on the phone.

3. *Be focused yet flexible.* Don't spread yourself too thin. Do one thing at a time but know when doing two things at once, like listening to a book on tape (audiobook) while commuting, is okay. Be flexible and open to revising your goals or activities based on new information.

4. *Rejoice in your fans and in your mentors.* Seek out, invest time in, and give sincere thanks to those who celebrate and help *you*--your values, your capabilities, your work, your relationships.

5. *Become a creative time manager.* Take the time to master effective time management. The skills will take you far and help you feel less stressed and able to lead a more balanced life.

6. *Keep physically fit.* Being out of shape, or in ill health, makes you less efficient.

7. *Use the ABC approach.* A. Knowing what you've got. B. Knowing what you want. C. Using A and B to get what you want by asking "who, what, where, when, why, and how".

8. *Use the verb-noun principle.* Simplify your goals and determine your short- and long-term priorities by dividing your goal into a noun and a verb. Just two words. "Finish book." "Write report." "Call hotel." "Learn software." "Hire publicist."

9. *Listen to your inner voice about how to spend your time* **right now.** What would you want to do with your time if you found out you had just two months to live? Unless you would say, "exactly what I'm now doing," why not do *now* whatever you've put off?

10. *Empower yourself.* Of course chance and fate are factors, but focus on how much control you *do* have. Remember *you* are the master of your life—and your time.

Basic principles

11. Concentrate. Eliminate self-made interruptions and distractions. Minimize interruptions imposed on you by others, especially automatically talking whenever you get a phone call

even if it is an inconvenient time for you.

12. Categorize your work, school, household, and personal responsibilities; focus on doing what you have to, and want to do, one task at a time.

13. Break down major tasks into small ones so: a) the work is more manageable; b) you can reward yourself for completing each step; c) you can keep better track of your progress; d) you will reduce the tendency to do too much at once; and e) you can set more realistic deadlines to complete each small step.

14. Be careful about basing decisions on the wrong information or on forming alliances with saboteurs in business or in your personal life, potential causes of mismanaged time.

15. Find your "hidden" time, and guard it carefully, such as going to bed an hour later, getting to work an hour earlier, waking up two hours earlier, or more productively using commuting time.

16. Don't worry and fret about the future or feel guilty about the past. Be aware of how the past teaches you, and how your current plans and efforts can improve the future.

17. If you don't know, find out, or ask someone who does whose opinion and knowledge you respect and trust.

18. Use your judgment and follow up as needed– on phone calls, on inquiries, on whether or not a fax was successfully received, on submissions.

19. Deal with crises immediately, before they become overwhelming obstacles to your goals.

20. Figure out the best way to handle each situation—by phone, by mail, by E-mail, or in person.

21. If there are major changes coming up in your life, adjust your time budget to accommodate them.

22. Group and complete similar tasks together.

23. Promise less, deliver lots more.

24. If possible, return phone calls the same day.

25. Do what you have to do first, not what is easiest.

26. Find out what others want you to do. Make sure, as long as you agree with their demands, that you first give them what they ask for, and then do anything extra.

27. Watch out for the "little" things that may have a tendency to fall through the cracks or, if ignored, may become "big" things.

28. There is a place within each of us where creative and innovative work is nurtured and developed. It is usually necessary to have inner calm, not chaos, for optimum thinking, efficiency, and to maximize your ability to concentrate.

29. Effective time managers make everyone, and everything, seem as if she or he (or it) is her or his only concern at that moment.

30. Be prepared ahead so when the time comes to do something it doesn't take you longer than necessary.

31. Read instructions carefully to avoid wasting everyone's time including your own.

32. Of course you should wear a watch, or be near a clock that is visible to you, but make sure whatever time piece you are depending on is accurate and reliable down to the exact minute. Put a clock in every room, including the bathroom.

33. You often do not know what is going on in someone else's life so be patient until you find out why a call is not returned, a fax, letter, or E-mail is not answered. Be patient and let them contact you. If you must get an immediate answer, *graciously* follow-up.

34. It takes the same amount of time to be pleasant to others as to be nasty, but pleasant and nice will get you much further.

35. A little pressure is a motivator; too much pressure usually shuts people down so be realistic about what you can and cannot accomplish, and set realistic deadlines.

36. Know yourself – your strengths, your weaknesses, what works best for you, and take what is special about you into account in your business and personal activities.

37. Become attuned to your body's energy highs and lows. When are you most alert? tired? able to concentrate? Try to plan your daily and evening activities around your natural body rhythm.

38. If you know what you should be doing (but you're not doing it, for whatever reason), you're a lot better off than most, who are in such a fog they do not even know that they don't know what they should do or how they might best spend their time *now*.

39. The more you do, the more you *can* do.

40. Sometimes you have to slow down, at least temporarily, in order to go faster in the long run. Learn to recognize when it is time for such a deliberate respite.

41. Learn speedreading as well as how to read material quickly, especially business writing and nonfiction, highlighting key points.

Goal setting

42. Figure out what will make the difference in your career, or in your personal life, and do that FIRST. Focus your energies on that specific project or relationship. Only go on to your next goal, or project, when you have completed the PRIORITY task at hand.

43. Write down your short (daily) and longer-term goals.

44. Focus, focus, focus.

45. Create a professional and a personal or family mission statement. What do you really value? Write down your mission statement. Date it. Review and revise it periodically.

46. Having enough time is both a reality, and a subjective perception. If you are unrealistic about how much you can accomplish in any given period of time, you will always feel as if you are "out of time." Set realistic and attainable goals.

47. Use special days, such as your birthday, New Year's Day, or your work starting date anniversary to reassess how you are handling your goals. Date each assessment and keep it stored in your "Everything Notebook," planning calendar, diary, or journal.

48. Don't waste time reinventing the wheel. Learn from the examples of others and then make your goals to do it better, faster, or in a different way than anyone else.

49. Create a business plan for your job, business, or career. Refer back to it on a regular basis to assess your progress.

Organizing

50. Develop a system for tracking your daily activities, such as a "things to do" list.

51. Eliminate clutter. Allot time for periodic sifting and sorting: discard, give away, or sell surplus possessions.

52. Organize your office and home so everything is accessible;

use *active* and *inactive* criteria for placing items.

53. Use an organizing principle for organizing your files: alphabetically, by number, color, chronologically, etc.

54. For a few, a messy desk is the sign of genius. For most, a messy desk is a sign of disorganization and neglected paperwork. Budget regular time to file and clear off your desk.

55. Get into the habit of dating what you are working on so it will be easier to keep it organized. Date written material on the front or back; incorporate a date into the name of a computer file.

56. To avoid lateness, give yourself an extra 10 or 15 minutes to get to appointments.

57. If you need additional help organizing and getting rid of clutter, take a course or a seminar, hire a time management consultant, read articles or books, or watch a related video.

58. Use the annual Getting Organized Week, sponsored by NAPO (National Association of Professional Organizers), the first week of October each year, as a target date.

59. Create your own days or dates, on a weekly, monthly, or annual basis, to clean off your desk, out your files, your closets, or to overhaul your organizing system.

60. Have handy the names, addresses, phone numbers, and, pick up schedule for charities, recycling, or resale shops that will welcome your old stuff or reading materials to get rid of your clutter.

Overcoming time management obstacles (time wasters)

61. If you have a tendency to do too many things at once, wait till you finish something before tackling the next project.

62. Learn to say "no" easily, politely, and without guilt.

63. If you have a tendency to procrastinate, make sure you give yourself a deadline with "mini-deadlines" along the way.

64. Sometimes delay is good (and not procrastinating) such as waiting to reread something before submitting it. But if you are really procrastinating, don't feel guilty about it, which will probably lead to more procrastinating.

65. Make whatever you are procrastinating about the first thing you do in the morning. Do not go on to anything else until you

have that priority task completed.

66. If you are a perfectionist, shift your drive from unattainable perfection to striving for excellence, a more realistic goal.

67. If you have a problem with lateness, time exactly how long each task (dressing, commuting, etc.) takes you; make an appointment with yourself to leave at a certain time so you will be on time.

68. If you stay on the phone too long, keep a clock or egg timer near your phone. Notice how much time is passing and learn to handle phone conversations in a more succinct way.

69. If you're always running late in the morning, do everything sooner — wake up earlier, eat breakfast earlier, and leave your house or apartment earlier.

70. Remember, in terms of lateness, that there are, however, cultural differences. As French and Spanish businesspeople noted, fifteen minutes late in their countries is not considered "late" the way it would be in the United States.

71. Find out as far in advance as possible what family responsibilities you have to deal with so you can budget work or personal time for those commitments.

72. Plan for better use of commuting or business travel time. Keep handy in your car or attache case, tapes, reading and writing material, a computer, or a portable tape recorder.

73. If fear of failure is holding you back, put your energy into doing more preparation and training to build up your confidence (which will help overcome a failure fear.)

74. See criticism as feedback, rather than criticism. If the feedback is valuable, use it. If not, ignore it.

75. It's unproductive to defend yourself if you were in the wrong. If appropriate, apologize, learn from your mistake, and move on without ruminating over the situation.

76. Boredom may be a signal that there are certain tasks you should be delegating.

77. Learn what obstacles to effective time management (time wasters) slow you down, such as complaining or perfectionism, and work on overcoming each and every one.

Equipment and Technology

78. If you plan to get new or upgraded equipment or systems, remember to budget time for the learning curve or time it may take to master the new equipment and way of working. Allot time on a regular basis for a technology hardware or software upgrade day.

79. A personal computer (PC) is the #1 time-saving office equipment so get the fastest, easiest to use machine you can afford. Take the time to really master the hardware and the software that you use. Back-up your files in multiple ways, such as on a floppy disk and an Iomega® Zip disk, even storing an extra back-up disk of what is on your hard drive outside of your office.

80. Make sure you have access to a fax machine, the #2 piece of time-saving office equipment. When sending a fax to an office, get a second fax number as "back up" if the first one is always busy. If possible, have a separate phone number for the fax machine.

81. Keep up with technology and how it can revolutionalize the way you do things (and help you save time). Your competition is certainly keeping up with technology and equipment advances. Read the "Circuits" section in *The New York Times, Wall Street Journal* technology reports, or popular computing magazines.

82. Consider if a conference call will save you time and money instead of an in-person meeting involving long distance traveling.

83. When you use the Internet, focus on what you initially intended to do or find out; avoid all the tempting unrelated paths.

84. Take a typing course so you increase how fast you can type on a computer or typewriter.

85. Consider using voice recognition software: speech is recognized by special software so words are transcribed without typing.

86. If possible, have back up equipment: a second printer, computer, fax machine, or scanner. That way if any piece of equipment breaks down and needs to be repaired, you will be able to keep working without lengthy "downtime" waiting for repairs.

87. Always have at least one traditional, non-portable, phone. In that way, if you lose your electricity, you will still be able to receive or place phone calls.

88. Use devices that are convenient to carry, such as the SwissCard™ from Victorinox®, which enables you to have a scissors, pen, tweezers, and other useful tools in a handy credit-card size plastic container that will easily fit in a wallet or suitcase.

Work time

89. Whether or not your company asks for a regular progress report, create one for yourself. Look over your daily "to do" lists. Study your short- and long-term goals. Where are you achieving what you want? What needs work?

90. Take the time to stay up in your field: attend conferences, read, network, take courses or seminars, or go to school.

91. Watch for signs of burnout and stress. Adjust your work schedule, and work load, accordingly.

92. Inform callers on your voice mail of the date when you will return to your office if you will be away for one entire workday.

93. Create uninterrupted or "quiet" work time.

94. Put the time into developing and maintaining a positive relationship with those pivotal to success at work or in a business or profession: subordinates, boss, co-workers, colleagues, customers, clients, professional associations, or employees.

95. Develop and maintain a database of work-related information so you can quickly locate clients, customers, products, vendors, suppliers, as well as information, resources.

96. Remember these six business protocol principles: be on time; be discreet; be courteous, pleasant, and positive; be concerned with others, not just yourself; dress appropriately; use proper written and spoken language. [See J. Yager, *Business Protocol*.] The Internet makes any business today an international one. Find out what business protocol and time management customs, need to be considered when conducting business internationally.

97. Make sure each meeting you call is necessary. Have clear goals and a written agenda. Start, and end, on time.

98. Web sites offer the opportunity to make descriptive material such as a resume or list of available products or services available; you can save the time and cost sending out basic material.

99. From time to time, you'll do everything "right," and you will still miss a deadline. Revise your schedule since the quality of your work is more important than speed. (But if this happens more than once in a great while, work on your time management skill of scheduling so you set more realistic deadlines in the first place.)

Delegating

100. For each and every task or assignment, you need to know when, if, how, and to whom to delegate.

101. Watch for seasonal or cyclical patterns to your work flow. You might need help only at certain times of the year, or just one or two days a week.

102. Give credit to those you delegate to.

Shopping

103. Frequent stores, restaurants, service centers, or banks during non-rush or off-hour times. (You generally will not find lines at the post office when it is raining.)

104. Try to shop infrequently, stockpiling necessary supplies, and avoiding last-minute dashes for a missing item.

105. Utilize time-saving delivery services whenever possible, including shopping over the phone, by mail, or over the Internet.

106. Use a credit card as a time-saving convenience—not to get into debt—for phone, mail order, or secure Internet purchases that you might otherwise have to make in person.

107. Keep handy catalogues of your favorite mail order companies, a list of web site addresses, or phone ordering numbers.

108. Sometimes you just have to shop in person so try to make it fun: include friends, children, exercise, or eat out.

Office or household maintenance

109. Reduce clutter. Eliminate everything lacking a practical, material, or nostalgic purpose. Create a place for everything.

110. Take some time to make your home or office maintenance free. Whenever you make a purchase, consider a product's upkeep, durability, or time-saving features, such as self-cleaning ovens.

111. Intentionally invite visitors or guests to your office or home to force you to have a target cleanup date.

112. If you absolutely cannot maintain your office or home on your own, find a cleaning service to do it for you.

Holiday time

113. Create a master list of names and budget for giving gifts.

114. If your children will have holiday time off from school, try to match your work vacation time with theirs.

115. Address your holiday cards all at once or a few at a time, but finish by mid November; mail early in December.

116. If you plan to send a business holiday gift, and need to customize or imprint it with your logo, select it over the summer. You'll probably get a discount and also avoid the late Fall rush.

117. Consider sending Thanksgiving or New Year's cards as your company holiday greeting card.

118. Use the holidays as an opportunity to update your personal or business database or address book.

Personal time

119. Value your leisure time and put effort into it but without over-planning or getting obsessive about it. Make the time to do what you enjoy whether it is reading, writing, going to the movies, learning a musical instrument, traveling, or cooking.

120. Taking the time for lunch, or to prepare nutritious, satisfying dinners, or to exercise is time well spent.

121. *Really listen* to your family and get to know them.

122. Don't let negative people drain your time or your psyche.

123. No matter how busy you are at work, try to take vacations, especially with your family when your children are young. If you cannot get away for a week or two, at least take a long weekend.

124. Relax during your personal time so you'll live longer, have more fun, and return to work refreshed.

125. Spend as much time as possible with your loved ones -- your mate, your children, your extended family, your friends.

SELECTED BIBLIOGRAPHY

ADLER, ALFRED. *What Life Should Mean To You*. NY: Putnam's, 1931, 1958.

ASLETT, DON. *Is There Life After Housework?* Cincinnati, OH: Writer's Digest Books, 1992.

BARKAS, J.L. See Yager, Jan.

BARKLEY, NELLA with E. Sandburg. *The Crystal-Barkley Guide to Taking Charge of Your Career.* NY: Workman, 1995.

BLANCHARD, KENNETH, and S. JOHNSON. *The One Minute Manager.* NY: Morrow, 1982.

BLISS, EDWIN C. *Getting Things Done*. NY: Bantam, 1976.

BOLLES, RICHARD NELSON. *What Color Is Your Parachute?* Berkeley, CA.: Ten Speed Press, 1999.

COOPER, A. M. with D. Trammell. *Time Management for Unmanageable People*. NY: Bantam, 1994.

COVEY, STEPHEN R. *7 Habits of Highly Effective People*. NY: Simon & Schuster, 1990.

_____ with A. R. MERRILL and R.. MERRILL. *First Things First*. NY: Simon & Schuster, 1994.

DAVIDSON, J. *The Complete Idiot's Guide to Managing Your Time*. NY: Alpha Books, 1996.

DAVIS, Flora. *Living Alive!* Garden City, NY: Doubleday, 1980.

DOUGLASS, M. and D. DOUGLASS. *Manage Your Time, Manage Your Work, Manage Yourself.* NY: AMACOM, 1980.

DRUCKER, PETER F. *The Practice of Management*. NY: Harper, 1954.

EISENBERG, RONNI, with KATE KELLY. *Organize Yourself!* 2nd ed. NY: Macmillan, 1997, 1986.

ELLIS, ALBERT, and W. KNAUS. *Overcoming Procrastination*. NY: NAL, 1979.

ENSIGN, PAULETTE. "110 Ideas for Organizing Your Business." San Diego, CA: OSI, 1991.

FRANCIS, J. and G. MILBOURN, JR *Human Behavior in the Work Environment*. Santa Monica, CA.: Goodyear, 1980.

FRANKL, VIKTOR E. *Man's Search for Meaning*. NY: Pocket, 1939, 1963.

FREUDENBERGER, HERBERT J., with G. RICHELSON. *Burn-Out*. Garden City, N.Y.: Doubleday, 1980.

GABARRO, JOHN J., and J. P. KOTTER. "Managing Your Boss." *HBR* (Jan-Feb 1980): 92-100.

GOLDFEIN, D. *Every Woman's Guide to Time Management*. Milbrae, CA: Les Femmes, 1977.

HALL, EDWARD T. *The Dance of Life.*. Garden City, N.Y.: Anchor, 1983.

HEMPHILL, BARBARA. *Taming the Office Tiger.* Washington, D.C.: Kiplinger, 1996.

HOBBS, CHARLES R. *Time Power.* NY: Harper & Row, 1987.

JACOBS, MARCIA. *The Excuse Book.* Los Angeles, CA.: Price/Stern/Sloan, 1979.

KESSELMAN-TURKEL, J. and F. PETERSON. *Study Smarts*. Chicago, IL.: Contemporary, 1981.

KORDA, MICHAEL. *Power!* NY: Ballantine Books, 1975.

_____ . *Success!* NY: Ballantine Books, 1977.

KOTTER J. P. "What Effective General Managers Really Do," *HBR* (Nov—Dec 1982):156-67.

KUBLER-ROSS, ELISABETH. *On Death and Dying*. NY: Macmillan, 1976, 1969.

KUSHNER, HAROLD S. *When Bad Things Happen to Good People.*. NY: Avon, 1981.

LAKEIN, ALAN. *How to Get Control of Your Time and Your Life*. NY: NAL, 1973.

LEHMKUHL, DOROTHY. *Organizing for the Creative Person*. NY: Crown, 1994.

LEVINSON, H. "When Executives Burn Out." *Harvard Business Review* (May-June 1981): 73-81.

LOWELL, FLORENCE, and N.L. BROWNING. *Be a Guest at Your Own Party*. NY: M. Evans, 1980.

MACDERMID, S.. "Improvising New Careers." Purdue University news service, February 1999.

MACKAY, HARVEY. *Pushing the Envelope*. NY: Ballantine, 1999.

MACKENZIE, R. ALEC. *The Time Trap.* NY: McGraw-Hill , 1972.

MAYER, JEFFREY J. *Time Management for Dummies.* ® Foster City, CA: IDG Books, 1995.

MACKENZIE, R. ALEC, and KAY CRONKITE WALDO. *About Time!* NY: McGraw Hill, 1981.

MOSKOWITZ, R. *How to Organize Your Work and Your Life.* Garden City, N.Y.: Doubleday, 1981.

McQUADE, WALTER, and ANN AIKMAN. *Stress.* NY: Bantam Books, 1975.

OAKLEY, ANN. *The Sociology of Housework.* NY: Pantheon, 1974.

OFFIT, AVODAH K. *Night Thoughts.* NY: Congdon & Lattes, 1981.

ONCKEN, WILLIAM, JR., and D.. WASS. "Management Time," *HBR* (Nov-Dec 1974): 75-80.

PETERS, THOMAS and ROBERT WATERMAN JR. *In Search of Excellence.* NY: Harper, 1982.

RAND, AYN. *The Virtue of Selfishness.* NY: NAL, 1961.

RICHARDSON, G. "Learn to Structure Personal Time Needs," *Bottom Line Personal,* 7/15/80.

RONEN, SIMCHA. *Flexible Working Hours.* NY: McGraw-Hill, 1981.

SCHIFFMAN, MURIEL. *Gestalt Self Therapy.* Berkeley, CA: Bookpeople, 1971.

_____. *Self Therapy.* Berkeley, CA: Bookpeople, 1967.

SCHUR, JULIET. The Overworked American. NY: Basic Books, 1993.

SCHUR, S. "How to Organize Your Home." 38-min. video. NY: SpaceOrganizers.

SCOTT, DRU. *How to Put More Time In Your Life.* NY: NAL, 1980.

SEDLACEK, KEITH, and M. CULLIGAN. *How to Avoid Stress Before It Kills You.* NY: Crown, 1979.

SHEERAN, JAMES J. *How to Skyrocket Your Income.* NY: Fell, 1976.

SHULEM, JULI. *Home-Based Business Mom.* Santa Barbara, CA: Newhoff Publishing, 1998.

SILBER, LEE T. *Time Management for the Creative Person.* NY: Three Rivers, 1998.

SYMONDS, MARTIN. "Victims of Violence." *AJP,* vol. 35 (Spring 1975), pp. 19-26.

TANNEN, DEBORAH. "That's Not What I Meant!" NY: Ballantine, 1987.

TAYLOR, HAROLD L. *Making Time Work For You.* NY: Dell, 1981.

TEC, LEON. *Fear of Success.* NY: NAL, 1978.

_____. *Targets.* NY: NAL, 1980.

THORPY, M. and J. YAGER. *Encyclopedia of Sleep and Sleep Disorders.* NY: Facts On File, 1991.

WAHLROOS, SVEN. *Excuses.* NY: Macmillan, 1981.

WHEELIS, ALLEN. *How People Change.* NY: Harper, 1973.

WHITE, B. and E. MADARA. *Self-Help Sourcebook.* Denville, NJ: Am. Self-Help Clearinghouse, 1998.

WILMOT, WILLIAM W. *Dyadic Communication,* 2nd edition. Reading, MA.: Addison Wesley, 1979.

WINSTON, STEPHANIE. *Getting Organized.* NY: Warner, 1978.

_____. *The Organized Executive.* Rev. ed. NY: Warner, 1994.

WINTER, ARTHUR, M.D. and RUTH WINTER. *Brain Workout.* NY: St. Martin's, 1997.

YAGER, JAN. (a/k/a J.L. Barkas) *Business Protocol,* Wiley, 1991.

_____. *Friendshifts®: The Power of Friendship and How It Shapes Our Lives.* Stamford, CT: Hannacroix Creek Books, 1997.

_____. "Is Someone Trying to Block Your Advancement at Work?" *National Business Employment Weekly,* 12/11/94. (Reprint at http://www.JanYager.com)

_____. *Making Your Office Work for You.* NY: Doubleday, 989.

_____. *Victims.* NY: Scribner's, 1978.

YOUNG, PAM, and PEGGY JONES. *Catch-up on the Kitchen.* NY: Warner, 1983.

_____. *Sidetracked Home Executives.* NY: Warner, 1981.

ZEROF, HERBERT. *Finding Intimacy.* Minneapolis, MN: Winston Press, 1978.

ZERUBAVEL, EVIATAR. *Hidden Rhythms.* Chicago, IL: University of Chicago Press, 1981.

Index

ABC approach, 126, 165
Active, 2, 10, 72, 73, 75, 136, 156, 160, 164
Adler, Alfred, 55
Agenda, 111, 172
American Self-Help Clearinghouse, 53
Anger, 2, 49, 52, 60
Appointments, 64, 70-71, 99, 147
Asimov, Isaac, 15
Aslett, Don, 159-160
Assignments, 32, 105, 126-127, 173
Associated Press, 123
Audiobook (cassette tape), 24, 25, 164

Babysitter, 107, 142, 151, 152
Balanced life, 2-3, 6-8, 13, 139-142, 165
Baldrige, Letitia, 106-107
Barkas, Janet *See* Jan Yager
Barkley, Nella, 105
Be a Guest at Your Own Party, Lowell, 148
Beeper, 8, 9
Behavior modification, 56
Bliss, Edwin C., 115
Bolles, Richard, 134-135
Books, 5, 9, 39, 61, 82-83, 107, 133, 151, 169
Boredom, 6, 44-47, 86, 104, 109, 101, 170
Boss, 48, 50, 51, 64, 80, 101, 104, 107, 108, 113, 172
Breaks *See* Efficiency Breaks, Vacation
Burnout, 6, 7, 110, 135, 172
Business *See* Company, Small business owner, Work
Business Protocol, Yager, 97, 110, 172
Business protocol, 106, 167, 172
Business travel *See* travel
Busywork, 65-66, 120

Calendar, planning, 70-71, 75, 76, 82, 138
Career *See* Work
CD-ROM, 83
CEO, 9, 105, 107, 137 *See also* Executive
Change, 3, 4, 7, 30, 56, 166
Childcare *See* babysitter, working father, working mother
Children, 2, 3, 6, 13, 56, 128, 152-153, 139-142, 157, 158, 174
Chores, 27, 141, 153, 157
Cleaning, 140, 159-161
    family activity, 154, 160
    service, 157, 174
Clients, 35, 64, 99, 103, 129, 130
    See Relationships, work.
Clock, 117, 118, 167
Closets, 64, 155, 156, 157, 169

Clutter, 63, 67, 71, 76-79, 82-83, 168, 169
Clutterers Anonymous, 57
Coffee, 88, 108, 147
Communication, 104, 144, 150
    at work, 104, 112-113
Commuting, 24-27, 83, 164, 166
Company, 3, 4, 35, 48, 69-70, 77, 78, 79, 85-87, 88, 95, 98-99, 100-102, 105, 107, 121-123
Complaining, 27-29, 54, 170
Compulsive talkers, 6, 29, 86, 95-96, 108-109
Computer, 7, 8, 9, 17, 25, 61, 72, 83, 89, 90-95, 169, 171
Computer disk, 62, 73, 76
Concentration, 3, 51, 165
Conferences *See* meetings.
Control, 20, 28, 30, 36, 40, 48, 64, 99, 103, 107, 143, 165, 167
Correspondence, 9, 2, 19, 27, 45, 46, 69-70, 75, 76-79, 88-90, 104, 139, 166
Coworkers, 3, 6, 13, 26, 50, 64, 104, 106, 113, 139
    See also Relationships, work.
Creative person, 80, 114-155, 127-129
Creative procrastination, 19
Creative time management, 1-13, 119
    benefits, 1-3, 4, 9, 165
    definition, 1
    examples, 4, 8, 119
    principles of, 9, 10-13
Creative Time Management for the New Millennium, Yager, 4, 9
Crisis, 52, 64, 166
Criticism, inability to take, 42-44
Crystal Barkley Corporation, 105
Customers, 64, 99, 129-130.
    See also Relationships, work.

Database, 172, 174
Davis, Flora, 119
Daydream, 24, 26, 118
Day-Timer ® Organizer 2000, 76
Deadlines, 2, 12, 31, 59, 62, 105, 123, 166
Decision-making skills, 4, 67-68, 166, 168, 169
Decorating, 158-159
Delegating, 33-34, 47, 52, 88, 102-107, 128, 130, 154, 157, 170, 173
Depression, 2, 46, 51
Desk, 67, 81-82, 125, 129
Devaluing (or overvaluing) activities, 37-39
Diamond, Lynn, 42-43
Disorganization, 63, 64, 67, 71
    See also Organizing.
D-O I-T N- O-W, 12-13, 164-165
"Do" lists. *See* Lists
Doing too much at-once, 11, 14-16, 23, 45, 54, 56, 81, 120, 169
Douglass, Merrill E., 68-69

Drop-in visitor. *See* Visitor interruptions
Drucker, Peter F., 35, 61
Dyadic Communication, Wilmot, 113

Education *See* **Learning, Student**
Efficiency breaks, 7, 71, 102, 168
E-mail, 9, 13, 27, 39, 45, 83, 93-94, 166, 167, 172
Emotional blocks to time management, 31-60
Employees, 64, 103, 105, 106 *See also* Work
Employers, 2, 85, 107 *See also* Boss
Encyclopedia of Sleep and Sleep Disorders, Thorpy and Yager, 119
Endymion, 143
Energy highs and lows, 110, 119, 167
Entertaining, 147-149
Equipment, 81, 90-98, 171-172
Errands, 7, 27, 141, 160-161
"Everything Notebook, 72-73, 168
Excuses, 30
Executive, 8, 50, 71, 81, 100, 102, 107, 120, 121-123, 130, 140
Exercise, 2, 7, 25-26, 45, 102, 118, 119, 143, 144-145, 146, 165, 173
Exhibitor magazine, 112
Expectations, 29, 48, 86, 166

Failure, fear of, 32, 34-36, 134, 154, 155, 170
Family, 6, 51, 53, 54, 67, 100, 120, 128, 148, 150-153, 160, 174
Fatigue, 46, 81, 102
Fax machine, 45, 83, 90, 95, 166, 171
Fear of failure. *See* Failure, fear of
Fear of success. *See* Success, fear of
Feedback, 42-44, 170
Filing, 5, 55, 61, 62, 64, 73-76, 78-79, 81, 136
"First Inquiry." *See* Mayo, Elton
Fischer, Theodore, 72
Flexibility, 84, 165
Flexible working hours 7, 123
Focus, 11, 12, 70, 164-165, 166, 168
Follow-up, 62, 105, 139, 166, 167
Food, 140, 147, 162-163, 173
See also Lunch, Overweight
France, 117, 170
Frankl, Viktor E., *29*
Franklin, Benjamin, 1
Freelancers, 5, 7, 123-127
Friends, 2, 4, 6, 13, 19, 26, 53, 54, 61, 67, 128, 144, 147, 148, 149-150, 174
making time for friends, 149-150, 173
Friendshifts, Yager, 149
Fun, 135, 143, 173, 174

Getting Organized Week, 169
Getting Things Done, Bliss, 115
Goals, 8, 16, 23, 26, 29, 35, 137, 168

long-term, 9, 11, 26-27, 114, 137, 165
setting of, 10-11, 69, 114, 168, 165, 170
short-term, 11, 12, 115-116, 137, 165
Goldfein, Donna, 49
Guilt, 47-48, 141, 166, 169

Habits 54-57
Hawthorne Effect,116
"Hidden" time, 118, 137, 141, 166
Hobby, 145-146
Holiday time, 110, 134, 147, 153, 168, 174
Homemakers , 139-142
Home office, 7, 77, 83-84
Household, 140, 153-163, 173-174
chores, 151, 153-160
How People Change, Wheelis, 54
Human Behavior in the Work Environment, Frances and Milbourn, 102
Human resource manager, 101
See also Manager

Impatience, 39-41
Inability to say "no," 14, 16-18, 49, 154
Inactive, 72, 75, 156
Internet, 8, 9, 13, 23, 44, 69, 83, 93-95, 171, 172
Interruptions, 7, 13, 64, 71, 165, 167
self-made, 167
telephone, 5, 9, 66-67
visitor, 98-99
Is There Life After Housework?, Aslett, 159-160

Jealousy, 41-42
Job seeker, 17, 95, 135-139
Jones, Peggy, 56, 141

Keats, John, 143
Kesselman-Turkel, Judi, 132
Kipling, Rudyard, 86
Korda, Michael, 88
Kubler-Ross, Elisabeth, 52
Kushner, Harold S., *29*

Lakein, Alan, 89
Lamping, Dolores, 129
Lateness, 2, 20, 57-60, 111, 169, 170
Laundry, 161
Leeds, David, 102
Lehmkuhl, Dorothy, 129
Learning, 13, 107, 130-134
Lee, Mary Dean, 123
Leisure, 4, 6, 13, 44, 47, 61, 143-146, 174
Letters. *See* Correspondence
Levinson, Harry, 105
Levinson Institute, 105
Library, 9, 82, 108 *See also* Research
Listening, 64, 104
Lists 5, 15, 69-70, 138, 148, 168

for entertaining, 148
  to do, 5, 15, 69-70, 138, 168
Living Alive!, Davis, 119
Love, 51-54, 150-152
Lowell, Florence, 148
Lunch, 50, 65, 84, 86, 102, 108, 119, 151, 173, 174

MacDermid, Shelley, 123
Mackay, Harvey, 123
Madara, Edward J., 53
Magazines, 26, 61, 77, 82-83, 107, 115
Magnetic diskette, 62, 76
Mail. *See* Correspondence
Making Your Office Work For You, Yager, 79-80
Maltz, Maxwell, 56
Manager, 81, 105, 123, 130 *See also* Executive
Marriage, 2, 151-152
Mayo, Elton, 102, 116
McKenzie, Cecilia, 78
Mealtime, 152 *See also* Family, Lunch
Meetings, 44, 47, 62,67, 84, 85, 110-112
Mentors, 165
Messies Anonymous, 57
Microwave, 90, 162
Mission statement, 168
Mismanagement of time, 14, 114, 118, 166
  See also Time wasters
Mistakes, 35-36, 48, 75, 102, 106
Money, 1, 6, 9, 41, 54, 77, 87, 102, 103, 130, 139, 161, 107, 171
Movies, 147, 174

NAPO See National Association of Professional Organizers
National Association of Professional Organizers, 82, 169
National Speakers Association, 25
Neighbor, 13
Networking *See* Relationships, work
Newspapers, 82-83, 94, 115, 161
  See also Reading, Research
*Night Thoughts,*Offit, 152
Night Thoughts, Young, 14
Nine-to-fivers, 121-123
Note taking, 64, 90, 132-133 *See also* Student

Oakley, Ann, 140, 153-154
Office
  health concerns, 81
  home, 7, 77, 83-84
    organizing, 79-82, 173-174
  workers, 121-123
Offit, Avodah, 152
OK4R System, 132
Oncken, William, Jr., 105
One Minute Manager, Blanchard and Johnson,
43
OneStep Connect Personal Organizer, 76
Optical Recognition Software (OCR), 94
Organization. *See* organizing
Organizing, 13, 61-85, 156-157, 166, 156-157, 168-169 *See also* file systems
  at home, 83-84, 156-157, 168
  at work, 76-83
  disorganization, 63, 67, 71
  getting organized, 61-85, 166, 168
  office, 79-82
  Organizing for the Creative Person,
Lamping and Lehmkuhl, 129
Overweight, 6, 32, 37

Pacing, 2-3, 6-8, 134, 135, 167
Paperwork,14, 20-21, 66, 76, 88-90
Parenting. *See* Children
Parents, 2, 13, 47, 141
Pareto's 80/20 Principle,11, 129
Part-time work, 7, 123, 142
  See also freelancers, self-employed
Partner *See also* Romantic relationship
Patch Products, 118
Pauk, Walter, 132
Peebler, Charles, 9
Perfectionism, 14, 20, 31-34, 39, 55, 103, 110, 154, 170
Personal time, 67, 143-163, 174
Peru, 117
Peterson, Franklynn, 132
Pets, 13
Phantam Rickshaw, 86
Phone. *See* Telephone
Photocopy machine, 40, 90
Physician, 145, 161
Pile filing, 76, 81
Planning, 1, 20, 58-59, 66, 71, 107, 119, 134, 163, 167, 168 *See also* goals
  electronic, 64, 72, 76, 138
  long-range, 114
  planning calendar, 64, 70-71, 75, 82, 131, 138
  reasons for, 64, 131, 134, 135, 167
Platonic Questions, Plutarch, 164
Plutarch, 164
Poor Richard's Almanac, Franklin, 1
Power, Korda, 88
Practice of Management, Drucker, 61
Principles of creative time management
  ABC, 126, 165
  creative time management, 1, 9, 10-13
  Pareto's 80/20 Principle,11, 129
  verb-noun, 11-12, 70, 165
Priorities, 10, 12, 15, 33, 48, 65-66, 68, 73, 104, 114, 118, 158, 165, 168

Procrastination, 13, 14, 18-20, 54, 55, 58, 66, 77, 89, 134
    solution to, 18-19, 28, 88
Productivity, 7, 13, 42, 50, 51, 63, 66, 80, 84, 102, 116, 118
Professor. *See* Teacher
Progress reports, 46, 61, 114-115
Promises, 166
Promptness, 63 *See also* Lateness
Psychocybernatics, Maltz, 56
Psychotherapy, 29, 51, 52, 56
Pushing the Envelope, Mackay, 123

Quiet time, 172

Rand, Ayn, 48-49
Reactive, 2, 10, 136, 164
Reading, 23, 25, 26, 29, 45-46, 86, 105, 143, 167, 174
    finding time for, 23, 26, 131, 174
Relationships, 13, 50-54, 164
    personal, 50-54, 58, 147-149
    romantic, 13, 50-54, 145, 147, 150-152
    work, 58, 99, 84, 102-110, 138
    See also Children, Sexual Intimacy, Spouse
Relaxation, 2, 3, 26, 54, 115, 174
    See also Burnout, Vacation
Reports, 61, 79, 105, 111, 114-115, 134-135
Research, 9, 33, 49, 71, 73, 101, 133
Retirement, 38, 120, 144
Rewards, 2, 18-19, 39, 45-46, 79, 145
Richardson, Gisele, 153
Romantic relationship, 13, 50-54, 151-152

Scanner, 94, 171
Scheduling, 1, 58, 62, 65, 64
Schiffman, Muriel, 109
School *See* student, teacher
Secretary, 67, 89, 96, 107, 122
Searching, 62-63
Selective attention, 15
Self-actualizing, 50
Self-employed, 70, 119, 124-126
Self-esteem, 32, 37, 38, 42, 113
Self-evaluations, 3, 33, 102-103, 115, 130-131
Self-fulfilling prophesy, 113
Self-help groups, 56-57
Self-Help Sourcebook, White and Madara, 53
Selfishness, 48-50
Selflessness, 48-50
Self-Therapy, Schiffman, 109
Sexual intimacy, 151-152
Sheeran, James J., 144
Shopping, 7, 50, 119, 153, 162-163, 173
Sibling, 13, 141 *See also* family
Sick days, 101-102
Sidetracked Home Executives, Young and Jones,

56, 141
Silber, Lee, 129
Sleep, 26, 102, 118, 166
Small business owner, 129-130
Socializing, 108, 147-149
Sociology of Housework, Oakley, 140, 153-154
Spain, 170
Speedreading, 41, 132, 168
Speedwriting, 132
Sports. *See* Exercise
Spouse, 13, 29, 128, 147, '50, 151-152, 162, 174 *See also*Romantic relationship
Stress, 2,3, 4, 9, 1, 25, 26, 45, 81, 100, 110, 141, 172
Structuring Time
    Balancing work and home life, 139-142
    Creative person, 127-129
    Executive time, 121-123
    Freelancers, 123-127
    Job Seekers, 135-139
    Nine to fivers, 121-123
    Self-employed, 124-127
    Small business owners, 129-130
    Students, 130-134
    Teachers, 134-135
Student, 5, 6, 8, 47, 107, 117, 130-134
Study Smarts, Kesselman-Turkel and Peterson, 132
Success, 1-2, 37, 116
    fear of, 32, 36-37, 134, 154, 155
    measuring, 116
Success, Korda, 88
SwissCardᴛᴍ 172
Symonds, Martin, 52

Tape recorder, 29, 89
Teacher, 17, 61, 109, 117, 134-135
Tec, Leon, 36
Technology, 8-9, 72-73, 90-93, 171-172
Teenagers, 6
Telephone, 4, 5, 7, 13, 17, 20, 22-23, 47, 55, 56,58, 59, 66-67, 72, 84, 86, 88, 95-96, 165, 166, 171
    answering machine, 59, 96
    answering service, 96
    cell phone, 8, 90
    conference call, 171
    portable phone, 97, 171
    voice mail, 22, 59, 121
Television,13, 16, 39, 146-147
Templates, 89
Theophratus, 117
"Things to do" lists. *See* Lists, "to do"
Thorpy, Michael J., 119
Tickler file, 75-76, 138
Time
    alone, 141-142, 147, 151, 153

budget, 120
concept of, 117, 120, 170
creative, 127-129
hidden, 118
lag, 126-127
log, 59, 87, 160
personal, 141, 142, 143-163
structuring, 120-142
wasters, 13, 14-20, 169-170
Time management
as skill, 3-4, 165
at work, 85-116, 119, 120-135
creative, 1-3, 4, 8, 9, 10-13
household, 153-163
personal, 143-163, 174
principles, 10-13, 164-165
125 top tips, 164-174
Time Management for the Creative Person,
Silber, 129
Time wasters, 13, 14-30, 62-63, 114, 122, 169-170
bad habits, 54-57
being in love, emotional issues, 51-54, 167
boredom, 44-47, 170
commuting and travel, 24-27
complaining, 27-29, 170
devaluing (or overvaluing) activities, 37-39
disorganization, 54-57, 63-66
doing too much at once, 11, 14-16, 45, 81.
122, 169
excuses, 30
failure to prioritize, 23-24
family responsibilities,
fear of failure, 34-36, 134, 154, 170
fear of success, 36-37, 134, 154
guilt, 47-48, 169
impatience and low frustration tolerance,
39-41
inability to say "no," 14, 16-18, 49, 169
inability to take criticism, 42-44, 170
Internet, 9, 11, 13, 69, 93-95, 171, 172
jealousy, 41-42
lateness, 57-60, 170
paper work, 14, 20-21, 66, 88-90
perfectionism, 14, 31-34, 39, 55, 170
procrastination, 13, 14, 18-20, 28, 45, 54,
55, 58, 134, 169
selflessness, 48-50
telephone, 13, 22-23, 56, 95-98, 170, 171,
173
television, 13, 22-23, 146-147
To do lists, 64, 68-70, 138, 168
Trade show, 112
Travel, 7, 18, 24-27, 58, 69, 144
Tribond®118

Trust, 104, 105, 149

TV *See* Television
Typewriter, 91, 171

Unemployed *See* **Job seeker**

**Vacation, 8, 53, 64, 99-102, 109, 118, 124,
135, 144, 149, 151, 153, 174**
Values, 41, 48, 50, 87, 104, 143, 152
Verb-noun principle, 12, 70, 165
Victims, Yager, 52
Video cassette recorder, 23, 146-147
Virgil, 31
Virtue of Selfishness, Rand, 48-49
Visitor, 83, 84, 147-149, 174
Visitor interruptions, 80, 98-99
Voice mail, 22, 59
Voice recognition software, 89
Volunteer, 13, 29, 143, 150, 152-153

Waiting *See* **Lateness**
Wall Street Journal, 115
Walsh, Tim, 118
Wass, Donald, 205
Watch, 167
Web site, 94, 172
www.expedia.com
www.elibrary.com, 94
www.napo.net, 82
www.selfgrowth.com, 57
www.JanYager.com, 182
What Color Is Your Parachute? Bolles, 134-135
What Life Should Mean to Me, Adler, 55
Wheelis, Alan, 54
White, Barbara J., 53
White House, 106
Wilmot, William, 113
Work, 4, 6, 9, 13, 21, 51, 38, 46, 47, 61, 85-116,
172 *See also* Flextime, Freelancers
goals, 114-116
part-time, 142
Workaholism, 5, 6, 53-54, 109, 110, 143-144
Working father, 5, 46, 139, 142, 154
Working mother, 3, 7, 120, 122-123, 139-142,
153-154
Writer, 38, 80, 114-115, 119, 125
Writing , 27, 28, 30

Yager, Jan, 52, 79-80, 110, 119, 149, 172, 182
Young, Edward, 14
Young, Pam, 56, 141

Zerof, Herbert, 152
Zip disk, 171

About the Author

Dr. Jan Yager is the author of more than a dozen books including these four business books: *Making Your Office Work For You* (Doubleday, 1989), the award-winning *Business Protocol* (Wiley, 1991), *How to Write Like a Professional* (Arco/Simon & Schuster, 1985), and *Creative Time Management* (Prentice Hall, Inc., 1984; Japanese edition, Mikasha Shobo, 1991).

For more than two decades, Dr. Yager, the former J.L. Barkas, has led time management seminars for groups as diverse as real estate brokers, television executives, small business owners, administrators, managers, self-employed writers, new mothers, and elementary and middle school children, as well as conducting extensive original research in time management and workplace issues including her survey of 234 working men and women.

Dr. Yager has a Ph.D. in sociology from The City University of New York (1983), a masters in criminal justice, and a year of graduate work in psychiatric art therapy. She is a member of the National Association of Professional Organizers (NAPO), the National Speakers Association, and other associations. Dr. Yager has taught at Penn State, Temple University, The New School, and the University of Connecticut, Stamford campus.

Frequently interviewed by the media, Dr. Yager's articles have appeared in *Parade, The New York Times, McCall's, National Business Employment Weekly, Redbook,* and *Working Woman.*

Dr. Jan Yager is a married working parent with two school-age sons who is able to achieve a successful balanced life by applying each day the creative time management principles that she developed and that are espoused in this book.

To share your comments about this book, or to find out about Dr. Yager's time management consulting or available dates for addressing your company or association, contact:

Dr. Jan Yager
P.O. Box 8038
Stamford, CT 06905-8038
(203) 968-8098 Fax (203) 968-0193
E-mail: jyager@aol.com
On the web: http://www.JanYager.com

HJ
2381
.P39
1993

Costly
Returns

The Burdens of the U.S. Tax System

James L. Payne

SOUTH PLAINS COLLEGE LIBRARY

 PRESS

Institute for Contemporary Studies
San Francisco, California

© 1993 James L. Payne

Printed in the United States of America on acid-free paper. All rights reserved.
No part of this book may be used or reproduced in any manner without written
permission except in the case of brief quotations in critical articles and reviews.

The Institute for Contemporary Studies is a nonpartisan, nonprofit, public policy
research organization. The analyses, conclusions, and opinions expressed in ICS
Press publications are those of the authors and not necessarily those of the
Institute, or of its officers, directors, or others associated with, or funding, its work.

Inquiries, book orders, and catalog requests should be addressed to ICS Press,
243 Kearny Street, San Francisco, CA 94108. (415) 981-5353. Fax: (415) 986-4878.
For book orders and catalog requests call toll free in the contiguous United States:
(800) 326-0263.

Distributed to the trade by
National Book Network, Lanham, Maryland

Edited by Tracy Clagett
Cover designed by Ben Santora

Library of Congress Cataloging-in-Publication Data

Payne, James L.
   Costly returns : the burdens of the U.S. tax system / James L.
Payne.
     p.   cm.
   Includes bibliographical references and index.
   ISBN 1-55815-202-4 (cloth). — ISBN 1-55815-215-6 (paper)
   1. Taxation—United States—Costs. I. Title.
HJ2381.P39 1993
336.2'00973—dc20   92-19854
                                                      CIP

Contents

Tables and Figures   vii

Foreword   Robert B. Hawkins, Jr.   ix

Introduction: Self-Inflicted Injury   1

1 Does the Helping State Help?   7

2 Compliance Costs   15

3 Enforcement Costs: Audits and Correspondence   35

4 Enforcement Costs: Litigation   53

5 Enforcement Costs: Forced Collections   67

6 Disincentive Costs   87

7 Evasion and Avoidance Costs   103

8 Governmental Costs   119

9 Emotional, Moral, and Cultural Costs   127

10 Tax System Burdens: Summary and Trends   149

11 The Culture of Taxing   163

12 Making Taxpayers Count   179

Appendix

Social Cost Analysis   195

The Burden of Initial Enforcement Contacts   199

Tax Rates and Tax System Costs   211

Notes   219
Index   257
About the Author   265

Tables and Figures

Table 1   Activities Involved in Tax Compliance   17

Table 2   Estimates of Tax Compliance Burden for 1985   21

Table 3   Fees for Preparation of Individual Tax Returns   28

Table 4   Summary of Tax Compliance Costs, 1985   29

Table 5   Compliance Times for Selected Tax Forms and Schedules   31

Table 6   Tax Enforcement Activities, Initial Contacts, 1985   37

Table 7   Rates of Audit Coverage, 1990   39

Table 8   Cost of Initial Enforcement Contacts, 1985   40

Table 9   Summary of Tax Litigation Costs, 1985   56

Table 10   Private Sector Costs of Forced Collections, 1985   84

Table 11   Estimates of the Disincentive Costs of Taxation   90

Table 12   Tax Evasion and Avoidance Costs, 1985   118

Table 13   Governmental Costs of the Federal Tax System, 1985   120

Table 14   Federal Tax System, Available Revenue Collected, 1985   123

Table 15   Costs of the Federal Tax System, Summary   150

Table 16   Indicators of Change in the Tax
Compliance Burden, 1980s   154

Table 17   Audits, Audit Personnel, and Tax
Court Cases, 1940–1990: Tax
Enforcement Trends   156

Table 18   Penalties, Levies, and Liens,
1978–1990: Tax Enforcement Trends   157

Table 19   Witnesses at Congressional Tax
Administration Hearings, House Ways
and Means Subcommittee on Oversight,
1987–1988   165

Table 20   Pro-IRS Voting on Compliance and
Enforcement Measures, Senate Finance
Committee, 1982–1986   176

Table A1   Social Costs of Initial Enforcement
Contacts, 1985, Detail   202

Figure 1   Trend in Negative Rating of the
Internal Revenue Service   162

Foreword

DEBATE IS CRITICAL to the workings of a self-governing and self-correcting society. This book will make an important contribution to the strength of our democracy through the vigorous public debate it is sure to stimulate.

James L. Payne wants Americans to know how much the federal government really costs them—and why. In *The Culture of Spending,* published by ICS Press in 1991, he showed how well-meaning members of Congress come to view increased spending as the solution to virtually every problem. In *Costly Returns* he demonstrates the true cost of raising the benignly termed "general revenues" that fuel these expenditures. Before, he told us where it goes; now he tells us how the government gets it—and at what price to the society.

The Internal Revenue Service claims that it runs an efficient system that costs the country well under 1 percent of revenues collected. But Payne's research establishes that our tax system is far more costly than anyone has previously believed. He details thirty different costs that are completely outside governmental expenditures for tax collection. The total of all these costs added together was more than $500 billion in 1990—or an amazing 65 percent of net tax revenues. In other words, every dollar we pay in taxes really costs us $1.65. Government never counts this sum, because it is paid almost entirely by the private sector. No tax bill placed before Congress ever shows this extra burden, and no one has ever had a chance to vote on it.

The monetary costs of the tax system are bad enough; but Payne shows that the system can also inflict intense psychological and emotional pain on the American people. According to the IRS, the U.S. tax system is voluntary. Payne affirms, however, that it is in fact highly coercive. In forcing compliance with the "voluntary" tax system, the IRS deals arbitrarily with taxpayers, invades privacy, denies civil rights, and heaps other abuses on American citizens.

This book extends the persuasion theory of policy making first advanced in *The Culture of Spending*. Payne explains that tax policy is made in a highly biased environment in Washington, where tax officials dominate the debates on tax regulations and where the voice of the taxpayer is seldom heard. This one-sided representation produces a mindset that focuses on raising revenue and ignores the pain and suffering of taxpayers. Payne proposes a novel way to redress this imbalance and begin to make taxpayers count: Require the IRS to compensate people for private sector costs it forces on them. A program of cash payments would at least, Payne notes, begin to make tax officials aware of the burdens of a destructive system.

Payne has given us a revolutionary look at the tax system. The monetary, social, and moral tolls he describes are antithetical to democratic values. In fact, Payne believes that the combined effect of tax system burdens has become so great that it is time to rethink the entire issue of taxation and its place in a self-governing society. His book will have a profound effect on the analysis and evaluation of government programs and is bound to provoke far-reaching debate on both the tax system and the role of government in the modern world.

Robert B. Hawkins, Jr., President
Institute for Contemporary Studies

Costly Returns

Introduction:
Self-inflicted Injury

Such energy wasted! What other films, what other books, what other songs go unsung while those hours and months and years pour down plush rat-hole offices of attorneys and accountants and advisers and counselors and consultants paid in desperation for help?

—Richard Bach, in *The Bridge across Forever,* referring to his four-year struggle with the IRS over a tax debt

SOCIAL SCIENTISTS AND POLICY MAKERS are concerned with hurts. Indeed, it might be said that the main activity of the scientists is to study hurts and that the principal purpose of policy makers is to alleviate them. Homelessness, unemployment, malnutrition, child abuse, illiteracy, poverty—the list of harms and deprivations that are studied, quantified, and debated goes on and on. Yet in the list of injuries that government noisily addresses, there is a singular omission: the harm that government itself does to citizens in collecting taxes.

I speak not of the burden of taxes, that is, the money that citizens send to the Internal Revenue Service. The taxes themselves are publicly debated. What is ignored is the burden of the tax system, the pain and suffering caused by the process of forcing Americans to pay these monies. The dollars that make their way to Washington do not flow effortlessly there. Citizens have to be prodded; and all this prodding, and dealing with the prodding, costs the American people dearly.

One who learned this truth in painful fashion was Richard Bach. Author of the best-seller *Jonathan Livingston Seagull*, Bach found himself with over a million dollars in royalties and no taste for financial management. He hired accountants and money managers and left matters to them. A midnight call from his fiancée—actress and screenwriter Leslie Parrish—revealed his mistake. She had just found out that the managers had lost most of his money; and, at the same time, they had neglected a tax problem that had turned into a threatened IRS seizure of all his property. Bach wondered, "Why did I hire these professionals? Surely I didn't need to hire experts for anything so simple as getting my property seized by the IRS. I could have done that by myself."

The tax dispute soon became a worst-of-all-possible-worlds predicament. Bach didn't have the money to settle the alleged tax debt; the IRS refused to enter into any installment agreement so that he could pay it off gradually; yet the IRS also delayed seizing his property. Visits to attorneys and letters to IRS officials failed to break the impasse. While the threat of seizure dangled over his head, Bach refused to write, fearing that his words would be snatched from his typewriter as "property" by federal agents. He also put off marrying, on the advice of his attorneys, so that the IRS could not lay claim to his fiancée's savings. Bach explains how the deadlock paralyzed their lives for four years: "No stories, no books, no screenplays, no films, no television, no acting, no production—nothing of the lives we'd lived before battle-with-government became our full-time occupation."[1] (He finally broke the deadlock by declaring bankruptcy, losing his home and the rights to his books.)

About ten years ago, I too was the object of an IRS enforcement action. It was small potatoes compared to what Richard Bach went through, but it left a big impression. I received a CP-2000 letter that declared I hadn't paid the right amount of taxes and which threatened collection action against me if I failed to give satisfaction. Naturally, having a gun pointed at my head spurred a high level of activity. I burrowed into my tax records, fashioned a theory to explain the IRS's blatantly wrong accusation, and drafted and redrafted a two-page, single-spaced letter. After months of nervous waiting, an IRS form letter arrived saying there was no tax liability after all.

My feeling of relief was mingled with irritation: my government had forced me into many hours of anxious labor, into using my best brainpower to figure out a foolish clerical error. Who was keeping track of this social waste? Who was working to see that it didn't happen again?

The answer, I gradually realized, was no one. Within government itself, there is no systematic desire to know about, and no systematic effort to alleviate, the burdens of operating the tax system. The Internal Revenue Service, the General Accounting Office, and the U.S. Congress pay lip service to the ideal of taxpayer service while calmly endorsing and extending a system characterized by appalling irresponsibility and waste. For most social scientists, the burden of a tax system on human beings is a nonproblem: there is no discipline on the subject, no textbook, no journal. A handful of scholars have studied aspects of this burden, but no one in academia has thought it important to draw the different findings together. The result is that no one knows, not even approximately, what it costs to operate the U.S. tax system.

The reluctance of the popular media to dwell on these burdens is nothing short of astonishing. The tax system causes countless human tragedies every year. These tragedies come in all shapes and forms, from massive worker layoffs to the creation of hundreds of thousands of victims of erroneous IRS penalties, liens, and levies. There are stories of careers wrecked, families broken, and businesses destroyed. Yet for the popular media, so eager to muckrake about substandard housing or drought in the farm belt, the sufferings caused by the tax system are all but invisible.

One illustration of the gap in public awareness is the widespread ignorance about tax system statistics. When it comes to a problem like unemployment, everyone—journalists, scholars, politicians—knows within a percentage point or two the current figure. We explain this high level of awareness by saying that unemployment is a social hurt important to know about, a suffering also significant as an index of the general health of the economy. If a president "allows" the unemployment rate to increase one point, he is hectored by politicians and commentators.

Now consider the statistic on IRS levies, that is, the number of bank accounts and paychecks forcibly seized by the IRS every year to settle what it believes (often incorrectly) are tax debts. Surely this is a social hurt comparable to unemployment, to have your savings snatched by federal agents, so that your checks bounce, your credit is destroyed, and your financial plans are ruined. The statistic on levies is also important as an index of political malaise: it reflects the degree to which citizens are unwilling or unable to cooperate with the demands of their government.

Yet who knows, even roughly, the number of IRS levies last year? Was it 1,000, or 10,000, or 100,000? Might it even be as high as 1,000,000? You can ask tax specialists and political economists to estimate this number and you will find, in almost every case, that they are completely in the dark about what it might be. People are also uninformed about its trend, unable to guess whether over the past ten years the number of levies has remained constant, increased by a little, or possibly doubled.

We could understand the lack of interest if the figure were trivial, if only a few people were affected each year. But it is not so. The numbers on tax enforcement burdens are staggeringly large. The statistic on levies illustrates the point. Even if you guessed the highest figure I mentioned, you were still low, for the actual number was 2,631,000 levies issued in 1990.

The same point applies to trends. If tax enforcement activities were stable, with no significant trends to alarm the public, reporters could be excused for ignoring them. But there has been no such stability. The U.S. tax system is undergoing breathtaking changes. The tax compliance burden, owing to a flurry of thoughtless tax legislation, has grown at an alarming rate; and tax enforcement programs have exploded like bombs in the midst of the American people. The number of IRS levies issued has not increased a mere 10 or 20 percent; it has not doubled. Since 1980 it has more than quadrupled!

The burden of the tax system is a policy issue of first importance. After all, this burden is a hurt government certainly can do something about, since it is entirely caused by government. Before they address far-flung social and economic harms, policy makers have a duty to look to their own house, to alleviate the unnecessary injury they themselves are causing through thoughtless management of the tax system. The public, also, ought to demand that officials attend to tax system injuries. Before we blame a president for a 6 percent unemployment rate, let us first hold him responsible for three million erroneous CP-2000 letters.

The tax system is the foundation of government. Until we thoroughly understand the injuries it inflicts and the sacrifices it demands, we cannot rationally use government to address any problem.

◆ 1 ◆

Does the Helping State Help?

IN THE MODERN WORLD, government is seen as the machine for solving social problems. It takes wealth from some sectors of society and transfers it, in the form of cash, goods, or services, to others suffering from a disadvantage. In some cases, the disadvantage is poverty; and many programs now exist to provide nominally poor individuals with income, food, and housing. But poverty is by no means the only problem the federal government seeks to address. It has become a major supplier of funds to many segments of American society, from farmers to college students, from corporations to art museums. It supplies a veritable banquet of benefits for the entire country.

In evaluating the operation of a mechanical system, we focus on efficiency. The important question about any system of transferring energy is, how much do you get back for what you put in? If the outputs are too small in relation to the inputs, then the machine must be repaired, or exchanged for another that works better.

The point also applies to the national fix-it machine of government. How efficient is it in making its transfers of resources? How much does it give back to the citizens in comparison with the burdens it places upon them? This issue is critically important in the modern era of the trillion-dollar welfare state. We cannot assume that, simply because government is trying to help, it actually leaves

7

people better off. The transfer system may involve so much friction—and hence waste—that even beneficiaries of government helping programs end up worse off.

The costs in governmental transfer systems are of two kinds: (1) the waste that occurs in attempting to disburse government funds to their intended use and (2) the waste of the tax system that collects the money. The first type of cost is generally recognized. It is widely understood that "bureaucracy" is inefficient, that, in one form or another, it wastes much of the funds given it to accomplish a certain objective. If we appropriate, say, $10 billion to a government housing agency, some of the funds will go into administration, record keeping, and report writing, and more money will be lost through unwise purchases and even outright fraud. In the end, we will get much less than $10 billion of housing.

Although the waste of bureaucracy is generally appreciated, the burdens of the tax system go largely unremarked. To a large extent, this is because people confuse the *burden of taxes* with the *burdens of the tax system*. The burden of taxes is the money that leaves the taxpayer's pocket and is spent by government. When we read about a $10 billion housing program, the $10 billion represents the burden of taxes, resources taken from the public and transferred to this other use.

But this is not the only cost of the housing program. The money being spent did not fly into the Treasury on wings of its own. It had to be extracted from society by the tax system, and the operation of this system entails numerous direct and indirect burdens. The contention of this book is that these burdens are very large— shockingly large. Once this point is realized, it raises major questions about tax policies, about spending policies, and about the viability of government as a "helping" institution.

The Findings

Before we turn to these questions, let us review this book's main conclusions about the burdens of the U.S. tax system. I have identified more than thirty different kinds of costs or wastes that the operation of the tax system places on society. Among the quantifiable costs, one of the most important is the tax compliance burden: the red tape that businesses and individuals must go through to file returns and pay taxes. This burden includes record keeping, data processing, learning about the tax code, and filling out forms and supporting documents. The cost of these activities, as documented in Chapter 2, amounts to 24 percent of net taxes collected, or well over $200 billion in 1990 terms.

Further burdens include the private sector costs of dealing with IRS enforcement initiatives: participating in audits, responding to deficiency notices, tax litigation, and forcible collection practices. The monetary costs of these burdens are estimated in Chapters 3–5.

Another major cost is the economic disincentive effect. By taking away the fruits of labor and capital, the tax system acts to discourage working and investing. The result is to diminish the production of goods and services, leaving the country poorer than it otherwise would be. In Chapter 6 we review the economists' calculations of this cost. The most dependable overall estimate for the disincentive effect is 33 percent of net taxes collected.

Further burdens involve the waste inherent in tax avoidance and evasion (Chapter 7). These include the costs of selling and managing the many different kinds of tax avoidance devices, including retirement tax shelters, estate tax shelters, and offshore tax shelters. The governmental costs of tax collection, especially the cost of running the Internal Revenue Service, prove to be relatively small (Chapter 8). Virtually all the costs of operating the U.S. tax system are shifted onto the private sector; they appear nowhere in the government's budget.

When all the monetary costs of operating the U.S. tax system are added together, the total comes to 65 percent of net tax revenues, or over $500 billion in 1990 terms. Naturally, this figure incorporates a number of estimates and should therefore be treated as a preliminary result, not a final answer. This book is a first effort to map out a vast, obscure realm.

Though this figure is approximate, this does not mean it is exaggerated. As the reader will see, I followed the practice of favoring lower estimates, and I also omitted estimates for many of the more obscure costs. Furthermore, I did not attempt to quantify a number of important moral and emotional costs of the tax system (discussed in Chapter 9). These include burdens such as the anxiety the tax system generates and the transgressions against civil and constitutional rights that are part of the tax system. For these reasons, my 65 percent figure is about as conservative an estimate of tax system costs as one is likely to arrive at.

This figure, conservative as it is, opens our eyes to the fact that the cost of government programs has been seriously understated in policy discussions. Because of the overhead costs of running the tax system, every federal program costs the country 65 percent more than the announced budgetary cost. The $10 billion housing program actually represents a sacrifice of $16.5 billion; a congressman's $125,000 salary actually costs the country $206,000, and so on. The burden of the tax system is a policy issue of major importance.

Inbred Tax Policy

Realizing the size of the tax system burden provokes the question, How did costs get so high?

In broad terms, the answer is that the U.S. federal tax system has been seriously mismanaged by policy makers who largely ignore the cares and concerns of taxpayers. As I explain in Chapter 11, the tax system is controlled by tax officials and a handful of congressional allies who have been indoctrinated to the tax officials' worldview. This collective "culture of taxing" makes tax administration policy without hearing from taxpayers and, in most cases, without seriously considering how they will be affected by policy decisions. The polestar of tax decision making in Washington is "protecting the interests of the government."

It is easy to see where this progovernment bias leads. Each year, dozens of new tax compliance and enforcement possibilities arise, proposed in the form of legislation, or Treasury Department regulations, or IRS rules and practices. Almost all of these measures embody this underlying conflict: if approved, they would make life more difficult for taxpayers, but they would make business more lucrative for tax collectors. Since tax collectors dominate the decision-making system, the result is a steady stream of changes that favor their perspectives at the expense of taxpayers.

An example of this pattern is the rapid growth of the federal tax surveillance system. Down through the years, novelists and science-fiction writers have speculated about the frightening potential that electronic data management affords for government control. It used to be difficult to take their warnings seriously, at least as applied to a democratic country. Surely, one thought, free people would never consent to have their privacy stripped away and their behavior monitored from the cradle to the grave by a government law enforcement agency.

Guess what? Big Brother is here. The Internal Revenue Service does indeed monitor U.S. citizens from the cradle to the grave. It forces employers, financial institutions, and a multitude of other payers to report virtually every significant financial transaction of every person. This information is mastered by IRS central computers, which collate the data and merge it with information from other state and federal data banks to detect transgressions. The citizen is then punished by computer-generated letters demanding payment, or by computer-generated seizures of funds. The electronic system is supplemented by an informants program, which induces citizens to spy on each other in exchange for government cash rewards. This comprehensive system of surveillance and control, presumptuous yet highly error-prone, frightens and frustrates large numbers of Americans.

Who voted for Big Brother? U.S. taxpayers were certainly never given a choice. They never saw any election or referendum in which they could express their opinion on the subject. The desirability of having a pervasive tax surveillance system was never debated in Congress, never discussed in the media, and never studied in the schools. How did it happen, then? The answer is that tax officials wanted it, to aid their tax enforcement and collection activities. Over several decades, they quietly included its components in their legislative and regulatory proposals, and congressmen quietly acceded to their recommendations.

The solution to controlling the tax authority and bringing the costs of the tax system under control is, at least in principle, simple to describe. The system needs to be restructured so that taxpayers and their concerns are fully represented in the decision-making process. With the tax-official mentality so deeply entrenched in Washington, this may not be an easy task. In Chapter 12, I explore the changes in perspective that are needed.

The Self-Subsidy Problem

As we noted earlier, modern government is seen as a helping institution. Its evolution over the past century has been constantly to increase the number of citizens it tries to help through direct and indirect subsidies. The poor were one of the first groups to be targeted, then came the elderly, then farmers, then the unemployed, then small businessmen, then college students, then scientists, then artists, and so on. Today, it is becoming difficult to find an economic sector or population group that government does *not* subsidize.

Unfortunately, the funds for all these helping programs do not come from the sky. The wealth that government disposes comes from the citizens themselves. Therefore, as government expands the size and number of its helping programs, it is bound to get into a situation where it is taxing the same people it is trying to help in its subsidy programs. In effect, it causes them to pay for their own benefits.

It is clear that this condition of self-subsidy is today rampant. The poor, who are the target of so many federal helping programs, pay taxes to support those programs at every turn. If a poor person works even one day, he pays a Social Security wage tax. He also pays federal taxes on phone service, gasoline, tires, cigarettes, and alcohol. And he pays the part of other taxes, such as corporate income tax, that gets shifted into prices. The same pattern holds for all the other beneficiaries of federal largesse. Farmers, the elderly, working parents, small businessmen—all contribute enormous sums in taxes.

None of this would be a problem if federal transfers of wealth were perfectly frictionless, with no waste or distortion in either the collection or disbursement process. This is apparently what the Washington policy-making community assumes. If you take $1.00 from a farmer in taxes and then give him back $1.10 in various subsidy programs, the assumption is that he is 10 cents to the good.

Once we include the real-world costs of operating the transfer system, we see how destructive the pattern of self-subsidy can be— even to targeted beneficiaries. If, in the above illustration, the true cost to the farmer of paying $1.00 in taxes is actually $1.65 (owing to his tax compliance burden, disincentive effects, and other costs) then the tax/subsidy system leaves him a net loser to the tune of 55 cents. And, of course, everyone else who has paid taxes to fund the agricultural subsidy is a total loser, bearing both the tax burden and the tax system cost.

Because government transfer systems have overhead costs, sound policy requires that decision makers take great care to avoid, or at least to minimize, the self-subsidy problem. In both the House and Senate chambers the injunction ought to be emblazoned on the wall in the largest possible letters: "Thou shalt not tax and subsidize the same thing." Because legislators are unaware of tax system costs, they fail to grasp this principle and hence squander national wealth at a prodigious rate through the virtually indiscriminate extension of taxing and spending programs to all sectors of society.

Death, but Not Necessarily Taxes

A third issue raised by tax system costs concerns alternative fund-raising systems. Traditionally, taxation has been viewed as an inevitable feature of the human condition. As Benjamin Franklin's aphorism goes, "In this world nothing is certain but death and taxes." This view, more than anything, may account for the public's lack of interest in the tax system and the social harm it causes. People consider the tax system an immovable part of the landscape. Reformers neglect its abuses because they assume that nothing can be done.

This view is shortsighted. A tax system is not a God-given constant. Taxation—the public extraction of funds through the use of force and the threat of force—is only one type of fund-raising system. There are voluntary fund-raising systems and techniques as well. Charitable and philanthropic giving has been a significant source of public funds for thousands of years. In ancient Greece, according to tax historian Charles Adams, philanthropy was the main source of funding for community projects. Through a practice called "liturgy," wealthy, prominent citizens made public gifts of buildings, military equipment, bridges, plays, and festivals. The system, says Adams, was "the voluntary alternative to progressive taxation."[1]

Another early case of charitable giving occurred in the Christian community under the Roman Empire. Through voluntary giving, the persecuted Christians collected funds that were spent, as a contemporary observer reported, "to feed the poor and bury them, for boys and girls who lack property and parents, and then for slaves grown old, and shipwrecked mariners, and any who may be in the mines, on the penal islands, in prison. . . ."[2] The Jews of that time had a similar system of charitable giving. The success of these voluntary arrangements was an embarrassment to Roman officials. The emperor Julian complained in a letter to his pagan priests that it was "disgraceful that, when no Jew ever has to beg, and the impious [in pagan eyes] Galileans support not only their own poor, but ours as well, everyone can see that our people lack aid from us."[3]

In the United States, philanthropy has been a significant source of public funds, a tradition extending from colonial times down to the present. In 1990, total charitable giving amounted to $122.57 billion.[4]

Within the broad field of voluntary fund raising, one encounters a host of techniques. There is the use of games of chance, like lotteries and bingo. There is door-to-door solicitation. There is mail solicitation. There are "profit-donating" arrangements, like thrift shops and bazaars in which the proceeds of commercial sales go to charity. There are arrangements of many kinds for death bequests. Many churches and clubs practice "stewardship giving"—giving based on an internalized recognition of need (and therefore involving virtually zero fund-raising costs).

Experience shows that taxation is just one possible way of raising funds for public purposes. It is an ancient system, of course; but this gives it no perpetual claim to our support. People can *choose* their fund-raising arrangements. They can decide which system they would like to phase out and which they would like to strengthen. If taxation is the best way to raise funds, this system must prove itself on a rational basis.

If we are to compare the tax system with other fund-raising arrangements we need to know about its costs. In the past, this issue has been mired in obscurity and misinformation. By supposing that IRS budgetary costs were the only costs of the tax system, generations of politicians, scholars, and journalists were misled into believing that the U.S. tax system was a virtually frictionless machine for collecting funds. Alongside this system, which was said to cost "less than 1 percent" of the taxes collected, many of the voluntary fund-raising systems did not compare favorably.

It is time to reopen this issue and to clear away the prejudice and misinformation of the past. A lively and searching debate needs to take place over the desirability of expanding and strengthening the tax system at the expense of other fund-raising arrangements. The first requisite for such a debate is a realistic picture of the tax system's burdens.

Compliance Costs

THE INTERNAL REVENUE SERVICE reported that for the tax year 1988 it distributed over eight billion pages of tax forms and instructions to American taxpayers. This works out to be a stack 208 miles high. If you prefer linear measurements, these sheets laid end to end would stretch 694,000 miles, or twenty-eight times the circumference of the earth. An impressive accomplishment!

The feat performed by the IRS, however, is nothing compared to what American taxpayers do. They have to read these instructions and fill out these forms. The magnitude of *this* task, tax compliance, makes distributing 694,000 miles of forms seem insignificant. For a glimpse of what tax compliance involves, let us examine one small aspect of one specific case.

A free-lance writer in Anywhere, U.S.A., is mailing an article to a magazine that he hopes will publish it. After he pays the postal clerk he asks for a receipt. The clerk enters the amount of postage (85 cents, let us say) on the printing calculator, which produces a piece of paper, which the clerk tears off and then stamps with the official post office seal. The writer carefully puts this slip of paper in his billfold and takes it home. There he takes it out of his billfold, goes to a filing cabinet, locates a file entitled "postage receipts" and drops the slip of paper alongside the other slips that have been gathered day by day in the same manner. Later in the year, he will empty out this file, spread the receipts on his desk and add them up with his calculator. Then he will add them up again to be sure, and he will get a different number. Then he will add them a third time, and get a third number.

The tax system is responsible for all of this activity. This system requires the writer to account for his income, which, in turn, requires him to account for the costs of operating his business, and the 85-cent postage charge is a cost of earning income as a writer. None of this activity would have taken place if there had not been an income tax code. The writer would not have asked for a receipt, nor transported it, nor filed it, nor tried to add it.

All around the United States, workers and businesses are engaged in similar activities. The nature of each enterprise causes variations in the duties performed, but the general outlines are the same. From the largest corporation to the smallest, part-time home worker, people are busy carrying out activities required by the tax system. This tax compliance activity represents *work*. It takes up time and attention; and, except in very rare cases, citizens find no intrinsic satisfaction in it. Filing and calculating are not attractive as hobbies.

How much is this work worth? If the activity had been performed in exchange for money, we would know. If the government had offered the writer, say, $200 in exchange for compiling all these receipts and if he had voluntarily accepted this offer, then we could say that $200 is the compliance cost in this case.

But with tax compliance, we do not have a voluntary transaction, a point which is often overlooked. "Taxation," as economist Joel Slemrod points out, is "a system of coercively collecting revenues from individuals who will tend to resist."[1] Because tax compliance labor is "conscripted," it becomes necessary to use an indirect technique to estimate its value. This technique involves determining the amount of time taxpayers spend on compliance activities, and then supplying an appropriate estimate for the monetary value of this time.

Components of the Tax Compliance Burden

Before turning to studies of the tax compliance burden, we should review the activities it includes, as listed in Table 1. Many of these

TABLE 1   Activities Involved in Tax Compliance

Record keeping
  Organizing data collection systems
  Collecting and appraising data
  Synthesizing data

Learning about tax requirements
  Studying tax form instructions, tax books, pamphlets, and articles
  Seeking interactive instruction in telephone calls and visits to IRS, discussion with friends
    and volunteers, classes, training sessions
  Finding and using a paid tax preparer

Preparing the return
  Making appropriate computations
  Filling out tax forms and schedules
  Copying and sending the return

Tax planning
  Studying tax requirements, books, articles, etc.
  Discussing tax avoidance with tax adviser and others
  Drafting tax management plan

tasks are quite involved. In record keeping, for example, one cannot even begin without a system for organizing the collection of data. For a large firm, this can involve a million-dollar investment in data-processing systems and in accountants and programmers to set them up, to debug them, and to modify them. The small taxpayer needs a plan for record keeping, as well as equipment—such as a filing cabinet—and a place to put it.

Burdens of data collection are often hidden and are often displaced in unrecognized ways. For example, when the free-lance writer asks the postal clerk for a receipt, the compliance burden includes not only his time in waiting for the receipt, but the clerk's time in supplying it, as well as the cost of electricity needed to run the printing calculator, depreciation on the calculator, even the cost of paper on which the receipt is printed. This same writer is likely to have a charge account at the local stationery store, mainly to meet tax accounting requirements: it provides him with a monthly summary of his spending for office supplies. Although this account reduces his own data collection costs, these are now displaced onto the store, which bears the burden of keeping these records for him.

Tax planning is included as one aspect of the tax compliance cost. This cost, it is true, is not required by the the income tax laws.

In this study, however, distinctions between mandated and optional costs are not relevant. We are calculating the total social cost of the tax system, that is, all the expenditure of resources caused by that system. If the tax system prompts individuals to expend time and money on reducing taxes, or even on evading taxes, this time and money represents part of the social cost, or waste, of the tax system (see the Appendix, "Social Cost Analysis").

In a later chapter we will focus on the actual costs of tax avoidance and evasion. The costs alluded to in Table 1 cover only the planning aspects of tax sheltering. They are included here because they tend to occur in connection with compliance. For example, many accounting firms include tax-planning suggestions when they prepare tax returns—which is one reason why their charges for this service are much higher than those of a simple tax preparer.[2]

Studies of the Compliance Burden

Early efforts to estimate the private sector burden of tax compliance were limited in scope. These studies focused only upon the actual preparation of the tax return. They downplayed or ignored the record-keeping burden, which, as we will see, is about half of the compliance burden. They also ignored the burdens of learning about tax requirements, another significant task. A further defect was the reliance on estimates rather than direct surveys of taxpayers.

Not surprisingly, these studies returned low estimates for the compliance burden. A 1944 study of this type estimated the compliance burden for individuals at 1.2 percent of federal tax revenues; a 1969 study along the same lines estimated the burden at 2.4 percent of income tax revenues; and the Commission on Federal Paperwork estimated the 1977 tax compliance burden on individuals at 3 percent of income tax revenues.[3] Before its calculations were supplanted by the Arthur D. Little study (described later in this section), the Internal Revenue Service used its own estimate of the compliance burden. This estimate considered filling out the tax form to be the only tax compliance activity.[4]

Three studies have used taxpayer surveys to measure compliance activities, and these have yielded a much higher estimate of compliance costs. A 1964 study by economist John Wicks, based on

118 questionnaires returned by Montana taxpayers, concluded that the taxpayer time and money spent complying with federal income tax requirements amounted to 11.5 percent of the taxes paid.[5]

Economists Joel Slemrod and Nikki Sorum did a similar study of Minnesota taxpayers in 1983, based on 600 questionnaire replies. They found that the average total cost of state and local income tax compliance was $379 per household. They readjusted this figure to correct for an apparent overweighting of higher-income households in their sample; this gave a nationwide estimate of $275 per household, or more than 7 percent of total federal and state income tax revenue.[6]

The third survey-based study, the one we will use to develop our estimate of compliance costs, was undertaken by the Arthur D. Little organization for the 1983 tax year.[7] It was commissioned by the Internal Revenue Service to comply with the 1980 Paperwork Reduction Act, which required government agencies to assess the private sector burden of complying with their regulations.

The Arthur D. Little study represents a landmark in measuring the tax compliance burden, setting a high standard in both comprehensiveness and theoretical elegance. Its strengths include the following:

1. The survey covered businesses as well as individuals, something no other survey of the tax compliance burden has done. The failure of other studies to include businesses has given a distorted view of the tax compliance burden even as it concerns the individual income tax. A large part of the compliance burden for this tax is borne by businesses which serve, in effect, as unpaid tax collectors and tax record keepers for individuals. Businesses must be added to the picture to obtain a valid estimate of compliance costs.

2. The polling organization (Opinion Research Corporation) was given access to IRS files of individual and business taxpayers so that a sample of these could be directly constructed. This avoided the problems of sampling along some other lines— such as residence—and then having to adjust results to be representative for taxpayers.

3. The survey covered the entire United States, thus avoiding the difficulties of converting local results into nationwide estimates.

4. The survey had large samples: 3,831 usable individual questionnaires and 1,474 business questionnaires. The return rate on the individual questionnaires was an especially high 65.2 percent, perhaps because the questionnaire was presented as a quasi-official IRS survey. (The return rate in Slemrod and Sorum's Minnesota survey of individual taxpayers was 32.65 percent.) The return rate for business taxpayers in the Little study was 36.8 percent. Knowing the nationwide taxpayer profile from the IRS files, the survey analysts were able to readjust survey results for biases caused by differences in return rates of subgroups in the sample.

5. The survey asked for and reported the amounts of time spent in each tax compliance subactivity.

6. The methodology of the Little study provides a way to calculate the compliance burden for any tax form, including new ones. It also enables analysts to calculate the total compliance burden for all the forms in a given year, given the IRS figures on how many taxpayers filed each form or schedule. Thus, the Little study gave the IRS the methodology to recompute the compliance burden each year, simply by running the computer program with updated information about the tax forms and their respective number of users (see Chapter 10 for the yearly trend in these figures). Table 2 shows the results of the Little study's calculations for 1985, our target year for compiling overhead costs. They show that the total compliance burden for 1985 was 5,427,000,000 hours.[8]

The Little study focused only upon the *time* taxpayers spend in tax compliance activities. It explicitly excluded all monetary costs to the taxpayer, such as money paid for supplies, computer, telephone, office space, postage, or tax information books.

Biases in the Arthur D. Little Study

Before we use the Little estimate to calculate the monetary burden of tax compliance, it is helpful to review some of the features of the Little study that might have resulted in a bias one way or the other.

One issue concerns the accuracy of the self-reported times. When people are asked to declare how much time they spend on

TABLE 2   Estimates of Tax Compliance Burden for 1985

	Millions of hours of work
Individual taxpayers	
Record keeping	783
Learning about tax requirements	313
Preparing	553
Copying and sending forms	164
Subtotal	1,813
Business taxpayers	
Record keeping	1,957
Learning about tax requirements	196
Obtaining materials	133
Locating and using preparer	207
Preparing	1,034
Copying and sending forms	86
Subtotal	3,614
Total	5,427

NOTE: Totals do not add because of rounding.
SOURCE: Arthur D. Little, Inc., *Development of Methodology for Estimating the Taxpayer Paperwork Burden* (Washington, D.C.: Internal Revenue Service, June 1988), p. I-7, table I-1.

tax compliance activities, are they accurate, or do they misstate the actual time? It appears that there may be tendencies both to overstate and to understate. There probably would be a tendency to exaggerate the time taken for specific, recognized activities. If a taxpayer actually sat at a table for four hours one evening filling out his return, he might report this as five hours or six hours. He might overlook the time he spent away from the table getting a sandwich, for example. Also, his annoyance with the activity might lead him to exaggerate.

Against this tendency to overreport is a tendency to overlook many types of tax compliance activities when they take place in small, undramatic ways. Take the case of the free-lance writer and his postage receipts. It is most unlikely that he will recall and report the time spent asking for the receipt, since it involves an almost negligible ten seconds, let us say. Nor would he recall time it took to go to his filing cabinet, take out the receipt, and put it in the correct folder, which might be another ten seconds. But these small activities add up. If this writer asks for and files 100 receipts a year, he has spent over half an hour on just this activity.

One compliance task that is almost certain to be underreported is learning about tax requirements. Throughout our lives, we spend a great deal of time reading about tax requirements and discussing tax issues with friends and acquaintances. All this attention is unlikely to be specifically recalled as tax compliance labor.

Learning about tax requirements crops up in our culture in other ways. For example, the IRS distributes an "Understanding Taxes" instructional package for high schools. In 1990, over four million students studied tax requirements through this course.[9] Their other studies had to be shortchanged, of course, to make room for this activity. Tax requirements are also disseminated in radio and TV programs, sometimes in the form of full-length programs distributed by the IRS, sometimes as part of general advice on money management. Tax requirements are also taught in some college courses.

On balance, then, the self-report of tax compliance activities would seem to have two offsetting biases: the tendency to exaggerate intense work done on a frustrating task, and the tendency to overlook smaller tasks and "background" tax compliance activities.

There is one major feature of the Little study that leads us to suspect a bias of understatement: its IRS funding. When a consulting firm is hired by a government agency, there is a natural tendency for the firm to bias its findings in the direction desired by the agency.[10] On the subject of the tax compliance burden, the IRS interest lies in understating it, to keep the Internal Revenue Service from getting bad press as a cause of woe to the public.

This underreporting bias does seem to have crept into the Little study in several ways. For example, many of the "time reported" boxes in the questionnaires were left blank by the respondents. Technically, these are missing data and, strictly speaking, should be eliminated from calculation. In many such cases, however, the authors substituted a value of zero for this missing information, on the grounds that this was probably what the person who filled out the questionnaire intended.[11] This procedure seems defensible, but it does run the danger of biasing the results downward: some of the missing data entries that were converted to zeros could have been positive values. Another practice that imparted a downward bias was that of discarding entries of extremely high reported compliance times and, in other cases, trimming high reported times to "more reasonable" values.[12]

Another source of bias concerns the use of an invalid "diary" study that was averaged in with the results from the questionnaire study. This operation appears to have reduced the calculated individual tax compliance burden by 22 percent.[13]

Comparison with the results of two independent studies of individual compliance times further confirms the understatement in the Little study. The Slemrod and Sorum study calculated an individual tax compliance burden of 2.13 billion hours in 1982.[14] A survey by Julie H. Collins and her colleagues of 219 taxpayers in Oklahoma and Pennsylvania indicates a total individual compliance burden of 2.02 billion hours in 1987.[15] The Little study's figures for individual compliance times—1.594 billion hours in 1983 and 1.813 billion hours in 1985—are significantly below these other results.

Another feature of the Little study that leads to an underestimation is the exclusion from the tax compliance burden of all record-keeping and accounting activities going into statements of profit and loss and other basic financial statements, even though the authors themselves recognized that many small businesses and self-employed individuals "prepare this type of information only to meet business tax requirements."[16]

Another bias toward understatement was the exclusion of tax planning. Both individual and business taxpayers were specifically instructed not to include as part of the paperwork burden "time spent on financial planning, even though it may have been tax-related."[17]

On balance, it seems that the Little study does have an overall bias toward understating the federal tax compliance burden, perhaps by about 20–30 percent.

Valuing Tax Compliance Time

To make a monetary estimate of the tax compliance burden, we need to convert the times of the Little study into dollars. How much is tax compliance time worth?

Let us answer the question first for the business taxpayers. Imagine the case of a company that at one point has no federal tax liabilities at all, and therefore no personnel devoted to tax compliance activities. It now learns that there is to be a federal tax system with a certain number of compliance hours of work to be done. How much will it have to pay for this work on a per-hour basis?

Its first costs will be for the labor, which will involve some mix of less skilled clerical workers and more skilled accountants, lawyers, and managers. The hourly labor cost to the corporation will be more than the hourly wages these workers are paid. It will also include many overhead costs. These include labor fringe benefits and employer-paid labor taxes, as well as many capital expenditures and services. The company will have to build office space for these new workers; supply office furniture, computers and other equipment, bathrooms, and lunchrooms, as well as payroll and accounting services; and pay for heat, light, and telephone services. In other words, the cost of the additional tax compliance employees will involve a host of nonlabor costs. What would be the best way to estimate this total cost?

If the company were already involved in the financial services industry, so that the mix of employees and their activities closely resembled the employees and activities in the new tax compliance unit, we could estimate hourly costs from the rest of the firm. We would simply take the firm's total costs and divide these by the total number of employee hours. This would give us the hourly cost of running the firm per average employee. This method would not be valid for a production firm that had major costs in the purchase of raw materials, or capital costs for things like blast furnaces that would not be needed for the tax compliance segment. But if the firm's business already consisted of processing data and documents, then the average cost for this activity gives a good estimate of the labor costs for tax compliance activity.

One organization to use as an example for estimating the hourly cost of processing tax documents is the Internal Revenue Service. In structure and activity, the IRS resembles a private corporation's tax compliance unit. It has a mix of personnel ranging from clerks and data entry personnel to accountants, lawyers, and managers, and the main function is the processing of tax-related information. If we take the total IRS costs for 1985 and divide by the total employee hours worked, the average cost was $21.14 per hour.[18]

There is reason to believe that this figure is a low estimate of the hourly cost of tax compliance labor for a private firm. The IRS has no capital cost, and a private firm always faces this cost in one form or another. If a private firm took out a loan to build the new tax compliance wing and buy the computers and equipment for it, it would have a loan-servicing cost of, say, 10 percent over the cost of these facilities. When the IRS acquires new facilities and equipment, the cost of these is simply appropriated by Congress, with no additional capital cost included. Also, it appears that IRS budgets understate its true pension and personnel management costs.[19]

These considerations suggest the need for a private sector comparison. One comparison is an accounting firm. Such a company would have no inventory, no raw material costs, and no capital equipment other than that relevant for processing financial documents. A good example would be the largest accounting firm in the industry, Arthur Andersen, Inc. In 1985, its employee cost per hour was $35.47.[20]

One can argue that this figure is either too low or too high as an estimate of hourly costs for business tax compliance, but on balance I believe it gives a fair reflection.[21] Indeed, in one respect, this figure is not merely an estimate of what businesses pay for tax compliance work but a direct measure of this cost. The overwhelming majority of businesses, 85 percent, have professional accounting services like Arthur Andersen prepare their tax returns, and therefore for tax preparation services they are literally paying the revenue per employee hour cost we have just calculated.[22]

To be sure that our estimates stay on the conservative side, however, I have elected to combine the Arthur Andersen–based figure with the IRS-based figure in a simple average. This gives us a figure of $28.31 as the hourly tax compliance cost for business taxpayers in 1985. The use of this figure enables us to calculate the cost of the 3.614 billion 1985 business tax compliance hours at $102.31 billion.

The Value of Individual Tax Compliance Work

Valuing individual tax compliance hours presents a number of difficulties. The first impulse would be to use the nationwide average total compensation-per-hour figure, which was $13.70 in 1985.[23] This figure understates the true value, however, for several reasons. First, the tax compliance burden falls disproportionately on the more skilled individuals such as professionals, entrepreneurs, and executives, who have the more complicated tax situations. The hourly compensation figure of these individuals is much higher than the nationwide average. A study of the tax compliance burden in Australia suggested that the weighted average wage for individual compliance work was some 60 percent above the nation-wide average wage.[24] Applying this correction to the $13.70 per hour compensation figure indicates that the individual tax com-pliance figure should be around $22.00 per hour.

Even this figure would be too low, however, because it does not include overhead costs of materials and facilities. In order to perform tax compliance duties, individuals need facilities just as business tax workers do, and their cost needs to be figured in. Several million taxpayers use a home computer to prepare their taxes, and scores of millions use their telephone to call the IRS for guidance.[25] The government is not a volunteer organization to which the taxpayer should be expected to donate the partial use of his home, desk, car, filing cabinets, or other personal possessions. This use should be charged on a free market, businesslike basis.

How should this overhead cost be measured? A survey ques-tion asking taxpayers to report their out-of-pocket costs would iden-tify only discrete purchases, such as tax books; the fractional use of facilities, such as home floor space, would be left out. One solu-tion is to turn to the business compliance cost we have just calculated. This figure does contain all associated overhead costs.[26] It also appears to be close to the figure we would expect if a com-prehensive measure of the value of individual compliance time could be applied.

There is another argument for using the business compliance cost to value individual compliance time: fairness. When the government confiscates an asset or conscripts labor, the appropriate payment should be the market-determined price for that asset or labor. Since the government is forcing individuals into the tax com-pliance business, it seems reasonable to say that their services are worth what business tax compliance services are worth. For most taxpayers, compliance is a difficult, stressful job, probably quite unlike their daily employment. They are struggling with complex decisions that affect thousands of dollars in taxes or penalties, or even a prison sentence. As one taxpayer I interviewed put it (complaining that the time estimates on IRS forms are way too low), "I find that I pace a lot. I do something one way [on the form], and then I think, 'No, wait, maybe I should really do it this way.' So I change it. Then I think about it some more and realize I want to do it the first way. It consumes weeks!" In addition to being stressful, tax compliance work is highly complex, forcing the citizen to grapple with technical and abstract matters that baffle even accountants and lawyers. It is unrealistic to value this frustrating intellectual work at a wage rate established for a simpler, less demanding job that the taxpayer may happen to hold.

To many readers, the figure of $28.31 per hour will seem rather high as an estimate of the value of individual compliance time, especially when compared with the hourly wages for many ordinary jobs. However, a lower figure could be arrived at only at the expense of the truth, by leaving out some aspect of the real cost of tax compliance work. It may help explain this point to review the reasons why a typical reported wage rate of a low-income worker is an invalid reflection of the social value of tax compliance work.

First, reported wages understate real wages because of the omission of employer-paid labor costs and fringe benefits. Second, reported wages never include the cost of materials and facilities that are necessary to make the work possible. This overhead cost must be included to correctly value taxpayer compliance work, whether of businesses or individuals. Third, the individuals doing most of the compliance work are highly skilled workers whose time is much more valuable than that of the average worker. Finally, tax compliance work is remunerated at a very high level—because it involves unusual difficulties and responsibilities.

When all these considerations are included, they produce the conclusion that tax compliance is an especially high-grade, demanding type of work with a social value in the range of the $28.31 per hour we have calculated. Only by ignoring one or more of these considerations can a researcher obtain a much lower figure.[27] Using this $28.31 figure to value the 1.813 billion hours of 1985 individual tax compliance time gives this work a value of $51.33 billion.

The Cost of Paid Preparers

In the Little study, the cost of using paid preparers was included in the business taxpayer survey by recording their times as part of the total time. Therefore, this cost is already contained in our estimate of the business compliance cost. In the individual taxpayer survey, the time of paid preparers was excluded.[28] Therefore, in order to complete our estimate of the tax compliance burden we need to include this cost.

Table 3 gives some average figures for tax preparation charges. The 1988 figures for public accountants (non-CPA accountants) are useful for illustrating typical lower charges for simple returns, as well as the regional variation in tax compliance charges. The East and West coasts, especially in their big cities, appear to have very high charges compared to the central United States and less urban areas. The H & R Block figures for 1985 and 1988 give another picture of the "budget" segment of the tax return preparation industry.

TABLE 3   Fees for Preparation of Individual Tax Returns

	Average fee per return (dollars)
Public Accountants (non-CPA), 1988	
Form 1040, not itemized	
Northeast	70.00
South	59.00
North Central	51.00
West	68.00
Average	62.00
Form 1040, itemized	
Northeast	186.00
South	147.00
North Central	119.00
West	186.00
Average	159.50
H & R Block	
1985	45.39
1988	49.21
Money magazine	
1988 test	779.00
1989 test	865.00
1990 test	1,012.00
1991 test	1,282.00
Slemrod and Sorum, adjusted to 1985 (see text)	127.81

SOURCES: National Society of Public Accountants (NSPA), *Income and Fees of Accountants in Public Practice: A 1988 Survey Report* (Alexandria, Va.: NSPA, 1988), p. 25; H & R Block, *1985 Annual Report*, p. 7, and *1988 Annual Report*, p. 7; Greg Anrig Jr., "Even Seasoned Pros Are Confused This Year," *Money*, March 1988, p. 135, and "The Pros Flunk Our New Tax-Return Test," *Money*, March 1989, p. 116; Denise M. Topolnicki, "The Pros Flub Our Third Annual Tax-Return Test," *Money*, March 1990, p. 90; Teresa Trich and Deborah Lohse, "The Pros Flub Our Tax Test (Again!)," *Money*, March 1991, p. 97.

The *Money* magazine figures give the average preparer cost for the magazine's tax return exercise given to fifty preparers each year. The (hypothetical) taxpayer for whom the return was prepared in both years was an upper-middle-income taxpayer with a moderately complex tax situation, so these figures illustrate preparation costs for the higher end of the spectrum. The preparers were a mix of low-cost preparers like H & R Block, medium-cost IRS enrolled agents, higher-cost local CPAs and a few preparers from national CPA firms, which tend to have the highest costs.

The figure we will use to estimate the nationwide average individual tax preparation cost for the 1985 tax year is $127.81. This is based on the finding from the Slemrod and Sorum study, adjusted for inflation and regional variation.[29] In 1985, 45.22 million individual returns were done by tax preparers.[30] Hence, the cost for this labor was $5.78 billion.

This estimate completes the tax compliance cost picture, which is shown in Table 4. The summary shows that the burden of federal tax compliance in the tax year 1985 was $159.42 billion, or 24.43 percent of available revenue collected. In other words, to deliver $1.00 in spendable funds to Congress, the tax system causes the waste of 24.43 cents' worth of resources by businesses and individuals in tax compliance activities.

Irrational Policy Making

As this figure shows, tax compliance represents a large burden on citizens, a burden that amounts to a further tax. Unfortunately this burden is largely ignored by policy makers and tax administrators. Their institutional responsibilities lead them to focus upon how

TABLE 4   Summary of Tax Compliance Costs, 1985

	Billions of dollars	As a percentage of available revenue collected[a]
Business taxpayer compliance costs	102.31	15.68
Individual taxpayer compliance costs	51.33	7.87
Paid preparer costs	5.78	0.89
Total	159.42	24.43

a. The available revenue collected was $652.557 billion in 1985. The derivation of this figure is explained in Chapter 8.

much revenue enters the Treasury and how much it costs the government to collect it. As I will explain in Chapter 11, taxpayers are virtually unrepresented in the system, so their sacrifices and frustrations tend to be ignored in laws and regulations. The consequence is this enormous compliance burden, a burden that drags down the same economy that policy makers keep saying they want to stimulate.

In addition to being large, the tax compliance burden is also unequal: certain taxpayers face a much higher compliance burden than others. This inequality causes unfairness and inefficiency and often defeats the purposes of other government policies. We can illustrate these points by considering two groups of taxpayers with unusual compliance burdens, self-employed workers and small corporations.

Self-employed workers are an important source of flexibility and growth in the American economy. It is the self-employed worker, often beginning part time, who opens up new businesses and new services for the community: computer repair, tutoring, dressmaking, dog grooming, photography, and a thousand other services and products, many quite innovative. Many of society's most creative individuals operate in self-employed status, including inventors, artists, writers, and consultants. Self-reliant, independent workers have been seen as the backbone of the political and social fabric of the nation. These are the country doctors, the small farmers, the corner grocers. Self-employment represents a special dream for Americans: starting your own business and becoming your own boss.

Tax compliance costs represent a direct challenge to this dream, for, as the tax system now operates, the self-employed bear a disproportionate fraction of these costs. An indication of this burden is suggested by Table 5, which shows the compliance burdens associated with some common tax forms and schedules, including those that self-employed workers are required to fill out.

Compare the relative burdens. An ordinary employee of a firm or government agency fills out a 1040 form and, let us assume, also has enough savings to require a Schedule B. Therefore, his tax compliance time is

	Hours
Form 1040	9.28
Schedule B	1.28
Total	10.56

TABLE 5   Compliance Times for Selected Tax Forms and Schedules

Document	Hours
Form 1040	9.28
Schedule A (Itemized Deductions)	4.57
Schedule B (Interest and Dividend Income)	1.28
Schedule C (Profit or Loss from Business)	10.81
Schedule D (Capital Gains and Losses)	3.27
Schedule E (Supplemental Income)	6.18
Schedule F (Farm Income or Loss)	17.67
Schedule SE (Social Security Self-Employment Tax)	
Short form	0.97
Long form	1.75
Form 1040-ES (Estimated Tax for Individuals)	3.22
Four quarterly vouchers and payments	0.67

SOURCE: Internal Revenue Service, *1988 Forms and Instructions: Form 1040,* p. 3; and *1040-ES Estimated Tax for Individuals, 1989,* p. 1. Quarterly payment times are estimated to be the same as the sending time (10 minutes) for the 1040-ES form, multiplied by 4.

See what the burden is for a self-employed worker with the same income level and assets. He has the form 1040 and Schedule B, just like the employee, but he also has a Schedule C (or Schedule F, if he is a farmer), and Schedule SE. Furthermore, he is required to make quarterly estimated tax payments, which means he has to fill out form 1040ES, and fill out and send off the payment and payment vouchers four times each year. As a result, his compliance burden looks like this:

	Hours
Form 1040	9.28
Schedule B	1.28
Schedule C	10.81
Schedule SE (short)	.97
Form 1040ES	3.22
Quarterly payments	.67
Total	26.23

Thus, the self-employed worker has a tax compliance burden two and one-half times that of the employee.

Actually, this comparison understates the burden on the self-employed worker. First, it excludes the cost of paid preparers, which will run higher for the more complicated tax situation of the self-employed. Second, it excludes the cost of general bookkeeping. Many self-employed workers have no real need for a profit/loss statement and would not, in the absence of tax requirements, invest in the record-keeping and accounting activities this requires. For these taxpayers, the tax compliance burden for the Schedule C should be set not at a mere 10.81 hours but at scores or even hundreds of hours.

Finally, the above calculation assumes that the self-employed worker does not hire any other workers. In many cases, self-employed workers use at least some temporary or part-time help; and this multiplies their tax compliance costs, since they have to keep records for and file documents and payments in behalf of these workers. (The compliance burden estimate for the employer's quarterly federal tax return, Form 941, is 22.03 hours.) When all these factors are considered, the average tax compliance burden on self-employed workers is many times the 26.23 hours calculated for the simplest case noted earlier.

Did Congress intend to lay such an extreme compliance burden on the self-employed sector? Consider the case of farmers, who, as Table 5 indicates, have an especially complicated tax schedule to fill out. Over the past half-century, Congress has poured scores of billions into the farm sector in an attempt to assist farmers and, especially, to preserve the family farm. Yet the tax compliance burden falling on farmers has been especially great. The small family farms have been forced to adopt extensive record-keeping systems they would otherwise do without, and have been forced to bear heavy compliance burdens for their few, often part-time, employees. Their failure or inability to keep up with all these compliance responsibilities has put them in the path of audits, penalties, criminal investigations, and costly litigation. This financial and psychological burden is bound to be a major factor in driving the small family farm out of business. By ignoring tax compliance costs, Congress has been undoing with one hand what it has been trying to accomplish with the other.

Once a disproportionate compliance cost burden has been identified, it should be the task of policy makers to correct it by lessening the paperwork burden on the affected group. In making these adjustments, officials cannot be guided only by considerations of the tax revenues that might be lost. It is this myopic perspective, which prevails in both Congress and the Treasury, that creates the disproportionate compliance burdens in the first place. The government official considers only government revenues and government costs and ignores private sector costs.

A good example of this myopia concerns the regulations imposing estimated tax forms and quarterly payments on self-employed workers. This system requires self-employed workers to calculate in advance their yearly earnings and then deposit quarterly the tax due on these expected earnings. From the point of view of the Treasury, this system accelerates tax payments and results in slightly higher revenues. If one considers only the government's interest, this is a beneficial arrangement. If one includes the burden on the public, however, it is highly inefficient. It sets some seven million taxpayers working to learn about, make calculations for, and fill out estimated tax forms, and then forces them to submit over 35 million estimated tax forms and quarterly payment vouchers.[31] Owing to confusion or forgetfulness, many of these submissions displease IRS clerks and computers, causing the generation of over three million penalties. These lead, in turn, to new burdens as penalties are appealed (successfully in over 120,000 cases), or go unpaid, to become collection cases, with all the burden this implies for the taxpayer.[32] It is difficult to believe that this additional burden on the self-employed would have been imposed if tax officials had weighed compliance costs along with revenue aspects in drafting these requirements.

Another type of taxpayer that bears a disproportionate tax compliance burden is the small corporation. Small companies must carry out virtually all the tax compliance activities that larger companies do, but they have a much smaller revenue base over which to spread their compliance costs. This pattern has been thoroughly documented for the British tax system by Cedric Sandford and his colleagues, and probably applies to an even greater degree in the United States.[33] The result is unintended harm. Small corporations are important for introducing competition into otherwise oligopolistic industries; and they are a source of innovations, new products, and new jobs. In recognition of their value, Congress has approved numerous programs to subsidize small businesses. Yet, at the same time, it imposes tax compliance burdens that penalize the small firms more than the corporate giants.

Insensitive to this issue, tax officials continue to increase compliance burdens with little regard to their economic cost to small firms. One set of regulations that has only a small revenue benefit yet imposes great compliance burdens, particularly on small firms, is the body of rigorous reporting and depositing requirements for employee tax withholding payments. These payments must be deposited monthly and, if over $3,000, must be deposited within three banking days.[34] By relaxing the depositing times by a few days and reducing the frequency of deposit, officials could significantly lessen the compliance burden, at very little loss of revenue—and also at a savings from reduced penalty disputes.[35]

Other requirements that impose a significant compliance burden for a minor revenue gain are the uniform capitalization of inventory regulations. These result in a small, one-time advance in tax revenues, while putting a perpetual burden on the firm to make complex calculations to revalue its production inventory.[36]

These examples illustrate the general point that officials in charge of the U.S. federal tax system are ignoring the problem of tax compliance costs. This lack of interest is reflected in the annual reports of the Internal Revenue Service. These volumes are laden with statistics about revenue raised and administrative activities undertaken, but they contain not one figure reflecting the compliance burdens placed on taxpayers. This omission is astonishing when you consider that the private sector's compliance cost, as given in Table 4, is over thirty times the entire budget of the Internal Revenue Service!

Gradually, this one-sided perspective may change. Congress has passed various "paperwork reduction" measures over the years, and the Office of Management and Budget has issued regulations in an effort to carry out these intentions. Often, these efforts bear little fruit. For example, the Paperwork Reduction Act of 1980, as implemented by OMB, has all federal agencies submit an information collection budget to OMB, which then compiles a national Information Collection Budget. This activity seems to have degenerated into an empty exercise.[37]

This act, nevertheless, does have to be given credit for at least one victory. It pushed the IRS to commission the Arthur D. Little study of the tax compliance burden. That study, as we have seen, documented the enormous burden of complying with the federal tax system and thus represents a start at recognizing the problem.

✦ 3 ✦

Enforcement Costs:
Audits and Correspondence

COMPLIANCE WITH THE TAX CODE is motivated by threats of punishment. These threats include both official sanctions—monetary penalties; seizure of bank accounts, homes, businesses, vehicles, or other property; and prison terms—and informal punishments, including damage to the taxpayer's reputation and credit rating, unreasonable demands for information, and the undue prolongation of tax investigations. The taxpayers who are the object of these enforcement actions bear a burden, a burden which is part of the cost of operating a tax system.

Contemplating this harsh aspect of the tax system is not pleasant, and this is one reason why tax officials tend to ignore enforcement costs. Their uneasiness is reflected in their misuse of words. Although the tax system is coercive, based, ultimately, on physical seizures and physical restraints, officials never refer to it as such. Instead, they call it "voluntary." The resulting newspeak leads to amusing logical contradictions that dot the official tax literature. For example, in introducing the discussion of criminal investigation, the 1987 IRS *Annual Report* declared: "Voluntary compliance with the tax laws in the United States self-assessment system of taxation relies heavily on the deterrent effect of successful criminal prosecutions."[1] Another example is the declaration of senior House Ways and Means Committee member Representative Charles Rangel: "It is clear to me . . . that what makes a voluntary system work is the fear of sanctions and penalties."[2]

Another reason why enforcement costs are disregarded is the tendency of tax officials to believe that these burdens are "deserved." At the IRS headquarters in Washington, I asked an official in the Office of Planning, Finance and Research if there were any studies dealing with the private sector burden of participating in audits. She was indignant that I should even consider this a burden. "It's their own fault," she said. "They wouldn't be examined if they followed the law. I've been filing taxes for seventeen years, and I've never been examined."

This declaration contains two errors. First, this official was misinformed about IRS practices. In most cases taxpayers are not selected for audit because they have "done something wrong." The tax return itself would seldom provide adequate information for such a conclusion. They are selected mainly on the basis of "discriminant function" (DIF) formulas which express the probabilities that recoverable tax revenue will be contained in that class of return.[3] Since these are only probabilities, a significant number of returns subjected to audit will be found to be in compliance with tax law. In 1990, for example, some 173,000 examinations produced a "no change" result, and 82,000 more taxpayers were found to have overpaid their taxes.[4] Nevertheless, these innocent taxpayers had to go through the burdens associated with an audit.

The more important point, however, is that the guilt of taxpayers is not relevant in a social cost analysis. Any cost that is caused, inspired, or triggered by the tax system is part of the burden of that system. Whether the individual spends millions fighting the tax system or is innocently trapped by the tax system makes no difference: in each case the expenditures can be laid at the doorstep of the system. In the absence of this system, this consumption of resources would not have occurred (see the Appendix, "Social Cost Analysis," for an elaboration of the social cost idea).

This perspective is especially applicable for modern tax systems, which are so artificial in their demands. In the case of simple crimes, like theft or murder, it might make sense to include enforcement burdens as part of the proper punishment a (guilty) defendant ought to bear. By their misdeeds, the transgressors have placed themselves beyond the pale of society's concern, so that we do not regret the enforcement burdens placed on them. But in modern tax systems, the transgressions are so far removed from common standards of right and wrong that it makes no sense to treat a tax violator as a subhuman whose burdens are no longer of concern to society. To use a five-year depreciation schedule instead of a seven-year one is hardly a crime against humanity. Hence, the burdens of tax enforcement are properly counted as social costs.

To simplify the discussion of enforcement costs, I have divided them into three categories: (1) burdens associated with the initial contacts made by the tax collection authority in audits and correspondence, (2) burdens associated with tax litigation, and (3) burdens associated with the forced collection process. The first category, the audits and assessments, will be treated in this chapter. The follow-on phases of enforcement—litigation and collections—will be treated in the subsequent chapters.

Table 6 summarizes the initial contacts, showing the number of taxpayers affected for 1985, the year being used for all our

TABLE 6   Tax Enforcement Activities, Initial Contacts, 1985

Initial contacts	Number of affected taxpayers
Examinations	
Office audits	814,213
Field audits	519,292
Mail audits	125,241
Service center corrections	558,876
Criminal investigations	6,065
Information Returns Program (computer matching)	4,100,000[a]
Nonfiling notices	3,000,000
Penalties not included elsewhere	8,785,000[b]
Total number of taxpayers affected by initial enforcement actions	17,909,000

a. This figure is taken from Frank Malanga, director, Research Division, Internal Revenue Service, "The Relationship between IRS Enforcement and Tax Yield," *National Tax Journal* 39 (September 1986), p. 335. This figure is preferred over the *1985 Annual Report* figure of 3.6 million, in view of the carelessness with which figures are handled in the *Annual Report* narrative section (see footnotes 14 and 15). The Malanga figure for nonfiling notices is the same as that given in the *Annual Report*, 3.0 million.
b. See the Appendix, "The Burden of Initial Enforcement Contacts," for the derivation of this figure.
SOURCE: Except as indicated above, the figures are taken from Internal Revenue Service, *1985 Annual Report*, pp. 12, 18, 67.

calculations. According to this tabulation, some 17.9 million tax-payers were affected. This figure represents nearly one-fifth of all taxpayers.

The Great American Nightmare

The taxpayer audit, or "examination" as the IRS prefers to call it, is a major source of gallows humor in American culture. Surveys show that most taxpayers spend at least some time worrying about this "Great American Nightmare," as one writer calls it.[5] This anxiety has several causes. For one thing, an audit means an invasion of privacy, as a stranger pries into how you earn and spend your money. Furthermore, this prying stranger wields the coercive apparatus of the state. In the face of this overwhelming power, the taxpayer often feels defenseless, almost naked. Another factor that contributes to the unpleasantness of an audit is guilt. Many taxpayers, probably a majority, have cut some kind of corner in connection with their tax return and fear the punishment, and the embarrassment, of being found out.

In contrast to Sweden, where all taxpayers are examined, or Denmark, where over half of the taxpayers are audited each year, the United States practices a limited audit policy, examining only a tiny fraction of returns.[6] In the 1960s, this audit rate was about 4 percent. It has been falling since that time, so that by 1990 the aggregate rate was 0.80 percent.[7] This decrease in audit coverage, which has occurred despite substantial increases in IRS audit personnel, is the result of several factors—especially the growing complexity of the tax code, which makes audits take longer.

The IRS examines returns in all taxpayer categories to maintain deterrence; however, it emphasizes examination of returns where more income is involved and where greater complexity is more likely to produce a major discrepancy between tax owed and tax paid. Table 7 gives the 1990 rates of audit coverage for selected categories of tax returns.

In estimating the burden of audits, it is important to distinguish between an office audit and a field audit. In an office audit, the taxpayer—usually with a rather simple tax situation—goes to the IRS office with his records. These examinations tend to be rather short, averaging a little over three hours, and are usually conducted by tax auditors, the non-CPA category of IRS examination official.[8]

TABLE 7 Rates of Audit Coverage, 1990

Category of tax return[a]	Percentage audited
Individual	
Under $25,000	0.44
$25,000–$50,000	0.74
$50,000–$100,000	1.09
Over $100,000	4.71
Individual small business	
Under $25,000	1.36
Over $100,000	3.38
Farmer	
Under $100,000	1.30
Over $100,000	2.69
Corporation	
Assets under $50,000	1.08
Assets $100,000–250,000	2.00
Assets $1–5 million	4.35
Assets $10–50 million	19.47
Assets over $250 million	72.50
Exempt organizations[b]	3.30
Estate	
Under $1 million	13.00
Over $5 million	57.58

a. For individuals, income figures are total positive income before deductions; for businesses and farmers, income figures are gross receipts.
b. The figure given is the audit rate for exempt organizations that filed tax returns.
SOURCE: Internal Revenue Service, *1990 Annual Report*, p. 28.

The field audit takes place either at the taxpayer's place of business or at the office of the lawyer or CPA handling his account. These audits tend to be quite long, continuing over a period of many days or weeks. In the case of a large corporation, the examination can go on all year. Field examinations are generally conducted by revenue agents, the CPA-level examiner.

The third category of examination, the mail query from the service center, requires the taxpayer to respond with appropriate documentation in connection with some questioned aspect of the return.

One of the costs of participation in an examination is representation. Taxpayers may have CPAs, lawyers, or other designated persons represent them, or accompany them, in an audit. One IRS official in the examination division estimated that proportion of office audits with representation is about 25 percent, while the proportion of field audits with representation is about 75 percent.

To gauge the cost of this representation, I interviewed a number of tax practitioners to learn their charges for typical cases. From this survey, I have arrived at an overall average figure of $350 for office audit representation and $1,500 for field audit representation.[9]

In the Appendix, "The Burden of Initial Enforcement Contacts," I present the time and cost estimates of audits. As summarized in Table 8, these estimates put the average burden of an office audit at $690 and of a field audit at $2,397.

Criminal Investigations

The tax compliance action that probably best deserves to be called the Great American Nightmare is not the audit but the criminal investigation. Each year the IRS initiates about 6,000 of these actions, in which the taxpayer is targeted for a possible prison sentence. Criminal investigations go on for a long time, usually years, during

TABLE 8   Costs of Initial Enforcement Contacts, 1985

	Millions of dollars
Office audits ($689 each)	561
Field audits ($2,397 each)	1,245
Mail audits ($343 each)	43
Criminal investigations	ne
Information Returns Program ($210 each)	859
Nonfiler program ($126 each)	377
Penalty/penalty abatement ($210 each)	1,845
Service center corrections ($210 each)	117
Representation in connection with IRP notices, nonfiling notices, and penalty abatement	ne
Correspondence sweeps	ne
Refund correspondence	ne
Payment document reporting burden	493
Total, initial enforcement contacts	5,540

NOTE: ne = not estimated.
SOURCES: The Appendix, "The Burden of Initial Enforcement Contacts," and Table A1

A tax lawyer, who defended a law firm under criminal tax investigation, gave this account of the costs:

The punishment starts on the day that the investigation is commenced. For three years you are in prison, before you start. For three years people are going around flashing a criminal investigation badge and saying, "We are investigating Walter Blum for possible tax crimes." The subject hears of the investigation from his friends and associates, and from anybody that he cares about and those who don't care about him, for three years. By the time it's over, many clients are relieved to be going before a judge for sentencing. . . . You cannot measure the cost (even though there was an acquittal, at least of the principal in the law firm), the cost of that investigation. The downside, in terms of lost opportunities, lost clients, lost reputation, goes beyond any analysis.

SOURCE: Harry K. Mansfield, "The Role of Sanctions in Taxpayer Compliance," in *Income Tax Compliance* (Reston, Va.: American Bar Association, 1983), p. 403.

---

which time the taxpayer's entire life and business may be profoundly injured (see box).

I will not estimate the monetary costs of criminal investigations, since the number of cases is too small to affect our aggregate figure. About half of the investigations result in criminal prosecutions in court; the cost of this phase will be included in tax litigation in the next chapter. As the tax lawyer I have quoted notes, the real costs of criminal tax procedures are nonmonetary, a point we pick up in Chapter 9.

Dealing with the "Orwellian Monster"

The advent of computers and data-processing machinery has meant that the IRS can deal with many enforcement issues in an impersonal and mechanical fashion. From the IRS point of view, these automated systems save money—and insulate IRS employees from angry citizens. From a social cost perspective, however, these

A California tax lawyer describes the IRS computer enforcement system:

The IRS has in recent years totally eliminated human contact and response. It is now an invisible all-powerful Orwellian monster, which is always correct and the taxpayer is a "cheat." The first contact is a brusque demand for additional income taxes due, based on data which even sophisticated tax preparers have difficulty understanding. . . . Letters with information or explanation supplying data to justify taxpayer's position disappear into a vast "Black Hole" at the IRS center. Subsequent demands generated automatically by computers keep coming again and again to the taxpayer without any indication that replies have been made to the original demand.

SOURCE: Letter of Kurt Anker, lawyer and CPA, *Taxpayers' Bill of Rights* (Hearings before the Subcommittee on Private Retirement Plans and Oversight of the Internal Revenue Service of the Committee on Finance, U.S. Senate, 100th Cong., 1st Sess., April 10 and 21, 1987), part 1, p. 280.

automated systems are extremely burdensome, as well as frustrating and anxiety-provoking (see box).

The largest of the computer-based enforcement techniques is the Information Returns Program, also called the "underreporter" program. In this program, which affects about four million taxpayers each year, IRS employees attempt, with the aid of the computer, to match income payer reports with taxpayer income declarations. If the clerk operating the system feels that a payment is not reported, he activates a program that automatically sends a notice of proposed tax adjustment to the taxpayer, the CP-2000 letter. The taxpayer must either pay the amount demanded or respond in a way that aborts an automatic sequence of further letters, deficiency notices, and collection proceedings.

In the nonfiler program, which affects about three million citizens each year, computer matching is used to detect individuals who have apparently failed to file an income tax return, and a computer-generated letter is sent to each one. The letter threatens an escalating sequence of enforcement actions unless the citizen either files a return or explains to the satisfaction of IRS clerks why he has not.

"Half of What We Do Are Errors"

It is not possible to assess these automated enforcement systems without stressing the fact that they are extremely error-prone. When it comes to making mistakes, silly mistakes and lots of them, the IRS probably exceeds the record of any government bureaucracy, including the military.

A reading of the IRS's own annual reports reveals this problem. These formal, glossy publications, where, one would think, top managers are trying to put their best foot forward, are studded with misprints, contradictory tables, and misleading claims.[10] Consider the following passages on the Automated Collection System. The 1987 *Annual Report* (p. 23) declared that "the Automated Collection System (ACS) completed its third full year of operation and increased in effectiveness to the point that 65 percent of all delinquent account dispositions were resolved through full payment." One year later, the 1988 IRS *Annual Report* (p. 21) again stated that "the ACS completed its third full year of operation and increased in effectiveness to the point that 65 percent of all delinquent account dispositions were resolved through full payment."

This error reveals both a human failure and a system failure. The individual who lifted the sentence from one year's report to the next had enough initiative to change it slightly by abbreviating "Automated Collection System" but failed to realize that a year had passed, requiring an update. But this copy should have been reviewed by managers, who should have caught the defect. (The actual claim about the 65 percent success for ACS would be untrustworthy in any case, a typical example of the careless statistical manipulations IRS officials engage in to puff their programs.)[11]

The carelessness that characterizes the "front office" of the organization is found to an even greater degree at the operational levels. In answering taxpayer questions, the IRS telephone information service gives the wrong answer to taxpayers 36 percent of the time.[12] A study of the Philadelphia Service Center in the third quarter of 1984 found that some 26,000 business taxpayers who made correct and timely payments were improperly accused of defaulting on their obligations.[13] In 1983, the IRS put 700,000 miscoded interest and dividend reports on the computer master file.[14] IRS employees themselves suffer from the inefficiency. Their own payroll system generates a high number of mistakes, with as many as 15,000 uncorrected payroll errors logged at one time.[15]

The IRS is not the only one to blame for garbled information. Taxpayers and businesses contribute their share of errors. Many of the errors are unintentional. For example, flawed computer software used by over fifty banks to report dividend and interest payments caused erroneous data to be given to the IRS on approximately one million taxpayers.[16]

Other errors are intentional, caused by taxpayers seeking to protest or trammel what they see as a police state tax system. Some submit bogus tax returns or incorrect taxpayer identification numbers. Another practice is the filing of payment reports that assert a taxpayer received a payment, such as a stock dividend, that did not occur. Under the Information Returns Program, these bogus reports will trigger an unjustified IRS enforcement action. The IRS claimed to have identified 2,000 such fraudulent 1099 payment report forms in 1989.[17] The number that go undetected is probably many times that figure.

This issue points up a general problem with the automated enforcement systems. By ignoring elementary judicial safeguards, these systems permit a great deal of false and unjustified state action. For example, these systems deny the right of the accused to face his accuser. Without this safeguard, it is possible for some individuals, by filing false 1099 forms, to use the enforcement system of the IRS to harass their personal enemies. Another obvious safeguard done away with in computer-based enforcement programs is the presumption of innocence. These systems assume the taxpayer is guilty of transgressing until he can convince IRS officials otherwise.

Many studies have documented the extensive errors in the computer-based enforcement programs. One analysis of the nonfiler program in 1972 revealed that only 9 percent of all notices sent out resulted in securing delinquent tax returns from nonfilers who owed significant tax. All the other cases represented some kind of miscue: the IRS had an incorrect address, or the taxpayers were not required to file, or owed no tax, or had already filed and the IRS had garbled its information on them (see the Appendix, "The Burden of Initial Enforcement Contacts," for a summary of this study). A decade later, another study indicated an even higher level of miscues: only 2 percent of the targeted nonfilers were nonfilers who owed significant tax.[18]

In 1988, a study by the General Accounting Office into the IRS's business nonfiler program was aimed at explaining why nearly three-quarters of these investigations represented a blind alley. The main answer was that these investigations were based on some kind of error. In 15 percent of the cases, the IRS had erroneously issued two employer identification numbers for the same employer and ended up chasing a ghost of its own creation. In 19 percent of the cases, the employers had no tax obligation (yet burdensome regulations required them to file anyway). And in 16 percent of the cases IRS clerks failed to delete invalid filing requirements, which, as the GAO noted, "will likely result in future unproductive investigations."[19]

In 1987, the General Accounting Office surveyed a random sample of 718 pieces of IRS correspondence, including letters assessing additional taxes, sent to taxpayers from the Fresno, Kansas City, and Philadelphia service centers. It found that 31 percent of the cases contained "critical" errors—such as providing incorrect information or making an erroneous entry in the taxpayer's account, while another 16 percent of the cases involved less critical mistakes.[20] Even congressmen were shocked (see box).

Congressman Christopher Shays (R-Conn.), upon hearing about the IRS error rate from GAO testimony:

I am not used to these kinds of hearings where I learn that 47 percent of all written responses to taxpayers is incorrect or that I learn that 36 percent of the noncomputer kind of responses, the personal contacts over the phone are incorrect. It just raises some questions in my mind that I haven't been able to sort out yet. I wonder, if we can make such a colossal number of mistakes, how would that translate in the other things we haven't looked at . . . ?

It is not that we are trying to fine tune and say 10 percent is the error rate and let us get it down to 5. We are saying it is close to 50 percent. . . . I can't even say it, it is so astounding. Half of what we do are errors.

SOURCE: *Serious Problems Exist in the Quality of IRS Correspondence with Taxpayers* (Hearing before a subcommittee of the Committee on Government Operations, U.S. House of Representatives, 100th Cong., 2d Sess., July 13, 1988), pp. 85, 86.

This 47 percent error figure compiled by the General Account-ing Office probably understates the true error rate because the GAO's research orientation is biased toward understating the injuries the IRS does to taxpayers. The GAO does its research from within IRS service centers and looks at the world through the eyes of IRS administrators. It does not survey taxpayers to see IRS programs through their eyes. This means that the errors it detects are those that can be seen from an IRS viewpoint. There are many more errors, however, that would be detectable only from the tax-payer's point of view, if one knew facts not available at the IRS office. In the Information Returns Program in particular, the error rate seems well above the GAO's 47 percent figure. A 1990 Gallup poll of *Money* magazine subscribers found that of those receiving correspondence about tax due, 69 percent reported that the correspondence was wrong.[21]

The errors in the computer enforcement program would not be so troublesome if the government were bearing the cost of correcting them. Unfortunately, this is not how the system works. As noted earlier, computer enforcement programs function on a guilty-until-proven-innocent basis. Taxpayers are ''accused'' of wrongdoing in notices that may be anywhere from 50 to 99 percent incorrect or inapplicable. Since these notices are coercive, threaten-ing eventual seizure of property unless the taxpayers clear them up, the taxpayers are compelled to grapple with them, and to keep writing and phoning to get the errors corrected.

Many inefficiencies in the computer-based programs are caused by the fact that the taxpayer is cut off from the person who made the original decision to send the notice. The computer-generated letter gives either no name at all or a fictitious name. Another problem is that the clerks who send the notices never see what they are sending. The form letters are called up by code, from an inventory of about 500 letters, and printed out in another location. All these gaps in the system mean the taxpayer often runs into a blank wall in attempting to resolve a dispute (see box). In recent years, the IRS has expanded a separate program, the Problem Resolution Program, designed to grapple with the Kafkaesque mix-ups originating in the enforcement bureaucracies. In 1990, officials in this program reportedly handled 379,000 cases.[22]

In the Appendix, ''The Burden of Initial Enforcement Contacts,'' I have compiled estimates for the private sector burden of the

A tax lawyer describes the problems of dealing with erroneous IRS correspondence:

The typical IRS response is, unfortunately, no response, even after repeated, good-faith efforts by the taxpayer to resolve the dispute. The notices continue to be generated, and the taxpayer's frustration continues to grow. To compound the taxpayer's frustration, these notices are often ambiguous, providing virtually no detail to substantiate the IRS's claims or even the nature of the purported liability.

SOURCE: Statement of James D. McCarthy in *Taxpayers' Bill of Rights* (Hearings before the Subcommittee on Private Retirement Plans and Oversight of the Internal Revenue Service of the Committee on Finance, U.S. Senate, 100th Cong., 1st Sess., April 10 and 21, 1987), part 1, pp. 180–81.

computer enforcement programs. The results are summarized in Table 8. For the Information Returns Program, the average cost of dealing with the IRS CP-2000 letter was $210 in 1985, with the total program burden being $859 million. In the nonfiler program, the burden was $377 million.

A third type of enforcement activity that depends partly on computer systems is the application of filing and payment penalties. Here again, many of the IRS actions are erroneous or unjustified. One GAO study conducted in 1989 found that 20 percent of the filing penalties issued were incorrect.[23] As I have explained, this GAO figure would understate the number of penalties that taxpayers feel are incorrect. Naturally, the high error rate leads to many taxpayer protests. Since the late 1970s, there has been a formal system of penalty appeals, through which a taxpayer can seek abatement, that is cancellation, of an unjustified penalty. Currently, about 45 percent of all penalties are contested by taxpayers (see the Appendix, "The Burden of Initial Enforcement Contacts"); in 1985 the IRS abated 21 percent of all penalties, recognizing that they had been erroneously assessed.[24]

To understand what can be involved in a payment penalty case, consider the 1985 experience of the Rohm & Haas Company. The IRS mislaid its $4.5 million payroll tax deposit check and assessed a $47,000 penalty against the company. Getting the IRS to find and admit its error occupied five corporate accountants, and took seven letters and a visit to the IRS office by corporate officials.[25]

As explained in the Appendix, "The Burden of Initial Enforcement Contacts," the social cost of the penalty–penalty abatement system has been assessed by treating it like the IRP program. Thus, each case is estimated to involve a private sector burden of $210, for a total of $1.845 billion. This figure does not include the actual penalties assessed or paid, since these transfers do not figure in a social costs analysis (see the Appendix, "Social Cost Analysis").

The burden of the service center corrections has been estimated by using the same estimates as for the IRP program. In the computation of the burdens of responding to the automated enforcement systems, I have not included the cost of representatives—accountants, lawyers—who are sometimes involved in these cases.

Another category of initial enforcement contacts is correspondence "sweeps." These are IRS mail-outs whose purpose is to remind each recipient of some compliance duty that may apply in his case. They are often couched in terms that require, or seem to require, a response, even when they are irrelevant to the taxpayer. For example, one nonprofit group received a "request for your tax return" in November 1989. This computer letter demanded a form 941 (Employer's Quarterly Tax Return) or a full explanation for why the form had not been filed, "within 10 days." In this case, the organization was not, and never had been, an employer.

Sweeps are sent blind, with the IRS having no basis for supposing that the recipient is not in compliance with the tax code. At least in the Information Returns Program, in theory the IRS has evidence of taxpayer wrongdoing. With a sweep, there is not even this presumption of guilt. The IRS targets a group which, it feels, may include some noncompliers, in the hope of jolting one or two into complying. This seems rather irresponsible, forcing ninety-nine unaffected taxpayers to respond to a spurious accusation in order to motivate one noncomplier.

An illustration of how burdensome and inefficient this scatter-gun approach can be is provided by a GAO study of a mail-out to some 46,000 "potential nonfilers" in California in 1975. The mail-out was based on a crude attempt to match federal and state records. A follow-up on a sample of recipients found that only 1.75 percent of the total number of recipients were true nonfilers who were made to file by the sweep. The remaining 98.25 percent of the notices were either unnecessary, creating a burden for the taxpayers who had to respond to them, or were unsuccessful for some other reason, such as being returned as undeliverable.[26]

It is difficult to estimate the burden of correspondence sweeps, since there appears to be no tabulation of how many the IRS undertakes each year.

Another burden we should mention concerns complications in obtaining tax refund checks. In 1988, the Treasury refunded $100 billion to some eighty-five million taxpayers. Though the refund process seems less error-prone than other aspects of the tax system, mistakes still do occur. The IRS may fail to issue the appropriate refund, and this puts a burden on the taxpayer to clear up the difficulty.

Finally, an additional burden of the computer-based enforcement systems, especially the Information Returns Program, comes in the information reporting requirements. The computer matching system requires payers to report transactions to the IRS and to the recipients of those payments. There are now over eighty payment-reporting requirements, requirements that compel businesses and individuals to render some one billion payer reports. Using data developed by the American Bankers Association, the cost of meeting these payer reporting requirements can be conservatively estimated at $493 million in 1985.[27]

The Forgotten Taxpayer

The total private sector burden of initial enforcement contacts, as shown in Table 8, comes to $5.54 billion for 1985. To put this figure in perspective, it was over 50 percent higher than the budgetary cost of running the entire Internal Revenue Service in the same year.

To some extent, this burden is an unavoidable cost of maintaining compliance with the tax system. There is no doubt, however, that it is compounded by the approach to tax enforcement that makers of tax policy have adopted. This approach emphasizes revenue collection in the short run and tends to ignore the burdens on taxpayers.

As I noted in Chapter 2, this perspective grows out of the "culture of taxing," Washington's subculture of tax officials who are insulated from the problems and perspectives of taxpayers. In their view, the injury done to the taxpayers in the enforcement process, even injury to completely innocent taxpayers, is of little or no importance. A dramatic illustration of this myopia is the manner in which tax officials evaluate the effectiveness of different enforcement programs.

IRS officials present calculations that purport to show that for each dollar spent on an enforcement function, many more dollars are collected in taxes. Congressmen and officials from the General Accounting Office accept these figures and leap to the conclusion that expanding IRS enforcement activities would produce "a painless reduction in our bulging deficit."[28] The result has been a rapid expansion of the IRS enforcement activities.

To illustrate the distortion in these analyses, let us look at the program that tax officials and tax committee congressmen are especially pleased with, the Information Returns Program. In a typical demonstration, the director of the IRS research division calculated that in 1985 this program had a yield-to-cost ratio of 11.8 because its "yield" was $2.3 billion in additional taxes collected and the "cost" was only $192 million.[29]

A close examination of this calculation reveals a number of omissions and distortions. First, it makes the error, which virtually all IRS calculations of this type make, of confusing "assessed" taxes and penalties with actual payments.[30] The $2.3 billion figure is the amount initially assessed. Much of this assessed amount would go unpaid, mainly because, as we have noted earlier, it was incorrectly assessed and eventually reversed. In addition, some assessments would be misaddressed or ignored by the addressee. Judging from the results of similar programs where true yield has been compared to initial assessments, we can say that only about 40 percent of the original assessments under IRP are actually collected.[31] Hence, the IRP program had a tax yield of something like $920 million, not $2.3 billion.

The most important error in this yield-to-cost calculation is that it totally ignores the burdens of the program on taxpayers, the human beings the IRS is supposed to be serving. The analysis includes only the budgetary costs to the IRS. Wearing these blinders, nothing prevents IRS officials from concluding that even genocide would have a favorable "yield-to-cost" ratio: one simply kills taxpayers (the appropriations for the bullets would be quite small) and confiscates their wealth.

Obviously, a responsible tabulation of the costs of any enforcement program must include the costs of the program to taxpayers.

In the case of the IRP, the monetary burden alone, as estimated in Table 8, is $859 million. This must be included as one of the costs of the program. Another cost to the public is the burden of supplying all the payer information documents on which the IRP depends. As just noted, this cost was at least $493 million in 1985.

One additional correction should be made before we recalculate the yield-to-cost ratio. In the IRS calculation, the budgetary cost is given as $192 million, but this figure represents an understatement of the social cost. As this book shows, there is an overhead cost to operating the tax system, a cost which, we will see, amounts to about 65 cents for every dollar collected and spent by the federal government. To make an accurate statement of the social cost of any government program, this overhead cost must be added to the actual budgetary cost. Thus, if the IRP costs $192 million tax dollars, the total social cost for this amount, including the cost of collecting the $192 million, is $317 million.[32]

With these numbers in hand, we can now make a realistic estimate of the true yield-to-cost ratio of the Information Returns Program. The yield was $920 million in tax revenue; and the costs were $317 million to operate the IRS component, $859 million in citizen labor and overhead in responding, and $493 million in payer reporting costs. This makes the total cost $1.7 billion. Hence, the yield-to-cost ratio is 0.55, indicating an extremely destructive program.[33]

A high tax yield-to-cost ratio is not necessarily good:

It is important to realize that a tax yield-to-cost ratio is not a social benefit-cost analysis. Although the costs are social costs—resources consumed by the enforcement activity—the tax collected is not a social benefit but merely resources transferred from one holder to another. Therefore, a high yield-to-cost ratio does not mean that the tax enforcement activity is a socially beneficial one. A yield-to-cost ratio of 1.0, for example, would not represent an acceptable, break-even result. It would identify a highly inefficient, highly destructive enforcement system, a system that is consuming one dollar of resources every time it shifts one dollar from the taxpayer to the government.

The IRP program may have a disappointing yield in economic terms, but can it not be justified from the standpoint of deterrence? Doesn't it help frighten citizens into paying their taxes, and increase tax collections in this fashion? This is the position of tax officials. In their view, IRP notices "provide presence."[34] They make the citizen feel that Big Brother is always watching.

The problem with this theory is that it overlooks the quality factor. Fear of an impersonal Big Brother rests on the perception that Big Brother is competent. The automated enforcement systems with their irresponsible notices tend to convince taxpayers that "the computer" is a fool, and their difficulties in attempting to clear up their problem suggest that it is a particularly dense fool. The rational responses to a dense and foolish system are (1) to attempt to outwit it or (2) to ignore it, on the grounds that nothing you do will make any difference. These responses reflect the exact opposite of the attitude enforcement officials wish to cultivate.

Furthermore, a tax authority that presents itself as Big Brother runs the risk of losing political support. The image of an impersonal, relentless governmental Authority is extremely unattractive. Congressional hearings are studded with unflattering references to the Internal Revenue Service, comparing it to "the Gestapo," or "the KGB." Tax specialist and former IRS agent James D. McCarthy summarized the changing sentiment: "Our self-assessment system was the pride of the world at one time, and I think it is now being changed into a police state system, based on computer matchings."[35] Tax officials are being penny-wise and pound-foolish in reaching for the apparent efficiencies of automatic systems without considering their effect on public perceptions of the organization.

All the arguments—economic, moral, and political—are strongly in favor of drastically scaling back computer-based enforcement systems like the Information Returns Program, to a level where they can be accurately and personally administered. If the makers of U.S. tax policy could step out of their "culture of taxing" cocoon and start including taxpayer burdens in their thinking, they would apprehend the point immediately.

✦ 4 ✦

Enforcement Costs: Litigation

ONE OF THE REMARKABLE FEATURES of the federal tax system is the number of opportunities it affords taxpayers to appeal decisions made by tax enforcement officials. In one sense, these many review procedures are healthy, giving the taxpayer a means of protesting destructive and arbitrary actions. From the standpoint of system costs, however, these appeal opportunities present a problem: to the extent that taxpayers make use of them, they add to the labor and expense of dealing with the tax system. This expense is especially high since it involves dealing with a rule-oriented bureaucracy implementing complex regulations. In protesting a decision one cannot simply appeal to "common sense" or to "reason." To obtain a hearing, taxpayer objections must be put in proper technical form; and mastering this form, or paying someone else to master it, can represent a significant burden.

In this chapter, I estimate the costs for the main types of tax litigation, including the appeals of examination results, U.S. Tax Court cases, refund litigation, criminal trials, and other tax-related court cases. It is important to remember that virtually all of this litigation is triggered by the initial IRS enforcement contacts, especially examinations. Hence, it represents a further cost stemming from the tax authority's enforcement activities.

Audit Appeals

In about 75 percent of the IRS audits conducted today, the result is a finding of additional tax due. The taxpayer can pay this amount and be free and clear of his obligations. Instead of paying the additional tax, however, the taxpayer may choose to contest the finding of the auditor. The usual first step of appeal is the formal examination appeal provided for in the IRS regulations. In 1985, there were 91,134 of these appeals, a figure that is typical for the 1980s.[1]

About 7 percent of all audits are appealed.[2] The cases being appealed, incidentally, are the ones involving higher amounts of tax. For example, in 1980, the average deficiency for all audits (individuals and corporations) was $5,600; however, the average deficiency for audits that were appealed was $45,000.[3] The appeals process, and tax litigation generally, is largely the domain of wealthy taxpayers who have large amounts at stake and who are therefore willing to invest large amounts in litigation to defend their position.

The audit appeal system, begun in 1927 and organized in its current form in 1978, is a proceeding in which the taxpayer or his representative disputes one or more findings of the IRS audit before an appeals officer who is an IRS official. About 80 percent of these appeals cases are settled by agreement between the taxpayer and the IRS, usually in a compromise. In the cases that remain in disagreement, the taxpayer typically pursues his position by filing in Tax Court. Although the audit appeal is an informal hearing, the preparation and argumentation are legal in character. The appeal cannot be based, as the IRS instructions point out, on "moral, religious, political, constitutional, conscientious, or similar grounds." Instead, the taxpayer is required to submit "A statement stating the law or other authority on which you rely."[4]

Since the taxpayer must make a legal case based on the revenue code or court decisions, he is likely to require expert representation in the audit appeal situation. The representative would generally be either a lawyer or a certified public accountant. Given the legal character of the appeals system, even some CPAs feel themselves out of their element. One CPA specializing in work for small corporations reported that he always turns audit appeals over to a tax lawyer: "You'd be a fool not to involve an attorney," he declared.

This attitude makes sense, since appeals are decided on the "hazards of litigation." Every audit appeal is potentially a Tax Court case, and the appeal officer is hearing the appeal with this in mind. Hence, to win an appeal, or to obtain a favorable compromise decision, one needs a representative who can mount persuasive legal arguments. In preparation, many audit appeals amount to Tax Court cases: the attorney puts together the documentation, research, and argumentation that he will take to the Tax Court if a favorable decision is not obtained in the audit appeal.

How much does this representation cost? In an effort to arrive at a figure, I interviewed a number of tax lawyers and CPAs. On the basis of their reports, I estimate the average cost for representation in an audit appeal at $7,000.[5]

In addition to the representation cost, the taxpayer also must devote some of his own time to the process. His activities include weighing the pros and cons of pursuing an appeal, finding the representative, meeting with him before and after the appeal conference, and supplying data and documents. In addition, some taxpayers also attend the hearings—although this appears to happen in a minority of cases. Most representatives urge their clients not to attend the conference, on the grounds that the client might say something unhelpful to his cause or become combative and prejudice his case.

How much taxpayer time is involved in the average appeal? In the absence of specific surveys, we must make an educated guess. The minimum time would seem to be around eight to ten hours (just one meeting with a representative, including travel time, could easily consume a working day). The maximum time, especially if the taxpayer contacted several possible representatives or became deeply involved in researching the rights and wrongs of his own case, could be several hundred hours. For our purposes here, I will employ the estimate of twenty-five hours of taxpayer involvement. This seems a conservative figure to use to cover all taxpayer activities associated with an audit appeal. These twenty-five hours can be valued at the rate developed in Chapter 2 for taxpayer compliance time including overhead costs, $28.31 per hour for 1985. This figure could be well below the market value of the time of many of the wealthy individuals involved in the audit appeal situation. However, to maintain consistency, I will continue to use this figure to reflect the value of taxpayer time. This figure, it should be remembered, also includes taxpayer overhead costs: telephone, travel, meals away from home, and so on.

Some fraction of taxpayers represent themselves in IRS audit appeals (the IRS officials I interviewed were reluctant to estimate this proportion).[6] In these cases, the representation costs would be absent, while the taxpayer involvement time would be greater. Since special treatment of these "self-represented" cases would not significantly alter our overall result, I have not made allowance for them. In this estimate, all audit appeals are assumed to involve a representative.

Table 9 shows the result of the estimates concerning the private sector cost of audit appeals. In 1985, the average cost of an audit appeal was $7,708—$7,000 for the representation and $708 for the taxpayer's own time and related costs. Therefore, the total private sector cost for all 91,134 audit appeals was $702 million.

TABLE 9   Summary of Tax Litigation Costs, 1985

Activity	Average representation cost (dollars)	Average taxpayer time and overhead (dollars)	Average cost per case (dollars)	Number of cases	Total cost (dollars)
Audit appeals	7,000	708	7,708	91,134	702,000,000
Tax Court, regular cases	35,000	2,265	37,265	34,258	1,277,000,000
Tax Court, small cases	0	3,397	3,397	14,884	51,000,000
Refund litigation	35,000	2,265	37,265	1,023	38,000,000
Criminal prosecutions	70,000	4,530	74,530	2,334	174,000,000
Appeals court cases	70,000	4,530	74,530	411	31,000,000
General litigation	35,000	2,265	37,265	25,628	955,000,000
Private letter rulings	2,000	0	2,000	26,049	52,000,000
Exempt organization determinations	2,000	0	2,000	59,497	119,000,000
Total				255,218	3,399,000,000

SOURCE: Internal Revenue Service, *1985 Annual Report*, for the number of cases in each category, as follows: audit appeals, p. 66; Tax Court, p. 39; refund litigation, p. 39; criminal prosecutions, p. 42; appeals court cases, p. 40; general litigation (court), p. 41; private letter rulings, p. 37; exempt organization determinations, p. 70.

Tax Court Cases

Originally established as the Board of Tax Appeals in 1924, the U.S. Tax Court is the principal legal arena for federal tax cases, receiving about 40,000 new cases each year.[7] These cases are initiated by taxpayers who have failed to obtain a satisfactory decision from the audit appeals process and by taxpayers who bypass the audit appeals process and petition the Tax Court directly. The Tax Court is advantageous, from the taxpayer's point of view, because the tax in dispute need not be paid until after the Tax Court decision. A further advantage is its overloaded condition. The forty-odd judges in this system (who travel to some seventy-five cities to hear cases) actually try only about 900 cases (not counting small tax cases). The overwhelming majority of cases have to be settled by the IRS informally through negotiations. The result of this pressure to settle means that the IRS may yield to the taxpayer as part of the effort to clear away the backlog. This is not to say that the Tax Court itself has any bias toward taxpayers. The judges are former government officials, and a majority are former IRS employees.[8]

Although few Tax Court cases go to trial, cases must be prepared as if they would, because they are negotiated on the strength of facts and arguments developed on behalf of the taxpayer. Tax lawyers point out that it is the preparation of the case—developing the legal background, taking depositions from witnesses, and so on—that represents the major work, not the court appearance itself. In practice, this means the taxpayer will retain a tax attorney to handle his case (except in the small tax cases, which, as we note below, will be assumed to be unrepresented). To estimate the legal costs for the average Tax Court case, I interviewed a number of tax attorneys from around the country.[9] I obtained a wide range of estimates, going from $2,000 when a mere filing was performed to $300,000 for major cases. In some cases, the fees are much higher. One knowledgeable tax attorney estimated that every year there are "dozens" of Tax Court cases in which the legal fees exceed one million dollars.

After weighing the different estimates, I have decided to use the figure of $35,000 as the average figure across all cases.[10] This figure is in the range frequently mentioned by respondents as the typical cost.

In addition to the legal costs, pursuing a Tax Court case requires taxpayer time—time spent on finding legal assistance, on collecting data and documents, on conferences with the attorney, and on discussions with friends and associates. Since these cases go on for many months, even years, it is likely that the taxpayer often spends considerable time and effort reviewing his case and going over it with others. One attorney reported that in a typical major case, the client would spend six days in conferences with him and another two days to prepare testimony if the case were actually going to trial. Another attorney noted that a client might spend fifteen working days preparing records and documents needed for the case. In major cases, the documentation burden can become staggering. An attorney who observed the Tax Court proceedings involving the Hunt brothers (of Texas silver investment fame) reported that entire van-loads of documents were delivered to the court.

In the absence of surveys of taxpayers in the Tax Court situation, taxpayer involvement has to be estimated. Following our practice of leaning toward conservative estimates, I put this figure at eighty hours, to be valued at the $28.31 per hour we are using throughout this study for 1985 taxpayer time (including overhead). This gives us a figure of $2,265, which includes not only taxpayer time but the cost of all work done for the taxpayer (by bookkeepers, secretaries) and all overhead costs, such as those for any equipment usage, travel, or lodging.

Combining the representation cost and taxpayer involvement cost gives $37,265 as the average cost for a Tax Court case. Multiplying this figure by 34,258, the number of regular Tax Court cases received in 1985, yields $1.28 billion as the private sector burden of these cases.[11]

Small Tax Court Cases

Within the Tax Court system, there is a provision for dealing with small cases, involving less than $10,000, in a less formal manner. In these cases, which cannot be appealed, the taxpayer may represent himself, and it appears that this occurs in about half of these cases.[12] To estimate the burden of these cases, we shall assume that they are all unrepresented and that the taxpayer expends

120 hours preparing for them and participating in the process. This would include time spent in deciding whether to pursue the case, time spent gathering records and data, time spent consulting with friends, business associates, and professionals to plan and review his approach, and time spent traveling to and participating in Tax Court or IRS appeals conference proceedings. Using the $28.31 per hour figure to value these 120 hours makes the taxpayer burden for these types of cases $3,397. Hence, the total burden for the 14,884 such cases in 1985 is $51 million.

Refund Litigation

Another way the taxpayer can appeal an IRS assessment is to pay the tax and then sue for a refund in federal district or claims courts. The importance of this route has declined over time, partly because it is disadvantageous to pay the tax first. Another disadvantage of the regular federal courts is that cases are defended by Justice Department attorneys, not IRS attorneys, as in proceedings of the Tax Court. As one tax lawyer explained, "[the Department of] Justice has a bad reputation of attempting to litigate. They have a lot of young lawyers on unlimited expense accounts who string things out." Although this tends to make refund litigation more expensive than a case in the Tax Court, we will simply use the same figures developed for the Tax Court to apply to these cases. Hence, the 1,023 refund litigation suits received in 1985 represent a private sector burden of $38 million.

Criminal Tax Litigation

Each year, Department of Justice attorneys conduct about 2,500 criminal prosecutions of taxpayers in federal court, of whom about 2,000 are convicted and 1,200 receive prison sentences. The cost of defending against these actions apparently runs much higher than the cost of the typical Tax Court case. One lawyer put the cost at $75,000 to $100,000. In one instance, a taxpayer who was the object of a criminal prosecution told a congressional committee that his cost to defend against the federal action was $6 million.[13] For our purposes here, we shall put the representation cost and client time for a criminal tax court case at twice that of the average

Tax Court case. Hence, the 1985 burden of criminal cases is $74,530 per case, or $174 million for the prosecutions completed in 1985.

In many ways, this figure understates the real burden of criminal tax prosecutions. The taxpayers who have been through this process—which usually goes on for years—find it a harrowing, even catastrophic experience that causes many kinds of secondary costs, including unemployment and unemployability, medical problems, and family breakup. Probably no satisfactory monetary accounting can be made of these burdens.

The same is true for the cost of a prison sentence. If sentenced, the taxpayer has been deprived of some years of his working life, and this deprivation must be laid at the doorstep of the tax system. If that system did not exist, the "crime" he committed would not exist. Although a calculation could be made for the forgone earnings represented by a prison sentence, it seems that this economic aspect is trivial compared with the moral and psychological burdens.

The Arbitrary World of Criminal Tax Prosecution

Another nonmonetary cost of criminal tax prosecutions is their inherent injustice. The basic problem is that huge numbers of Americans are "guilty" of criminal tax evasion; that is, they willfully misstate what they know to be the facts in order to lower their taxes. Public opinion polls find that at least one-fifth of respondents will admit to cheating.[14] The actual number of tax cheaters is, of course, larger than this figure, since most people have the good sense not to give strangers evidence that might be used against them in a criminal tax prosecution.

The tax law itself is so complex and ambiguous that the "crime" of tax evasion is often a matter of interpretation (see box). Given the complexity of the law and the large number of violators, criminal tax prosecution becomes an arbitrary, subjective realm where guilt exists largely in the eyes of the government officials who choose to target one taxpayer and not another. One New York tax attorney, who previously worked for the Justice Department as an assistant U.S. attorney prosecuting tax cases, recalls that this point was made quite frankly in his first days at work. Pointing out the

---

The IRS's top legal authority on international tax havens explains why tax evasion is an ambiguous crime:

At times, the transactions are so complicated and the information gathering problems so difficult that it may not be possible to distinguish between the various categories [of tax evasion or tax avoidance]. The lines become murky because the law is murky and the information is incomplete. . . .

In truth, often the question of whether a tax haven transaction is legitimate or illegitimate, whether it is tax avoidance or tax evasion, is in the eyes of the beholder.

SOURCE: Internal Revenue Service, *Tax Havens and Their Use by United States Taxpayers: An Overview.* Report to the commissioner of internal revenue submitted by Richard A. Gordon, special counsel for international taxation (Washington, D.C., January 12, 1981), pp. 59, 61.

---

window at the people walking along on the street, his supervisor said, "See all those people? Each one is guilty of something. Your job is to find out what, and to prove it."

This subjectiveness undermines the principle of the rule of law. Individuals are prosecuted for criminal tax evasion, not because they have done anything that millions of others have not done, but because a government official chose to single them out. One way to provoke the attention of criminal tax investigators is to criticize taxation or the tax system. Each year the IRS targets for criminal prosecution some 200 "illegal tax protesters," individuals who have engaged in civil disobedience of the tax laws on some grounds of principle. These include protesters from the right who contest the constitutionality of the income tax and those from the left who object to defense spending. These individuals have only done what hundreds of thousands of other Americans have done— for example, failing to file a tax return. Yet the hundreds of thousands are let off with fines, while the "tax protesters" are prosecuted for criminal tax evasion.

Another way to get caught up in the criminal tax process is to be informed upon by a "friend," or family member. The IRS has a program of advertising for and paying rewards to those who turn in tax evaders. It appears that, to a large extent, these informants' reports drive the criminal tax process.[15]

Another basis for the selection of cases for tax prosecution is social prominence. A General Accounting Office report on how criminal tax cases are pursued explicitly reports this criterion: "CID [IRS Criminal Investigation Division] management also emphasizes the importance of investigating taxpayers who are highly visible in the community and who allegedly violated tax laws."[16]

In other words, if A and B do exactly the same thing wrong, A, who is prominent, will be prosecuted, while B, who is obscure, will not. To some extent, this policy helps the IRS gain political support: it plays the role of demagogue, bringing down the "high and mighty" that many people envy. But this practice of targeting prominent citizens for "tax crimes" contradicts the ideal of justice, which is to treat all citizens equally.

The arbitrariness in the prosecution of criminal tax cases is a strong argument for abolishing all criminal penalties in the tax realm, and relying solely on civil penalties.

Judicial Appeals

Decisions of the Tax Court and other federal courts are appealed, to both federal appeals courts and, in a handful of cases, the Supreme Court. To estimate the cost of these actions, we will use the same $74,530 figure we applied to criminal trials. Hence, the 411 appeals cases in 1985 cost $31 million.

General Litigation

In addition to the cases already discussed, the tax system generates a large number of other cases which the IRS chief counsel classifies under the heading of "general litigation." One large group of cases in this category involves bankruptcies, where the government litigates to extract tax monies and is countered by other creditors. Another large group of cases involves the enforcement of summons: the IRS attempts to force someone—say a bookkeeper—to testify against a taxpayer, and the taxpayer challenges the summons in a legal action. Other cases include suits against the government for negligence in tax collection. For example, the IRS may place a lien in error, freezing a blameless taxpayer's bank accounts so that he cannot pay his bills. This might cause a business failure, and the taxpayer might sue the government for negligence. Another type of suit involves privacy and freedom of information issues: taxpayers use the courts to force the IRS to disclose information relevant to their tax circumstances.

Rather than attempting to estimate the costs of each of these types of cases, it is simpler to use the estimate already developed for Tax Court cases and assume that these general litigation cases approximate, on average, the same degree of legal work and taxpayer involvement. If this $37,265 per case figure is used, the total private sector burden of the 25,628 general litigation court cases received in 1985 was $955 million.

Noncourt Rulings, Opinions, and Determinations

In addition to the court cases, the operation of the federal tax system involves a large number of rulings and determinations. Most of this activity falls in the following three categories.

1. Private Letter Rulings

Taxpayers can write the IRS to ask about the propriety of a particular action that they would like to take. The most common of these actions is a change of accounting method. These requests go to the IRS Chief Counsel unit, which, after reviewing the relevant legal points, issues a ruling for that taxpayer alone. Currently, the number of these requests is running at about 25,000 per year. Preparing these requests for private letter rulings—developing the necessary data and argumentation and putting them in the correct form—is nearly always a job for a tax professional. One source reports that the legal fees for private letter rulings are often in the neighborhood of $10,000.[17] I will employ the more conservative estimate of $2,000 as the average cost of preparing these requests.

2. Requests for Tax-exempt Status

Many fraternal, educational, and charitable organizations apply for and obtain official tax-exempt status. These requests are running at the rate of about 60,000 per year, and the total number of exempt organizations on file with the IRS is now over one million.[18]

Obtaining a tax-exempt ruling involves a rather complicated set of instructions and procedures. If handled by an attorney, it appears the cost would be in the order of several thousand dollars. Organization leaders may avoid this cost, but only by substituting their own time. It should be noted that the application for exempt status requires a number of documents that a nonprofit group may not have and that it might have to expend considerable time assembling. These include a formal statement of purposes, a budget, and bylaws. It seems reasonable, therefore, to estimate the average burden of an organization's application for exempt status at $2,000, whether or not professional assistance is involved.

In recent years, the IRS has been charging a "user fee" for exempt-organization determinations, a fee that is about $300 for a small local organization. Although it is a burden on the voluntary organizations involved, a user fee of this kind does not figure in our analysis of social cost, since the money is simply transferred from one hand to another. (The imposition of the user fee has added slightly to the paperwork burden, however. An additional step, mailing back the fee, has been added to the process.)

3. Determinations on Employee Plans

To preserve the tax-exempt status of their employee benefits, the plans under which these are conferred must meet legal requirements. To protect themselves, employers may file with the IRS for "advance determination letters" on the acceptability of their plans. The IRS receives some 150,000 of these requests each year.

The cost of preparing these requests is a part of the process of setting up tax-exempt benefit arrangements for employees. For this reason, the cost is included in the estimates of the administrative overhead costs of retirement tax shelters, discussed in Chapter 7.

The Growing Burden of Litigation

The total private sector cost of tax litigation comes to $3.4 billion, as shown in Table 9. Although this is only 0.52 percent of tax revenues collected, it is a substantial sum for what should be a minor, incidental aspect of a tax system.

Indications are that this burden is increasing rapidly. The growth in the number of Tax Court cases illustrates the pattern. In the period 1940–1949, the average annual number of cases received was 3,797.[19] This figure increased to around 30,000 cases per year in the 1980s. The trend in other categories of litigation is similar. For example, in 1971, the IRS chief counsel reported 12,600 general litigation cases; in 1990 the figure was 41,166.[20]

One source of this growing litigation is the growing complexity of the tax code. Congressmen and regulation writers have created an ever-growing forest of rules and regulations within which the taxpayers and tax authorities can play an ever-expanding game of hide-and-seek. The tax code today now contains some 7,600 pages of regulations and continues to expand every year.

Restraining the prolific tax code writers—even if it could be accomplished—would not put an end to the growth of tax litigation. There is another, almost cosmic, process at work: the desire to humanize and restrain the exercise of force by state officials. Our culture is hostile to political arrangements that give government officials unlimited power over citizens. A tax system, by its very nature, involves many such arrangements. As time goes by, citizens and politicians take conscious notice of one or another of these areas of abuse. Little by little, legislators, administrators, and courts introduce modifications that give citizens the power to restrain the actions of tax officials.

However much we might applaud this evolution toward more humane patterns of administration, we have to note that it involves a growing cost: more rules and regulations have to be written that define and restrain the actions of officials, and that means more disputes and more tax litigation.

To illustrate this process, consider the evolution of summons enforcement disputes. The IRS often wants to force third parties, such as accountants or bookkeepers, to testify against taxpayers by summoning them to give evidence or produce records. In earlier times, the IRS would have this summons issued without notifying the taxpayer involved. Thus the taxpayer would often be unable to make any move to stay an unjustified gathering of evidence against him. This inequitable procedure was changed in the Tax Reform Act of 1976, which required the IRS to give the taxpayer notice of a summons against a third party.

While this change limited IRS abuses, it also had an impact on litigation. In its 1977 annual report, the IRS Chief Counsel unit correctly predicted what would happen: "It is anticipated that this new statutory right will increase summons proceedings."[21] The number of summons enforcement cases went from 1,877 in 1975 to 3,698 in 1977—and on to 8,254 in 1990.[22]

A large and growing burden of litigation may well be an inescapable feature of a modern tax system. The public is becoming increasingly uneasy about arbitrary administrative actions. Hence, regulations and procedures are developed to restrain these abuses. But these same regulations and procedures open the door to more disputes and a growing burden of litigation.

✦ 5 ✦

Enforcement Costs:
Forced Collections

THE FORCED COLLECTION PROCESS represents the foundation of the tax system. The fact that the tax authority will physically seize money and property from taxpayers gives meaning to all the other enforcement activities.

Every year over a million taxpayers are involved in forced collections. Yet in spite of its great importance, the forced collection process has gone unstudied and even unremarked. The seizing of taxpayer assets is one of those ugly social processes that we would rather not think about. But if we seek an informed understanding of the burden of taxation, we do have to think about it. Forced collections are one of the big negatives of a tax system. Citizens are subjected to a disagreeable experience, their assets wrested from them in a most frustrating way. Bank accounts are taken; paychecks attached; and cars, homes, and businesses seized. Sometimes taxpayers try to protect their property using force of their own, and violence results. To say that the state is entitled to pursue this collection activity does not lessen the pain to the individuals involved. Furthermore, in many cases, the state is acting against its own rules, undertaking a forced collection action against a citizen in error. It should also be noted that the personnel the government hires to undertake this work are not always the most considerate (see box).

Reckless drivers are sometimes sentenced to work in hospital emergency wards, so that they may witness the distressing consequences of the behavior they have engaged in. Something of the same philosophy ought to be applied to big-spending policy makers. They need to take a close look at the forced collection process to see the pain and suffering taxpayers go through in order to raise the money they are spending.

Burdens in the Collection Process

A social cost analysis of forced collections is rather complex, because it involves a number of different burdens. To begin with, the cost that seems most obvious, the asset seized, is not a social cost at all. If the IRS levies $1,000 from a bank account, or seizes a $1,000 car, there is no net social cost. The taxpayer's loss is counterbalanced by the government's gain.

The social costs of collections stem from the consequences and implications of the seizure. To illustrate, let us consider a simple case where the IRS has impounded a $1,000 automobile. In such a case the taxpayer would make some effort to find out what happened and to get his car back. All such efforts are *resistance costs.*

A former IRS collection agent describes the mentality of fellow collection agents in what he calls the ''American Gestapo'':

Some [agents] were vicious—they'd brag back at the office, ''Boy, did I make that guy jump,'' or ''I had that woman crying when I told her I'd put her on the street with her kids.'' One agent who bragged about padlocking some guy's business said the man was so upset he asked, ''How do you expect me to pay now?'' The agent said, ''I told him, Go get your wife to peddle [herself].''

SOURCE: Statement of former IRS collection agent Mike Klein, quoted in Art Harris, ''The Tax Man and the Big Sting,'' *Washington Post,* April 16, 1989, p. F4.

They include thinking about the problem, discussing it with others, calling IRS officials, making trips to IRS offices, and filling out documents and dispatching them. Resistance costs also include the hiring of accountants, lawyers or other representatives to pursue the taxpayer's case.

A second burden is the *asset deprivation cost*, the waste caused by being denied the use of the asset in question. In the case of a seized car, the taxpayer cannot drive to work, and thus his productive labor is lost. In the case of a padlocked business, the asset deprivation cost would be the earnings that the business would have made if allowed to operate.

The asset deprivation cost is most severe when a physical asset is seized, but it can also be present when a bank account is frozen or levied. This action destroys the taxpayer's ability to fulfill contractual obligations: his checks bounce, and creditors may take action, including lawsuits, to recover funds that the taxpayer had intended to pay them.

A collection case that involved a dramatic asset deprivation cost occurred at a nursing home in Toledo, Ohio, in February 1989. To collect back taxes, the IRS levied the nursing home's funds, forcing it to close immediately, during a winter cold snap. In the hasty relocation of the 199 residents, 18 died. Senator Howard Metzenbaum (D–Ohio) demanded an explanation and was told by the IRS that the seizure was "extremely routine."[1]

In order to lessen the asset deprivation cost, the taxpayer will usually attempt to replace the seized asset. In the case of the seized car, the taxpayer may buy another car. The simple market value of this substitute car will not figure as a social cost, but the expense of acquiring it in the circumstances is the *asset replacement cost*. This would include the time and expense of shopping for another car, and the time and effort of the car salesman.

Another burden in many collection actions is a *credit impairment cost*. A collection action can indicate impending insolvency; whether it does or not, most creditors, and credit-rating services, treat it as a black mark.

Probably the greatest cost of a collection action is the emotional burden. The taxpayer may experience frustration, anxiety, humiliation, or rage. His life may be thoroughly disrupted. He may lose his job, or his family. He may develop mental or physical illnesses as a result of the stress of the collection process.

"The Bloody Body Going down the Street"

To a considerable extent, the burdens of the forced collection process depend on the orientation of officials. They can follow a policy of minimizing their impact, by stressing sensitivity, courtesy, and carefulness in their dealings with taxpayers. Partly by accident and partly by design, the U.S. system does not have this orientation. Instead, officials act in ways that send costs higher than they need to be.

At the bottom of this problem is the "deterrence" philosophy of IRS officials. Although for public consumption IRS officials keep saying that compliance with the tax system is voluntary, it is clear that they believe no such thing. In their view, it is the threat of punishment that makes the tax system work (see box).

Deterrence means instilling fear, causing the taxpayer to be afraid of the consequences of running afoul of the tax authority. It therefore follows that the more burdensome the taxpayer's experience with the tax enforcement system, the better the deterrence. This orientation is most pronounced in the collections division because of the greater presumption of guilt. In the initial contact phases of enforcement, such as audits, IRS workers know that large numbers of innocent taxpayers are involved. In collections, it is

---

At a conference of tax system insiders, one IRS official put the organization's position on voluntary compliance bluntly:

Those of you who believe that most of the voluntary compliance that we have, to whatever degree we do have it, results from patriotism or true voluntarism probably also believe in the tooth fairy. (Laughter.)

Most of us that are in the business believe that what degree of voluntary compliance we have . . . results in a large part because people recognize that there is a risk if they don't comply. . . .

Our objective ultimately is deterrence.

SOURCE: Statement of Charles Gibb, director, Office of Planning and Development, criminal investigation division, Internal Revenue Service, in Internal Revenue Service, *Conference on Tax Administration Research January 1985* (Washington, D.C., 1985), vol. 2, p. 84.

much easier for officials to believe they are dealing with the enemy, willful tax evaders who threaten the foundations of the tax system. Thus, an ingredient of personal hostility is added to the idea that hurting taxpayers strengthens the system (see box on page 72).

The deterrence approach has led to—or permitted the continuation of—a number of highly destructive practices. For example, collection employees are often evaluated on the basis of the number of seizures and other "energetic" collection actions they make. Since 1973, this practice was supposed to have been banned by the IRS's own regulations, but it has persisted nevertheless.[2] Collections managers want taxpayers punished, and they instruct officers to behave accordingly. In 1980 over eighty IRS revenue officers in the collections division of the Detroit district signed their names to public letters protesting the "undue pressure" on revenue officers "to take actions against taxpayers. . . ." For the IRS management, they claimed, "seizure is no longer a means to an end; the seizure statistic is an end in itself."[3] A collections group manager in Virginia "keeps a chart of his Revenue Officers' enforcement statistics by ranking. . . . The Revenue Officers in his group try to serve a lot of levies and make a lot of seizures so they won't be ranked last."[4] In 1987, a Los Angeles revenue officer testified that his group manager prominently displayed outside his office a sign that said, "Seizure fever; catch it."[5]

Other destructive collection practices include the following.

"No equity" seizures.   The IRS may seize a piece of property that the taxpayer does not own but is using, such as a leased delivery truck being used in the taxpayer's business.[6] This will yield no revenue to the government, but it will cause great inconvenience to the taxpayer.

"Sacrifice sale" seizures.   The IRS may seize a taxpayer asset and then sell it for a fraction of its value.[7] The result is that the taxpayer's loss is much greater than the taxes owed and collected. Hence, the taxpayer's anger, and desire to resist, is much greater.

Refusal to accept installment plans.   By demanding all of the tax debt at once, the IRS can destroy a going business and wind up with less money than if it had accepted an installment arrangement.[8] But the taxpayer is made to suffer.

How IRS Collection Officials View Their Work

Statement of a collection officer before a Senate committee in 1980:

To exhibit any sensitivity to and understanding of the taxpayer's current individual circumstances is anathema. . . .

When the question of priorities comes up, [IRS] management replies that: "The maximizing of revenue is not a priority. The priorities are compliance and making an example of delinquent taxpayers through seizure." This statement was actually made by two branch chiefs.

This attitude of punishing citizens permeates the entire management cadre. The manager in Ann Arbor has stated that he does not care if he has to close up half the businesses in Ann Arbor in order to get compliance. . . .

This same manager has also referred to some business taxpayers as "dens of thieves." The management's guiding principle seems to be that if we apply very heavy-handed enforcement, we will dissuade other potential tax delinquents.

Statement of a former IRS collections division manager before a Senate committee in 1987:

You [the collection officer] get caught up emotionally in championing the cause of voluntary [sic!] compliance. In other words, you want to be a tough cop. . . . You want to go out there and demonstrate to the public—and this is important—understand the underlying philosophy—you want to go out and demonstrate to the public that tax protesting movements or not paying their taxes is wrong, that as a part of the American citizenry, as a part of the American Government, you must pay your taxes.

And therefore, they go out and use this enforcement tool to demonstrate to other people who see the bloody body going down the street that this is in effect a deterrent to noncompliance.

SOURCES: Statement of Warren J. Ingersoll, Jr., *IRS Summary Collection Policy Impact on Small Business* (Hearings before the Subcommittee on Oversight of Government Management of the Committee on Governmental Affairs, U.S. Senate, 96th Cong., 2d Sess., July 31, 1980), pp. 33–34. Statement of Joseph B. Smith, Jr., *Taxpayers' Bill of Rights* (Hearings before the Subcommittee on Private Retirement Plans and Oversight of the Internal Revenue Service of the Committee on Finance, U.S. Senate, 100th Cong., 1st Sess., April 10 and 21, 1987), part 1, p. 111.

Failure to notify taxpayers of intended collection actions.   By surprising the taxpayer with a lien or levy, or a seizure of property, collection officers give the taxpayer no time to correct IRS errors or to arrange his affairs to accommodate the IRS demand.[9] The hasty collection action increases taxpayer anger and financial loss.

Efforts to publicize collection actions.   IRS officials may deliberately spread information of the collection action to the general public, by using ostentatious "warning stickers," for example, or by mentioning the action in interviews with the taxpayer's coworkers or neighbors. One Idaho revenue agent was praised in an IRS memo for inducing a Twin Falls newspaper to publicize the names of local taxpayers who had IRS liens filed against them.[10] For taxpayers, publicity about enforcement actions adds to embarrassment and anger and increases credit impairment costs as well as resistance costs.

The Error Machine

As we saw in Chapter 3, IRS systems for gathering data and proceeding against taxpayers are highly flawed. The result is large numbers of incorrect or unjustified actions. In collections, just as in other enforcement realms, these erroneous actions are a major cause of needlessly high burdens. Not surprisingly, mishandled computer systems are a main part of the problem. The IRS employs one of these systems in the collections division, the Automated Collection System. In addition to being error-prone, the ACS seems to be harder to deal with (see box on page 74).

The error rate in IRS collection actions may be nearly as high as the 50-plus percent rate found in the underreporter program. One tax practitioner testifying on the collection process in 1987 said, "Computer-generated notices should not be legal. The computer has gone bad again just within the last month or so, and the last three notices I have received for clients have all been wrong."[11] In the same hearing, Senator Pryor (D-Ark.) observed that the committee had found "hundreds of cases" of erroneously assessed liens and levies.[12] (Even IRS commissioner Larry Gibbs conceded that levies are "occasionally" issued "in error.")[13]

The number of erroneous levies runs at least into many thousands, according to one GAO study. Examining a sample of

An author advising accountants how to handle collection cases explains the difficulty of dealing with the Automated Collection System:

An ACS levy can usually be released only by someone at the ACS center. These are not walk-in facilities, and any release must be worked out over the telephone, which is usually a cumbersome and frustrating experience for both taxpayer and representative. Whenever possible, you should request that the case be moved from ACS status and assigned directly to a Revenue Officer group. . . .

SOURCE: Robert S. Schriebman, "How to Handle IRS Levies: The Basic Rules," *The Practical Accountant*, November 1987, p. 36.

ACS cases in 1986, the GAO projected an error rate of 2.8 percent, or 12,400 taxpayers whose assets were wrongly seized because IRS clerks had applied payments to the wrong period, or to the wrong tax return, or had mistaken one taxpayer for another.[14] As noted in Chapter 3, studies of this kind understate the true error rate because the GAO works within IRS offices and detects only those errors visible from that vantage point.

Case Histories

To give the reader a feel for collection activities and the burdens they involve, it is helpful to review a sample of these cases, as drawn from congressional testimony and other sources.

The Thomas L. Treadway case was featured in the 1987 Senate hearings on the Taxpayers' Bill of Rights. Although an extreme case of taxpayer abuse, it is by no means unique.[15] Treadway was audited in 1981 and assessed an additional $247,000 in taxes, penalties, and interest. The case itself wound its way to the appeals conference where, two years later, it was reversed by the IRS appeals officer. In the meantime, however, the IRS examiner issued a "jeopardy assessment."

Some background is needed to understand this action. The U.S. tax system operates outside a number of basic constitutional principles. One of these is due process. Taxpayer property can be seized without due process of law, that is, without any trial, hearing, or court action. So as not to leave taxpayers entirely at the mercy of tax officials, Congress has established rules and procedures which tax cases are normally to follow. Taxpayers are supposed to get notices of intended IRS actions, are to be given the right to appeal, and are to receive other courtesies and safeguards. However, these rules and procedures may be suspended by IRS officials whenever, in their judgment, the collection of the revenue is jeopardized.

Since there is no standard of proof, and not even a formal process for deciding when the collection of the revenue is jeopardized, tax officials themselves can decide the question on the basis of their personal feelings toward the taxpayer. This is apparently what happened in the Treadway case. The examination officer took a dislike to Treadway and then alleged that the collection of Treadway's tax debt was endangered and made a jeopardy assessment. This meant that the collection officer could seize from *anybody* anything that, in his opinion, related to Treadway's possible debt.

In addition to filing a tax lien against Treadway, the collection officer seized some $22,000 from the bank account of his friend, Shirley Lojeski, on the (unfounded) suspicion that Treadway had passed money to her. To unsnarl the case, Treadway and Lojeski went through several legal actions including the use of the Freedom of Information Act to disclose that neither the examining officer nor the collection officer had any sound basis for his actions. After several years, they finally got all their money back from the IRS, although Treadway reported he still has to contend with "audits, harassment, and surveillance" from IRS officials (see box on page 76). Treadway put the total cost of legal and accounting fees to combat the IRS actions at "over $75,000."

Significantly, the IRS took no action against the agents who were guilty of hasty misjudgments and who also violated IRS regulations (the seizure should have had approval from the IRS legal counsel). One agent was even promoted. This appears to be a consistent practice. Officials who engage in indiscreet, illegal, or erroneous actions in the course of trying to "get" a taxpayer are not seen as bad apples, but as normal employees doing what collection employees are expected to do.[16]

An IRS collection officer, Warren J. Ingersoll, Jr., testified in 1980 about a number of business taxpayers forced into bankruptcy

Thomas L. Treadway summarized for a Senate committe the costs of his five-year experience with forced collection:

The outrageous and arbitrary actions of Agent Boandl and Officer Jessup have ruined our lives. . . .

I am now broke, I have no job, no insurance policies, and no car. At one time I had a very successful business in trash management, but the government has stripped me of everything, and everything they did was based on naive assumptions. . . .

After years into this nightmare we have lost many of our acquaintances, family and friends. Everyone assumes that the IRS *must* have had some basis for what they did.

Treadway's friend, Shirley Lojeski, a "totally innocent bystander," experienced similar problems because the IRS suspected her of holding money for him. Treadway reported that as a consequence of the IRS seizure of her savings,

She lost her health and life insurance policies because she did not have the money to pay the premiums.

She was threatened with foreclosure of her real estate because she couldn't make her mortgage payments.

She couldn't run her horse business because she couldn't afford to buy feed and other items.

She was sued by a supplier because she couldn't pay the bills.

She had to borrow money to buy her groceries and to make her mortgage payments.

She felt humiliated and degraded and became withdrawn.

She wouldn't leave the farm because she was ashamed to meet people, and for fear that Officer Jessup would come back to the farm and seize all her personal property.

SOURCE: Statement of Thomas L. Treadway, *Taxpayers' Bill of Rights* (Hearings before the Subcommittee on Private Retirement Plans and Oversight of the Internal Revenue Service of the Committee on Finance, U.S. Senate, 100th Cong., 1st Sess., April 10 and 21, 1987), part 1, pp. 60–67.

by hasty collections actions. The case of a firm in the health service industry illustrates the pattern. It owed $123,000 in back taxes

but had a cash flow problem because government programs—
Medicare, Medicaid, the Veterans Administration, and the State
of Michigan—had not paid their bills in a timely manner. Since
the business was under foreclosure pressure from one bank
and in the middle of arranging a new loan from a second bank,
the collection agent (Ingersoll) thought it best to refrain from
filing the tax lien and rely on an installment agreement. His IRS
supervisor, however, insisted that he file the lien. Ingersoll summarized the result:

> I filed the notice of tax lien, as ordered, and this act has caused
> the taxpayer nothing but trouble. . . .
>
> If the first bank does foreclose, what are the results? Obviously,
> the owners of the company will lose what they have worked for.
> But, in addition, we will have approximately fifty people out of
> work with a concomitant impact on their families, two hundred
> thousand residents in the county without an essential health ser-
> vice, and the government will get only what is left over from the
> bank and the SBA.[17]

This case illustrates how high the credit impairment cost of a collection action can be. If filing a tax lien prevents a business from
raising needed capital, then the entire business and many millions
of dollars of future earnings are lost.

In the preceding case, filing the lien was destructive, but it was
justified under the tax law. Many times, as we noted earlier, liens
and levies are filed in error (see box on page 78). One practitioner
noted that his charge for handling an erroneous notice case, which
might involve five or six phone calls ("and you don't charge by
high blood pressure rate"), would typically be $400–$500.

In many cases, possibly the majority, the tax debt is actually
owed and IRS officials act with reasonable competence in pursuing it. Nevertheless, the collection process still entails a great burden
to the citizen. Some of the aspects of this burden are noted by an
Idaho resident in her description of the collection process. Her case,
while a fairly typical one from the burden aspect, was unusual in
origin. The taxpayer was a social reformer who was building a concrete free-form house in the mountains, and who was also protesting the Vietnam War. She had written the IRS that although
she was paying the interest on her taxes, she would withhold

Tax Practitioners Describe Erroneous IRS Collection Actions

A former IRS agent in Washington, D.C.:

My latest case involved a person who had been employed for many years and opened up his own courier service; and his return was audited and the assessment was made as far as I can see within 10 days. . . .

He owed about $2,500. He went to the collection officer; no talk at all about an installment plan or anything. Get the money or we are going to take everything you have. He went to a dumb lawyer who put him in bankruptcy; went out of business, lost his business. He went on for a couple of years and finally came to us.

We looked into the thing, and we found that the IRS apparently had lost his Schedule A, his itemized deduction schedule. . . . We worked for about a year with him, got the Schedule A in, and it turns out that he got a $600.00 refund.

A CPA in Cincinnati, Ohio:

The client got a notice, or the bank called him up and said that the IRS from Cleveland had called up and put a lien for $900 on their bank account. This was a corporation that's always paid their bills. They're very profitable. They've paid a lot of taxes and they always try to pay everything on time. I forget how all this came about, but it was something that was the IRS's problem, it wasn't the client's problem. But they wouldn't pay any attention to that. They put a lien on the bank account, and that was not too good a reflection, from the client's standpoint as far as the bank was concerned. I called up Cleveland, I was a little irate. We got it resolved, but they just felt if the computer says this, it's right as far as they're concerned. They don't care what anybody else tells them.

SOURCES: Statement of former IRS officer, *Taxpayer's Bill of Rights* (Hearings before the Subcommittee on Private Retirement Plans and Oversight of the Internal Revenue Service of the Committee on Finance, U.S. Senate, 100th Cong., 1st Sess., April 10 and 21, 1987), part 1, p. 176. Author interview of CPA, 1989.

the balance due until after the war was over. She described the eventual IRS action:

> When I next went to town, I found that the Internal Revenue Service had confiscated all the money from my checking account causing a few checks to bounce. I had never had a check bounce before in my life. In addition they had placed liens against all my property and I found I was on the blacklist which was circulated to all local merchants. It took me several weeks to straighten all this out. . . .
> Dale Lee helped me unsnarl my name from the "poor credit" list and cleared the liens from my property. He paid my taxes for me (using my money of course).[18]

Another Idaho case illustrates how the collection cost burden is sometimes shifted to local government. Don and Helen Crisman were modern pioneers whose religious and philosophical convictions led them to live far away from modern society and to have no dealings with the state. Because they refused to pay federal taxes, the IRS took legal title to their home and land and sold it. The new owner then filed a civil suit seeking eviction of the Crismans from their home. When the court found in favor of the new owner, the county sheriff first sent a reconnaissance team to serve the eviction notice, and then, because of speculation that the Crismans might refuse to leave their home, sent a team of a dozen deputies. Though their resistance was only passive, the Crismans were booked on charges of obstruction and held in jail for two weeks (which costs the county $35 per day per prisoner). After several court hearings, they were finally released, as the sheriff declared, "We're satisfied they're not likely to engage in criminal activity."[19]

In this case, then, county judicial and law enforcement systems were made to bear a burden of many thousands of dollars in order to follow through on a collection action initiated by the IRS. Of course, the Crismans also bore a burden—which included their time and the asset deprivation and replacement costs associated with losing their home.

These monetary burdens pale beside the psychological and moral ones. For the Crismans, these include the emotional stress of being evicted from their home and land and being left destitute.

An incident in which a collection burden was shifted to local law enforcement agencies occurred in Minnesota in 1980:

The bank account of a farmer, Donald McGrath, was levied by the IRS for $39.65. McGrath, believing the levy to be erroneous, and unable to obtain an IRS explanation, instructed his bank not to comply with the levy. The bank ignored his request and sent the $39.65 to the IRS. McGrath sued the bank in district court and meanwhile held up his payments to the bank on a loan on a combine. The bank sent local law enforcement officers to repossess the combine, McGrath made a show of armed resistance, shots were exchanged, and McGrath was killed.

SOURCE: George Hansen, *To Harass Our People: The IRS and Government Abuse of Power* (Washington, D.C.: Positive Publications, 1984), pp. 24–28.

Voters and legislators are left pondering the moral irony of a system that drives some people from their homes in the name of raising funds to help the homeless.

The IRS policy of using the collection process to cause injury is not universally accepted, even within the organization. Some IRS collection officials have protested this approach and have apparently adopted a more "understanding" perspective in their own work.[20] A number of the more destructive collection techniques have been discouraged by law or regulation in recent years. The Taxpayers' Bill of Rights, passed in 1988, attempts to curtail many of these bad practices. My reading of this law indicates that most of its provisions are advisory and that IRS officials can ignore them if they so choose.[21] Nevertheless, this act, and other laws and regulations of recent years, does serve to encourage a more considerate approach on the part of IRS collection officials. Overall, the forced collection process exhibits a mixture of policies: trying to harm taxpayers in order to inspire fear, trying to collect funds without much thought about the social costs, and trying to collect funds in a way that limits the strain on the taxpayer.

Monetary Costs of Forced Collections

With this overview of forced collection activities in mind, we can now turn to the task of estimating the monetary cost. The collections division engages in three main actions: *levies*, *liens*, and *seizures*.[22]

A levy is an IRS demand on a third party, usually a bank or an employer, for funds belonging to a taxpayer. The IRS is able to make this demand without going through any legal process and, as we noted in the Treadway case, without any formal grounds whatsoever. According to current law, the taxpayer is supposed to have twenty-one days to respond to the intended levy; but in practice the actual time may be less.[23] Over the past decade, the number of levies has increased dramatically, going from 465,000 in 1979 to 2,631,000 in 1990.[24]

A lien is an IRS claim to legal ownership of an asset, such as a home, land, or a business, a claim that blocks its sale or disposition by the taxpayer. The lien itself does not transfer ownership, but it compels the taxpayer to take action to regain unhindered ownership of his property. The typical use of the lien appears to be as a device to "get the taxpayer's attention," and compel him to clear his account with the IRS. The use of liens has also been growing dramatically, going from 371,000 in 1979 to 1,114,000 in 1990.[25]

A seizure is the taking of a physical property such as a car, home, cash register, or business. As with levies, IRS officials make seizures on their own authority, without court approval. The number of seizures is about 20,000 per year, and this figure has not been increasing.

In estimating the burden of levies and liens, we will treat only the resistance cost, that is, the burden to the taxpayer of responding to the collection action.

In calculating the burden of levies, we must first arrive at an estimate of the number of taxpayers affected by levy notices, to take into account the facts that some taxpayers receive more than one levy and that some levy notices are spurious and never affect any taxpayer. Making adjustments for these factors gives us 671,000 taxpayers affected by the levy process in 1985.[26]

To estimate the amount of time these taxpayers spent responding to the levy action, we would prefer to have the results of a survey of a sample of these taxpayers. In the absence of such direct information it is necessary to supply an estimate. Obviously, the degree of taxpayer involvement will vary over a wide range. A few taxpayers (guilty or innocent) will allow their accounts to be levied with no response whatsoever, whereas a few will struggle against the collection action for years. The activities involved in reacting to and resisting a levy include reading and digesting notices; examining tax records and tax law; discussing the problem with friends and associates; contacting banks, employers, and IRS officials; finding and meeting with a lawyer, CPA, or other representative; submitting documents to banks and to the IRS, correcting bounced checks; reestablishing credit; and contending with other secondary consequences of the levy, such as bankruptcy proceedings and lawsuits by creditors.

Another cost for many taxpayers involved in levy proceedings is setting up and fulfilling installment payment plans. The IRS reports entering into 710,450 installment plans in 1988.[27] Such plans, as noted earlier, reduce some collection burdens, like the asset deprivation cost, but they do involve effort and attention from the taxpayer. IRS installment plans are especially burdensome because they are unilaterally renegotiable by the IRS: if the revenue officer believes the taxpayer can pay more, he can demand more. This requires the taxpayer to supply ability-to-pay information on a periodic basis. One taxpayer complained that his installment arrangement was so confining that "I have to get permission from the IRS to see my dentist."[28]

Reviewing these different activities, I estimate that the average taxpayer time devoted to responding to levy initiatives is 120 hours. This would amount to three weeks of work if performed on a nine-to-five basis. This figure is probably a small fraction of the total time the taxpayer spends *worrying* about the collection action. But worry is a psychological cost, which we are not including in this tabulation of monetary costs. Valuing these 120 hours at the figure established for 1985 compliance work plus overhead, $28.31 per hour, gives an average cost of $3,397 for resisting levies.

In addition to the taxpayer's own involvement, there will be some cost for representatives acting on the taxpayer's behalf. Again, this burden would span a wide range. Some taxpayers handle their own levy notices without assistance. Others pay only a hundred dollars to an accountant, who clears the problem up with one phone call, while still others pay lawyers tens of thousands of dollars. In the absence of a direct survey on this matter, an estimate is again required. I put this estimate at $500, a figure that is advanced as the average for all affected taxpayers, including those who use no third-party assistance.

When we turn to liens, it seems that the taxpayer burden would be similar to that of dealing with levies, since the steps involved are similar. Therefore, the same cost estimates will be applied. The number of taxpayers affected by liens, after excluding overlap and double counting, is estimated at 352,000 for 1985.[29]

Estimating the other costs—asset deprivation, asset replacement, and credit impairment—would be an extremely difficult task, beset by logical difficulties as well as by a lack of data.[30] It seems, on balance, that these costs are not especially large, and we may therefore omit advancing an estimate for them without greatly affecting our overall results.

Turning to the cost of seizures, we are again faced with the problem of too many unknowns. Although the burden of the average seizure is probably rather high, the relatively small number of seizures means that the total for this category is unlikely to be large in proportion to all the other costs and so, again, it can be ignored without greatly affecting the final tally.

Table 10 summarizes the monetary burdens of forced collections. The costs estimated add up to nearly $4 billion in 1985, or 0.6 percent of available revenue collected.[31]

The Dilemma of Forced Collections

Taxation in the modern era involves a major, and possibly fatal, contradiction. On one hand, the purpose of the state, and the purpose of its spending programs, has become that of trying to make life easier for citizens. We increasingly expect government to be nice to people. This perspective applies across all government activities: we expect the army to treat its soldiers well, we expect prisons to treat prisoners well, and so forth. Naturally, therefore, we expect the tax authority to treat taxpayers well.

This aim embodies a logical contradiction, however. A tax system, by its very nature, must do harm. It is not a voluntary system in which donors give as they please depending on their generosity. As congressmen and IRS officials point out, taxation is based on

TABLE 10   Private Sector Costs of Forced Collections, 1985

	Millions of dollars
Taxpayers affected by levies (671,000)	
Resistance cost	
Taxpayer time	2,280
Representation cost	336
Asset deprivation cost, asset replacement	
cost, credit impairment cost	ne
Taxpayers affected by liens (352,000)	
Resistance cost	
Taxpayer time	1,196
Representation cost	176
Credit impairment cost	ne
Taxpayers affected by seizures (25,000)	
Resistance cost, asset deprivation cost, asset	
replacement cost, credit impairment cost	ne
Total	3,988

NOTES: ne = not estimated.
For source and details of computations see Chapter 5, note 31.

fear, on making the taxpayer afraid that if he fails to comply, disagreeable punishments will follow. To back up this fear, the tax authority must punish citizens, that is, it must injure them.

If the number of citizens resisting the tax system is small, then the punishment aspect may be a minor consideration. But what happens when noncompliance starts to rise? The tax authority's impulse is to apply more punishment in an attempt to increase the fear coefficient of the system. In a despotism, this response would probably work. But in a free, humane society, people start criticizing these punishments because of the harm they do to the very citizens the government is supposed to be preserving from harm.

The IRS forced collection process is caught in this dilemma. A number of circumstances—high tax rates, declining respect for the federal government, growing self-centeredness of the citizenry—have led to growing collection problems. From 1978 to 1988, the total amount of uncollected taxes increased twice as fast as the total taxes collected, from $10 billion in 1978 to $59 billion in 1988.[32] The amount of uncollected taxes written off after the expiration of the six-year statute of limitations period is climbing at the same dramatic rate. In 1975, $176 million was written off; in 1984, the figure was $757 million.[33]

The IRS has responded by developing a vast computer enforcement and surveillance system and by dramatically increasing forced collection actions. But this reaction to noncompliance is compounding the problems. Because the United States is not a despotism, these redoubled enforcement measures are being criticized, with the result that the IRS loses citizen cooperation and political support. Furthermore, these harsh measures contradict the humane thrust of our cultural evolution. The feeling is growing that taxpayers have rights that should be protected, that harming taxpayers in the collection process is wrong. As we noted, some IRS officials agree with this position; and, I expect, more will join their ranks in the future.

An illustration of this dilemma is seen in the growth of installment payments. From a pure deterrence point of view, tax collectors should not allow them. They want taxpayers to fear that everything they value will be abruptly and painfully seized if they fail to obey the tax authority. Allowing installment plans communicates that the tax authority is sensitive to taxpayers' problems, and hence encourages future delinquency. One statistic about installment plans is suggestive in this regard: of the 710,000 taxpayers involved in these plans in 1988, some 123,000 defaulted.[34] It would appear that quite a few taxpayers aren't particularly worried about disappointing the IRS these days.

In the short run, there is much that makers of tax policy can do to lessen enforcement burdens without changing the deterrence climate, especially by reducing errors and improving communication. But they have to realize that, ultimately, compassion and taxation cannot fit in the same box. Sooner or later, the question will have to be faced: Can a society increasingly reluctant to inflict pain on its members sustain a tax system based on fear?

✦ 6 ✦

Disincentive Costs

FROM THE STANDPOINT OF THE TAXPAYER, every tax amounts to a penalty for engaging in the activity being taxed. It raises the effective price of the activity and thus discourages it. With certain consumption taxes like the so-called sin taxes on alcoholic beverages and cigarettes, policy makers recognize this penalizing aspect and make deliberate use of it. Taxes on these harmful products are set high partly to discourage their purchase.

Unfortunately, there is not enough sin in society—or rather, not enough taxable sin—to enable governments to raise the revenues they desire. Hence, governments find themselves taxing legitimate, constructive activities. Down through history, quite a variety of innocent, helpful actions have been taxed: raising crops, importing and exporting goods, traveling from place to place, buying and selling property, even putting windows in houses. The lawmakers' aims have been to raise money, but the fact remains that, at the same time, they discouraged the activities they taxed.

In the U.S. federal system, taxes are levied principally against labor and against the earnings from capital (including profits, interest, dividends, and capital gains). Labor and investment are, of course, the foundation of the prosperity of the nation. Therefore, taxing them—penalizing them—does harm to the country. Economists speak of this harm as a "deadweight loss," or an "excess burden," or a "welfare cost." In this presentation, we will call such effects the "disincentive costs" of a tax system. In this way we focus on the point that taxes are discouraging people from deploying labor and capital as productively as they otherwise would.

The simplest way to visualize this harm is to imagine what would happen under tax rates of 100 percent. Let us take the case of labor first. Suppose the government's income tax were set at 100 percent of earnings. Assuming that this is an effective tax rate and that there is no evasion, what happens to the amount of labor performed in society? Workers go to their factories and offices, toil all day long, and are then paid exactly nothing. Whatever they have earned is entirely taken away in taxes and transferred to the government.

It seems clear that under this arrangement, workers will stop going to factories and offices. This 100 percent tax, in effect, reduces wages to zero. The result would be that zero, or nearly zero, work would be performed. Perhaps a few dedicated, idealistic people would show up to work at zero wages—some nurses in hospitals, for example—but in general, work as we know it would cease. This, in turn, would mean that production in the official money economy would cease.

Workers would stay at home and either waste their time doing nothing constructive at all, or they would try to provide for themselves the goods and services they formerly purchased. Since in trying to do their own farming, carpentering, weaving, and other economic tasks, workers would be highly inefficient, a dramatic drop in production would occur and, hence, a corresponding drop in the standard of living.

What if the income tax rate were 99 percent instead of 100 percent? The effect, obviously, would be nearly the same. A little official labor in the taxed money economy would occur, but most workers would not respond to an effective wage rate that was almost indistinguishable from zero. As the tax rate was lowered, more labor would be put forward, until, at an income tax rate of zero, where workers would be allowed to receive all the fruits of their efforts, the maximum amount of labor in the (more efficient) money economy would occur.

The same point would apply to investment. If 100 percent of the profits from investments were taken away in taxes, then investment would be perfectly discouraged. The result would be no new plants or offices and no repairs of existing capital equipment, at least as far as the taxable money economy was concerned. Anyone with any savings would either consume them or invest them in some aspect of personal home production. Again, the ultimate result would be a drastic decline in production and standard of living.

The disincentive effect of taxation is now widely recognized, not only by economists but also by many policy makers. It is recognized that high taxes stifle economic growth and that one way to "get the economy moving" is to lower tax rates. This point is supported by a considerable body of evidence from many countries around the world.[1] For example, a careful study of the Swedish experience by economist Charles Stuart found that the increasing tax rates on labor in the period 1959–1977 accounted for 75 percent of the decline in the growth rate of Swedish GNP.[2] Sweden's socialist politicians have themselves accepted the logic of the tax disincentive effect, moving in the late 1980s to lower tax rates in an effort to spur economic growth.[3]

Empirical Calculations of Disincentive Costs

Only recently have economists begun to make calculations of the precise size of the disincentive effect, or what they generally call the "marginal excess burden" of the federal tax system. One motive for these studies has been the need for a correct benefit-cost analysis of government programs. The standard practice in this type of analysis has been to assume zero fund-raising costs for government funds. Hence, if one spent $10 million on a government irrigation project that returned $11 million in total calculated benefits, this would be said to have a benefit-cost ratio of 1.1 (11/10) and would be considered a wise use of public funds.

The error in this logic is that it assumes the $10 million would be raised without any cost. The tax system is assumed to be a frictionless machine for collecting money at no harm or inconvenience to anyone. We are beginning to see how unrealistic this assumption is, of course. The first overhead cost that attracted the attention of economists was the disincentive effect. They realized that the tax system would distort incentives and cause some loss of production. The value of this lost production should be included in benefit-cost analyses to make correct decisions about the value of government projects. Hence it became necessary to estimate, in monetary terms, the disincentive cost of taxes.

The calculations made of the disincentive effect are estimates of the marginal cost of the distortion. This is the cost of raising one additional dollar in taxes, at the existing tax level. Table 11 shows the findings of a number of studies of the marginal excess burden of taxation.[4] As the reader might expect, there is a considerable variation in the results obtained. These differences can be traced to a number of factors. First, the studies treat different taxes, which have different disincentive effects. Second, the studies use different models to express the relationships involved. And finally, the calculations incorporate different estimates for real-world variables, such as the elasticity of supply for labor and capital and the specific, relevant tax rates. In earlier days, these "parameter estimates" were quite crude and imprecise; ongoing empirical research is gradually reducing the uncertainty about these values, so that the calculations of the disincentive cost are more dependable.

The early studies of the disincentive cost of taxation tended to yield rather small figures, largely as a result of their restrictive focus and inadequately specified models. One of the first of these was

TABLE 11   Estimates of the Disincentive Costs of Taxation (marginal excess burden)

Study	Taxes covered	Disincentive cost[a] (percentage)
Browning (1987)	Labor	31.8–46.9
Hausman (1981)	Labor	28.7
Stuart (1984)	Labor	24.4
Gordon and Malkiel (1981)	Capital gains	123.0
	Corporation	139.0
Gravelle and Kotlikoff (1989)	Corporation	84.0–151.0
Ballard, Shoven, and Whalley (1985)	Comprehensive	33.2
Jorgenson and Yun (1990)	Comprehensive	46.0

NOTE: For method of calculating disincentive cost and for full facts of publication for the studies cited, see Chapter 6, note 4.

a. The disincentive cost, or marginal excess burden, is expressed as a percentage of the amount of tax collected. For example, the Ballard, Shoven, and Whalley figure of 33.2 percent means that for each additional dollar of tax collected, the additional cost to the economy is 33.2 cents.

advanced by Michael Boskin in 1975, following a model developed by Arnold Harberger, which focused on the cost of discouraging labor in the regular economy. His calculations put the loss at 6 to 13 percent of tax revenues.[5] Another early estimate was that of Edgar Browning, in 1976, which focused on the disincentive effects on labor. He found the loss to be 9 to 16 percent of tax revenues.[6] A decade later, after correcting an error in the original model and adopting what he felt were more realistic parameters, Browning obtained results that tripled his earlier estimates: the disincentive effect was 31.8 to 46.9 percent of tax revenues (as noted in Table 11.)

Another problem in making calculations on the disincentive cost of labor taxes is that the effect can vary considerably from one person to the next, depending on the life circumstances of each. For example, full-time workers who are heads of households are less sensitive to taxation effects. The labor supply behavior of married women, on the other hand, is much more sensitive to tax effects. They are much more likely to stop working when taxes take a larger share of their wages.

The Hausman study, which was based on data from the University of Michigan Panel Survey on Income Dynamics, is especially valuable in documenting these different effects. Hausman found that the disincentive cost for married men aged twenty-five to fifty-five was 21.8 percent of taxes collected for workers earning $6.18 per hour and 54.2 percent for workers earning $10.00 an hour. For married women, the disincentive cost was 58.1 percent of taxes collected for a worker earning $4.00 per hour. Hausman calculated that the overall average disincentive cost for the entire sample was 28.7 percent of taxes collected, as noted in Table 11.

Hausman also found that the main cause of the disincentive effect came from the progressive feature of the income tax, from the fact that the more an individual works and earns, the higher his tax rate becomes. According to his calculations, a flat tax rate of 14.6 percent for all workers (which would raise the same amount of revenue as the current system) would have a disincentive cost of only 7.1 percent of taxes collected, one-quarter the size of the 28.7 percent figure for the existing system, which incorporates progressivity.[7]

The disincentive effect of taxation on various forms of capital income is a complex topic. The consensus appears to be that the taxing of capital generally produces more severe disincentive effects because capital can be more flexibly redeployed than labor. Taxing capital gains, for example, has long been recognized as economically harmful. The disincentive effect of a tax on capital gains is compounded by the fact that the effect of inflation is not adjusted for. This means that holders of assets have to pay a tax even when they have actually lost money relative to inflation. One study of a sample of 30,000 taxpayers in 1973 found that this group of taxpayers paid $439 million in taxes on illusory, inflation-caused, capital gains.[8]

The combined effect of the "inflation tax" along with the capital gains tax discourages individuals from investing in new business opportunities. For example, when higher tax rates for capital gains were adopted in 1976, the flow of capital to new ventures practically stopped. Whereas in 1968 more than 300 new high-technology companies were founded, in 1976 none were formed.[9] One calculation made by Chase Econometrics Associates showed that a capital gains tax rate of 49 percent would cost the economy 440,000 jobs, compared with the number of jobs tht would be created under a capital gains tax rate of 25 percent.[10]

It is not surprising to find, then, that the empirical calculations indicate a high disincentive cost for capital gains taxation. The estimate of Gordon and Malkiel noted in Table 11, 123 percent, indicates that every dollar raised from the tax on capital gains costs the economy $1.23 in lost production. A similar figure was suggested by Michael Boskin in a 1978 study. He estimated the cost of the tax system in discouraging savings at $50–60 billion, or about the same amount that was raised in taxes on savings.[11]

The tax on corporations appears to be the most distortive and inefficiency-causing levy in the federal tax system. Economists point out that it has several destructive effects. Perhaps the most obvious effect is that, like the tax on capital gains, it discourages investment in new plant and equipment.[12] A second inefficiency springs from the fact that while corporations pay taxes on profits, which would be returned to shareholders in the form of dividends, they do not pay taxes on the interest they pay to bondholders. This leads corporations to prefer a financial structure that favors debt over equity. By focusing on the inefficiency cost of this distortion, Gordon and Malkiel obtained a disincentive cost of 139 percent for the corporation tax, as noted in Table 11.

Another effect of the corporation tax is that it penalizes joint economic endeavors, which are more efficient, as compared with less efficient production at the individual level. If a group of people join together in a corporation to make shoes, let us say, this invest-ment is taxed at a higher rate than if each worked alone making shoes. Pursuing this theme, Jane Gravelle and Laurence Kotlikoff estimated the disincentive cost of the corporation tax at between 84 and 151 percent of taxes collected, as noted in Table 11.

Given the disincentives imposed by the taxes on capital income, and the waste caused by taxing different forms of capital income at different rates, some economists question whether capital taxes raise any revenue at all. These taxes can hurt the economy so much that other tax revenues fall by more than the tax on capital collects. This is the conclusion of economists Roger Gordon and Joel Slemrod, who made a quantitative study of this issue. Their calcula-tions for 1983 showed that "abandoning entirely any attempt to tax capital income while leaving the tax law otherwise unchanged would have resulted in a slight rise in government revenue."[13]

Comprehensive Estimates

The figures discussed in the preceding paragraphs are estimates of the burden of particular types of taxes. For this study, we need an estimate of the combined disincentive effect of all federal taxes. Fortunately, two teams of specialists in public economics have worked on developing such a comprehensive estimate. Their two results are shown in Table 11. One team, Charles L. Ballard, John B. Shoven, and John Whalley, obtained the estimate of 33.2 per-cent; the other, Dale W. Jorgenson and Kun-Young Yun, obtained the estimate of 46.0 percent.

In order to decide which of these figures to use, we have to explore what they represent. In studies of marginal excess burden, there are two basic approaches to computing the disincentive cost of a tax.[14] The approach of Ballard, Shoven, and Whalley assumes that the tax dollars being raised are used to finance an additional government spending program like a highway or a battleship. The approach underlying the Jorgenson and Yun study assumes that the tax dollars are directly added to the incomes of consumers in some kind of welfare benefit. In this second approach, the disincen-tive effect is higher, since increasing a person's income will tend to weaken his motivation to work.

If one seeks an estimate for the disincentive effects of the overall tax-and-spend system, then probably an average of these two figures would be appropriate, since some government spending goes to buy goods and services and some goes to cash transfers. This book, however, is about the burden of the tax system alone. We focus only on this cost and leave the specification of the wastes that might occur on the spending side to be estimated elsewhere.

Because of this focus, we seek a figure that reflects the pure disincentive effect of the tax system and leaves out any additional disincentive effect that might come as a result of how the money is spent. This is the Ballard, Shoven, and Whalley figure of 33.2 percent. The meaning of this figure is that if tax rates are raised to produce one additional dollar of revenue, the consequence will be 33.2 cents' worth of lost production.

In evaluating this figure, we should note first that it depends on the parameters used in the general equilibrium model, especially the assumed elasticities for labor supply and savings. The authors experimented with several plausible values for these terms and came up with a range of figures for the marginal excess burden, from a low of 17 percent of taxes collected to a high of 55.9 percent of taxes collected. The 33.2 percent estimate is their calculation using the middle estimates for labor supply and savings elasticity, the ones in which they placed greatest confidence.

A factor that leads us to treat the Ballard, Shoven, and Whalley estimate with some caution is that it includes state and local taxes as well as federal levies. Although these other taxes are smaller than the federal taxes, and generally have similar marginal excess burdens, their inclusion means that we do not have a pure estimate for the federal tax system alone.

Another problem—which affects any econometric estimate of this nature—is that no allowance is made for tax evasion and tax avoidance. The calculations assume that the official tax rates apply to every unit in the economy. In practice, some units face lower tax rates, either because of outright tax evasion or because of a special, legal loophole written into the tax code. Such a loophole lowers the effective rate of taxation for the taxpayers involved. The failure to include tax avoidance means that econometric estimates yield higher burden figures than may actually apply.

Still another problem with trying to arrive at an exact figure for the disincentive effect of the tax system is that the system is always being changed. Each change in a tax rate would produce a change in the size of the disincentive effect. The Ballard, Shoven, and Whalley study was based on the tax code as it existed in 1973, and therefore their calculations may somewhat misstate the disincentive effect in another year, such as 1985, our target year.

Although the 33.2 percent figure may have flaws, its validity as an approximate estimate is still strongly supported by the fact that it falls within the range of estimates that others have made, especially the estimates for the disincentive effect of labor taxes. Since labor taxes are the most important in the federal system, accounting for about three-quarters of federal revenues, the labor effect should be the predominant one.[15]

Although economists have not settled on a precise figure for the marginal excess burden, it is clear that there is an enormous disincentive effect in the raising of federal funds through taxation. In pursuing their calculations, economists have begun to alert government agencies to the fact that the existing benefit-cost analyses of their programs are grossly misleading. It is incorrect to assume that a government dollar costs a dollar. As Ballard, Shoven, and Whalley point out, their findings suggest "that many projects accepted by government agencies in recent years on the basis of cost-benefit [sic] ratios exceeding unity might have been rejected if the additional effects of distortionary taxes had been taken into account.[16]

Disincentive Costs of Tax Law Changes

In the western tradition of theorizing about taxation, the tax-making process is generally assumed to be rational and coherent. Each philosopher, academic, or politician who advocates a new tax, or a tax law change, assumes that the tax authority will be intelligent and farsighted in implementing his suggestion. Indeed, the whole theory of using a tax system to fund needed community services assumes that makers of tax policy are competent and responsible.

This may be an overly optimistic assumption. There is nothing in human nature, or in the logic of collective decision making, that assures that, let us say, the 535 human beings that make up the U.S. Congress will always produce sound decisions. There might be times in the history of a nation when these 535 people happen to be shortsighted or misinformed. Or perhaps the people themselves are adequately thoughtful, but a complex decision-making system produces disorderly, inconsistent results.

Disorderly tax policy has characterized the U.S. federal system for several decades. The clearest indication of this state of affairs is provided by the policy makers themselves, who, as documented in Chapter 11, are not aware of most of what they are approving and sometimes reverse outright what they have enacted a few months earlier.

One aspect of a disorderly tax-making process is the frequent revision of the tax code, as legislators respond to momentary political impulses and lobbying campaigns. In recent years, Congress has plunged into a veritable orgy of rewriting the tax code. In every year there are some changes, and major revisions have occurred about every two years: 1976, 1978, 1981, 1982, 1984, 1986, and 1988. Such changes greatly increase costs of compliance and enforcement, of course. Taxpayers and tax practitioners have to spend time learning about the changes, and new regulations mean confusion and uncertainty about tax requirements. Hence, audits take longer and are more likely to be contested in appeals and Tax Court cases. Those practicing tax-avoiding investment and estate strategies must consult anew with lawyers and alter their holdings to take advantage of the new code.

In most cases, these costs of tax law changes should already have been included in our tabulations of the respective costs, at least in principle. For example, the time taxpayers spend learning about the frequently changing requirements should show up in measures of compliance time, and the extra time tax lawyers must spend to master a changing tax code should show up in their legal fees.

One cost of frequent tax law changes that would not be included in any other category of overhead costs is the effect on economic planning. Tax changes disrupt arrangements people make for the efficient use of labor and capital. As economists Alan Auerbach and James Hines put it, ''In the uncertain business of planning for U.S. corporate investment, one of the few reliable forecasts one can make is that the tax law will change before any new investment outlives its usefulness.''[17]

These frequent changes in the tax law cause waste, as efforts and investments made at one point are undermined by later changes (see box). The depressing effect of uncertain tax policy would probably be greatest on investment decisions that have to be made on assumptions about the tax climate many years, even decades, into the future. To compensate for the uncertainty in tax rates, investors will require a higher margin of expected profit before undertaking long-range projects. In other words, the ultimate effect of tax uncertainty is a disincentive to investment.

A similar disincentive effect applies to labor. Workers have to make decisions about careers, about job and location changes, about marital status and family size, and about the timing of retirement. A decision that is optimal under one set of tax rules and rates becomes suboptimal when tax rates change—but the worker may now be locked in to his choice. Hence, the worker has to take the

---

I asked an accountant who specializes in tax problems of small corporations about the frequent changes in the tax code:

Q: Does it affect planning? For example, when someone makes an investment decision or something?

R: Oh you can't plan. There's no way you can plan. You don't know what the tax law's going to be this year let alone next year. And they make things retroactive. . . .

We've got a client, fellow about sixty years old. He was trying to sell his company to his employees and he came up with an ESOP [employee stock ownership plan]. One of the attractions of an ESOP from a financing standpoint is that the banks get to deduct 50 percent of the interest income, . . . and the bank passes part of that on to the customer in the way of a reduced rate.

They started on this last September, and they were getting fairly close. . . . But then in the middle of June, Rostenkowski [D–Ill., Chairman of the House Ways and Means Committee] entered a bill that would exclude that exemption. . . . So this client of ours, they're caught in the middle of it. There wasn't a whole lot of leeway in the deal to start with, and if they have to pay more interest . . . I'm not sure that he can swing it with that.

SOURCE: October 1989 interview.

possibility of tax law changes into account, and this discourages him from making the most efficient economic choices.

An effort to estimate the cost of uncertain tax policy has been undertaken by Jonathan Skinner. Using a general equilibrium model of economic activity, he calculated the work and savings decisions that would be made under conditions of tax certainty and then compared them with the decisions that would be made taking into account the actual variability in tax rates over the period 1929–1975. His overall finding was that "the annual loss of uncertain taxation, expressed as a proportion of 1985 U.S. national income, is $12 billion."[18] This figure amounts to 1.84 percent of available tax revenues collected.

There are several reasons to believe that Skinner's estimate is an understatement of the full disincentive cost of tax uncertainty. For one thing, the period used to measure that uncertainty, 1929–1975, had fewer changes in the tax code than has been the current pattern. Second, Skinner's computations focused only upon the uncertainty in general tax rates for wages and interest. It did not, and could not, take into account the ever-changing array of specific loopholes, regulations, depreciation rules, and other provisions that bear on investment decisions.

Despite these reservations, it is probably best to use this low figure as our estimate in view of the novelty of Skinner's work. His model and its application may undergo reinterpretation and refinement in the future, so it is preferable to stay on the conservative side with a smaller estimate. As it is, the figure more than justifies Skinner's conclusion that "the cost of extensive tinkering with the tax code should be recognized."[19]

Disincentive Costs of Compliance

In Chapter 2 we examined the compliance costs of the federal tax system, that is, the value of the resources expended in learning about the tax code, keeping records, submitting documents, and so on. This proved to be a very substantial cost, amounting to 24.43 percent of tax revenue raised. As we noted, this burden amounts to a further tax on the businesses and individuals concerned.

As a further tax, this burden has a disincentive effect on economic activity. That is, the threat of having to bear tax compliance costs discourages workers and investors from being as productive as they otherwise would be. Probably the greatest burden on Mom-and-Pop businesses like motels, groceries, and farms is not taxes but tax compliance burdens. To avoid these burdens, many owners—unwilling to put in the time, attention, and nervous energy that grappling with the tax system requires—simply close their businesses. I noted one such case when my computer repairman, the only provider of this service in town, closed his business. The owner was an older man on a retirement income who did computer work part time. His sole reason for shutting down the repair service, he explained, was the burden of tax compliance. An extremely honest person, he felt morally bound to follow all tax requirements and keep the exact, careful records needed to fill out his tax forms, and to make all the tax deposits. As he put it, "It got beyond me. I was spending all of my time with the taxes, and it just wasn't worth it." Now the town is without his services, so that in the event of breakdowns, computer users suffer more waste and lost production.

Another compliance disincentive effect occurs when successful self-employed individuals contemplate expanding their business to include employees. The tax red tape these changes involve would often deter this evolution. As a result, society loses the higher productivity that these business expansions would bring.

Economists have not yet attempted calculations of what they would call the marginal excess burden of tax compliance costs—a not surprising state of affairs, since tax compliance costs themselves have gone unrecognized until very recently. The point has been discussed by British economist David Collard, who points out that this cost is probably higher than one would at first suppose. Since the compliance cost affects the taxpayer as a further tax, it in effect raises his tax rate, and this will have an exponential effect on the marginal excess burden. For this reason, Collard argues, the disincentive effect of compliance costs is likely to be "non-trivial."[20]

In the absence of calculations of this cost, we will have to leave it as one of our unestimated burdens. We should keep in mind that this figure is a significant cost, perhaps on the order of 10 percent of the value of tax revenues collected.

Are Tax Systems Rational?

For the disincentive effects that have been estimated, the total comes to 35.0 percent of tax revenues—33.2 percent for comprehensive economic effects and 1.8 percent for the effect of tax code uncertainty.

This finding prompts the natural question: Can this burden be lessened by rewriting the tax code? The experienced observer cannot answer this question with an enthusiastic affirmative. To some degree policy makers and their economic advisors can make progress in reducing the more extreme disincentive effects in the tax code. It is certainly worth making efforts in this direction. But as a practical matter, a fully rational tax system may be out of reach. In a democratic country, at least, too many popular misconceptions get in the way.

Consider, for example, the tax on corporations, a tax with an extremely high disincentive effect. The attempt to tax this impersonal economic entity has given rise to a host of distortions and inefficiencies. In addition to the effects mentioned in this chapter, the corporation tax leads to significant tax avoidance costs, as corporations undertake complex and wasteful financial maneuverings designed to lower their effective tax rate.

To abandon the corporation tax, however, politicians and the public would have to get over their tendency to anthropomorphize corporations. As long as corporations are seen as persons, there will be political pressure to make them pay "their fair share" and, reflecting the envy that plays so important a part in the tax code, to punish them for being so large and wealthy.

Corporation taxes are among the most destructive yet are politically fashionable. At the other extreme, we find that the least destructive tax is highly unfashionable. This is a poll tax, a fixed, lump-sum tax on individuals. Because it is not tied to anything the individual does, the poll tax does not alter behavior. It does not penalize labor, or investment, or starting a business, or making any kind of purchase. Another advantage of the poll tax is that it is extremely simple to administer, with very low compliance costs. Furthermore, it is a highly explicit tax, one that allows taxpayers to see clearly what they are paying for government services.

This, it appears, is one of the main reasons why it is disliked. Politicians and the public want to view government as a cornucopia, a something-for-nothing machine. To keep this illusion going, taxes need to be unnoticed or indirect, or people have to assume that other, richer, people are paying much more than they are. The poll tax does not meet these illusion-sustaining requirements, and for this reason it is widely disliked. When the government of Margaret Thatcher in Great Britain introduced a poll tax in 1990 to fund certain local government expenditures, the tax was strenuously opposed, and it was later abandoned.

In conclusion, although a rational, efficient tax system may be possible to describe in theory, there is considerable doubt whether it could ever be attained, given the role of illusion and emotion in political affairs.

✦ 7 ✦

Evasion and Avoidance Costs

There is nothing sinister in so arranging one's affairs to keep taxes as low as possible. Everybody does so, rich and poor; and all do right, for nobody owes any public duty to pay more than the law demands; taxes are enforced exactions, not voluntary contributions. To demand more in the name of morals is mere cant.

—Supreme Court justice Learned Hand

JUSTICE HAND'S DECLARATION points up a basic contradiction in the theory of taxation. To function efficiently, the tax authority needs citizen cooperation. It needs taxpayers who are prompt, honest, and helpful in fulfilling tax requirements. Yet a tax system is poorly positioned to elicit this cooperation. It takes money by force, and the use of force undermines its moral claim to taxpayer goodwill. This is Justice Hand's point.[1] In a tax system, the contributors are, *and are legally expected to be*, out for themselves. Tax systems, by their very nature, wear a "Cheat me" sign.

When the effort to "keep taxes as low as possible" is done in a legal way, it is called *tax avoidance*. When it takes forms contrary to law, it can be called *tax evasion*. Actually, the line between the two is quite difficult to draw. Most taxpayers sense what Justice Hand declared, namely, that paying taxes is only a legal requirement, not a moral duty. Hence, the difference between tax avoidance and tax evasion hinges on legal technicalities. Since these technicalities have, in the modern day, become complex and obscure, the line between tax avoidance and tax evasion is further blurred. In recognition of this ambiguity, some writers in this field combine the two aspects under one term, tax "avoision."

In a social cost analysis such as we are undertaking here, the legality or illegality of the tax-avoiding activity has no bearing. In either case the "avoision" will involve a cost in the form of work or wasted resources, and that is what we want to measure.

By my reckoning, there are some eight different tax avoidance and evasion activities that entail social costs. Each cost is quite difficult to estimate, given the paucity of available data. The purpose in this chapter is to lay out the dimensions of the topic and to make a first, rough estimate of the burdens involved.

Underground Labor and Production

It is useful to start our exploration with the so-called underground economy, since this topic enables us to clear up some important issues. Economists define the underground economy as economic activity that is not reported in the usual measures of national income and which should be added to the measure of Gross National Product.[2] Through a number of indirect techniques, they have arrived at estimates of the size of this underground sector. These estimates range from 4 to 22 percent of GNP for the United States in 1976.[3]

One of these indirect techniques is based on tax audits. Through careful audits in what is called the Taxpayer Compliance Measurement Program, or TCMP, the IRS attempts to identify how much income is being concealed from the government. A recent TCMP audit indicates unreported income of $406.4 billion in 1987 and a "tax gap" of unpaid federal taxes on this amount of income of $71.2 billion.[4] These figures, based only on taxpayers the IRS has a documentary basis for investigating, probably understate the extent of unreported income and unpaid taxes.

Whether accurate or not, such measures of understated income have little bearing on the social cost of tax evasion. In this accounting, it should be remembered, it makes no difference *who* winds up with the money. The alleged $71.2 billion in unpaid taxes that was not turned over to the government stayed in the pockets of taxpayers. Since we treat the government and the taxpayers as equally meritorious recipients of funds, there is no net cost to society in the actual amounts of tax evaded or avoided.

The social cost of underground economic activity, therefore, does not have to do with the taxes paid or unpaid. It applies to the work or waste incurred by operating underground and trying to hide one's activity from the tax collection authority. Three of these costs are bartering, exclusion from the banking system, and limits to business growth.

The tax system is oriented toward exchanges in which the values of things are established in money terms and the transactions recorded (and usually reported to the tax authority). One way to avoid taxes is to avoid these money exchanges and trade goods and services directly. Some of this bartering may be legal, some may be illegal. For example, house-swapping clubs and baby-sitting clubs appear to be legal, whereas the IRS considers exchanging labor services to be illegal. Whatever the case, bartering enables citizens to avoid leaving a record for the tax authority to trace.

Bartering is inefficient, however. Since a person may not really want the item he receives in the exchange, he winds up underutilizing this item, or he has to bear additional administrative and marketing costs to get it transferred to a consumer who is willing to exchange something of greater value to him. In the accounts of the underground economy, this overhead cost appears clearly (see box on page 106). Though barterers are often pleased with themselves (it's remarkable how hard some people will *work* to cheat the government), one cannot overlook the burdens they bear in arranging their deals.

Another burden of underground operation is the limitation on the use of the banking system. Since the IRS forces banks to report taxpayer identification numbers for all accounts, anyone who opens an account is generating a lead for the IRS to pursue. Furthermore, IRS agents have access to all banking records, including checks. Therefore, the underground worker or businessman must generally steer clear of the banking system. Often, this means that the businessman cannot accept checks or credit cards—which limits business. Or, if checks are accepted, the businessman has to employ more costly means to deal with them—such as driving across town to cash them at the bank of origin. Furthermore, in having to shun

An "off the books" printer describes a typical barter transaction:

I got a new air conditioner put in with no money at all changing hands. First, I paid for part of it in printing for the guy. Next, I had another customer who wanted to pay me for a job with a solar unit, which his company makes. I didn't want the unit, but I wondered if the air condition-ing man might be interested. He looked at the set-up, and decided that he could sell it to another customer of his, and get paid for the installation, too. He took it, and that's how I got my air conditioner for nothing.

SOURCE: Adam Cash, *How to Do Business "Off the Books"* (Port Townsend, Wash.: Loompanics Unlimited, 1986), p.121.

the legitimate banking and investment outlets, the underground businessman has no convenient way to put idle capital to use.

Another cost of doing business underground is that it limits business growth. The underground businessman has to turn away orders from larger firms and public entities that might report him, he has to be cautious about advertising, and he has to be cautious about hiring workers who might report him. Furthermore, raising capital is difficult. The worker who is trying to stay off IRS computers is limited in his ability to take higher-paying jobs in all those firms that do report to the IRS. In a number of ways, then, being underground causes workers and businesses to limit their productivity.

Estimating the social cost of the burdens of going underground involves a number of problems. First, we want to estimate the cost of only that activity driven underground by the tax system. Some businesses are driven underground more by licensing requirements and other regulations than by the tax system. Illegal businesses—drug dealing, for example—are driven underground by laws aimed against them, and therefore their burdens should not figure in calculations of the overhead cost of the tax system. Illegal aliens are driven underground mainly by immigration laws.

A second issue concerning the burden of underground activities is their partial character. Very few American workers are entirely underground. The typical pattern is some underground activity combined with above-ground dealings. People who barter seldom barter for everything. Many workers have two jobs, one of which is on the books, and one of which is not. This blurring of the two spheres creates further difficulties in making estimates.

Another point to keep in mind is that the underground worker avoids tax compliance costs. This represents a genuine benefit in a social cost analysis: society is richer to the extent that the underground worker is not wasting resources keeping tax records, filling out forms, and otherwise spending time and effort on compliance activities. Another gain from underground activity is the removal of disincentive costs. Because he knows he will not pay taxes, the underground worker is likely to work harder, thus increasing the social product.[5]

Given the empirical and conceptual problems in making a social cost accounting of the burdens of tax-avoiding underground economic activity, it is clear that any estimate, at this point, will have to be quite "dirty." The method I will use focuses on individuals who are not filing tax returns. This approach gives us a way to improve measurements in the future. By concentrating on nonfilers, we focus on the individuals who, in principle, can be counted and whose burdens can—again, in principle—be known through empirical surveys.

Using a 1979 GAO study of nonfilers, I have calculated the number of significant nonfilers in 1985. These are nonfilers with tax liabilities that are not trivial, who can be considered to be underground workers consciously evading the tax system. This number works out to be 4.3 million.[6] Of this number, I estimate that half, or 2.15 million, are tax-motivated significant nonfilers, that is, individuals whose underground status is caused mainly by the federal tax system. The other half is made up of nonfilers who are presumed to have been driven underground by other regulations, such as local business and zoning laws, drug laws, and immigration laws.[7] The net burden, in terms of social costs, on these tax-related significant nonfilers is estimated to be 10 percent of their income, estimated at $20,000 per year, the nationwide average income in 1985.[8] This makes the social cost of tax-caused underground activity $4.3 billion. This is an extremely conservative estimate, but it follows our pattern of erring on the side of caution, especially when ambiguities preclude a firm estimate.

Investment Tax Shelters

Numerous features of the tax code make it advantageous for investors to place their money in artificial investment opportunities that have tax advantages but little or no economic return. Sometimes, these tax shelters are created deliberately by Congress, which decrees that a certain type of investment—let us say, windmills intended to produce electricity—be given a tax break. More commonly, however, the investment tax shelter is created through the clever application of the tax code to produce a legal tax advantage for investors in a particular category. Such arrangements are almost always quite technical, involving complex accounting arrangements whereby the assets and liabilities of a financial entity are arranged and rearranged through leases, loans, and different levels of ownership. The investor need not understand any of the mechanics of these arrangements. From his point of view, what is being sold is a tax savings which is supposed to be legal.

One example of an investment tax shelter was the so-called silver butterfly, a commodity tax straddle that became popular in the mid-1960s. By making offsetting buy and sell moves in the commodity futures market, brokers could provide their clients with paper losses that reduced their taxes.[9]

Naturally, there is work and risk involved in putting these tax shelters together. Lawyers and accountants have to prospect the tax regulations to find the appropriate loopholes, and they have to put together the investment vehicle to mine these lodes. They have selling expenses of bringing the investment opportunity to the attention of investors, and they must invest their time and reputations in countering the challenges of tax officials.[10]

From the point of view of social cost, these activities represent wasted effort caused by the tax system. Talented specialists and entrepreneurs are expending time and energy, not in creating anything of value to society, but in helping some taxpayers lower their tax bill. The social cost of investment tax shelters is not measured by the amount of money invested in them, nor in the tax savings they generate. The social costs consist of (1) the time and effort expended selling and administering them, and (2) the less productive use of capital they involve.

Using two methods of estimation, based on IRS identification of "abusive tax shelters," I have arrived at a figure of $3.8 billion as the social cost of investment tax shelters in 1985.[11]

The Tax Reform Act of 1986 made a number of changes, especially in the passive loss requirements, that discouraged the formation of investment tax shelters of the kind prevalent before that time. It is clear, however, that tax shelter activity has not ceased. In one suit filed in 1989, for example, the IRS alleged that a California investment firm sold $356 million in questionable investments designed to lower investors' taxes by $1 billion.[12] Another sign that tax shelters are here to stay is the fact that now, with form 8264, the IRS officially registers them! This seems an illogical stance for a tax authority that has also held that investment tax shelters represent a criminal violation of the tax code.[13]

Estate Tax Shelters

In addition to taxing wages, income, and corporations, the federal government also levies a tax on estates. As the law is currently written, the federal estate tax falls on amounts over $600,000 and is graduated from 20 to 55 percent of the amount of the estate. The estate tax appears to be the most evadable of all federal taxes, so evadable that it has been explicitly called a voluntary tax: you pay it only if you want to.[14]

To evade the estate tax takes a little more than desire, however. It requires the services of estate and trust lawyers who know how to make the necessary arrangements. It is remarkable what these alchemists of tax avoidance can do with grantor retained income trusts, irrevocable life insurance trusts, generation-skipping trusts, conservation easements, installment sales, lease-backs, and all types of corporate arrangements and recapitalizations. With such devices, estate tax lawyers are able to reduce the effective tax rate on estates to 3 or 4 percent, instead of the 20 to 55 percent written in the tax code.[15]

This legal assistance costs something, of course, and this burden represents a social cost of the tax system. Highly trained professionals with fine minds are expending their energies in a task that would not exist but for the tax system. An estate lawyer in the Spokane, Washington, area reported that his basic charges for avoiding estate tax are predicated on arranging three trusts: an irrevocable living trust, for which he charges $1,500–$5,000 to draft; an irrevocable life insurance trust, which costs $500–$1,000 for each spouse; and a grantor retained income trust, which costs a minimum of $1,500. He will assess, in addition to these charges, recording and registration fees, which will run about $300, and often a charge of $250–$500 to obtain a private letter ruling from the IRS approving of the trust arrangement.

Furthermore, there are reporting and management requirements for the trusts. If a trust has a corporate trustee, such as a bank, lawyer, or accountant, the standard management fee is 1 percent of the market value of trust assets per year. A corporate trustee will typically charge $350 for each quarterly tax return on a trust and $750 for the year-end return. In this lawyer's own practice, he found that his charges tended to run to 0.17–0.25 percent of the total value of the estate being tax sheltered; he believed that in higher-cost areas such as California this figure would run to 0.50 percent.

One way to estimate the nationwide cost of estate tax avoidance services is to focus on the lawyers who are at the heart of this industry. The American Bar Association has a special section for attorneys who deal with these matters, entitled Real Property, Estates, and Trust Law. In 1988, this section had 30,093 practicing attorneys.[16] Of course, attorneys in this field do not work only on estate tax avoidance; they also work on matters of probate, property transactions, wills, and inheritance arrangements established for reasons other than tax avoidance. The estate attorney quoted above estimated that about 30 percent of his time was devoted to estate tax avoidance work; we will apply this reduction to the figure for the total number of practicing attorneys. The Altman and Weil survey of the legal profession found that the average revenue per lawyer in 1987 was $178,707.[17] Therefore, putting these figures together, the value of legal work for avoiding estate taxes can be calculated at $1.6 billion.[18]

This figure does not include the labor of other participants in the estate tax avoidance picture, such as banks, accountants, and appraisers; and it does not include attorneys who are not registered in this ABA section but who may do estate tax work. Nor does it include any estimate of the value of the taxpayers' time in finding and working with estate tax lawyers. In recognition of these points, the $1.6 billion figure is increased 25 percent, to $2 billion. This figure is our estimate of the administrative cost of estate tax sheltering activities.

Retirement Tax Shelters

Probably the most important single loophole in the federal tax structure concerns pensions and retirement savings. Since the enactment of the Employee Retirement Income Security Act in 1974, many types of retirement savings have been exempt from federal taxation, including pension systems of large companies, Keogh plans for smaller companies, and IRAs and SEPs for individuals.

Tax-sheltered retirement income plans involve several types of costs. Perhaps the most obvious one is the compliance burden. The government makes extensive reporting and record-keeping demands and has imposed numerous requirements that must be met for an income-sheltering plan to qualify for the tax exemption. Hence firms and specialists have come into being that offer retirement tax exemption products. Just as in the case of investment tax shelters, these firms have to devise and sell the income-sheltering plan, guarantee its legal viability (often by obtaining a special private letter ruling from the IRS), sell it, and administer it (an activity that includes yearly filing of form 5500). These activities represent a social cost of the tax system.

A second cost of retirement tax shelters has to do with their indirect feature. Any pension system, whatever its reason for being adopted, entails overhead administrative costs. Money that could have been paid to the worker, for him to control, save, and dispose of directly, is being placed in the hands of a third party, to be disbursed according to certain rules. This third party must be compensated for its record-keeping and disbursing activities. Furthermore, the additional layers of bureaucracy between the worker and his money add more work and confusion in recovering it.

Since pension systems entail overhead costs, their forced or induced creation by government necessarily implies additional burdens on the society. Perhaps some social or political purpose is being achieved by these induced pension systems, but this point does not alter the fact that administrative burdens are being added as well. Hence, when the tax system is used to create more pension arrangements than would otherwise exist, the overhead costs of these arrangements should be attributed to the tax system.

We cannot lay all costs of retirement plans at the doorstep of the tax system, however. In the absence of tax deductions for retirement income, some firms would still have pension plans for their employees. (One private pension specialist I interviewed estimated that 90 percent of the existing private pension plans were tax-break-induced, while 10 per cent would exist without the tax exemption.)

Another factor that complicates the cost picture is that pension plans are subject to additional, nontax regulations. Pension laws attempt to guarantee fairness and dependability of private pensions. It is unclear to what extent this aim has been achieved, but at least some of the paperwork burden in operating pensions must be traced to this legislative intent, not tax-related features.

The charges for tax-sheltered retirement programs can be of three types: set-up fees, which are one-time charges for establishing a plan; contribution fees, which are commissions based on new money contributed to the plan; and asset management fees, which are commissions based on the total savings in the retirement fund. The taxpayer may not necessarily see all three charges, but they will figure somewhere in the cost picture. For example, the Fidelity Investment Company of Massachusetts offers firms with 50 to 500 workers defined contribution plans that have typical set-up fees of $2,000–$5,000, and yearly charges ranging from $4,300 to $10,700. These charges convert to fees of approximately 1.1 to 4.7 percent of funds contributed.[19] Not appearing in any charges are the asset management fees taken from the individual funds in which the retirement money is invested. A pension specialist for small firms in Sacramento, California, places all costs in a yearly fee of $600 per plan plus $15 per participant. For a typical eight-employee firm, this amounts to a fee of about 4 percent of retirement funds contributed.

To estimate the administrative burden of tax-sheltered retirement programs, it is simplest to express this burden relative to gross contributions. In 1988, total contributions to private defined-benefit pension plans, involving thirty-two million participants, was $50 billion.[20] In addition, some $43.5 billion was contributed to Keogh and IRA plans.[21] The total, $93.5 billion, can be taken as representing the contributions flowing into tax-system-caused retirement income shelters. For an overall average administration fee (including set-up costs, reporting costs, asset management costs, and taxpayer involvement) I will adopt the figure of 2.5 percent of contributions. Hence, the total overhead cost of retirement tax shelters is calculated to be $2.3 billion.

Foreign Tax Havens

Anyone who believes that a tax system is a simple, rational way of raising funds for public purposes should explore the law and practice governing international financial dealings. Whether this aspect of taxation ever could have been handled in a simple, sensible way is an academic question. The law, erected through seventy years of piecemeal adjustment, today defies the capacity of administrators to understand or apply it (see box).

The complexity in the international tax field is rooted in the fact that the United States cannot tax foreign entities. Therefore, if U.S. citizens or corporations place their money in these entities, the profits cannot be taxed at the source. By the time these earnings are repatriated to the U.S. taxpayer, their form can be changed so that they escape taxation or face a lower effective tax rate. This basic loophole has been added to by Congress, which has periodically sought to encourage or guide various aspects of international commerce by additional tax provisions and tax treaties.

Since 1913, Congress and offshore tax avoiders have played a game of leapfrog. Congress has attempted to close some loopholes, mostly with the use of murky, subjective tests to distinguish between legitimate and illegitimate uses of tax havens. Corporations, investors, and promoters then jump ahead to more sophisticated techniques that better disguise their tax-evading purpose.

Complexity in international taxation:

Areas in which the Statistics and Income division of the IRS attempts to guide tax policy making include the following: corporation foreign tax credit, foreign corporation information returns, domestic international sales corporations, interest charge domestic international sales corporations, foreign sales corporations, U.S. possessions corporations, foreign personal holding companies, individual foreign tax credit, individual income earned abroad, excluded income from U.S. possessions, foreign trusts.

SOURCE: Internal Revenue Service, *SOI Bulletin*, fall 1988, pp. 25 ff.

For example, in 1921, Congress decreed that a foreign subsidiary of a U.S. corporation could not accumulate earnings abroad "beyond the reasonably anticipated needs of the business."[22] Naturally, this stricture was simply an invitation to corporate managers to invent, on paper, projects to justify the need for the accumulated earnings they happened to have.

On balance, the tax collectors seem to be on the losing end of this game of leapfrog. Tax evasion and avoidance through the use of foreign financial arrangements has apparently increased quite dramatically in recent years.[23] No doubt, the increased use of foreign tax havens is partly motivated by the higher U.S. tax rates, which make it more worthwhile to pursue these exotic opportunities. Tax haven vehicles now include dozens of arrangements which, if done carefully, are essentially legal tax evasion devices. These include foreign trusts of many different varieties, transfer pricing, tax haven corporations, holding companies, trading companies, and investment companies. Along with tax havens, in this category of international tax avoidance, we will also include money laundering, that is, the use of banking systems to hide the origin of funds from tax authorities. Although some money laundering takes place on a domestic basis, it appears that most of it involves international financial transactions.

The game of leapfrog played with foreign tax havens has its cost, however. Lawyers, accountants, and promoters are needed to find loopholes, to construct investment organizations and instruments, to certify them as (apparently) legal devices, and to sell them to investors. One organization that promotes the formation of tax-sheltering contractual companies based in the British West Indies charges from $2,800 to $14,000 to establish the companies and a trustee fee of from $250 to $750 per year.[24]

To a corporation, the tax advantages of having a foreign branch have encouraged the formation of these units beyond what would be economically justified. Congress has further encouraged the creation of foreign branches of U.S. businesses with specific tax breaks. For example, since 1986, smaller companies have been encouraged by a tax exemption on their foreign export sales to form "foreign sales corporations." Incorporating an FSC in the U.S. Virgin Islands with a resident administrator is said to cost an initial $1,300 with an annual charge of $2,000–$2,500 for a company with less than $5 million in sales.[25]

Since there are so many loopholes in the international tax law for corporations, the effort to tax foreign earnings of these entities may be futile. This is the conclusion of a study of how U.S. corporations repatriate their foreign earnings, by James Hines and Glenn Hubbard: "The present U.S. system of taxing multinationals' income may be raising little U.S. tax revenue, while stimulating a host of tax-motivated financial transactions."[26]

In estimating the social cost of tax havens, we should focus on the administrative overhead. That is, we wish to estimate how many bankers, bank clerks, lawyers, accountants, salesmen, translators, and others are at work shifting funds into arrangements that avoid taxes. Administrative costs also include the work and travel of taxpayers and corporate officials who spend time and money setting up the arrangements and monitoring them. As already noted, the actual taxes avoided by these arrangements represent no net social cost, and therefore we ignore this aspect. In addition, for the sake of simplicity, we also assume that the investments themselves are as economically productive as other investments. Therefore, the actual capital flows do not figure in our calculations of social cost.

Obviously, any estimate of social cost in this area is necessarily crude. My method for arriving at a figure is to estimate the total foreign flow of U.S. tax-avoiding funds and then estimate administrative overhead costs as a fraction of these.

For an estimate of the funds, we can begin with some findings by IRS researchers into the international funds in tax haven countries. These are some twenty-two areas that are especially favored by tax-avoiding investors because they levy little or no taxes on foreign holdings and their banking regulations permit a rather high degree of privacy. These countries include Switzerland, the Bahamas, the British West Indies, Hong Hong, Liberia, Luxembourg, Bermuda, Panama, and Singapore. Reasoning that tax-avoiding funds would pass through the banking systems of these countries, IRS researchers compiled estimates of the size and growth of foreign deposits in these areas. Their figures for the period 1968–1978 show a dramatic rise in foreign deposits.[27]

The researchers reasoned that the funds in the Western Hemisphere tax haven banks would be predominantly U.S. funds, and would therefore reflect the magnitude of U.S. tax avoidance activity in foreign locales. This seems a serviceable assumption. To be sure, there would be substantial U.S. funds in other areas, especially Switzerland; but these amounts would be roughly counterbalanced by the fact that some of the foreign funds in Western Hemisphere havens would be non-U.S. Hence their figure of $159.5 billion in the Western Hemisphere tax havens can be taken as an estimate of U.S. international deposits in all tax haven areas.[28] When extrapolated to 1985, the tax year that is the focus of our analysis, this international deposit figure becomes $344 billion.[29] As an estimate of the total of U.S. money seeking tax havens, this figure contains a number of distortions, but it appears to be a useful rough estimate.[30]

What is the cost of moving funds into international tax-sheltering arrangements? Obviously, these vary according to the amounts invested and the complexity of the arrangements. After surveying a number of illustrative examples, I have decided to estimate this figure at 2.0 percent of the funds involved.[31] Thus, $1 million placed in a foreign country for the purposes of reducing taxes is estimated to cost $20,000 in the services of people such as bankers, accountants, and currency traders to get it there in safe and useful form. This $20,000 will also include the time and expenses, including travel, of taxpayers and corporation officials in making the arrangements.

This 2.0 percent figure is multiplied by our estimate of the total funds seeking offshore tax advantages, $344 billion, to give a social cost of $6.9 billion. As already noted, this estimate is crude; but it at least provides a first approximation of the burden of this large and growing type of tax avoidance activity.

Other Tax Avoidance Costs

In addition to the burdens already noted, there are several other types of tax avoidance costs that we should note. Since they would be quite difficult to estimate, and would generally be rather small, we will not attempt to provide monetary estimates for them.

Investment Lock-in

In order to avoid paying tax on the appreciated value of property, investors may refrain from selling it even though it would otherwise be advantageous to do so. In such cases, the tax system must be held responsible for the costs or losses inherent in the failure to make a prompt sale. For example, a New York retiree who is planning to move to Florida may delay selling his home for six months so that the capital gain will fall in the following year, thus lessening his tax bill. The social cost of this tax avoidance strategy would include both personal inconvenience (having to endure another winter in Brooklyn), and economic waste—for example, paying rent on an apartment in Florida that goes unused.

It is clear that investment lock-in does occur, at least concerning the sale of securities, and economists have made a considerable study of this phenomenon.[32] However, they have not yet turned their attention to calculating the social cost of this effect.

Investment Churning

Just as there can be tax advantages to not selling an asset when you want to, there can also be tax benefits to selling when you would otherwise want to hold the asset. What the taxpayer might do in this situation is sell the asset, in order to establish a point for tax purposes, and then repurchase it. The social costs in this situation are the buying and selling costs. A certain amount of this tax-motivated churning occurs in the securities field, where buying and selling costs are relatively low.

Tax Lobbying

One way of avoiding taxes is to have the tax law rewritten so that it exempts you! In a well-ordered tax system, such as prevailed until the 1970s, this would be an inefficient, impractical tactic. Legislators realized that customized tax exemptions would disgrace them—and bring the tax system into disrepute; therefore, they almost always said no to requests for specific tax breaks. Furthermore, the tax code was changed infrequently, giving less opportunity for new loopholes. In recent years, the tax code is almost constantly revised, and legislators write hundreds of specific exceptions into tax bills. Since these clauses can be worth millions of dollars, firms, industries, and associations are willing, in turn, to pay large sums to lobbyists, and to the campaign funds of politicians, to get them. These funds represent a waste of resources caused by the tax system as currently operated.

Summary

The tabulation of the social costs of tax avoidance and evasion is given in Table 12. The total burden adds up to $19.3 billion in 1985, or 2.96 percent of net available revenue collected. Although this is a significant amount, it may seem unexpectedly small. But it should be remembered that this figure is the social cost of tax evasion, that is, the waste or cost to society as a whole. This figure should not be confused with the flow of funds in tax avoidance realms, a flow that involves many hundreds of billions.

TABLE 12   Tax Evasion and Avoidance Costs, 1985 (billions of dollars)

Underground economic activity (inefficiences of barter, inefficiencies of banking, and limits to expansion)	4.3
Investment tax shelters (administrative costs and investment misallocation)	3.8
Tax-sheltered estate management (administrative costs)	2.0
Tax-sheltered retirement plans (administrative costs)	2.3
International tax avoidance (tax havens and money laundering)	6.9
Investment lock-in	ne
Investment churning	ne
Lobbying for tax exemptions	ne
Total	19.3

NOTE: ne = not estimated.

✦ 8 ✦

Governmental Costs

IN ADDITION TO THE BURDENS of the tax system on the private sector, which have been enumerated in the previous chapters, there are also governmental costs. These are the expenditures for the various agencies that carry out tax collection and enforcement functions. Although these costs are relatively small, they need to be noted to complete the picture of tax system burdens.

These expenses, for the year 1985, are given in Table 13. The main component is the cost of operating the Internal Revenue Service, which was $3.6 billion in 1985. In addition, a number of other units of the federal government play a role in the tax system. The Tax Court (which is administratively located under the legislative branch) is a special court system for federal tax cases. In addition, the federal judicial system—district courts, claims courts, appellate courts—is also used by the tax system to handle criminal cases, refund litigation, and many thousands of other tax-related cases. The fraction of the judicial system occupied by tax work is calculated to be 12 percent.[1] Hence, 12 percent of the cost of the judiciary should be attributed to the tax system.

Although IRS attorneys handle litigation before the Tax Court, most of the rest of the federal tax litigation is handled by the Justice Department. The Tax Division in the Justice Department handles most of the civil tax cases, while the U.S. attorneys handle, among

TABLE 13   Governmental Costs of the Federal Tax System, 1985 (millions of dollars)

Agency	Expenditure
Internal Revenue Service	
personnel and benefits	2,631.4
other expenses	986.0
Total, Internal Revenue Service	3,617.4
U.S. Tax Court	21.5
Federal judicial system	
(12% of $1,040,415,000)	124.8
Department of Justice	
Tax Division	32.8
U.S. attorneys (12% of $300,237,000)	36.0
U.S. marshals (12% of $139,708,000)	16.8
Witness expenses (12% of $40,732,000)	4.9
Federal prison system (12% of $522,932,00)	62.8
Total, Department of Justice	153.3
Department of the Treasury	
Departmental office (50% of $96,968,000)	48.5
Financial Management Service (11% of $246,285,000)	27.1
Total, Department of the Treasury	75.6
Direct and indirect legislative costs	ne
Total, governmental costs	3,992.6

NOTE: ne = not estimated.
SOURCES: Internal Revenue Service, *1985 Annual Report*, p. 71; U.S. Office of Management and Budget, *Budget of the the United States Government, Fiscal Year 1987: Appendix* (Washington, D.C., 1986) pp. I-A25, I-O3, I-O8, I-O11, I-S1, I-S8; *Departments of Commerce, Justice, and State, the Judiciary, and Related Agencies Appropriations for 1987* (Hearings before a subcommittee of the Committee on Appropriations, U.S. House of Representatives, 99th Cong., 2d Sess.), part 3, p. 4; *Departments of Commerce, Justice, and State, the Judiciary, and Related Agencies Appropriations for 1986* (Hearings before a subcommittee of the Committee on Appropriations, U.S. House of Representatives, 99th Cong., 1st Sess.), part 7, p. 80.

other cases, the criminal litigation. The U.S. marshals serve the federal court system as process servers, guards, and custodians of defendants in criminal trials. It seems reasonable to allocate the expenses of these units to the tax system at the same 12 percent rate used for the judiciary.

Those convicted of crimes against tax regulations and given prison sentences (1,338 individuals in 1985) are incarcerated by the federal prison system.[2] Attempts to assess the fraction of prison costs attributable to tax offenders suggest that the 12 percent figure used for the judicial system gives a satisfactory estimate.[3]

Another agency, the Financial Management Service of the Treasury Department, plays a significant role in the tax system in issuing IRS refund checks (some 78 million in 1985). The fraction of the work of the FMS devoted to this function is calculated to be 11 percent.[4]

Finally, there is a management cost for the Treasury Department. As the most important subdivision of the Treasury, the Internal Revenue Service utilizes management resources at the departmental level for drafting legislation and regulations, for compiling statistics and reports, and for budgeting. The Treasury Department units dealing entirely with taxes include the Office of Tax Analysis and the Office of Tax Legislative Counsel. The fraction of Treasury management costs devoted to tax policy, legislation, regulation, and IRS management is estimated at 50 percent of Treasury's front office expenses.

These various costs are added up in Table 13, giving a total of $3.993 billion in 1985. This figure represents a conservative accounting of the governmental cost of operating the federal tax system. For one thing, IRS budget figures understate employee pension costs.[5] We have also omitted costs pertaining to the higher decision-making levels. In Congress, tax matters and tax legislation occupy a significant component of congressional time, staff work, and office space etc. One way to estimate this fraction is to base it on the House Ways and Means Committee, the committee that deals with tax legislation and whose thirty-six members are on no other major committee. Using this as an index, we could say that 8 percent (36/435) of congressional business is tax business. Hence, 8 percent of the cost of Congress (including the cost of elections and election campaigns) should probably be attributed to the tax system. A similar calculation could also be done for the presidency, including executive branch agencies such as the Office of Management and Budget.

Calculating Available Revenue Collected

Estimates of overhead costs of the tax system are best expressed in relative terms to enable us to judge the overall impact of these costs. The reference point that most analysts use to compute this relative burden is the tax revenue collected. This seems the most useful way to present burden results, and it is the one adopted in this study. It is important in making this calculation, however, to employ the correct definition of tax revenue. Unfortunately, most presentations, including IRS and Treasury sources, do not correctly specify this amount.

The first distortion found in many purported tax revenue figures is the use of gross collections instead of net collections. Gross collections are all money taken in, whereas net collections are the funds that remain after tax refunds and interest have been paid. The IRS emphasizes the use of the gross collection figure. In IRS annual reports, the gross collection figure is prominently featured as representing the overall accomplishment of the agency and is often labeled "revenue" or "collections." The IRS also uses the gross collections figure to compute the relative governmental cost of raising funds, and this figure is accepted even by Treasury specialists as a valid one.[6]

This practice embodies a serious distortion. The proper reference point for the burden of a tax system is the net amount collected, the funds available to be spent by government. If the tax system takes in, say, $100 billion but returns $100 billion in refunds, it should not be given credit for collecting anything. To assess the relative burden of costs of a tax system one should use net collections, that is, gross collections minus the payment of refunds and interest. Since refunds and interest have been running at about 10 percent of gross collections in recent years, this point is not unimportant.

Another refinement makes less of a difference in the result but is important theoretically: the exclusion of governmental tax collection costs. The aim of taxation is the collection of funds that will be available for government policy makers to spend. The funds that are spent by government agencies in collecting taxes cannot be counted as available funds. If the funds they collected were merely enough to cover their expenses, then *no* usable revenues have been collected. Therefore, funds consumed in the operation of the tax system should be subtracted from the net collection figure. This will yield a figure I call available revenue collected, which is the proper one to use to assess the various overhead costs of a tax system.

Table 14 shows the calculation of this available revenue figure for 1985. This is the figure, $652.557 billion, used throughout this

TABLE 14   Federal Tax System, Available Revenue Collected, 1985
                     (billions of dollars)

Gross tax collections	742.872
Refunds	− 84.560
Interest payments	− 1.762
Net tax collections	656.550
Governmental costs	− 3.993
Available revenue collected	652.557

SOURCE: Compiled from Internal Revenue Service, *1985 Annual Report*, pp. 9, 56, and table 8.1.

book to calculate the relative burden of the different tax system costs in 1985. If we use this figure, the relative governmental cost of operating the federal tax system in 1985 was 0.61 percent of available revenue collected. This is a small figure, indicating that very little of the cost of the tax system shows up as a governmental expense. As will be seen from the summary given in Chapter 10, the private sector burden is about 100 times this 0.61 percent figure.

Trends in Governmental Costs

At first glance, it would seem that the governmental cost of operating the tax system should be relatively constant. Once the tax agency has been set up and staffed, it should be able to do its job with the same resources, even as tax rates and tax revenues increase.

It is something of a surprise to discover that this has not happened at all. The governmental costs of operating the tax system have been rising sharply. One index of growth is the increase in personnel. The number of IRS employees has more than doubled in the past thirty years, going from 51,047 workers in 1960 to 112,987 in 1990.[7] Even after it has been adjusted for inflation, the cost of the IRS has more than tripled, rising from $1.227 billion in 1960 to $4.244 billion in 1990 (using constant, 1983 dollars). There is no sign of this trend's abating. The federal budget for 1991 stipulates an 18 percent increase in IRS spending compared with the 1989 figures.[8] This pattern of rapid expansion has meant that IRS costs have risen even faster than tax revenues, at least in recent years.[9]

Causes of Growing Inefficiency

The usual pattern in economic institutions is that unit costs normally fall. The failure of the IRS to match this pattern suggests that, in one form or another, it is subject to a growing degree of inefficiency. Since over the past thirty years the IRS has introduced automated systems, the growing inefficiency is especially remarkable.

There appear to be several explanations for this pattern. The first is increasing waste in IRS operations, owing to poor management and growing problems with employee morale and motivation. In the previous chapters we have seen how error-prone many IRS systems are. The result is a burden on citizens—and a further burden on the IRS as employees attempt to unravel the original mistakes. In the Problem Resolution Program, for example, the IRS has some 300 employees whose main job is attempting to straighten out mistakes made by other employees.[10] IRS Commissioner Fred T. Goldberg declared in 1990 that "The cost of poor quality and correcting mistakes in the system is in the hundreds and hundreds of millions of dollars a year."[11] The Service has difficulty hiring quality personnel. Newly hired accountants score in the bottom fifth of a standardized entry level test, and beginning lawyers come from the bottom half of their law school classes.[12] Turnover is extremely high. In the Manhattan district, for example, 30 percent of the accountants hired in 1988 had quit by mid-1989; the overall level of turnover in the organization is 11.3 percent.[13]

The personnel problems go much deeper than the need for higher compensation. The civil service system, which effectively prevents managers from discharging employees with poor attitudes, is one great impediment to developing a capable, highly motivated staff. Another impediment is even more intractable: the unattractiveness of the job. Taking money away from one's fellow citizens is not an appealing task to begin with; and today, with the tax bite so large and IRS intrusions and errors so manifest, the IRS is viewed with great skepticism. In one survey of attitudes toward fifteen federal agencies, the IRS ranked lowest, even below the CIA.[14] Increasingly, the IRS is less able to appeal to patriotism to attract and retain workers.

A second explanation for growing inefficiency is the increasing complexity of the tax system. The rapidly growing number of regulations and procedures means that workers in the tax collection authority must do more work to accomplish the same tax collection step, and this, of course, impairs efficiency. The growing complexity of the system has also meant that more labor must be devoted to informing the public about the tax code: the tax manuals take more time to write, and the public has more questions to be answered. In addition to the growth in the tax code, the IRS has also been given other tasks, including administration of pension legislation (ERISA) and the collection of nontax debts, including child support payments and student loan obligations.

A third cause of inefficiency is increasing citizen resistance. In recent decades, it appears that the degree to which citizens respect and cooperate with the tax system has declined.[15] This trend has many sources. The tax system itself has become more complex and onerous, fraught with an increasing array of requirements and punishments that irritate citizens and try their patriotism. Tax levels have become higher and more objectionable. Large and seemingly irresponsible spending programs have undermined the appeal to civic duty. Whatever the reasons, the declining citizen cooperation means that employees in the tax collection authority must do more work to accomplish the same tax collection step. For example, audits take longer when citizens contest each point and make more threats to appeal, and tax processing is slowed down when citizens submit bogus tax returns.

Given the depth of these forces making for inefficiency, it seems unlikely that the adoption of more electronic systems will overcome the trend toward inefficiency. The IRS has probably reaped the main benefits of automation. Automated systems can replace rote tasks fairly easily, but as the task to be replaced grows more complex, and more subtle, it becomes increasingly difficult—and costly—to substitute machines. Having turned the simple tasks over to automation, the IRS is now finding it increasingly difficult to use automation to advantage.

One illustration of these limits is seen in the experience with the Automated Examination System, a project intended to automate the examination of income tax returns. A review by the General Accounting Office found this system had slipped six years behind schedule, its projected budget had nearly doubled (to $1.8 billion), and its benefits were "elusive."[16] A consensus developed on the futility of the system, and it was largely scrapped in 1989.

Efforts to use automation in sophisticated ways require that the employees using the system be highly motivated and highly trained. Otherwise the system can be wasted or even abused. For example, part of the Automated Examination System plan was to provide portable lap-top computers for 15,000 revenue agents in the expectation that "examiners will be able to use these computers to access all the pieces of information relating to the taxpayer's account: a tax issue, the latest tax law changes, court decisions, IRS rulings and analyses by professional tax services."[17] The flaw in such plans is they overlook the human element. Relevant information would not leap usefully out of the computer any more than it would leap out of the shelves of a tax law library. The agent would have to master the software for accessing material and then have the skills and intelligence to cull complex documents and correctly extract the relevant points.

The outlook, then, is for growing inefficiency in the IRS efforts to administer the tax regulations. Congress will probably attempt to check the deterioration in service by continuing to increase the funding of the IRS. But since the root causes of the growing inefficiency have relatively little to do with money, the result will probably be a tax authority that keeps getting larger and more costly but is still unable to render prompt, accurate service.

✦ 9 ✦

Emotional, Moral, and Cultural Costs

OURS IS A MATERIALISTIC SOCIETY, in which money talks. I have bowed to this orientation in this book by emphasizing the tabulation of the strict monetary costs of the tax system. These burdens, however, are not the only ones involved. There are also costs of an emotional, moral, and cultural nature, costs just as important as, or even more more important than, sacrifices we can put a dollar figure to. A complete assessment of the burdens of operating a tax system therefore needs to take note of them.

One of the difficulties in attempting to weigh nonmonetary costs is that their importance varies from one person to another. What one observer considers a tragic violation of principle can be seen by someone else as merely a nuisance—or no problem at all. In examining the moral and psychological burdens of the tax system, this relativism must be kept in mind. The listing that follows contains points that, in each instance, *some people* consider serious costs. They are not points that, in each case, everyone would be disturbed about.

The Use of Coercion

The importance of different perspectives is clearly illustrated in the first cost we address: the coercive basis of the tax system. A tax, by definition, is what you are forced to pay, and the meaning of "forced" is not figurative but literal: if you do not come up with the money, government agents will physically seize your property. If you resist, you will face SWAT teams with sawed-off shotguns and tear gas grenades.

The tax system's use of force is weighed differently by different observers. For many Americans, it does not appear to be a significant burden. They observe that force is already widely used by governments around the world. In this perspective, coercion is an enduring characteristic of collective life, something to live with, like cockroaches or the flu, not something to worry about or criticize. Besides, this view runs, the use of force by the tax system seems to involve relatively little actual bloodshed.

In other perspectives, however, the tax system's use of force represents a serious problem. For some thinkers, the use of physical force represents a great evil in the world, and therefore the intentional use of force, which the tax system involves, makes one a party to evil. For others, including many libertarians, the use of force to defend against force is acceptable, but to initiate the use of force to carry out some social or political aim is wrong. The tax system, they feel, involves this error. Tax collectors, in effect, initiate the use of force against peaceful citizens to get funds to carry out the aims of those in control of the tax system. The nineteenth century English "voluntaryist" Auberon Herbert made this point in his treatises against taxation (see box).

While philosophical objections are voiced by a small minority, large numbers of Americans have some, less focused, misgivings about the tax system's use of force. Tax officials themselves seem sensitive on this point, repeatedly substituting the word "voluntary" whenever "coercive" would be the correct one to use to describe the system they operate. This evasion suggests that these officials sense there is something wrong, or at least unappealing, about the tax system's use of force.

Encouragement to the Use of Force

The tax system's use of force provokes a number of destructive reactions. Many citizens see themselves as having a right to their property and to what they have earned. When the tax authority

---

Is taxation moral?

To compel any human being to act against his own convictions is essentially a violation of the moral order, a cause of human unrest, and a grievous misdirection of human effort. Of the immediate ill effects, of the waste, of the extravagance, of the jobbery, that are all born of the compulsory taking of taxes, I will not speak here. The first and greatest question is whether to help oneself to one's neighbor's property by force is or is not morally right.

SOURCE: Auberon Herbert, *The Right and Wrong of Compulsion by the State, and other Essays*, Eric Mack, ed. (Indianapolis: Liberty Classics, 1978), p. 164. In the same volume, in his essay "The Principles of Voluntaryism," Herbert lists twenty-nine objections to compulsory taxation (pp. 392–409).

---

uses force to take it away, some resist (see box). Forcible responses by citizens are making tax collection a dangerous business. The number of assault and threat incidents involving IRS employees has been rising dramatically, from 400 in 1981 to 988 in 1985.[1] In some respects, tax collection resembles a war: certain categories of tax employees are even demanding hazardous duty pay.[2]

How one weighs the citizen violence provoked by the tax system depends, of course, on one's perspective. One can say that citizens are getting exactly what they deserve for resisting the government's

---

Who started these fights?

An Oklahoma taxpayer was arrested for threatening two revenue officers who were attempting to seize his truck. The taxpayer brandished a pistol while threatening and ordering the revenue officers from his property.

An Indiana taxpayer was convicted for assaulting two revenue officers during a seizure of his automobile. The taxpayer struck both revenue officers and kicked one of the officers after knocking him to the ground.

SOURCE: Internal Revenue Service, *1975 Annual Report*, p. 69.

---

exercise of its lawful powers. Or one can see it as a tragic secondary violence caused entirely by the government's initiation of force. However one interprets them, the violent reactions to the tax collecting process do constitute a social cost of the tax system. Not one of the 988 threat and assault incidents mentioned earlier in this section, for example, would have occurred if there had been no tax system.

Anxiety

The tax system makes extensive use of deterrence, that is, threats: threats of seizing the taxpayer's funds, his home, his business— or of putting him in jail. Deterrence may be efficient from the standpoint of the tax collection agency, and it may even be necessary; but we have to note that it involves a social cost, namely, anxiety for citizens (see box).

This cost would not be particularly significant if the tax system involved a simple, definite obligation. If the United States used a poll tax, where each person owed a flat sum, most taxpayers would suffer little anxiety. In paying this lump sum, they would know that they had done everything the law required and that they

---

A former IRS official begins his book on the IRS by describing how deterrence feels to the taxpayer:

Are you crazy? A total paranoid to think that *they* really do know everything about you? That given half a chance, the IRS will wipe you out and send you to jail?

No, I can assure you, there's nothing paranoid, even neurotic, about feeling that way. Mental instability in no way creates that state of fear and loathing. What you feel exists for good reason: the IRS has worked hard to put it there.

Nothing is more central to the IRS strategy of tax collection than scaring you, the taxpayer, and keeping you that way.

SOURCE: Paul N. Strassels, *All You Need to Know about the IRS: A Taxpayer's Guide* (New York: Random House, 1981), p. 3.

were therefore beyond the reach of any punishment. The current federal system is quite unlike this. It is extremely complex and ambiguous. This means that many taxpayers have reason to worry about whether their tax returns are "right." Most of them have cut corners, knowingly or unknowingly, in record keeping, in reporting, and in interpreting the tax law. Furthermore, the IRS is so error-prone that even blameless taxpayers have reason to fear harassment and punishment.

One indication of the magnitude of the anxiety fostered by the tax system is seen in the response to offers of audit insurance. The term is misleading, since the protection can cover only the expenses of representation in the event of an audit. This insurance cannot shield the taxpayer from penalties, nor from criminal prosecution, nor from additional taxes. Nevertheless, taxpayers are eager to buy it. One accounting firm in New Jersey offered audit insurance for $75, and only to clients who had simple tax situations and who were especially meticulous in their tax affairs. Of 350 clients to whom the insurance was offered, 300 purchased it. Since only one of these "safe" 300 returns was audited, the plan was almost pure profit.[3]

Stress

Extreme critics of the tax system flatly declare that taxation is theft. In one sense, they are incorrect. Theft is a forcible seizing action outside the law. Taxation, on the other hand, is established and regulated by law. It is a legal method for raising funds.

But in a rougher, practical sense, the tax critics do have a point. Most taxpayers probably have a relatively smooth working relation with the tax authority and take the operation of the system in stride. But to some individuals, especially those in the midst of an enforcement action, taxation can *feel like* theft. Property is being taken away involuntarily, and often under highly unpleasant circumstances.

This point easily goes unnoticed. The prevailing theory is that government is supposed to help citizens, to make their lives easier through its grants and subsidies. Politicians don't like to be reminded that this system of helping also entails a large measure of hurting. Whatever one feels about the importance or necessity of public spending, the fact remains that a definite injury is done to citizens in collecting the funds. The various tax enforcement activities put millions of Americans under considerable stress, stress that leads to illness, marital breakdown, even suicide (see box).[4]

The hard-heartedness of IRS agents is necessary. Tax collection procedures can and should be less stressful than they are, but one cannot let the collection system become sensitive to the problems of taxpayers. Otherwise, tax collectors would soon discover that almost everyone has problems: people have dental bills they can't pay, and leaking roofs they can't afford to fix, and cars that need repairs. In our system, only the congressman can be Mr. Nice Guy, the one who listens to hard luck stories and devises ways to alleviate them. In order to raise funds, tax collectors have to be Mr. Mean.[5]

When the tax collection bears on businesses, the effects are often far-reaching, resulting in stressful difficulties for employees, suppliers, and the community being served. The IRS closes thousands

---

The IRS as a source of stress:

I want to tell you about a client who owes $12,000 to the Internal Revenue Service. The IRS had been on her case to pay. I met with the revenue officer. I told her she can't pay because she was going through extremely emotional times and doesn't know when she will work. Her husband beats her up. She threw him out. The family environment is not good. The son, who is nine years old, tried to kill himself three times. The son is going to a psychiatrist. While I was explaining this to the revenue officer, she put up her hand and said to me: "Stop Mr. Smith. I have told you many times before I don't want to hear it. I don't care about her personal situation. All that matters is what is shown on this financial statement. That other stuff doesn't matter."

SOURCE: Statement of Joseph P. Smith, Jr., private tax practitioner and former IRS officer, *Taxpayers' Bill of Rights* (Hearings before the Subcommittee on Private Retirement Plans and Oversight of the Internal Revenue Service of the Committee on Finance, U.S. Senate, 100th Cong., 1st Sess., April 10 and 21, 1987), part 1, p. 139.

of businesses every year through collection procedures. Take the KilClean company in Columbus, Ohio, a cleaning services company. After a transfer of ownership, the proprietors discovered that the previous owners had a tax liability. An installment arrangement with the IRS was arranged, and repayment begun. In midwinter, however, during a time of slack business, the IRS felt tax payments were endangered and seized the business (even though bankruptcy had been filed in an attempt to halt the seizure). The IRS sold all the assets for what it could get, which was $31,000—about one-tenth of the company's yearly payroll. All forty-four employees were thrown out of work.[6]

Again, we should not suppose that this case represented wrongdoing. The IRS was doing what it is supposed to do: take money away from people. This process is unavoidably painful. Congress has implicitly recognized this truth by sanctioning many practices that in other contexts are considered uncivilized or unconstitutional. For example, the IRS is exempt from respecting bankruptcy proceedings. Of all creditors, it alone has the power to ignore an attempted restructuring in order to collect money.

Of course, many times IRS errors and ineptness compound the emotional burdens. Consider the case of Joan Kilburn, a hotel manager in Las Vegas. She was divorced in 1986, but in 1987 the IRS levied her wages and seized her home (which she had paid for with her own money) in pursuing a tax case against her former husband. The IRS failed to listen to her case or review her documentation that no tax liability was owed. She hired a tax practitioner and wrote to a Senate tax committee in an effort to get the matter straightened out. "Needless to say," she wrote, "this creates mental strain and anxiety as well as monetary expenses when one has worked all one's life to buy a house and to find that it is seized by the IRS without their doing any prior investigation."[7]

How one evaluates the harm of such episodes depends, of course, on how common they are, something which at this point is not easy to determine. Evaluation also depends on how one feels about state-initiated injury. For many, the personal tragedies caused by the IRS are simply frictional, the unavoidable broken eggs that the omelet of modern government requires. For others, there is something deeply shocking about a government deliberately inflicting injury upon the very citizens it is supposed to protect.

The Denial of Civil Rights

As just noted, Congress has concluded that in order for the tax system to function successfully, tax officials should be excused from many of the legal and civil restraints that apply to virtually all other public and private actors in our society. Among other things, the tax system is exempt from due process requirements: tax officials do not need court authority to seize taxpayer property. Although they generally follow set procedures in acting against taxpayers, they are not bound by them. The law itself allows for arbitrary action by enforcement officers; court cases have established that IRS officials are not even legally bound to follow the IRS's own internal regulations. This means that IRS officials can seize property and destroy businesses on the basis of personal prejudice, speculation, or even whim. How often such totally unjustified actions occur is, of course, hard to determine.

The federal tax system denies citizens self-incrimination protections. It forces the taxpayer to testify against himself, in submitting a tax return, in corresponding with tax officials, and in participating in an audit.

The federal tax system is exempt from the protections of injunctive relief. If federal agents are seizing property wrongly, or are even in the process of causing death (as in the Ohio nursing home case mentioned in Chapter 5), the taxpayer cannot halt the process by court order until the rights and wrongs can be cleared up.

The federal tax system does not adhere to the principle that the burden of proof is upon the prosecution. If a clerk in the Information Returns Program, relying on garbled data (or just as a joke), sends a taxpayer a CP-2000 letter alleging failure to report a payment, it is up to the taxpayer to prove that such a payment never took place. He is guilty of not paying his taxes until he can prove himself innocent. This means that the taxpayer has to try to prove a negative. If the firm that made the alleged payment is out of business, or uncooperative, gathering such proof may be impossible.

Of course, tax officials and legislators have been aware of the lack of civil protections and have gradually erected a quasi-judicial structure of regulations and procedures that attempt to protect civil rights. But these restraints are so written that they can, in the end, be overruled by IRS officials.[8]

As one index of the violation of civil rights, from 1980 to 1986 over 1,000 suits were filed against IRS employees alleging violation of constitutional rights.[9] None of these suits succeeded, given the IRS immunity.[10] The fact that so many suits were undertaken in spite of their futility indicates that IRS violation of civil rights is a significant problem.

Criminalization of a Victimless Crime

Crimes can be divided into two categories: those that have a definite victim and those that lack a direct injury, called victimless crimes. In the former category are murder, rape, and robbery, crimes in which everyone can clearly see who is being hurt by the wrongdoer. In the category of victimless crimes are acts like gambling, engaging in prostitution, publishing pornographic material, or smoking marijuana. In these deeds, it is not clear who, if anyone, is being hurt by the action. They are actions that lawmakers feel are unhealthy in a general way, or harmful to the person voluntarily engaging in them.

One school of thought contends that such activities should not be crimes, that is, they should not be punished using the state's police and criminal justice system. This, they say, is too severe and violent a way of handling these ambiguous transgressions. Those adopting this point of view will be especially disappointed with the federal tax system.

Tax evasion is perhaps the purest victimless crime. There is no specific human being who is certainly harmed when a taxpayer fails to report his income and pay his tax. Even theoretically, it is unclear who suffers from tax evasion. The IRS argues that tax evasion increases the taxes of other taxpayers (see box on page 136). This position seems both empirically and legally incorrect. As the U.S. budgetary process operates, any tax shortfall results either in more borrowing or in less spending. According to the Gramm-Rudman-Hollings deficit reduction act, any taxpayer's nonpayment of taxes must necessarily result in a reduction of federal spending. Hence, the IRS position contradicts federal law.

Regardless of who suffers from tax underpayment, this suffering is far more marginal and indirect than in any of the usual victimless crimes. Nevertheless, tax evasion is a criminal offense, for which some 3,000 citizens are prosecuted every year.

IRS recorded message explaining the tax informers program:

Our federal income tax system is based on voluntary compliance. This means that each of us is responsible for filing a tax return when required, and for determining and paying the correct amounts of tax. Some people break the law by not filing a return, or not reporting all their taxable incomes, or claiming higher deductions than they should. By doing this, *they cause the rest of us to pay more taxes than we should* [emphasis added], to make up the amount that these people do not pay. If you believe someone is violating federal tax laws, you should contact the local criminal investigation division of the IRS, or call the toll-free information number in your area. If you prefer, you may provide your information in writing to: Internal Revenue Service, Criminal Investigation, CI/IND/I, Washington, D.C. 20224.

You do *not* have to identify yourself. You may also be entitled to a reward.

SOURCE: Teletax option no. 108, "Tax Fraud—How to Report," recorded August 24, 1989.

The Use of Paid Informers

The IRS has a formal policy of offering cash rewards to informers who will turn in their friends, employers, or even parents for evading taxes (see box). In 1961, for example, 4,401 informers filed for cash rewards for denouncing tax violators. Most of their allegations turned out to be spurious: only 706 informers were actually paid.[11] Nevertheless, the number of informers seeking rewards has increased significantly, to 11,754 claims in 1989.[12]

Rewarding citizens to spy on other citizens is socially corrosive, for it trains them not to trust one another. Dictatorships, of course, aim to make citizens suspect one another, to prevent them from developing any personal or social loyalties among themselves, thereby leaving the state as the master of citizen affection. It is indeed puzzling that this feature of despised totalitarian dictatorships should be embraced by U.S. tax managers. Civilized countries do not use paid tax informants. An American Bar Association survey of sixteen other major Western countries found that only the United States had a system of paid tax informants.[13]

Invasion of Privacy

In a voluntary system of giving to worthy causes, each person is his own judge of what his fair-share contribution should be. In a tax system, on the other hand, the state sets the standards of giving, and state officials must enforce them by inspecting personal financial data that documents compliance with the tax code. In forcing people to give up data about themselves, the state is violating their privacy. Citizen privacy is also abridged by tax investigation and prosecution activities. Using both formal and informal sanctions, IRS agents force accountants to inform against their clients, they force bookkeepers to testify against their employers, and they force lawyers to reveal information about their clients.[14]

In recent years—in the name of enforcing the federal tax system—privacy has been broken down to a degree unimaginable even a generation ago. There are, by my best effort to count them, eighty-one specific types of personal information that third parties are required to report, under penalties of up to $100,000. These include the reporting of wages, dividends, interest, tax identifying numbers, foreign trusts, direct seller commissions, donated property, partnership interest, individual retirement accounts, retirement annuities, pensions, dividends amounting to less than $10, tips, oil production, and certain fishing boat crew members' share of fish caught.[15]

There are more fines to force payers to deliver this information promptly and on magnetic tape, so that it can be fed into IRS central computers. In 1988, the IRS acquired 913 million pieces of information, or about 9 for each taxpayer. IRS computers also link up with computers in the state tax enforcement agencies, pooling information. Now, even children are required to have Tax Identification Numbers, so that they are brought into the web of computer surveillance long before they reach the age of consent.

Significantly, this comprehensive system has not been adopted in any public, democratic way. There never has been a debate in the United States over whether to adopt a Big Brother tax enforcement system. As I explain in Chapter 11, the system has been implemented quietly and incrementally by a handful of tax administrators and senior members of congressional tax committees. As representatives of the culture of taxing these officials have aimed to enhance enforcement and collections, at the expense of many other values, including the citizen's right to privacy.

Arbitrariness

A key achievement in the history of government has been the development of the rule of law. This is the principle that the force of the state should be brought to bear according to universal rules that apply equally to everybody, not according to the subjective whim of an official. The advantage of the rule of law is that it makes official action predictable, and just: like cases are treated alike.

To a surprising extent, the federal tax system no longer adheres to the rule of law. At every level, officials are making arbitrary decisions that cause similar cases to be treated differently. One cause of this arbitrariness has been system overload. The tax system is now so complicated and so little respected that violations overwhelm it. Tax officials cannot possibly cope with all these transgressions; therefore, they must decide, on an arbitrary basis, which ones to pursue.

In Chapter 4, we saw how this overload undermines the judicial character of criminal tax prosecutions. Since the IRS catches hundreds of thousands of tax "cheats," it must use arbitrary and subjective criteria to treat a few of them as tax criminals and let the rest go, subject only to civil fines and penalties.

In the Tax Court, overload has led to a bargaining system whereby tax liabilities are adjusted on the basis of negotiation, not the rule of law. The Tax Court can decide only 700–800 cases a year, while tens of thousands of new cases enter the system every year. To unclog the court calendar, IRS lawyers offer deals to taxpayers to get them to drop their cases and pay a reduced amount of tax. For example, in estate tax, the IRS is willing to value shares in a closely held corporation at below their market value. One researcher who questioned estate tax lawyers reported, ''Our interviewees confirmed that the Internal Revenue Service regularly opens negotiations with discounts of 20–25 percent in minority interest situations and goes to 40 percent in settlements."[16] In the tax system, the value of many different kinds of assets is a function of how clever and persistent your lawyers are in bargaining with the IRS.

In other enforcement areas, overload has produced arbitrary practices of a statistical nature. For example, the collections division is unable to pursue all the overdue accounts; therefore, it separates cases into more and less lucrative. The cutoff point, which has been increased several times in recent years, is kept secret but appears to be around $500. If the delinquent taxpayer owes $499, he will get a series of threatening letters and then nothing will happen. But if he owes $501, he will get the threatening letters and then be subject to levy action.

The tax code itself embodies a massive departure from the principle of uniformity, from the principle that all citizens should be treated alike. Over the years, Congress has built exception upon exception into the tax code, until it has become common practice to write loopholes tailored for a single taxpaying entity. Tax law specialist Charles Adams summarizes the result: "The income tax law is so grotesquely lacking in uniformity that if this constitutional condition were ever applied, the whole tax law would be unenforceable."[17]

The demise of the rule of law may seem an abstract problem, but in the long run, it may be one of the most tragic consequences of the current overblown and mismanaged tax system. A tax system that operates on an arbitrary basis or at the behest of special interests will be seen as corrupt by citizens and will encounter their increasing opposition and resistance.

Abuse of Power

When a bureaucratic system departs from the rule of law, abuses of power become inevitable. Tax officials are given broad powers that they may exercise arbitrarily; being human, they sometimes use them for personal or partisan ends. For example, the official may harass a taxpayer with enforcement actions because he personally dislikes the taxpayer. Or the official may be bribed by one citizen to harass another. A case of this kind recently came to light in California, where one clothing manufacturer bribed IRS officials to institute a criminal prosecution against a competing firm.[18]

One factor that compounds the problem of abuse of power in the IRS is the reluctance of officials to take action to prevent it. This is a common problem in a law enforcement agency. Officials see themselves as an embattled "us" struggling against a law-breaking "them." When a taxpayer complains about mistreatment, the impulse is to side with the agent. Furthermore, all bureaucracies act to protect their image by covering up wrongdoing. A congressional committee looking into this problem in 1989 found a consistent pattern in the IRS of ignoring wrongdoing. Of twenty-five senior officials involved in recent bribery and information-selling scandals, only one was punished, and no one was prosecuted. The committee chairman concluded that instances of misconduct were not being brought out because of "a pervasive fear at all levels of the IRS over retaliation for the reporting of such misconduct; and a driving concern that publicly exposing wrongdoing by senior managers will tarnish the agency's public image and make its tax enforcement responsibilities more difficult."[19]

Infringement of Freedom of Speech

One abuse of power that tax officials have engaged in is to bring tax enforcement action against citizens expressing certain political views, thereby infringing upon their freedom of speech. Over the years, IRS enforcement has been directed against a number of both left- and right-wing political groups, from the National Council of Churches and the Fair Play for Cuba Committee to the Christian Anti-Communist Crusade and the Unification Church of the Reverend Sun Myung Moon (see box).[20]

The most consistent infraction of free speech occurs on the subject of taxation and tax policy. As just noted, IRS officials are defensive about their organization and their mission. In this respect, they are perhaps not unlike officials in the military or any other bureaucracy. But the difference is that the IRS alone holds levers of power and information over every citizen. If you speak out against the Department of Defense, or declare that war is wrong, there is very little the secretary of defense can do to punish you and deter others from doing the same thing. If you speak out against

An inside view of the 1982 conviction of the politically unpopular Reverend Sun Myung Moon on charges of tax evasion (for which he served a thirteen-month prison sentence):

Journalist Carlton Sherwood reports he was having drinks with two attorney friends who worked at the criminal division at the U.S. Department of Justice when the subject of Moon's Unification church came up.

What about the tax evasion and conspiracy case against Moon? I asked. Then they dropped the bomb.

"That was a bad case," one of the lawyers said.

"We never had a case," the other corrected. "All of the seniors in Tax [career, senior prosecutors in the Criminal Tax Division of the Justice Department] are still bitching about the prosecution which was forced down their throats. . . ."

Within hours I was pulling boxes of documents back out of the closet and reexamining records, particularly court files I had only given a glance to previously. To my utter astonishment and embarrassment, there they were, memos and letters authored by the Justice Department's own prosecutors, explaining in great detail why the government had no case against Moon or any of his followers.

In fact, the Justice Department's own chief of criminal tax prosecution not only argued strenuously against indictment but warned that if Moon was brought to trial on trumped-up tax evasion charges, the government might find itself in the embarrassing position of owing him a tax refund.

SOURCE: Carlton Sherwood, *Inquisition: The Persecution and Prosecution of the Reverend Sun Myung Moon* (Washington: Regnery Gateway, 1991), p. 12.

the Internal Revenue Service, or say that taxation is wrong, you are already in the grasp of the agency you are criticizing. The IRS has your tax return and it has powers to investigate and prosecute you without accounting to anyone for its action.

IRS officials monitor the media and identify individuals who criticize the tax system. These individuals may be placed on special lists and subjected to enforcement or surveillance.[21] The IRS also keeps lists of supposed tax protest organizations.[22] A seventeen-year-old boy who wrote a letter to the editor of a Buffalo newspaper on tax policy became the target of a fifteen-agent criminal investigation task force.[23] In Montana in 1978, the IRS district director announced that IRS agents would attend Montana taxpayer meetings, collect names, and run tax checks on those who attended. An Idaho man who published a letter in a local paper criticizing the growing burden of taxation was contacted by an IRS agent masquerading as a fellow tax critic. Using this deception, the IRS agent induced the man to turn over his tax criticism materials, and the IRS then investigated him.[24]

Sometimes, the IRS uses the information at its disposal to smear or undermine a critic. One of the most celebrated of such cases involved Senator Edward V. Long, whose Judiciary subcommittee investigated IRS abuses of power in 1966 and 1967. IRS officials leaked personal financial data about Long. This information wound up in a *Life* magazine story and probably was a main cause of Long's subsequent electoral defeat.[25] A similar case involved Idaho Republican congressman George Hansen, a severe critic of IRS abuses in the 1970s. In an effort to unseat him, local IRS officials leaked his personal tax record to newspapers and to his Democratic opponent.[26]

The harassment of critics of the tax system has a chilling effect on those who attempt to correct IRS abuses. Legislators are perhaps the most vulnerable, since they can ill afford the negative publicity that an IRS audit or investigation would bring. This point came out in the 1988 hearings on the Taxpayers' Bill of Rights (see box). One should not exaggerate the IRS intimidation, however. Many lawmakers have criticized the IRS with no ill effect.

Violation of Conscience

One reason why some people object to giving up their funds to tax collectors is that they feel that a particular government program is profoundly wrong or immoral, and it goes against their consciences to be implicated in it.

One program frequently objected to is military spending. Many individuals have protested against the tax system on the grounds that it makes them a party to war. In Chapter 5 we met Barbara

Intimidation of lawmakers by the IRS:

SENATOR PRYOR: Let me just ask you this one question, if I might. After your 1980 hearings, I hope you were not audited by the IRS. Were you, Senator Levin?

SENATOR LEVIN: I was not, but I must tell you I assumed I might be, given the history of some of our prior colleagues with the IRS. . . .

SENATOR PRYOR: Senator Levin, in the last several weeks I have visited informally with some of my colleagues, and I have said, ''You know, I hope you will really consider becoming a cosponsor of S. 604 [the Taxpayers' Bill of Rights]. We will send you all the information about what it does.'' And they say, ''You know, I really hope you have great success, but I don't know that I want to flag myself right now.'' That intimidation and fear of the Internal Revenue Service is present today in the Congress of the United States.

If we are intimidated or our colleagues are intimidated, just imagine what some of the very vulnerable small business people and small taxpayers of our country feel.

SOURCE: Senators David Pryor (D-Ark.) and Carl Levin (D-Mich.), *Taxpayers' Bill of Rights* (Hearings before the Subcommittee on Private Retirement Plans and Oversight of the Internal Revenue Service of the Committee on Finance, U.S. Senate, 100th Cong., 1st Sess., April 10 and 21, 1987), part 2, p. 10.

Rothacher, who suffered an IRS collection action because she withheld taxes in an effort to protest the Vietnam War. ''I was raised to feel responsible for my own actions or inactions,'' she explains. ''My tax dollars helped buy the gun used by Lt. Calley so am I not as guilty as he? How can a person of conscience survive in our day and age? There is simply no way to remain self supporting and not support war.''[27]

Another illustration of the same principle concerns abortion. If abortions or abortion counseling are governmentally funded, then the tax system forces individuals who consider abortion immoral to support the practice.

This criticism is sometimes answered by saying that without accepting the principle of involuntary participation, the funding of public activities would be impossible. This is not so. Any collective or public purpose, even war, can be funded on the basis of voluntary donations, whereby people give only to the causes they believe in. Perhaps a voluntary system would not bring in so much money; that may be an important consideration. We are simply observing that in turning to a coercive system—taxation—to raise funds, one cost is that it forces people to be implicated in activities that go against their consciences.

Congress has noticed this problem and made efforts to ease the burden involved. For example, the Amish believe that the Social Security system violates their creed and have refused to pay taxes into it. After decades of struggle, with the IRS repeatedly seizing the property of Amish farmers in attempting to enforce the tax laws, in 1965 Congress finally exempted them from the tax. Now, if you are Amish you don't have to pay Social Security taxes.

The Weakening of Voluntarism

One method of dealing with social and public problems is voluntarism, that is, to rely on funds given voluntarily by concerned citizens. Many advantages can be claimed for this approach. It involves citizens more closely in their own community's problems, and it cultivates the spirit of helpfulness.

For those who value voluntarism, the tax system poses some severe costs. First, all the funds taken from the public by the tax system are monies unavailable to be donated to charitable causes. Second, the tax system encourages an I-gave-at-the-office mentality. Having been forced to give to community needs through the tax system, citizens are less in the mood to give again to charities. Furthermore, they may feel that government is already addressing all social problems and that charitable giving is no longer needed.

Tax policy makers themselves agree on the harmful effects of the tax system on charitable giving and have, in consequence, established tax deductions for charitable donations. It is doubtful that these loopholes fully correct the problem, however. They taint charitable giving, turning it into a tax dodge instead of an expression of idealism. Furthermore, they make voluntary groups something of an extension of government, registered and regulated by the tax authority and dependent for funding on the tax code and its interpretation.

Promotion of Antisocial Attitudes

The last burden we will mention has to do with a rather subtle cultural issue. The tax system, as we have noted, is based on force. We know that, on a personal level, when one individual uses force to make another do something, this provokes a hostile and resentful attitude. The question is, Does the state's use of force in the tax system also generate hostile, antisocial attitudes?

This problem has been obscured in the United States by a strong tradition of tax idealism. In this perspective, public-spiritedness and community pride motivates citizens to contribute funds for the common welfare. When officials speak about the tax system as voluntary, this is the image they appeal to: a citizenry that *wants* to pay taxes and therefore doesn't need to be forced. This is the official position of the IRS, which declares in its *Annual Report* that "practically all Americans voluntarily report and pay their correct taxes. . . ."[28] In this perspective, the coercive aspect is needed only for the recalcitrant few, the "antisocial" individuals lacking in community spirit.

This idealistic view is not so farfetched as it sounds. Americans *are* public spirited. Over 90 million volunteer their time to help in their communities; voluntary giving for charitable and philanthropic purposes in this country tops $120 billion. The error in the tax idealism concept is that it fails to recognize that coercion undermines idealism. Suppose 99 people are contributing voluntarily to an organization like a church. What happens if we resort to the use of force to get one more person to contribute? At first, it may seem that we have not changed things very much. We still have 99 idealistic, voluntary contributors and just one unwilling, coerced donor. But soon the shadow of coercion falls on the other participants. They have to prove that they gave the "right" amount, which means they have to keep records, file returns, and defend themselves before examiners. Inevitably, the amount they want to give, on a voluntary basis, will conflict, even if slightly, with what the tax rules require. They have to be forced to comply, and in being forced, their motivation changes from idealism to self-protection.

In the long run, all tax systems lose their idealistic character. This, it seems, is what has happened in the United States. In an interview with an estate lawyer, I encountered a significant datum on this point. He estimated that he had dealt with 5,000 clients and prospective clients interested in estate and inheritance planning. From all these cases, he could recall only one where the clients actually wanted an inheritance arrangement that would include paying their fair share of estate tax. They were a husband and wife, both teachers in a state university all their lives, and they saw an obligation to support the government and its activities by contributing their taxes. The other 4,998 clients were all seeking to avoid estate taxes.

Another indication of the motivation of taxpayers is seen in the literature written by and for tax professionals. The treatments focus on techniques to reduce or avoid taxes. One seldom sees the position that taxes are needed to fund worthy community services and that it is therefore our duty to pay them cheerfully (see box).

A tax system may be set up with good intentions, but its actual operation would appear to have unhealthy effects on citizen attitudes. Take honesty. By making untrue declarations, the

---

The preface to a recent college textbook on federal taxes illustrates the selfish attitude toward the tax system that now prevails:

Your federal tax life is like a hockey game, with IRS guarding the goal while you try to score with your tax planning decisions. . . .

Of course, you can play the tax game on a strictly defensive basis. Then the best you can do is to stop IRS from scoring. That's the traditional approach to teaching taxes. Avoid this trap, sidestep that pitfall! Our approach to federal taxes goes beyond the defense, for the taxpayer can also take the initiative. Planning what happens is the taxpayer's competitive edge.

SOURCE: William L. Raby and Victor H. Tidwell, *Introduction to Federal Taxation*, 1987 ed. (Englewood Cliffs, N.J.: Prentice-Hall, 1986), p. ix.

taxpayer can often save himself a great deal of money. Further-more, these untrue declarations are not being made to a friend who merits trust but to a distant governmental authority that is using the threat of force to make the taxpayer answer. Especially if the tax system has lost its idealistic support, it can seem moral to lie to tax collectors. An income tax, especially, puts a strain on honesty, since it involves reporting many obscure, easily overlooked trans-actions. One of Will Rogers's best-known aphorisms was that "the income tax has made more liars out of the American people than golf has."

Lying induced by the tax system probably carries over, to some degree, into other realms. Once citizens have learned to lie from the tax system, where lying seems both profitable and moral, this argument goes, they will lie elsewhere: shoppers will cheat at stores, for example, and employers will cheat employees. One who made this encouragement-of-corruption argument against the income tax was the nineteenth-century British parliamentarian William Gladstone.[29]

It also seems that tax systems weaken sentiments of helpfulness and community spirit. A voluntary system of funding community purposes appeals to generosity, helpfulness, and duty and in this way reinforces these attitudes. In a tax system, the appeal—as idealism fades—is to force; and, of course, to be subject to force or the threat of force is an unpleasant experience. This negative reinforcement conditions citizens to be selfish and self-protective when community needs come knocking.

Our understanding of how and why social norms change is limited, and therefore firm conclusions about the tax system's effects on social attitudes are not possible. In a preliminary view, however, it does seem that the growth of the federal tax system has been associated with, and may well be a cause of, a growing self-centeredness in social attitudes.

Conclusion

The tax system is reached for, again and again, as the easy way to raise funds for worthy public purposes. Just about every com-munity service or need is addressed through it. Taxation, our public officials say, approvingly echoing Justice Oliver Wendell Holmes, is the price we pay for civilization.

The message of this book is that taxation is not an easy way to raise funds. It is very costly, costly not only in monetary terms but also, as this chapter shows, in emotional, cultural, and moral terms as well. The federal tax system is based on coercion. It encourages the use of force. It creates anxiety and stress. It violates civil rights, criminalizes a victimless crime, uses paid informers, invades privacy, abuses power, and infringes upon free speech. It departs from the rule of law. It compels violation of conscience. It undermines voluntarism, and it may even be weakening social attitudes of honesty and generosity.

Taxation may have been a minor nuisance in Oliver Wendell Holmes's day, in 1904, long before the adoption of the income tax. Now, grappling with a full-blown welfare state tax system, we are left pondering the converse of Holmes's dictum. Now we wonder whether civilization is what we pay for taxes.

✦ 10 ✦

Tax System Burdens:
Summary and Trends

USING THE DIFFERENT COSTS of the tax system detailed in the preceding chapters, we can now summarize the findings. The main monetary costs are displayed in Table 15. As the reader can see, these total $362.9 billion in 1985, or 65.01 percent of the available tax revenue collected.[1]

For many readers, this figure will seem surprisingly, even unbelievably, high. It should be noted that this result does not principally depend on my calculations and estimates. Its two main components, the overall economic disincentive cost and the total business compliance cost, are taken from other, highly regarded sources, the *American Economic Review* study and the Arthur D. Little study, respectively. For this latter study, I had to supply a figure for the hourly cost of business tax compliance work. This estimate, however, is a secure and defensible one: it is the literal per-hour employee cost experienced by tax compliance organizations.

These two components, the disincentive cost and the business compliance cost, amount to $258 billion, or more than two-thirds of the total shown in Table 15. The figures for the rest of the costs are perhaps more open to debate, since they depend on more approximate techniques of estimation. I believe that readers who

TABLE 15   Costs of the Federal Tax System, Summary (monetary costs, social cost basis, 1985)

Burden	Billions of dollars	As a percentage of available revenue collected
Compliance costs		
Businesses	102.3	15.68
Individuals	57.1	8.75
Enforcement costs		
Initial contacts	5.5	0.84
Tax litigation	3.4	0.52
Forced collections	4.0	0.61
Disincentives to production	155.3	33.20
Disincentive cost of tax uncertainty	12.0	1.84
Evasion and avoidance costs	19.3	2.96
Governmental costs	4.0	0.61
Total	362.9	65.01

NOTE: The figures in the second column are to be treated as marginal costs, while the total cost figures in the first column are based on average cost. See Chapter 10, note 1, for an explanation of the construction of this table.

follow how and why each estimate was made, however, will be satisfied that there is very little fat in the estimates and that, in many ways, they are extremely conservative.

It should also be remembered that not all of the monetary costs have been included in Table 15. This study has encountered some eleven other monetary costs, which, owing to the paucity of information, could not be estimated. Together, these could add something on the order of $50 billion to the figure given in Table 15.[2] Also omitted are the emotional, moral, and cultural costs noted in the preceding chapter. I have not attempted to put a monetary value to these, but efforts are possible in this direction. The anxiety the tax system creates, for example, represents a social cost just as much as the fear of crime or anxiety about cancer. By seeing how much people are willing to pay to lessen this anxiety—by purchasing audit insurance, for example—we could place a dollar value on this concern. Converting some of these emotional and moral burdens into monetary costs would greatly increase the figure shown in Table 15.

The proper interpretation of the 65 percent figure is that it is, at least roughly, a marginal cost figure. In other words, it indicates the cost of raising one additional dollar of tax revenue. It is important to recognize this point, to avoid making the error of assuming that tax system costs are fixed. When tax revenues increase, owing to higher tax rates or more taxpaying units (or both), tax system costs will increase along with them. The exact nature of this relationship is complex, owing to the many different types of costs going into the overall total. On balance, it appears serviceable to assume that tax system costs are proportional to tax revenues. This conclusion is explained in the Appendix, "Tax Rates and Tax System Costs."

Since tax system costs are roughly proportional to tax revenues, we can use the 65 percent figure given in Table 15 to estimate costs in different contexts. For example, it is reasonable to assume that each spending program should be assessed a proportional share of the tax system cost. If taxes are raised $10 billion to pay for another spending program, then an additional $6.5 billion in tax system costs is incurred.

A Half Century of Flawed Analysis

The fact that we are paying an additional 65 cents for every tax dollar collected and spent is a datum of great significance. As this finding is brought into our policies and analyses, it is bound to have a profound effect on how we think about government and government programs. To illustrate, it is useful to examine the implications of the tax system cost issue for one important topic in economics, the evaluation of government programs through the use of benefit-cost analysis.

Benefit-cost analysis is a way of deciding if government programs are worthwhile. The analyst is supposed to add up the monetary value of the benefits of the program and then divide this figure by the costs. If the resulting number is greater than one, it means that the benefits outweigh the costs. Since the 1930s, when it was first mandated in federal legislation, benefit-cost analysis of government programs has grown into a major branch of political economy. The federal government has spent enormous funds on such studies, studies that are accepted by congressmen, administrators, and journalists as scientific program evaluations.

All of these studies contain a serious flaw: they ignore the cost of raising government funds. When analysts compute the cost of the project or program, they start with the budgetary cost. In other words, they assume that a government dollar costs a dollar. In fact, as we have just seen, a government dollar costs $1.65, since there are overhead costs to running the tax system that collects the dollar. By ignoring this point, the analysts' calculations give government programs much higher benefit-cost ratios than are justified.

To take a typical example, consider the comprehensive benefit-cost analysis of the Job Corps program undertaken by the Mathematica company for the U.S. Department of Labor.[3] Through surveys and calculations, researchers determined that the social benefit of the Job Corps program was $7,399 per participant. This figure included value estimates of future earnings of corps members, reduced criminal activity and drug use, and other results of the program. (Being hired by the Labor Department to evaluate its own program, the authors bent over backwards to find benefits for the program.) Then the authors established that the budgetary costs of the program were $5,070 per corps member.[4] Using these figures, they calculated the benefit-cost ratio, as follows:

$$\frac{\text{program benefits}}{\text{program costs}} = \frac{\$7,399}{\$5,070} = 1.46$$

This was the basis for their conclusion that the Job Corps program "is a worthwhile public investment." They went on to say that the "Job Corps is an economically efficient use of public resources in the sense that the program provides a greater value to society than the value of the resources it consumes."[5]

This conclusion is incorrect, for it leaves out the social costs of running the tax system that collects the money to pay for the program. In order to have a Job Corps funded by government, people have to keep tax records, and fill out tax forms, and be subject to audits, and react in hundreds of other inefficient, burdensome ways to the tax system. A proper accounting of the cost of government programs must include these burdens. The cost figure of this study enables us to calculate a more realistic benefit-cost ratio for this program. Each dollar spent on the program actually costs society $1.65; therefore, the true social cost per corps member is $5,070 × 1.65 = $8,366. This gives us the following benefit-cost ratio:

$$\frac{\text{program benefits}}{\text{program costs}} = \frac{\$7,399}{\$8,366} = 0.88$$

Now we see, using the researchers' own methodology and figures, that the Job Corps is *not* a worthwhile public investment. It provides less value to society than the value of the resources it consumes.

This Mathematica study is not an isolated example. Ignoring tax system costs is the standard practice among benefit-cost analysts. In a recent, highly respected text on benefit-cost analysis, we find this declaration: "In the case of cash transfers, the usual convention is to regard the B/C ratio as unity."[6] In other words, if money is taken from A in taxes and given to B in the form of cash, we are to assume that there is no social gain or loss. Accepting this logic, generations of philosophers and politicians have embraced schemes of redistributing income, as if this were a harmless transaction that could only make society fairer.

Bringing the costs of the tax system into the picture exposes the social cost of income redistribution. In order to take a dollar from A in taxes, we impose a further burden of 65 cents in tax system costs. The true benefit-cost ratio of a simple cash transfer should therefore be calculated as follows:

$$\frac{\text{benefit}}{\text{cost}} = \frac{\$1.00}{\$1.65} = 0.61$$

(The actual benefit-cost ratio for a cash transfer will be even lower than this 0.61 figure, because there will be administrative costs and waste in disbursing the cash payments to the targeted beneficiaries.) By including tax system costs, we can mathematically demonstrate that the redistribution of wealth by government always involves a significant social cost. Redistribution by government may make society fairer by certain definitions, but it also definitely makes society poorer.

Benefit-cost analysis needs to be entirely reconstructed to incorporate the burden of the tax system. The government, which is paying for the studies, can promote this development. Congress or the Office of Management and Budget should require that all government-funded benefit-cost analyses include the cost of raising the governmental funds spent. Without this requirement, the public will be given—as it has been given for fifty years—studies that incorrectly overstate the value of government action.

Trends in Tax System Costs

The pattern of costs in a tax system is constantly changing, owing to evolutionary developments as well as deliberate modifications. To complete this study, it is useful to review the main trends.

The tax compliance burden has been increasing significantly over the past decade. Table 16 shows the computations made by the Arthur D. Little study for the years 1983–1985. These figures indicate a 25 percent increase in just two years. The IRS has taken over the Arthur D. Little data and methodology and has produced some altered estimates for 1983–1987, also given in Table 16. Knowing what we know about the pattern of distortion in IRS estimates, we can suppose that these figures probably understate the growth of the compliance burden.[7]

The 1986 tax reform act had offsetting effects on the compliance burden. It tended to reduce the compliance burden on certain low-income taxpayers. Between 1987 and 1988, some one million taxpayers stopped filing because their income put them below the income threshold, and some eight million used the standard deduction instead of itemizing deductions.[8] This easing of the compliance burden for the low-income taxpayers was also reflected in a leveling

TABLE 16   Indicators of Changes in the Tax Compliance Burden, 1980s

Tax year	Compliance burden, A. D. Little study (millions of hours)	Compliance burden, IRS recomputations (millions of hours)	Number of individual tax returns filed (millions)	Proportion of taxpayers using paid preparers
1981	—	—	95.4	41.4%
1982	—	—	95.3	44.2
1983	4,342	4,382	96.3	44.9
1984	4,973	4,714	99.4	45.5
1985	5,427	5,004	101.7	45.9
1986	—	4,916	103.0	46.6
1987	—	5,159	107.0	47.7
1988	—	—	109.7	47.0
1989	—	—	112.3	48.8

NOTE: Dash = not available.
SOURCES: Arthur D. Little, Inc., *Development of Methodology for Estimating the Taxpayer Paperwork Burden* (Washington, D.C.: Internal Revenue Service, June 1988), p. I-7; IRS recomputations: James T. Iocozzia and Garrick R. Shear, "Trends in Taxpayer Paperwork Burden," in Internal Revenue Service, *Trend Analyses and Related Statistics, 1989 Update* (Washington, D.C., 1989), p. 56; returns filed and use of paid preparers: Internal Revenue Service, *SOI Bulletin*, various issues.

off of preparer fees for this type of taxpayer. For example, the H & R Block average fee went from $20 in 1977 to $45.39 in 1985, a substantial jump even after one allows for inflation. By 1988, however, the H & R Block average fee had risen to only $49.21, an increase slightly less than inflation.[9]

For most taxpayers, and for businesses, however, the 1986 act had the opposite effect. This bill (and other 1980s legislation) resulted in large increases in tax compliance burdens: alternative minimum tax systems for both businesses and individuals, passive loss calculations, a host of layered depreciation systems and subcategories, and uniform capitalization of inventory, to name some of the major complexities. These changes are still being digested, as new regulations come out and tax practitioners struggle to learn them. For example, the first phase of the Treasury regulations implementing the passive activities provisions contained 268 pages that dealt with defining a "material participant" and another 100 pages defining (trying to define?) what constitutes an "activity."[10] The director of taxes of the Union Pacific Corporation, Robert T. Bonafide, concluded that the 1986 law made the corporate tax picture so complex that no IRS auditor would be capable of computing the "correct" tax for a company. "I am absolutely convinced," he declared, "that the examination process will result in chaos."[11]

A sign of this increased compliance burden is the jump in the preparer fees of the accounting firms that serve businesses and middle- and upper-income taxpayers. These fees, already increasing rapidly in the early 1980s, were given a substantial boost by the complexities of the 1986 tax act. This legislation spurred increases of preparer fees of 10 to 30 percent at smaller accounting firms and caused nearly a doubling of the fees of the major accounting firms.[12] A direct measure of the changing compliance burden for individuals comes from a 1989 study by Joel Slemrod and Marsha Blumenthal that can be compared with an earlier 1982 study (discussed in Chapter 2). They found that the average household spent 27.4 hours on taxes in 1989, a figure 26 percent higher than in 1982.[13]

Another indicator of the trend in the compliance burden is the proportion of taxpayers who seek the assistance of paid tax preparers. As shown in Table 16, this figure has risen significantly in the 1980s as more and more taxpayers are compelled by the complexities and confusions of the tax law to seek outside assistance.

The tax compliance burden has increased in another way: more tax returns are being filed. The increase in individual returns shown in Table 16 is over twice the rate of population growth.

The trend in enforcement costs is even more discouraging. Since the mid-1970s, the U.S. tax system has undergone a major transformation. As noted in Chapter 9, there are now some eighty-one financial reporting requirements that bring one billion pieces of information into IRS computers. Using these data, the IRS has greatly expanded its contacts with, and burdens upon, taxpayers in correcting tax returns, mail audits, nonfiling, and payment penalties. Although there has been a decline in the number of tax audits (Table 17) this does not reflect a lessening of pressure on taxpayers. As Table 17 also indicates, the number of employees in the examination division has increased substantially. What has happened is that returns have become so much more complex that auditors can do fewer of them. Fewer taxpayers are burdened with audits, but this gain is counterbalanced by the fact that the audits take longer to prepare for and last longer.[14]

A series that affords a useful picture of the trend in tax enforcement costs are the statistics on Tax Court cases, given in Table 17.

TABLE 17   Audits, Audit Personnel, and Tax Court Cases, 1940–1990: Tax Enforcement Trends

	Examinations	Employees in examination division	Tax Court cases received
1940–1949 (average)	—	—	3,797
1960	3,000,000	15,596	6,562
1965	3,303,000	19,854	6,842
1970	1,879,000	20,444	6,969
1975	2,172,000	26,386	11,206
1980	2,179,000	23,360	20,660
1985	1,459,000	24,798	49,142
1986	1,292,000	26,120	48,787
1987	1,296,000	29,243	43,496
1988	1,205,000	31,895	31,700
1989	1,144,000	31,315	31,850
1990	1,158,000	28,788	28,375

NOTE: Dash = not available.
SOURCE: Internal Revenue Service, annual reports, various years. Data for 1940–1949 Tax Court cases appears in *Annual Report of the Commissioner of Internal Revenue, Fiscal Year Ended June 30, 1950*, p. 55.

These cases are all generated by IRS enforcement actions and thus reflect enforcement pressures, as well as the degree of contentiousness and confusion in the tax system. The caseload peaked in the mid-1980s with a surge of tax shelter cases. Even discounting for this factor, there has been a sevenfold increase in this type of tax litigation over the past half-century.

Another picture of the growth in enforcement burdens in recent years is given by the comprehensive summary of penalties that the IRS began including in its annual reports in 1978 (see Table 18). This summary gives the penalties from all enforcement programs and hence reflects the overall incidence of enforcement contacts. The figures indicate that the number of penalties nearly doubled in the period 1978–1990. The number of taxpayers affected by these penalties is less than the number of penalties issued, since some taxpayers get more than one penalty, and some of the penalties are issued to "ghosts," erroneous computer entries that correspond to no real taxpaying entity. Adjustments for these factors might reduce the number of taxpayers involved to about half of the number of penalties, or about 14 million in 1990. The abatement rate is one indicator of the error level in the penalty programs.[15]

The statistics on levies and liens, shown in Table 18, indicate an astonishing rise in the rate at which the tax authority is bearing down on taxpayers. The number of levies—funds seized by the IRS—has nearly quadrupled and the number of liens has nearly tripled in just the past decade. As with the penalties, these figures involve some double counting and ghosts, and perhaps ought to

TABLE 18   Penalties, Levies, and Liens, 1978–1990: Tax Enforcement Trends

	Penalties assessed	Penalties abated	Abatement rate (percentage)	Levies	Liens
1978	15,390,687	1,426,326	9.3	444,912	348,480
1979	20,750,336	1,719,519	8.3	465,059	371,357
1980	19,593,765	2,028,717	10.3	611,000	445,000
1985	22,035,067	4,529,165	20.6	1,418,000	705,000
1986	22,913,557	4,331,979	18.9	1,617,000	767,000
1987	26,968,271	3,868,314	14.3	2,056,000	837,000
1988	26,589,303	3,562,997	13.4	2,153,000	838,000
1989	29,907,698	3,686,525	12.3	2,283,000	904,000
1990	29,677,206	3,741,656	12.6	2,631,000	1,114,000

SOURCE: Internal Revenue Service, annual reports.

be divided in half to reflect the number of taxpayers affected. Just as in the penalty realm, these increases in forced collections have been made possible by the computer-based enforcement systems the IRS now operates, systems that enable it to track taxpayer assets and accounts for enforcement purposes.

On the economic disincentive cost, most economists believe that the tax reforms of the 1980s did reduce the extent to which the tax system discourages work and investment. The most helpful changes in reducing the marginal excess burden of the tax system appear to be the lowering of the tax rate for higher incomes and the reduction of the tax rate on corporations. One study of the efficiency gain of the change in corporate tax rates of the 1986 act estimated that it accomplished a $31 billion gain in 1988 terms.[16] Other studies that have looked at the changes in tax rates for corporations and capital also support the idea that 1980s reforms increased efficiency.[17] A comprehensive analysis of the 1986 tax reform act by Jorgenson and Yun (discussed in Chapter 6) found that this legislation reduced the disincentive cost significantly.[18]

The overall picture of tax system costs, then, seems to indicate two offsetting trends in the 1980s: higher compliance and enforcement costs, and lower economic disincentive costs. The net effect would seem to leave the overall burden of the tax system at about the same level in 1990 as it was in 1985, that is, at about 65 percent of tax revenues collected.

Changing Attitudes toward the Tax System

In concluding this discussion of trends in the federal tax system, we should note what may be the most important trend of all: growing dissatisfaction. This frustration has several causes: burdensome complexities in the tax laws; overzealous, haphazard tax enforcement; frequent changes, which leave everyone unsettled and confused; a multitude of loopholes, which appear to be the product of corrupt congressional action; and, finally, questionable spending programs.

The importance of this last point should not be overlooked. It is wrong to treat the tax system as a structure independent of government spending. The public evaluates the tax system in terms of the spending programs it funds. If these programs seem needed and responsibly managed, then the tax system will have higher approval.

Unfortunately, this stricture has been largely ignored by the modern Congress, which has approved many questionable spending programs. In one nationwide poll in 1988, Americans were asked what proportion of tax monies they thought the federal government was wasting. The average answer was 46 percent.[19] Congress itself has not taken care to avoid the appearance of corruption. One example of this lapse is the spending congressmen have showered upon themselves in the form of pension benefits, staff, mailing privileges, and other perquisites. Though a tiny part of the budget, these expenditures undermine the legitimacy of the tax system. The manner in which Congress increasingly legislates spending programs for the benefit of specific groups further harms the tax system. Taxes are no longer seen as funds needed for comprehensive, national purposes but as part of a system of rip-offs operated by, and for, special interests.

This cynical view has become widespread; and it is held in elite, leadership circles as well as by the general public. For example, a former chairman of the president's Council of Economic Advisers, Herbert Stein, began a 1989 article in the *The Wall Street Journal* with this question and answer:

Q: What is a tax?

A: A financial burden levied by the government upon some citizens or residents of the country to provide benefits to others.[20]

An article appearing on the op-ed page of *The New York Times* expressed a similar sentiment. The writer was criticizing congressmen who pretended not to know that corruption was taking place in the Department of Housing and Urban Development: "Here's the great principle that Mr. Lantos and Mr. Frank, sitting in that hearing room in Washington, must pretend not to know: No American can get anything out of his Government unless he's rich enough to buy influence. All ordinary Americans know that."[21] The writer perhaps overstated what "all" ordinary Americans believe, but the underlying point is clear. Irresponsible spending programs generate cynical attitudes and weaken support for the tax system. The citizen has to ask himself, "If my tax monies are going to corrupt politicians and lobbyists, what duty do I have to pay them?"

A second cause of declining support for the tax system has been the complexities that Congress has thoughtlessly introduced into the tax code in recent years. Again, the criticism comes not just from the man in the street but from academics and tax specialists. Law professor Richard Doernberg, who declares that "The United States now has the most complex tax laws in the history of civilization," believes that the reason is "the process of buying and selling tax legislation." As Doernberg explains, "Status as a legislator confers on a politician the legal authority to help or hurt private interests through taxation. In exchange for being helped or for not being hurt, private interests will compensate legislators in a variety of ways."[22]

In testimony before a congressional committee, economist Richard Vedder stated the case against the tax system in forceful terms, calling the system "a complete mess" (see box). Political scientist John Witte, who also calls the system a mess, argues that the only hope for sound policy is to take control of tax policy away from Congress.[23] Brookings Institution tax experts Henry Aaron and Harvey Galper reach a similar judgment about congressional mismanagement of the tax system: "The U.S. tax system has become a swamp of unfairness, complexity, and inefficiency."[24]

One index of this complexity is the loss of certainty in the calculation of taxes. In recent years, *Money* magazine has held a

---

An economist evaluates the U.S. tax system:

If an enemy power bent on destroying our nation were somehow given the opportunity to devise our tax code with a goal of sapping the nation of its economic vitality, impairing the moral fiber of its people, wasting huge resources on unproductive administration, and causing division and frustration in its people, it could do little better than adopt our current Internal Revenue Code. . . .

The American tax system is a complete mess.

SOURCE: Statement of Richard Vedder, *Increasing Productivity and Administrability of the Tax Code* (Hearing before the Subcommittee on Oversight of the Internal Revenue Service of the Committee on Finance, U.S. Senate, 98th Cong., 2d Sess., September 17, 1984), p. 130.

contest in which fifty tax preparers, mostly certified public accountants, attempt to calculate the taxes for an upper-middle-class family with a rather complex tax situation. The results show that for this type of taxpayer, tax calculation today is essentially a lottery. In the 1991 test, the experts calculated tax bills ranging from $6,807 to $73,247, with 90 percent of the preparers coming up with tax bills deviating by more than 10 percent from the "correct" figure (of $18,724).[25] It is not surprising that citizens lose respect for a tax system that is so confused in its demands.

There is some evidence that the recent problems with the tax system have led to an increasing disposition to cheat on taxes. The Tax Compliance Measurement Program audits that the IRS has undertaken down through the years throw some light on this issue. These especially careful audits of a random sample of taxpayers are designed to reveal inaccuracies in tax returns. A simple method enables us to calculate the proportion of intentional tax understatement from the results of these audits. A test audit performed in 1949 indicated a deliberate understatement proportion of 20.5 percent. In the TCMP audit of 1985, the deliberate understatement proportion appeared to be 37.25 percent.[26]

Another indicator of attitudes toward the tax system is the public's evaluation of the Internal Revenue Service. In recent years, the Roper Organization has conducted a survey of public attitudes toward federal government agencies, including the IRS. Not surprisingly, the IRS comes out with the least favorable rating. The time series, depicted in Figure 1, shows a rather erratic pattern; but, overall, it indicates that the proportion of respondents reporting a negative attitude is increasing.

Does the IRS have a future?

When linear regression analysis is performed on the seven data points shown in Figure 1, it yields the following equation (R^2 = .32):

% with negative opinion = 1.25 (year) − 2438

This equation projects 100 percent negative opinion toward the IRS in the year 2030.

FIGURE 1   Trend in Negative Rating of the Internal Revenue Service

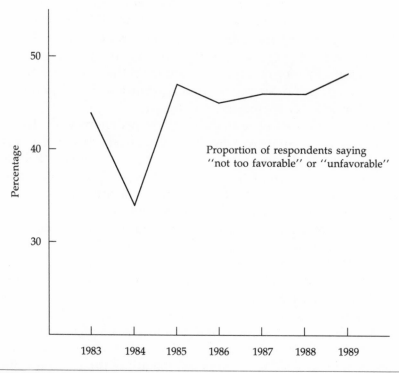

SOURCE: Figures for 1983–1987 courtesy of the Roper Center, Storrs, Conn.; figures for 1988 and 1989, courtesy of the Roper Organization, New York.

The federal tax system faces a number of difficult problems, none of which will be easy to repair: growing complexity, growing IRS enforcement pressures against taxpayers, growing resistance and evasion, and declining public support. These difficulties form a set of vicious circles with each problem contributing to the others. Given the mounting negatives, one begins to wonder whether the tax system can continue much longer without some major changes in direction.

✦ 11 ✦

The Culture of Taxing

IF ANTS ATTEMPTED TO EXPLAIN why so many of their kind are stomped on by elephants, it is almost certain they would miss the correct explanation. Important to themselves, ants would assume they are important to elephants. If they are stepped on, they would reason, it must be because the elephants intend to harm them.

Many taxpayers make this kind of mistake about the tax system. They assume that since tax regulations and procedures lay such a heavy burden on them, it must be because the officials who control it intend to abuse taxpayers. The actual explanation for much of this burden, however, is simpler: To a remarkable degree, tax policy makers are unmindful of taxpayers and their problems. They are like the elephants who simply do not see the ants.

This observation may at first seem puzzling, since it flies in the face of the American theory of government. The U.S. system is supposed to be democratic. Elected representatives are supposed to be attentive to the wants and cares of citizens. In theory, not one dot on one *i* should go into the tax code unless a majority of citizen-taxpayers approves of it. Unfortunately, it doesn't work this way. Citizens lack the time, motivation, and expertise to communicate successfully with their representatives on most issues. On a few points where there has been great publicity and the issue has taken the form of a single, simple question, a degree of democratic communication will take place. At any one time, there are but a few of these highly visible questions, which we can call conspicuous issues. On these issues, democracy can be said to "work," at least in an approximate way.

What is overlooked, however, is that conspicuous issues constitute a tiny fraction of the decisions made by government, especially in the modern era. Day by day, thousands of nonconspicuous issues are being resolved, and these decisions together make up most of what government does. On these decisions there is, for all practical purposes, no citizen input whatsoever.

I first realized the importance of this point several years ago when I studied how federal spending matters are decided in Congress. Although a few spending issues become conspicuous questions, most of them do not. They are dealt with in a quiet, routine process that is dominated by government officials themselves. In the appropriations committee hearings, for example, the main witnesses are the government administrators giving encouraging reports of their programs and presenting the need for more funds.

Who comes to Congress to counterbalance these prospending voices? Who comes to describe the waste, harm, and unfairness of the spending? Almost no one at all! There may be millions of citizens upset about spending, and many quite knowledgeable about abuses of specific programs, but they do not contact their representatives about it, not on the thousands of nonconspicuous spending issues that make up the bulk of the budget. The result is that congressmen are left immersed in a "culture of spending," a one-sided environment that indoctrinates them in favor of spending programs.[1]

As I began to study tax administration, I realized that much the same thing happens in the tax realm. Except in rare instances when a tax regulation becomes a conspicuous issue, there is virtually no input from taxpayers or critics of the tax system. The policy process is dominated by tax officials who impose their perspectives on tax committee congressmen and their staffs. The result is a "culture of taxing," a one-sided environment that emphasizes the government's collection of revenue and downplays or even ignores the burdens and frustrations of citizen-taxpayers.

We can see this one-sided pattern in the hearings of the tax committees. Table 19 shows the breakdown of the witnesses who

TABLE 19   Witnesses at Congressional Tax Administration Hearings,
House Ways and Means Subcommittee on Oversight, 1987–1988

Officials from the Internal Revenue Service	17
Officials from the General Accounting Office	12
Past IRS commissioners	6
Officials from the U.S. Tax Court	6
Representatives from the American Institute of Certified Public Accountants and other CPA organizations	3
Representative from the American Bar Association, Tax Section	1
Representative from the National Treasury Employees Union	1
Member of the House of Representatives	1
Total	47

SOURCE: Compiled from the four hearings of the Subcommittee on Oversight of the Committee on Ways and Means, U.S. House of Representatives: *Internal Revenue Service Operations* (February 6, 1987); *Administration's Fiscal Year 1988 Budget Proposals Relating to the Internal Revenue Service* (April 23, 1987); *1988 Tax Return Filing Season* (February 23, 1988); *Administration's Fiscal Year 1989 Budget Proposals Relating to the Internal Revenue Service and the U.S. Tax Court* (April 13, 1988).

appeared at the most important congressional tax administration body, the oversight subcommittee of the House Ways and Means Committee, in four ordinary hearings over a two-year period. It is revealing to see who testifies at these hearings. The largest group of witnesses is IRS officials. As pointed out in many places in this book, the IRS orientation is to stress raising more revenue through more tax enforcement and to ignore the burden of this increased enforcement on citizens.

The same one-sidedness appears in the next most important group of tax witnesses, officials from the General Accounting Office. The GAO is Congress's independent investigating agency, charged with producing objective and authoritative reports on governmental activities. The GAO has a large tax section. Every year it produces dozens of tax-related studies, and its officials testify many times before congressional committees on tax matters. When it comes to tax compliance and enforcement, the GAO bias is consistent and pronounced: enforcement is stressed and taxpayer burdens are downplayed.

One illustration of this bias is the absence of taxpayer burden studies. The GAO has made hundreds of studies of tax administration issues down through the years, but, as far as I have been able to determine, it has never made a single study of the burden of any compliance or enforcement procedure on taxpayers. Another indication of the bias is its yield-cost estimates for enforcement procedures. Like the IRS, the GAO *never* includes the burdens on citizen-taxpayers as as a cost in these calculations and estimates. The GAO has become, in effect, a lobby urging the IRS to put more pressure on taxpayers. In its 1988 tax studies, for example, the GAO made a total of thirteen recommendations to enhance IRS enforcement and surveillance of taxpayers, every one of which would have added to taxpayer burdens in time, money, and frustration.[2] It made not a single recommendation to scale back an enforcement or compliance activity for the purpose of reducing an enforcement or compliance burden on the public.[3]

These two groups of witnesses, IRS officials and GAO officials, dominate opinion formation on tax administration in Congress. Their impact is enhanced by several other participants who reinforce their orientation. One group that congressmen listen to with respect are former IRS commissioners, who, for the most part, have the same perspective of emphasizing revenue raising and ignoring burdens on taxpayers. Typical is this declaration of Donald C. Alexander, commissioner from 1973 to 1977, made in a 1988 hearing:

> It is good to see a long-overdue substantial increase in the Internal Revenue Service Budget. At last the Administration is viewing the Internal Revenue Service as a profit center, which indeed it is. Adding to IRS resources can result in four to seven dollars, or more, of additional revenue collected for every dollar spent.[4]

Because they overlook the economic burdens of their activities on taxpayers, tax officials tend to see enforcement measures as mere marketing devices, a way to increase the revenues of this ''profit center." Alexander urged the committee to add "new and greatly increased penalties" to the system—which had already increased penalties from 13 in 1954 to 150 in 1988.[5]

Another group of spokesmen in the tax administration picture are the representatives of the tax practitioner organizations, especially the American Institute of Certified Public Accountants (with some 240,000 members) and the Tax Section of the American Bar Association (with some 30,000 members). One might suppose that since these practitioners represent taxpayers in their struggles against government, their spokesmen would uphold the taxpayer position.

This tends not to be so. These organizations tend to support the IRS in its efforts to pressure taxpayers. For example, in the 1987 hearing included in Table 19 at which these representatives appeared, both the ABA and AICPA urged expanded IRS enforcement efforts in examinations, collections, delinquent returns, and document matching. Neither group made any mention of the additional burdens these programs would entail for taxpayers.[6]

Why are tax practitioners reluctant to champion the cause of the taxpayer? Part of the problem is that tax practitioners benefit from citizen compliance burdens. When the IRS raises the frustration level of taxpayers, through the use of more penalties and expanded enforcement techniques, this pressure translates into more business for tax practitioners. Even error-prone document-matching programs create snafus for practitioners to unravel. This is not to say that tax practitioners in general are unconcerned about taxpayer burdens. Privately, many of them are disturbed by the waste and folly of the system. But ordinary accountants and lawyers do not come to Congress on a regular basis to testify. They are, like the rest of us, citizens who tend to their own affairs. They are spoken for by their organizations in Washington, and these organizations accentuate, as pressure groups often tend to do, the self-interest orientation of their members.

What is most striking in this picture of the witnesses at the typical congressional tax administration hearing is who is *not* there, namely, the taxpayers. Even though they constitute a force of over 100 million citizens, tens of millions of whom are distressed, even outraged by the operation of the tax system, not one appeared to tell a tale of woe to the committee in charge of tax administration. Furthermore, there were no representatives of taxpayer organizations present to urge Congress to lower compliance and enforcement burdens.

The taxpayer position did not go entirely unmentioned in these four hearings, however. Two of the forty-seven witnesses did raise some concerns about the compliance burden. Representative Constance A. Morella (R-Md.) appeared to criticize the "fearsome" complexity of the new W-4 form; and one former IRS commissioner, Mortimer Caplin, warned about the proliferation of penalties and the antagonism this generates among taxpayers. Including these two statements in the picture, and finding the Tax Court witnesses and two others neutral on the subject of taxpayer burdens, we have this overall picture of the balance of testimony in these four hearings:

witnesses urging increased enforcement and surveillance pressures, ignoring the burdens of these pressures on taxpayers	37
witnesses neutral on the subject of taxpayer compliance or enforcement burden	8
witnesses urging consideration of enforcement or compliance burdens on taxpayers	2

This tabulation shows that the antitaxpayer message outweighed protaxpayer communications by nearly twenty to one. It is not surprising that most congressional tax committee members, exposed to this one-sided persuasion, absorb the IRS view. They become committed to the revenue enhancement approach to tax administration and tend to forget the burdens that enforcement measures entail in anxiety, time, and money for those on the receiving end.

Another group on Capitol Hill that tends to reinforce the IRS slant are the staff members of the various tax committees. These staffs have grown to enormous size in recent years: the House Ways and Means Committee has a professional staff of over eighty; the Senate Finance Committee has nearly forty; and the Joint Tax Committee, composed of senior members of the aforementioned committees, has over fifty. A former staff director of the Oversight Subcommittee of the House Ways and Means Committee explained how staffers become socialized by their continuous interaction with IRS officials: "Almost all of the time, we relied on information given to us by the IRS, hardly an unbiased source. Then, as the months go by, you get used to working with the agency's congressional liaison people and you begin to develop institutional and personal ties with them."[7]

Like the researchers in the General Accounting Office, congressional tax committee staffers have very little direct contact with taxpayers—and they don't suppose that such contact is important in doing their jobs. This came out in my study of one recent piece of antitaxpayer legislation, the move to extend the statutory collection period from six to ten years (see box). I asked a staff member

---

Extending the tax collection period: Did anyone consult the taxpayer?

The 1990 extension of the statutory collection period (from six years to ten) is a textbook illustration of how tax administration policy is now made. The measure injures taxpayers because it lengthens the period during which they suffer the uncertainty of not knowing when or how the IRS will pursue an old tax dispute. Since large numbers of these stalemated cases reflect IRS errors, legal ambiguities, and changed conditions (such as death or bankruptcy) that make the tax debt moot, there is a social gain in having a relatively short statutory collection period, allowing taxpayers to leave old disputes behind and get on with their lives.

There is no sign that this point of view ever entered the policy-making process. The measure, adopted in response to GAO prompting, was folded into the giant Omnibus Budget Reconciliation Act of 1990. No hearings were held on the measure, there was no debate about it in either house when it was passed, and no press comment. When I asked a Senate staffer handling the measure if there had been any outside input at all, he recalled that the Senate Finance Committee had received "one or two" letters. These he dismissed out of hand as being from "tax protesters." (To Washington officials of the culture of taxing, citizen anger about the tax system denotes citizen irresponsibility. Overlooked is the possibility that anger might be a sign of truly outrageous flaws in the system.)

of the Senate Finance Committee what effort was made to contact taxpayers to get their views. "None," he replied. "We don't usually contact taxpayers in any way to find out about their reactions to a particular clause. We just contact people in the area [that is, Washington tax system insiders]."[8]

The cumulative effect of the pro-IRS view that surrounds members of Congress is especially noticeable on senior legislators. Their commitment to this perspective can mean that they would rather avoid hearing taxpayers' complaints at all. It is significant to note, in this regard, that at the occasional hearings held by Congress to explore taxpayer burdens and IRS abuses, the senior congressmen stay away. Hearings of this kind are attended by relatively junior members and usually take place in committees other than the tax committees. The only case I have encountered where a senior member of a congressional tax committee attended a hearing on taxpayer burdens was the exception that proves the rule. It concerned a session of Senator David Pryor's (D-Ark.) subcommittee that was taking testimony on the 1988 Taxpayers' Bill of Rights. Senator Lloyd Bentsen (D-Tex.), the most senior Democrat on the full Finance Committee, and its chairman, was absent during the sessions in which witnesses came to describe IRS abuses. But at the April 21, 1987, session, Bentsen appeared. The only witness was a man Bentsen introduced as his "friend," IRS Commissioner Lawrence Gibbs, who appeared to defend the IRS and explain why the Taxpayers' Bill of Rights was unnecessary.[9]

When the Public Awakes

In broad terms, policy on tax administration is normally made by a small group of tax system insiders: IRS, Treasury, and GAO officials and the senior tax committee congressmen and their staff. In the overwhelming majority of instances, the tax administration clause, provision, or regulation is designed by IRS, Treasury, or GAO officials and is inserted into the legislation by the like-minded members of Congress. No one else, in Congress or outside it, has much to do with it, or even knows about it. Policy in this system is normally made so quietly that it is impossible for outsiders to see what is happening. All one sees are tax and budget laws containing hundreds of provisions, and reams of regulations, presumably consistent with these laws, issued by Treasury tax officials.

Every so often, however, a point of tax administration becomes a conspicuous issue, with interest groups making noise about it, with press comment on the subject, and with some constituents writing their congressmen. These cases are worth examining, because they illustrate how weak the culture of taxing is whenever tax policy making approaches an open, democratic pattern. They also illustrate how out of touch tax officials and senior tax congressmen are from the concerns of ordinary American taxpayers.

Interest and Dividend Withholding, 1982–1983

For many years, IRS and GAO officials had urged Congress to adopt measures to force payers of interest and dividends to withhold some of these funds and send them to the IRS.[10] Such a measure would give the IRS an enforcement advantage. Instead of having to track down taxpayers who had not paid taxes on interest and dividends, the IRS would start with the money, and the taxpayer would be forced to take action to get it back if it wasn't owed. As usual, the IRS failed to consider the monetary and psychological burdens of this measure to the private sector: the compliance burden on financial institutions and other payers, the confusion and litigation over proper implementation, evasion and avoidance costs, the denial of the sense of security in savings, and the invasion of privacy.

This withholding measure was one of many revenue enhancement proposals that officials from IRS, the Treasury, and the GAO had been advocating. In 1982, the Reagan administration, seeking ways to balance the budget without raising taxes, hit upon these proposals. These new enforcement requirements and penalties were incorporated into the 1982 tax act, which the administration strongly endorsed (see box on page 172). The interest- and dividend-withholding provision, however, ran into opposition. Some members of Congress realized how onerous this measure would be and tried to have a vote on it. In 1982, however, there had not been enough public attention to the matter. The tax committees prevailed in both House and Senate: they kept the issue buried in the comprehensive 1982 bill and refused to allow it to be examined and voted on separately. So it was approved when the entire bill was passed (see box on page 172).

Who approved Big Brother?

It is something of a surprise to discover that the Reagan administration did more to tighten the enforcement screws on U.S. taxpayers than any prior administration, pressing for the adoption of a flood of new penalties and reporting requirements, greatly expanding computer surveillance and enforcement programs, and supporting a 30 percent increase in IRS personnel.

This administration overlooked the points that (a) *every* surveillance or enforcement action entails a burden for the taxpayer and (b), since large numbers of errors are committed in all enforcement programs, these programs *always* entail abuses of many innocent taxpayers. Rather than being a painless way to raise revenues without raising taxes, enhanced enforcement generally represents a burden on taxpayers greater than an increased tax.

A congressman points out, during the debate on the 1982 tax bill, that the practice of passing massive bills with unexamined clauses contradicts democratic theory:

Most of the provisions in this bill have not been subject to hearings in either body. Most of the Members of this House had no opportunity even to see its 400 pages until just the day before yesterday. This is no way to legislate. . . .

No longer are Americans given the opportunity to be heard on matters which gravely affect their lives. No longer does legislation get careful study by the committees that have relevant expertise. Indeed, legislation of the most profound importance to this Nation is thrown together hastily, without study, put in omnibus bills and we are asked to vote on them as a package, without study, without hearings, without even the opportunity of the elected Representatives of the people to vote up or down on their various provisions.

SOURCE: Representative Richard Ottinger (D-N.Y.), *Congressional Record*, August 19, 1982, pp. H6549–50.

In the months that followed the passage of the 1982 act, however, financial institutions mounted a lobbying campaign against the measure. Savers wrote to their congressmen to complain about the withholding provision, and the media gave the issue some attention. The result was that in 1983, the provision for dividend and interest withholding was repealed by overwhelming majorities in both houses.

The episode illustrates how the tax insiders generally uphold the antitaxpayer position in Congress. In a critical 1982 House vote to prevent the dividend-withholding provision from being considered separately, members of the House Ways and Means Committee voted twenty-three to five to prevent a public vote. The rest of the House was slightly in favor of opening up debate on the question. The following year, it took a discharge petition, signed by a majority of House members, to compel the Ways and Means Committee to report the repeal provision so members could vote on it.[11]

The interest- and dividend-withholding provision is a thing of the past. But many other burdensome enforcement and compliance provisions of the 1982 tax act are fully incorporated into the current tax system. No one noticed them, no one complained about them, and the culture of taxing therefore had its way.

Automobile Logs

This issue closely resembled the withholding case. IRS officials argued that taxpayers who used their cars for both business and personal use were overdeducting automobile expenses. If taxpayers were forced to keep detailed, contemporaneous logs that accounted for each mile the car was driven, there would be less abuse. Once again, tax officials had made highly biased calculations about the additional tax revenue this compliance measure would generate; and, again, they ignored the burdens of this measure on taxpayers. These included the nuisance and compliance costs of keeping detailed logs, and the evasion and falsification they would almost certainly impel.

The auto log requirement was completely unnoticed when it was approved, in the 1984 Deficit Reduction Act. Apparently not one word was spoken pro or con on this issue when this legislation was considered, and the overall tax package that contained it was approved by overwhelming majorities in both the House and the Senate. After it became law, groups of self-employed people and small businessmen mounted a lobbying campaign against it; and the following year the auto log requirement was repealed, by a vote of 421 to 1 in the House and 92 to 1 in the Senate.[12]

A case like this opens an interesting question in democratic theory. What was the will of the electorate in this instance? In 1984, when nobody was taking any notice, the auto log requirement slipped through, approved by huge majorities. When some public comment and agitation brought the issue to the attention of members of Congress in 1985, they reversed their position. It seems clear that in the 1984 approval of the measure, democracy had nothing to do with it. It was an administrative action inserted into the legislation with the complicity of a few senior tax committee members and blindly approved by congressional majorities.

Automobile logs were defeated, but it should be noted that the 1984 Deficit Reduction Act contained many other tax compliance and enforcement measures, such as a measure that prevented simplified depreciation practices for small businesses and a measure that provided for burdensome quarterly payments of alternative minimum tax. These measures were not defeated. They went straight from tax administrators, courtesy of the culture-of-taxing legislators, into law. And today's tax system is more burdensome and costly because of them.

Section 89

Since many employee fringe benefits, especially pensions, are tax-exempt, tax officials are concerned that tax revenue is being lost through the provisions. If these exemptions are made harder to qualify for, the theory is, they will be used less. These points were the genesis of legislation approved as part of the 1986 tax act, that became Section 89 of the tax code. As it was to be implemented, all businesses with tax-exempt benefit plans would have to apply a complicated series of eligibility and benefit tests to their plans and file cumbersome reports certifying that the criteria were met.

As businesses began to grapple with the new regulations, they learned that the compliance burden was staggering: for a typical large company, costs of $300,000 to begin the record-keeping systems, and $100,000 each year thereafter.[13] Furthermore, the regulations were so extensive and ambiguous that they promised to provide an endless source of disputes and litigation.[14] Business organizations mounted a campaign for repeal of the regulations and, in September 1989, succeeded. Congress struck down Section 89.[15]

As with the interest-withholding provision, it was the House Ways and Means Committee that endorsed this burdensome compliance measure; and it was this committee and its chairman, Dan Rostenkowski, that had to be compelled by the rest of the House to accede to repeal. As with the withholding provision and the log book issue, the vote to repeal the onerous tax provision was overwhelming. Indeed, in the case of Section 89, the policy-making lapses were particularly flagrant. The measure was drafted by two Treasury officials, one of whom later admitted that no one had "fully assessed the real administrative difficulties that would be imposed on business." Not a single congressman sponsored the measure and no hearings on it were ever held. It was simply tucked into the giant 1986 tax act by Ways and Means Committee Chairman Rostenkowski, with most members of Congress being unaware of its existence.[16]

A Test of the Socialization Theory

Our review of the tax policy-making process suggests that members of Congress come to adopt the tax administrators' position by being exposed to their one-sided persuasion. If such a process of indoctrination is taking place, it follows that the legislators most affected will be members of the tax committees, and especially the senior members, who have had the longest exposure to the persuasion. This theory can be tested by examining legislative voting behavior on those roll call votes that clearly pit tax administrators against taxpayers. Such votes are rare, since, as we just noted, tax administration provisions seldom come to congressional attention as debatable issues. Examining the tax legislation of the 1980s, I have been able to find four roll call votes in the Senate bearing on tax administration that permit a preliminary test of the socialization idea.[17] According to this theory, Senate Finance Committee members should be more pro-IRS than other senators, and the more senior Finance Committee members especially so.

Table 20 shows the results of this test. Each Senate Finance Committee member is given a score of 1 for voting with the IRS position that emphasized enforcement or compliance and increased the burden on taxpayers, 0 for voting against the IRS position and in favor of taxpayers, and a score of 0.5 for abstaining or not voting. As the reader can see, the more senior members of the Finance Committee, those at least in their second terms at the time of the first (1982) vote, are the most pro-IRS, followed by the less senior members who, in turn, are more pro-IRS than senators who are not on the Finance Committee.[18]

TABLE 20   Pro-IRS Voting on Compliance and Enforcement Measures, Senate Finance Committee, 1982–1986

Senator	Year of entry	Interest withholding 1982	Tip income estimation 1982	Employee auto use 1985	Auto logs 1986	Total score
Senior committee members (over one full term in 1982)						
Long (D-La.)	1948	0	0	1	1	2.00
Packwood (R-Ore.)	1969	1	1	1	0	3.00
Dole (R-Kans.)	1969	1	1	1	0	3.00
Roth (R-Del.)	1971	1	1	1	0	3.00
Bentsen (D-Tex.)	1971	0	0	1	1	2.00
Danforth (R-Mo.)	1976	1	1	1	1	4.00
Chafee (R-R.I.)	1976	0	1	1	0	2.00
Average pro-IRS score, senior committee members (N=7)						2.71
Junior committee members (less than one full term in 1982)						
Heinz (R-Pa.)	1977	1	0.5	1.0	0	2.50
Matsunaga (D-Hawaii)	1977	0	0	0	1	1.00
Moynihan (D-N.Y.)	1977	0	0	0.5	1	1.50
Wallop (R-Wyo.)	1977	1	1.0	0	0	2.00
Durenberger (R-Minn.)	1978	1	0	0.5	0	1.50
Baucus (D-Mont.)	1978	0	0	0	0	0
Armstrong (R-Colo.)	1979	1	1.0	0.5	0	2.50
Boren (D-Okla.)	1979	0	1.0	0	0	1.00
Bradley (D-N.J.)	1979	1	0	1.0	1	3.00
Pryor (D-Ark.)	1979	0	0	0	0	0
Mitchell (D-Maine)	1980	0	0	1.0	1	2.00
Grassley (R-Iowa)	1981	1	1.0	1.0	0	3.00
Symms (R-Idaho)	1981	1	1.0	0	0	2.00
Average pro-IRS score, junior committee members (N=13)						1.69
Average pro-IRS score, rest of senators (N=80)						1.46

NOTE: 1 = pro-IRS, antitaxpayer vote; 0 = anti-IRS, protaxpayer vote; 0.5 = abstention or absence. See text and note 17 for a description of the issues voted on.

We should note in passing that the existence of this socialization process is an important argument for limiting the terms of members of Congress. Prolonged service on tax committees tends to make legislators overly susceptible to the arguments of IRS, Treasury, and GAO officials and therefore less mindful of the taxpayers they are supposed to represent.

Conclusion

The culture of taxing is, I believe, the main explanation for the large compliance and enforcement burdens in the U.S. federal tax system. The system is largely the domain of tax administrators and their congressional allies, who tend to undervalue the cares and concerns of taxpayers. Their isolation from the nation and its economic life have led them to adopt an enforcement mentality that results in a host of burdensome provisions and practices.

Sometimes, the shortcomings of these policy makers go beyond bias and border on irresponsibility. For example, the system includes tax officials and GAO researchers who, in their calculations of the costs of compliance and enforcement measures, never count the burden on taxpayers. The policy-making system includes tax committee leadership in Congress that does not permit public examination and discussion of the far-reaching legislation it urges Congress to adopt.[19] And, finally, it involves ordinary congressmen who, as is evident from their dramatic flip-flops in voting, are approving legislation they know nothing about.

Any reform to correct the harmful effects of the culture of taxing must take this irresponsibility into account. It will not be enough merely to tell the tax policy-making community in Washington that it has forgotten about taxpayers. The burdens of the tax system on the public must be projected so clearly that even careless, distracted policy makers cannot miss the point.

In the next chapter, I outline a proposal that, I believe, meets this requirement.

✦ 12 ✦

Making Taxpayers Count

POLITICIANS AND POLITICAL SYSTEMS gravitate toward the imposition of hidden costs. Cynical observers will say this is because politicians are out to hoodwink the public for selfish ends. A more charitable view is that politicians tend to be shortsighted; they lack interest in looking beyond surface manifestations. For them, costs that are out of sight are simply out of mind.

When it comes to taxation, the disposition to ignore hidden costs is especially pronounced. Politicians focus their attention on spending, on the good things they wish to do with government monies. The harm that is done in raising the funds is out of sight. This presents reformers with a difficult task: how can policy makers be made to take the costs of the tax system into account? How can they be led to remember the taxpayers?

The question is a policy issue of critical importance. The costs of the federal tax system, according to the calculations of this study, are 65 cents for every dollar of revenue collected. That is, in addition to the taxes Congress thinks it is levying upon the American people, it is imposing another burden equal to 65 percent of that. And this is only the monetary cost. The tax system imposes additional costs of a psychological, social, and moral nature.

To ignore these costs sets the stage for a destructive vicious circle. As more and more taxpayers resent these costs, their disposition to cooperate goes down. Tax administrators are tempted to

179

redouble surveillance and coercion in an effort to maintain compliance, taking us ever closer to a repugnant tax police state. Such a system, in turn, will lead to still more citizen resistance. Ultimately, the conflict will resemble an undeclared war between citizens and their government.

All Government Is Government by Insiders

The usual approach to correcting gaps in the policy-making process is to create some type of board, council, or commission. If X has gone unrepresented in the policy-making process, the theory goes, then we need a body specifically charged with noticing X. If tax system costs have been ignored, then why not create a body—in Congress, in the Office of Management and Budget, or in the Department of the Treasury—to speak out on the subject?

The error in this approach is that it treats symptoms, not causes. If a particular policy perspective has been overlooked in Washington, it is because the motives for its expression are weak. The creation of an additional political entity does not change those motives. What is likely to happen is that the same people with the same perspectives will control this new entity.

Imagine, for example, that we created a Tax System Cost Commission, charged with informing the rest of the government about the burdens of the tax system. Who would constitute the members and staff of this commission? Unless we took special precautions, the commission would be filled with well-indoctrinated members of the culture of taxing. These are the IRS, GAO, and Treasury Department personnel working in tax administration policy, and the members of Congress and congressional aides who share their perspectives. Their dominant bias, as detailed in this book, is to downplay or ignore the burdens that the tax system places on taxpayers.

We might, of course, specifically disqualify all such individuals from serving on this commission. But then who would the president appoint? He is not going to drive out to Nebraska and interview local, irate businessmen and farmers for the job. He would be guided by members of Congress, IRS officials, and the professional associations in making appointments, and these groups would recommend seasoned Washington insiders. The result would be bland, conformist individuals who could be counted on not to make waves.

Even if, by some miracle, this commission were staffed by outspoken champions of taxpayers, how long would they stay that way? Interacting day after day with IRS officials and other members of the culture of taxing, they would gradually be drawn into their orbit. The General Accounting Office illustrates this pattern. Although it is supposed to be objective, its officials and researchers have absorbed the ignore-the-taxpayer perspective that prevails in the Washington tax community.

In summary, it does not seem possible to create a governmental unit to represent taxpayers and their burdens in the councils of government. Such a unit, if created, is likely to be ineffectual; or, worse, it could become a further part of the culture of taxing that it was supposed to counteract.

It also seems unpromising to look to legislation that would urge tax officials to take burdens on taxpayers into account. One is tempted, for example, to propose a law providing for a taxpayer impact statement for every new tax rule, procedure, or regulation. This TIS would be required to detail the monetary, psychological, and moral burdens of the provision on taxpayers before it could be approved. The 1988 Taxpayers' Bill of Rights had several provisions of this nature, one requiring the IRS to compile an annual report for Congress on "the quality of taxpayer service provided," and another that provides for the federal Small Business Administration to review proposed IRS regulations for their impact on small businesses.

The fallacy of putting such pious hopes in legislation is that they do not affect anyone's perspectives. The participants go through the motions required by the legislation, but their attitudes remain unaffected. Congress may be sent an annual report discussing taxpayer service; but this is likely to be empty window dressing, unrelated to what the thousands of IRS workers who are responsible for taxpayer service are doing.

A good example of how legislative urgings can become a dead letter is the Paperwork Reduction Act of 1980. This law mandated yearly reductions in the paperwork burdens imposed on the public by the tax system and other regulations. Yet instead of reductions, the 1980s saw a huge increase in the federal paperwork burden. The evidence shows, then, that it will not be enough merely to urge, even in legislation, that the Washington tax community be sensitive to the concerns of taxpayers.

There is a reform that would accomplish this change in perspectives, however. It is a simple idea, easy to describe and easy, in most instances, to apply. But the spirit behind this reform is quite radical, so radical that we can assume that today's tax policy makers would be reluctant to consider it. I propose it, not in the expectation that it will promptly make its way into policy, but as an analytical device. Through examination of this idea we can see what the requirements are for a rational tax system, for a system in which burdens on taxpayers are automatically included in the making of laws and regulations. Showing how this reform would transform policy making reveals how far the current system has strayed from the principles of sound management and democratic decision making.

Taxpayer Compensation

In the modern world, our way of reflecting costs is through prices. For example, it costs effort and capital to produce milk. To reflect these sacrifices, milk has a price. You cannot go into a supermarket and walk away with as much milk as you like without paying anything. You must give money in exchange. Placing a price on milk keeps people from wasting it. If milk were free, people would use it to bathe in, for example, never stopping to remember the sacrifices made by the farmers to produce it.

The tax system involves considerable sacrifices by citizens, sacrifices in complying with tax regulations and in responding to tax enforcement procedures. Unfortunately, up until now, no price has been placed on this expenditure of effort. From the standpoint of tax officials, it is free. The predictable result has been that tax officials waste this labor. "Let us mail out a million notices," they say, "requiring taxpayers to respond. Perhaps many of these notices are wrong or irrelevant, forcing taxpayers into anxious, frustrating labor. That is not of concern to us."

The obvious solution to this pattern of waste is to *put a price on taxpayer effort and have the tax system pay for it.* In other words, the various actions the taxpayer is now forced to perform would be given a price, and the tax authority would pay the taxpayer this amount whenever it required them. For example, Congress would establish a payment for audits—let us say, $500 per day or part thereof. If a taxpayer were required to come in for an office audit that lasted part of one day, he would be given $500 for participating in it, above and beyond whatever adjustments or penalties were decided. If a business were examined for three weeks (fifteen days), then the IRS would pay it $7,500 after the audit was completed.

Although this compensation idea represents a novel departure, a close inspection reveals that it would correct many failings of a deeply troubled tax system.

Including Compliance and Enforcement Costs in Policy

A compensation program would necessarily and inescapably make tax officials aware of the burden they are placing upon citizens. The burden on taxpayers would appear as a direct budgetary cost, a cost as real to officials as the salary being paid to government clerks. This would cause them to make wise use of taxpayer time and effort. If the IRS were paying $500 a day for audits, for example, it would take care to see that the audits were justified and make an effort not to prolong them unduly. With a compensation plan in effect, it would be impossible for tax officials to make yield-cost calculations for enforcement procedures that ignore the burden on taxpayers—which, as we have seen, is what they *always* do today.

Tax policy makers at a higher level, including legislators, would be similarly affected. As the system functions today, Congress goes along (one is tempted to say "merrily") writing new tax clause after new tax clause with virtually no regard for the burdens these imply for taxpayers. The result, as we have seen, is a tax compliance burden of over five billion hours. The Section 89 legislation, discussed in Chapter 11, is an excellent illustration of this thoughtlessness. With a compensation scheme in effect, members of Congress would want to ask, and Treasury officials would be eager to calculate, how much work this would mean for taxpayers. With the citizen compliance burden coming straight out of the budget, congressmen would think twice about adding to it.

Another benefit of the compensation idea, perhaps even more important in the long run, is that it would convert the tax authority into a genuine *service* organization. In the modern era, a tax authority cannot function without a considerable degree of popular acceptance. To this end, the IRS has attempted to implement certain marketing techniques in an attempt to improve its image. But little has been done about the feature of the tax system that citizens find most objectionable: its enormous burdens of time, expense, and anxiety.

When a taxpayer today is called for an audit, he receives a pamphlet describing his rights. If he bothers to read the fine print of this document, he will discover that none of the injuries he really cares about are mentioned. He is still being forced to attend the audit against his will; his time, labor, and attention are still being forcibly extracted; his privacy is still being massively invaded; his savings are still at risk, dependent on the rather subjective findings of a hostile government official. He concludes that the pamphlet is window dressing to cover up a highly disagreeable process. He adds hypocrisy to his list of IRS failings.

See how his perspective changes if the notification of the audit also contains an announcement that the taxpayer will be paid $500 a day for participating. This payment tells the taxpayer that the IRS realizes that the audit experience is a burden. It says that the taxpayer is doing the tax system a favor by participating in the audit, which, of course, is the case. Once the taxpayer learns he is to be paid, he no longer feels helpless and trampled upon.

The compensation idea would also change the orientation of IRS officials: it would make them consumer-oriented. The compensating payments to taxpayers would be the largest part of the IRS budget. As a result, administrators would spend a great deal of time and effort figuring out how to limit this cost—which would mean, of course, limiting the burdens of their procedures on citizens.

The compensation idea has certain precedents. When the United States had a military draft in effect, forcing men to serve in the armed forces, it paid the conscripted soldiers a salary. Even though this labor was available "free," through the use of force, it was not deemed right to take it without any compensation. The same logic should apply to the tax system, for taxpayers are the last great remaining conscripts in our society. The government should not use its powers of coercion to force them to work for free.

One tax administration measure that already embodies the compensation principle is the refund interest provision incorporated into the tax law (Section 6611). Under this law, if the IRS delays more than forty-five days in paying a refund, it must also pay the taxpayer interest. The arguments in favor of this provision also apply to the compensation proposal: (1) Fairness: the IRS should pay for burdens it creates. (2) Public relations: taxpayers feel better if the IRS compensates them for the losses it causes. (3) Administrative efficiency: when the IRS has to pay for the burdens it places on citizens—in this case, the burden of a late refund—its officials will make a greater effort to avoid imposing these burdens.

Tying Down Loose Cannons

As documented throughout this book, tax enforcement programs today are highly error-prone. Tax officials have adopted the mentality of junk-mail marketeers who send out a blizzard of circulars in the hope of receiving a small number of usable responses. What IRS managers overlook is that they are not making voluntary solicitations. Their little brown envelopes represent the awesome coercive power of the state, causing the public a great deal of anxiety and frustration. Where an enforcement notice is wrong or unjustified, the citizen has been been subjected to an action approximating a false arrest: he has been incorrectly accused by government officials of wrongdoing. In some ways, the IRS accusation is worse than a false arrest since, unlike the judicial system, the tax system places the burden of proof on the accused.

In addition to moral and legal issues, there is a consideration of social efficiency. A false notice forces the taxpayer to undertake stressful and often extensive work to clear the matter up. A government that cared about its citizens would be eager to minimize this wasted effort. For these reasons, tax officials should be extremely careful to see that their actions are accurate. Even one mistake should be a cause for embarrassment, a forthright apology, and a strenuous effort to prevent a similar mistake in the future.

This ideal is ignored by U.S. tax managers. The underreporter notices are a case in point. These are the letters the IRS sends to millions of taxpayers every year accusing them of not paying enough taxes. A recent GAO study (which, as we have explained, can be expected to understate IRS errors) found that "for 1987, about half of the 6.2 million underreporter cases that IRS pursued were unproductive—that is, taxpayers did not owe additional taxes."[1] The tax policy-making community has known about the error rate in this program for years and has quietly accepted it. The GAO study that found that some three million taxpayers were needlessly harassed in 1987 did not denounce the program but declared it to be "cost-effective."[2]

Tax officials are equally complacent about other error-prone enforcement programs. In the nonfiler programs, where citizens are accused of not filing tax returns, only about one notice out of ten goes to a real nonfiler; nine out of ten are miscues, going to people who already filed, or who don't need to file, or who don't owe tax, and so forth. In certain correspondence sweeps, the error rate can run as high as 99 percent. In forced collections, even GAO studies show that at least tens of thousands of false actions are taken each year, actions in which the IRS seizes funds from the wrong taxpayer, or from taxpayers who have already paid their taxes, or from others who do not merit this treatment.

Erroneous and clumsy IRS enforcement programs are building resentment. They are like loose cannons rolling back and forth on the deck of the American ship of state, smashing into one group of taxpayers and then another. Year by year they create additional millions of angry, frustrated taxpayers, people who no longer wish to cooperate with the tax system. All the arguments reinforce the conclusion that making tax enforcement programs error-free must be a top priority. Under the current system, there is little incentive for anyone to worry about errors. With a taxpayer compensation program, officials would worry about them, since an erroneous or spurious enforcement action would entail a budgetary cost with no corresponding enforcement revenue.

The Revenue Enhancement Myopia

In recent years, federal budget managers have become magicians. They have been expected to find money to pay for increased spending programs without adding to the deficit and without increasing taxes. Sometimes, they have been able to do this by twisting assumptions or misrepresenting costs. Another method of squaring the budgetary circle has been to tinker with tax enforcement and compliance policy. By tightening one or another of these screws, government accountants can "find" slight revenue advantages to offset, on paper at least, some new spending drain. This practice of contriving changes in tax compliance in order to achieve so-called revenue enhancement has dominated tax administration policy in recent years.

This shortsighted approach has harmed the tax system. Instead of fashioning tax administration policy according to what is healthy for the entire tax system, members of Congress have looked only at what the clause or regulation would mean for government revenues. The result has been the imposition of many new burdens, many of which are quite irrational, and many of which have angered and frustrated taxpayers.

To illustrate, let's look at a typical tax system malfunction, the payroll deposit regulations. Employers who are forced to withhold income taxes and Social Security taxes from their employees are required to deposit these monies at financial institutions at certain times and in certain amounts. Over the years, officials discovered that the federal government would make a slight gain in revenue cash flow by forcing employers to make these deposits as quickly as possible. Therefore, they elaborated ever more stringent regulations in order to get the money to Washington sooner. One recent rule, approved by Congress in 1989, requires larger companies to deposit monies within one banking day.

As a result of this pressure for revenue, the deposit rules have become complex and burdensome. Under just one subsection of these rules, for example, employers are required to estimate their payrolls in advance, many times within a month, and make the required payments within three banking days of eight different days within the month—and these deposit days change every month. The requirements are so confusing that one-third of all employers are issued penalties for violating them each year. Even the IRS officials who administer the penalties can't figure them out: according to a GAO study, 44 percent of the penalties they assessed under these deposit rules were incorrect.[3]

Businessmen have complained about the complexity and burden of payroll deposit regulations for years, and GAO studies have documented their confusion. Yet Congress does not correct the problem. The Kafkaesque requirements are allowed to persist because of the revenue enhancement mentality. The rules have been adopted as a way of squeezing a few extra pennies from the tax system without actually raising tax rates. Since a genuine reform would have to give employers more time to calculate their tax liabilities and make deposits, this would mean (because of forgone interest income) slightly less tax revenue. Hence, Washington's culture of taxing will not consider a genuine simplification (though much energy has gone into proposing superficial reforms).

A taxpayer compensation arrangement would expose the irrationality of this approach. Enhanced compliance and enforcement are not free. They always create additional burdens on those who are subjected to them, and often these burdens are more onerous than a tax increase that raised equivalent revenue would be. The way to bring this point home to policy makers is to have these compliance burdens compensated by government payments.

In the case of the payroll deposit regulations, for example, one approach would be to pay employers $200, let us say, for each penalty dispute with the IRS, regardless of how the penalty issue was finally settled. Under this arrangement, the 10.4 million employer penalties issued in 1990 could cost the government over $2 billion in compensation payments. Another application of the compensation idea would be to reimburse employers for their time and trouble in making payroll deposits. If payroll deposits were costing the government, say, $500 each, tax managers would immediately see the wisdom of reducing their frequency.

Objections to Taxpayer Compensation

One objection to the compensation idea is that it constitutes a spending program—and that either spending for other programs would have to be cut back or taxes would have to be increased to pay for it. The point is correct, but it hardly constitutes a criticism. If one believes in any government spending programs at all, then, logically, the first spending program government must have is a program to compensate for the burdens of operating the tax system. Otherwise, officials may end up approving socially destructive spending programs.

We are dangerously close to this problem today. In Washington, the usual approach to spending programs is to ask, Whom do we want to help? From the standpoint of rational policy making, this is an incomplete question. It incorporates the fallacious view of government as a magical money source, when it is merely a transfer machine with substantial overhead costs. The proper way to pose the spending issue is with this question: What hurts are we going to inflict in order to help the social group we want to help? Policy makers will be guided to this question when tax system costs show up as budgetary costs.

With the true costs of spending programs made evident, it is quite likely that policy makers will find many programs much less attractive than before. Indeed, if they are rational, they *must* find the programs less attractive, since they will see that the costs are greater than they thought. This means that one of the consequences of an arrangement that compensated taxpayers for tax system burdens would be a lower level of government spending and, hence, lower taxes.

A close parallel to the idea of taxpayer compensation is the practice of compensating property owners when government seizes their land, as it does to build highways. This compensation program is a spending program, but one that everyone agrees is just and necessary, for two reasons. First, it is only fair that property owners hurt by the government project be compensated for their injury. Second, including the cost of condemned land makes policy makers recognize the true cost of highways and therefore discourages them from building as many as they otherwise would. Both of these points—fairness and social efficiency—apply to the involuntary takings that the operation of the tax system requires.

A second objection to the compensation idea, one that tax officials would certainly make, is that if the government had to compensate taxpayers for enforcement actions, it could not afford to engage in so many. For tax administrators, the ideal system is one which keeps close track of every taxpayer and detects and punishes every noncompliant one. In this way, perfect intimidation is maintained. Now, with the advent of computers, which greatly lower the tax authority's cost of comprehensive nationwide surveillance and enforcement, it seems they may be able to make their dream a reality.

The problem is that what is a dream for tax officials can be a nightmare for everyone else. Maximum tax enforcement, if carried out by an insensitive or inept tax authority, means maximum pain for citizens, pain in the burdens of the enforcement actions, and pain in the frightening feeling of being in the grasp of a hostile, all-pervasive bureaucracy. The compensation idea outlined here would make policy makers sensitive to this problem. If government has to pay citizens for its burdens and intrusions, then Big Brother quickly becomes Little Brother.

Washington on the Nile

How can we get public officials to listen to criticism? This perennial problem in democratic governance takes an especially challenging form in the case of the tax system. In ordinary government programs, people are supposed to be helped. Complaints are therefore taken as a sign that the program is failing and needs to be fixed. A tax system, on the other hand, is not a program to help people. It is a "program" to hurt them, to take their money away against their will. Complaints are therefore taken as a sign that the system is functioning normally. This perspective means that no matter how seriously mismanaged the tax system, legislators are disposed to discount criticism of it. They tend to assume that the tax system is doing its proper job and that taxpayer criticisms are groundless. This bias against taxpayers is compounded when legislators have spent many years interacting with tax officials and absorbing their perspective. The result, as we have seen, is a culture of taxing, a policy community strikingly insensitive to taxpayer viewpoints.

A dramatic illustration of this insensitivity was revealed in a 1990 hearing of the oversight subcommittee of the House Ways and Means Committee. Committee investigators had looked into how well businesses were complying with Section 6050I of the tax code. This clause, passed in 1984, requires everyone to report to the IRS all transactions that involve more than $10,000 in cash. It was one of the scores of reporting requirements added to the tax code in the 1980s as a way of helping the IRS maintain its surveillance of possible tax evaders.

The investigators went to nine different cities and posed as customers seeking to make cash purchases of over $10,000 without the transaction's being reported to the IRS. The items they arranged to purchase included a $250,000 condominium, a $17,000 Rolex watch, a $15,000 Mazda Miata, and a $22,000 antique mirror. Of the seventy-nine businesses approached, seventy-six agreed to make the sale without informing the IRS. What did this massive disobedience mean? Without hesitation, the congressmen blamed the noncompliant citizens. Their view was expressed by the subcommittee chairman, twenty-six-year congressional veteran J. J. Pickel (D-Tex.): "It is shocking that businesses throughout the country are routinely conniving with customers to violate the law."[4]

Democratic theory would suggest a different interpretation. Under this theory, congressmen are not pharaohs who force captive populations to do their bidding. They are supposed to represent citizens, to reflect their wishes in law. If large numbers of people are disregarding a law, it means a malfunction has occurred somewhere in the system. Perhaps the regulation itself is too obscure or too burdensome. Perhaps businessmen have lost respect for the IRS because of its past abuses and errors. Perhaps they have lost respect for U.S. congressmen and their policies! Whatever the explanation, when 96.2 percent of the affected citizens ignore a law, democratic legislators have a lot of soul-searching to do.

Today, they are not soul-searching. They are blaming the taxpayers. They see a tax system characterized by an alarming degree of opposition and noncooperation. They see a growing number of penalties, delinquencies, and forced collection actions. They know that something is going wrong, but they do not look to their own shortcomings for an explanation. Instead, they are stepping more firmly into the autocratic mold, adopting a hostile view of taxpayers and devising an ever-growing apparatus of regulation to force them to conform. After the subcommittee found out about the disregard of Section 6050I, they increased the penalties for violating this clause to a fine of $100,000.

What lies at the end of this road of constantly tightening tax enforcement and surveillance? In the modern age, a tax system is surprisingly vulnerable. An institution that traces its ancestry to the despotisms of the ancient world seems, at first glance, an immovable part of civilization. But one forgets: today, despotism is deplored. Citizens increasingly suppose they have the right to resist government's demands. In a dozen ways, taxpayer dissatisfaction can bring the federal tax system to its knees. Citizens may clog the system with legal disputes and protests. They may refuse to cooperate with the system, refuse to appear at audits, refuse to answer correspondence, refuse to file returns, and so on. They may practice civil disobedience on a wide scale. They may flood the system with bogus information. They may turn to violence against tax officials. The tax agency may become so discredited that it cannot attract competent, loyal employees. A political taxpayer revolt might dramatically restrict the system. These possibilities are not far-fetched; most of them have already begun to occur.

We are not in an age when policy makers can shore up a faltering tax system by cracking the whip. If officials expect the tax system to survive in anything like its present form, they need a change in perspective. They have to find a meaningful way to respect the sacrifices of the taxpayers, who are, after all, the foundation of the government.

Appendix

Social Cost Analysis

IN CALCULATING THE BURDEN of the tax system, this study employs the concept of social cost. The social cost of an institution is the net burden of the institution on society as a whole. For those costs that can be quantified, the institution's social cost is the monetary value of all resources that the institution causes to be expended. In the case of the tax system, social cost analysis aims at establishing the value of the resources—labor, land, capital—that would be available for other purposes if the tax system did not exist.

For example, if a person pays a tax accountant $250 to prepare his tax form, the resource being expended is the labor of the accountant, established at $250 in this voluntary exchange. If there were no tax system, this $250 worth of time, expertise, and associated overhead would not be consumed in this way—and would be available for other uses.

Take another illustration of a somewhat different kind. Assume a heart surgeon does thirty operations a year, each of which pays him $10,000. Suppose this doctor decides not to do a thirty-first operation because too much of the extra $10,000 he will earn will go to taxes. In this case, the tax system has caused labor worth $10,000 to be withheld. If the tax system did not exist, there would have been one more operation performed, worth $10,000.

Although the social cost concept generally corresponds to our intuitive meaning of cost, there are a few points where confusion can arise.

First, social cost analysis makes *no distinction in the value of a resource according to who holds it*, whether it be one individual, or another individual, or the government. That is, a dollar in anyone's hands always has the same value. This can be called the equal-value assumption.

In the world as we find it, this assumption might be highly debatable. We might say that John, who spends his money on comic books, is wasting his dollars, whereas Jack, who buys books on Shakespeare, is spending his money much more constructively. Hence, we feel that Jack's dollars are more socially valuable than John's.

The trouble with this view is, how do we prove it? How do we show that our evaluation of John's spending is anything more than a subjective prejudice? Furthermore, even if we did prove our contention in the case of John and Jack, that would be just the beginning, for there are also Bill, and Mary, and Steve, and millions of other individuals whose spending habits must be evaluated. The only way around this mind-boggling complexity is to say that a dollar equals a dollar, no matter who spends it.

The equal-value assumption also enables us to bypass comparisons of governmental and private spending. We assume that a dollar in the hands of government has the same value as a dollar left in private hands. Of course, when it comes time to evaluate a specific government spending program, then the benefits of it must be assessed and compared with the benefits of the private spending it precludes. But since we are focusing on the tax system and do not know to which use the tax dollars will be put, we proceed with the neutral assumption that private and governmental dollars have the same value.

The equal-value perspective means that transactions that are important to the actors have no significance in social cost analysis. For example, the actual amount of taxes that an individual pays does not figure one way or the other in a social cost analysis. Whatever the individual loses in taxes, the government gains; and since we agreed to treat all dollars as of equal value, no net change in total social wealth has occurred. We treat tax penalties in the same way. A $100 penalty assessed against a taxpayer is just like another tax: it is $100 less for the individual and $100 more for the government. Even if the penalty is assessed unfairly or erroneously, there is no net social cost—assuming there are no costs to paying or protesting the penalty. (If the taxpayer contests the penalty, then his efforts to challenge it will be social costs: they are expenditures of time and resources caused by the operation of the tax system.)

The equal-value principle also means that tax evasion in itself has no social cost. Any money withheld from the government is as valuable in the pocket of the individual as it would have been to the government. Tax evasion will involve a net social cost, however, if any resources are expended to accomplish the evasion. For example, if the taxpayer pays a tax shelter promoter to put his money in tax-exempt form, then such a payment represents a net social cost.

Second, since the aim of social cost analysis is to identify all the costs associated with an institution, *no distinction is made among the different reasons why social costs are incurred.* In analyzing a tax system, this means that one counts both costs for activities that are legally required, like keeping records or filing returns, and costs for activities that are optional, but still caused or inspired by the tax system. In this category are costs like using a tax preparer or contesting an audit result in Tax Court. At bottom, the tax system is responsible for both kinds of costs, the required and technically optional.

Third, *all taxpayers are human beings whose efforts and sacrifices need to be included* in a social cost analysis.

In some realms of law enforcement, we sometimes treat guilty citizens as deserving of the enforcement costs that fall upon them. For example, if a police officer shoots and wounds an armed robber who was in the process of committing a robbery, some would be inclined to say that the wound was a proper part of the punishment, and they would not think of it as a cost to society.

Adopting this point of view, one could say that any burdens that a guilty taxpayer has to bear should not be considered social costs. They are "deserved" punishments and as such represent no loss to society. It appears that some IRS officials favor this perspective. I think this view should be rejected on the following grounds:

1. Even for serious crimes, like armed robbery, it is not accepted. Police are not permitted to shoot robbers just because they are committing armed robbery.

2. The distinction between guilt and innocence is especially difficult to draw in tax cases, since the majority of cases involve some degree of innocence.

3. A tax transgression is not viewed by the majority of citizens as serious wrongdoing, and therefore it is not one for which they believe extra punishments are called for.

4. The number of tax transgressors is so large that violators form a significant part of society, perhaps even a majority. A social cost analysis that ignores their sacrifices obviously lacks comprehensiveness.

Following this logic, I have considered that the costs born by all taxpayers in responding to the tax system are social costs. This includes the burdens on those who intentionally resist tax requirements.

The Burden of Initial
Enforcement Contacts

IN THIS SECTION of the Appendix, I explain the enforcement burden estimates summarized in Chapter 3. The purpose of the discussion is twofold: (1) to arrive at the numerical estimates themselves, and (2) to identify issues and methodology involved in assessing enforcement burdens so as to assist future studies of these matters.

Audits

I estimate the burdens of the various kinds of audits as follows:

1. Office audits, unrepresented, preparation time.   In audits, the taxpayer expends time in two categories: preparation and participation. In preparation for the audit, the taxpayer will examine his return to see if he can find any flaws. One taxpayer who went through an audit on his own reported, "I spent the better part of two weeks going over my return." The taxpayer will also gather records and make computations that might bear on relevant issues. The typical audit announcement letter asks the taxpayer to bring a wide range of documents. Attempting to collect these can be a major chore. Finally, the taxpayer may discuss the case with friends, family members, and business associates to figure out his problems and how to handle them.

The time spent doing these things represents work, time and energy consumed because of the tax enforcement system. Until surveys reveal the number more accurately, we can only make a rough estimate of time spent in audit preparation. At one extreme, a highly anxious taxpayer might spend all his waking hours for several weeks trying to get ready for his audit, that is, something like 150 hours. Possibly there are some taxpayers at the other end of the scale who never give the audit any thought before they go to it. Leaning toward the conservative side, I will estimate this preparation time at 15 hours.

2. Office audits, unrepresented, participation time.   IRS figures indicate the average office audit consumed 3.8 hours in 1985 (the figure rose to 4.6 hours by 1988).[1] Audit participation also includes the travel times to the IRS office, which would typically be an hour or so each way, and some waiting time. Add to this the psychological strain associated with the audit, and the fact that the audit is scheduled during business hours. The result would normally be that the participation effectively consumes an entire working day.[2] Hence, I estimate 8 hours for participating in an office audit.

3. Office audits, represented, preparation time.   When representation is involved, it would seem that the taxpayer's participation should be somewhat less, since much of the responsibility and anxiety of an audit is transferred to the representative. This reduction is not necessarily too significant in actual hours, since the taxpayer still has to meet with the representative and discuss the case and has to assemble the required information. For example, one CPA estimated that clients spent four to six hours in conference with her before an office audit and an additional four to six hours gathering the requisite data on their own. On balance, however, it seems justified to set taxpayer preparation time for represented audits below that of unrepresented audits. I adopt a figure equal to two-thirds of the unrepresented preparation time, or ten hours.[3]

4. Office audits, represented, participation time.   It appears that in office audits, most represented taxpayers also appear, so there may be no time saving in the majority of cases. Since the represented taxpayer is attending the audit more as an observer, however, not as a solo performer, it would seem that the stresses would not be so great, so the entire workday would not be consumed. Therefore, the participation time for represented audits is set at three-quarters that of unrepresented audits, or six hours.

How much is this taxpayer time worth? Here we can employ the same figure developed in Chapter 2 for individual compliance time plus overhead: $28.31 per hour for 1985. The logic for using this estimate is given in Chapter 1. In the audit situation, the taxpayer is thrust into becoming a tax compliance worker, forced to do extremely stressful and distasteful work. Also, the taxpayer has to bear all the overhead costs of this type of work: work space, equipment, utilities, telephone, transportation, meals away from home, and so on. Finally, the audit burden falls disproportionately upon highly skilled, highly paid workers whose time is worth much more than a national average compensation figure.

The cost of representation in office audits is set at $350, as explained in Chapter 3.

With the figures supplied, we can estimate the burden of the different categories of office examinations as shown in Table A1.

5. Field audits, preparation time.   In field examinations, taxpayer preparation times would normally be much more substantial than for office audits. The estimate advanced here is that in unrepresented field audits, taxpayer preparation time is three times that of office audits, or 45 hours, and that for represented field audits, the time is two-thirds this figure, or 30 hours. This preparation time covers not just that of the taxpayer or owner of a business but the time of employees working for the business, such as bookkeepers or accountants. These are conservative estimates. For example, in one reported field audit, the respondent noted that along with the $11,000 representation cost was a $4,500 cost for the bookkeeper to develop the figures needed for the case. At the transformation figure we are using for tax compliance labor, this was a preparation burden of 160 hours, over five times the 30 hours we are assuming for such a case.

6. Field audits, participation time.   IRS figures indicate an average duration of 15.3 hours for field audits in 1985 (the figure

TABLE A1   Social Costs of Initial Enforcement Contacts, 1985, Detail

Audits	Dollars
Office audits	
Unrepresented (75% of 814,213, or 611,000)	
Preparation time (611,000 × 15hrs × $28.31)	259,000,000
Participation time (611,000 × 8hrs × $28.31)	138,000,000
Represented (25% of 814,213, or 204,000)	
Preparation time (204,000 × 10hrs × $28.31)	58,000,000
Participation time (204,000 × 6hrs × $28.31)	35,000,000
Representation cost (204,000 × $350)	71,000,000
Total, office audits (average cost = $689)	561,000,000
Field audits	
Unrepresented (25% of 519,292, or 130,000)	
Preparation time (130,000 × 45hrs × $28.31)	166,000,000
Participation time (130,000 × 15hrs × $28.31)	55,000,000
Represented (75% of 519,292 or 389,000)	
Preparation time (389,000 × 30hrs × $28.31)	330,000,000
Participation time (389,000 × 10hrs × $28.31)	110,000,000
Representation cost (389,000 × $1,500)	584,000,000
Total, field audits (average cost = $2,397)	1,245,000,000
Mail audits (125,241 × 12hrs × $28.31)	43,000,000
Information Returns Program (total 4,100,000)	
Notices paid without protest (36%) (1,476,000 × 4hrs × $28.31)	167,000,000
Notices contested (45%) (1,845,000 × 12hr × $28.31)	627,000,000
Notices not replied to (14%) (574,000 × 4hr × $28.31)	65,000,000
Notices not reaching taxpayer (5%) (205,000 × 0)	0
Total, Information Returns Program (average cost = $210)	859,000,000
Nonfiler program (total 3,000,000)	
Notices ignored or miscarried (41%) (1,230,000 × 0)	0
Notices resulting in tax return filings (22%) (660,000 × 0)	0
Notices contested (37%) (1,110,000 × 12 × $28.31)	377,000,000
(Average cost = $126)	
Penalty and penalty abatement procedures	
Total (8,785,000 at $210 per case)	1,845,000,000
Service center corrections	
Total (558,876 at $210 per case)	117,000,000

climbed to 22 hours by 1988).[4] In general, the taxpayer spends an equal amount of time in dealing with the revenue agent. In the case of an unrepresented field audit, the agent works mostly by himself with documents supplied to him, but someone in the office must be continuously available to get documents, answer questions, and make sure the auditor stays physically in bounds. Furthermore, the auditor's presence at a place of business often interferes with productivity, putting everyone on pins and needles. Also, the audit means that the owner or manager must stay close by to answer questions and supervise. This, of course, interferes with the productive use of time. It is not unreasonable, therefore, to set the taxpayer burden of participation in an unrepresented field audit at the estimated average length of field audits, or 15 hours for 1985.

In field audits with representation, the taxpayer is relieved of both the policing function and much of the consulting function, since this is taken over by the representative. There still is a need to supply additional documents and to consult with the representative and auditor during the progress of the audit. But overall, the taxpayer participation seems to be less. This figure will be estimated at two-thirds of the length of the average field audit, or ten hours.

The cost of representation in a field audit is set at $1,500, as explained in Chapter 3.

These figures enable us to calculate the private sector costs of the different kinds of field audits as shown in Table A1.

The mail audits are treated like contested cases in the Information Returns Program (see the next section).

Information Returns Program (Underreporter Program)

To assess the burden of the Information Returns Program we need to know the breakdown of the responses to the IRP notices. Through the Freedom of Information Act, the IRS supplied the following tabulation of IRP case disposals for 1985 (letter of February 22, 1990):

Agreed ("paid without protest")	2,154,752
No change (abatements)	795,762
Unagreed to higher levels	93,841
Defaulted (no response)	734,503
Total	3,778,858

This tabulation seems incomplete. There is no category for taxpayers who protested their notices but who were turned down by the IRS and then went on to pay the assessment. One tabulation of statistics on the penalty process showed that the number of unsuccessful appeals for abatement was three times the number of successful appeals for abatement.[5] A 1990 *Money* magazine survey of those affected by IRS computer notices found that 53 percent of those who challenged their assessments had them abated. This implies that 47 percent of those who contest notices are denied abatement. This survey also found that only 28 percent of those who received notices paid them without protest.[6] This figure contradicts the claim implied in the IRS figures for case disposals, that 57 percent (2,154,752 out of 3,778,858) pay without protest.

The high proportion in the "paid without protest" category is especially implausible in light of the high error rate in the IRP program. As noted in Chapter 3, the proportion of erroneous notices, as seen from the taxpayer's point of view, is probably well over 50 percent. Tax writer David Burnham notes that 1985 was a particularly bad year for accuracy, a year in which the IRS "sent out millions of erroneous dunning notices."[7]

To make these IRS figures plausible, therefore, it is necessary to create a category of taxpayers who protested their assessments in one or more letters but who did not succeed in having their penalties abated. The size of this group, following the finding of the *Money* poll, will be assumed to be the same size as the group that successfully challenged their penalties, 795,762. We will assume that this group of unsuccessful challengers has inadvertently been included in the "agreed—paid without protest" category.

This change enables us to recast the tabulation as follows:

Agreed without contest	1,358,990	(36%)
Contested		
abated	795,762	
unabated	795,762	
at higher levels	93,841	
Total contested	1,685,365	(45%)
Defaulted, response declined	530,000	(14%)
Defaulted, wrong address	204,503	(5%)
Total	3,778,858	(100%)

In this tabulation, I have separated the default cases into two categories: taxpayers who receive the notice, ponder it, and decide not to reply, because they can't understand it, or don't agree with it; and notices that never reach their destination. The division into these two categories is simply an educated guess. (Note that the number of notices this source claims were processed in 1985, 3,778,858, is different from the 4.1 million figure we are using as the number of notices sent out in 1985.)

With the response categories defined, I estimate the burdens in each category as follows:

1. Notices paid without contest.   In these cases the CP-2000 letter is not protested, either because it is correct or because the taxpayer judges that it is less burdensome to pay the assessment than to contest it. The taxpayer reads and digests the notice (which itself probably takes several hours); looks up his tax data; perhaps talks about it with friends, family members, or tax practitioners, but eventually fills out the form agreeing to the demand; writes a check; and mails it. In these cases, I estimate a taxpayer burden time of four hours. As always, we value this taxpayer time plus overhead at $28.31 per hour.

2. Notices contested.   In these cases, the taxpayer protests mainly because he believes the assessment is incorrect. When the taxpayer handles his IRP by himself, I estimate that the time consumed ranges from something like five to six hours to perhaps twenty to twenty-five hours. The lower figure assumes that the taxpayer sends only one carefully drafted letter, after reading and digesting the IRS letter, checking records, checking tax books and instructional materials, and discussing the case with others. The higher figure applies to cases where several letters and phone calls are involved, not only to the IRS but also to third parties to appeal for documentation. Between these two possibilities, I select twelve hours as the average across all cases.

3. Notices not replied to.   For these cases, I estimate the same burden as notices paid without protest. That is, the taxpayer reads the notice, tries to figure out what it means, and talks it over with others. Later on, this taxpayer may face additional burdens from the collections division; but these burdens appear in the tabulations for the burdens of collections.

4. Notices not reaching taxpayers.   Again, these might later involve burdens in connection with collections; but as they concern the IRP program, there would be no burden.

To simplify our calculations, we will assume that all the IRP notices are handled by the taxpayer himself, without representation. It is well to keep in mind that representatives are used in many cases. The cost of this representation varies considerably, depending on the difficulty the representative has in breaking through the bureaucratic barriers. One CPA, whose firm specializes in small corporations, described the process of correcting IRS computer actions this way:

R: Sometimes you go 'round and 'round. I don't try to [write] an answer to their computer notices, there's no point. In fact, they'll send out a letter with a fictitious name on it, and you try and call that person and they give you the run-around.

Q: You mean there isn't such a person?

R: There is no such person. It's a fictitious person. You try to find that person, but you can't. [You are told] you've got to write a letter. Then I go around and around. I try to call the district director. They never let you talk to them, but they finally give you somebody that can resolve the problem. I don't try to answer them with correspondence. It's a waste of time. If you try to do it with correspondence, you have to get someone who can make something happen. It's not that easy to find that person.

Q: Well after a while you must learn who they are don't you?

R: Yes, but by the time the next one rolls around, they've gone on to someplace else. . . .
     Basically, I'd say, the IRS tries basically to be helpful, though still there are exceptions. But it's just the system more than anything else.

The charges for handling IRP or other penalty abatement cases vary, depending on the practitioner and the difficulty of the case. My informal survey indicates an average figure of $250.[8]

Table A1 shows the costs of the Information Returns Program. The total monetary burden of the IRP program on taxpayers in 1985 is thus calculated to be $859 million, or an average of $210 per taxpayer across all cases.

Nonfiler Program

A survey conducted by the General Accounting Office in 1979 provides a useful basis for estimating the different outcomes in the nonfiler program. The researchers looked more deeply into 962 IRS nonfiler cases from 1972 to see what they actually involved. The cases, regrouped in categories that correspond to the different burdens on the taxpayers, are as follows:[9]

Status of affected taxpayer	Proportion of all cases	
Taxpayer owed significant tax, delinquent return secured	9%	
Taxpayer owed zero or insignificant tax, delinquent return secured	3%	Taxpayer compliance burden
Taxpayer owed a refund, delinquent return secured	10%	
Taxpayer had already filed, IRS error in assuming delinquency	8%	
Taxpayer had no obligation to file, IRS error in assuming delinquency	16%	Taxpayer enforcement burden
Taxpayer response, IRS fails to conclude case	13%	
Notices miscarried or ignored	41%	No burden
Total	100%	

From a tax collection point of view, only the first group—the 9 percent of cases representing "real" tax delinquencies—represents a success for the delinquent nonfiler program. In the other 91 percent of the cases, the tax authority is wasting its time or burdening citizens needlessly, or both.

For our tabulations of the burden of the nonfiler program, we will put all delinquent nonfilers together (22 percent of the whole) in one category. Although responding to the program represents a burden for them, it is a burden that should already have been included in our estimates of the compliance cost of filing a tax return, discussed in Chapter 2. Therefore, we will not attribute any additional burden for this category. For the 41 percent of the cases in which the notices miscarry (either because the addresses are bad or the taxpayers decline to respond) we will also assume no additional burden. This is a conservative assumption, since, as discussed above, the decision to disregard IRS notices may involve planning and discussion with others.

The burden of the nonfiling program, then, falls on the 37 percent of the taxpayers who are forced to respond to the IRS notices but who are not nonfilers. For these taxpayers, the nonfiling notices are treated as IRP notices contested without representation: the taxpayers must try to convince the bureaucracy that it has erred in accusing them.

Penalties and Penalty Abatement

The IRS issues large numbers of penalties each year, especially penalties for what it considers to be late or insufficient tax payments. The grand total of all penalties in 1985 was 22,035,067. This number includes penalties assessed by the other enforcement programs.[10] To arrive at the number of penalty cases exclusive of these other enforcement programs, we need to (1) correct the penalty figure so that it identifies the number of taxpayers, not penalties, and (2) exclude penalty cases already tabulated under other enforcement programs. When this is done, the result is 8,785,000 additional taxpayers involved with penalties.[11]

To calculate the taxpayer burden of responding to penalties, I will use the same parameters and estimates developed for the IRP notices, since the issues involved are quite similar. In other words, we will assume the same proportions of cases in each category (paid without protest, contested, defaulted) and the same respective times for taxpayer involvement. This means we can use the cost of $210 per case developed for the IRP program and apply it across the 8,785,000 penalty cases.

For simplicity, we disregard any representation costs that might figure in penalty cases. Given the difficulty of dealing with the IRS bureaucracy, these representation costs can often be considerable.

Testifying before a congressional committee in 1988, CPA Dale Demyanick, director of tax service for the National Federation of Independent Business, commented that in the penalty abatement process, the abatements often approximate the cost of obtaining them:

> Our experience has been if we correspond enough times and be persistent that many of the penalties will be abated due to reasonable cause. However, in order to go through this procedure numerous times to get the penalties abated we end up in the situation where the fees to the clients are more than the actual penalties that we are trying to get abated.[12]

Service Center Corrections

It appears that even in the simple area of checking tax returns for entry and computational errors, the IRS clerks frequently send out wrong notices. In the *Money* magazine survey of computer notices, tax professionals reported that the math error notice "is a major area of IRS goofs. . . ."[13] And of course these goofs, like those of the IRP program, are not easy to correct. If we treat service center corrections by using the same estimates as for IRP notices, the average burden per case is estimated to be $210 in 1985.

Tax Rates and
Tax System Costs

EFFORTS TO CORRECT INEFFICIENCIES and abuses in tax systems usually take the form of pointing to particular tax provisions that need to be changed. Although this approach has its uses, it generally fails to address the real problem. It is like bailing a boat without looking to see how the water is entering.

To treat the problems of the tax system, it is not enough to identify harmful regulations. Several decades of attempted tax reform in the United States underscore the futility of attempting to treat symptoms. Policy makers have been paying lip service to tax simplification, yet the system they manage has grown ever more complex and burdensome at the same time. It is important, therefore, to step back from the specific issues and look at the underlying causes of high tax system costs.

The main explanation for the problems in the U.S. system appears to be the mismanagement of the system. In Chapters 11 and 12, I have explained at length how this mismanagement has come about and what its consequences have been. There is another factor, however, that bears on tax system costs, one that applies to all tax systems, no matter how they are managed. This is the tax rate. In this section of the Appendix, I will explore this effect and its policy implications.

The Costs of Squeezing Harder

An analogy with a steam boiler helps us understand the connection between tax rates and the costs of operating a tax system. With such a system, one cannot simply double the pressure and leave everything unchanged. A higher pressure requires a more expensive system to contain it. One has to strengthen the boiler, or buy a stronger one, and upgrade all the supporting parts such as pipes, values, and gauges.

Taxation is another kind of pressurized system. The tax authority is trying to squeeze money out of the public, and the public is resisting. In this system, the tax rate represents the pressure level. The more money the tax authority attempts to raise from the same unit of property or income, the greater the resistance. Taxpayers expend more effort struggling against the bigger tax bite, and the tax system has to be strengthened to counteract this resistance, with more resources put into extracting funds from the unwilling taxpayers. Hence, the costs of a tax system are a function of the tax rates. Higher tax rates mean higher tax system costs.

What is the nature of this relationship? When tax rates go up, how fast do tax system costs increase? The precise connection would be difficult to specify, since it involves many different costs changing at different rates. Some of these costs increase in an exponential fashion. That is, if tax rates increase by 10 percent, then tax system costs will increase by more than 10 percent. Many other costs increase in a more-or-less proportional fashion: if tax rates increase by 10 percent, then the cost will increase by about the same amount. A few costs would increase in a fashion less than proportional to the tax rate, but a close examination suggests that these will be relatively unimportant.

In my judgment, when all the different costs are combined, the overall effect is that tax system costs are approximately proportional to tax rates, at least within the range of tax rates actually experienced. A review of the different costs helps explain this general conclusion.

Direct Effects: Disincentive and Avoidance Costs

Many of the connections between tax rates and tax system costs are immediate. The affected individuals start changing their behavior—and start incurring higher costs—as soon as they perceive the change in the tax rate. The economic disincentive cost is one such effect. As soon as taypayers see they are losing a greater share of their capital or labor to higher taxes, they withhold more of it.

In the formulas that economists use to calculate the economic disincentive cost of a tax (what they term the marginal excess burden), this cost is exponentially tied to tax rates, usually by a power of two.[1] That is, if the tax rate doubles, the disincentive cost will quadruple. The mathematical expression corresponds to our common-sense understanding: at low tax rates, the discouraging effect of taxes on production is minimal, whereas at very high tax rates taxation becomes prohibitive, virtually destroying the industry or activity being taxed.

Tax avoidance and evasion costs also respond in this direct manner. A larger tax bite motivates more taxpayers to avoid or evade taxes.[2] Since more money is at stake, taxpayers are willing to expend more resources in keeping their tax money from flowing to Washington. They will hire tax shelter promoters, for example, or spend more time keeping records and filling out forms so that they can take more deductions. Or they might expend more effort in hiding their income or assets.

Although economists have not calculated the relationship between tax rates and avoidance costs, it is plausible that this function is at least proportional. At low tax rates, not much effort goes into tax avoidance and evasion; as the rates climb, avoidance and evasion efforts climb as fast or even faster.[3]

Tax rates also have a direct effect on citizen resistance costs in most tax enforcement situations. Higher tax rates mean that more money is likely to be involved in any enforcement dispute, whether this be an underreporter notice, a collection action, an audit appeal, or a Tax Court case. When the stakes of the enforcement actions are higher, taxpayers will be more willing to devote more time and energy to obtaining a favorable outcome.

Indirect Effects: Compliance and Enforcement Costs

For some tax system costs, the higher tax rate has no immediate or direct effect. However, the higher tax rate sets in motion a process that indirectly increases them in the long run. Most compliance costs are in this category. Suppose a taxpayer with a given income suddenly finds the tax rate on that income has gone from 10 percent to 20 percent. In the short run, his compliance costs would seem unchanged. Whatever record keeping, learning about the tax code, and calculations he had to do at a 10 percent rate would be the same at the 20 percent rate. The same conclusion would seem to apply to enforcement costs: a change in the tax rate would not seem to affect the number of audits, correspondence, and collections or change their burden on the public.

If we inspect all the connections, however, we discover indirect mechanisms that cause the compliance and enforcement costs to increase. In general, these indirect links involve a three-stage process: (1) The higher tax rate causes greater tax evasion and avoidance; (2) policy makers alter the tax system in response to these pressures; (3) these modifications in the tax system add to system costs. Let us examine some examples of this process.

Compliance costs.   As just noted, higher tax rates lead to more tax avoidance and evasion. But the process doesn't stop there. Tax officials, seeing that the tax system is being undermined, move to shore it up by plugging the leaks. This takes the form of more regulations and procedures to supervise taxpayers more closely. To taxpayers, of course, this closer supervision means higher compliance costs: longer forms with more questions to answer, more formal justifications required, and more reporting requirements.

The history of the investment tax shelter issue illustrates the pattern. High tax rates made uneconomic "abusive" tax shelters advantageous to taxpayers. As these grew more popular, tax officials took steps to prevent them, for example in the "passive loss" regulations ushered in by the 1986 Tax Reform Act. These additional rules may have stemmed the use of abusive tax shelters, but only at the cost of complicating the tax code for millions of filers. One accountant in Tennessee reported that she now charges her clients an extra $50 per business on the tax return because of the extra work the passive loss regulations have caused. Other illustrations of the same pattern include the alternative minimum tax and the "kiddie tax." Adopted during the 1980s to stem certain forms of tax avoidance, they have added new layers of time-consuming complexity.

Litigation costs.   Another adjustment the tax authority makes to stem growing tax avoidance is to increase penalties for transgressions. But this adds costs to the system on the litigation side. An increase in the number of penalties means more opportunity for error or misunderstanding and, hence, an increase in the efforts citizens make to contest penalties. Making the fines larger—in order to strengthen their deterrent effect—means that more taxpayers will be disposed to challenge them.

Enforcement costs.   As higher tax rates drive more taxpayers to cut corners and evade taxes, the tax authority will be prompted to expand its efforts to catch them. It will initiate more enforcement and surveillance actions, and these increase the burden of the system on taxpayers.

Tax loopholes.   Taxation, by its very nature, does harm. If some of the interests suffering this harm happen to petition for relief, there is a good chance that legislators, being in the business of responding to dramatized suffering, will respond. This relief will take the form of a tax loophole, an exception written into the tax code to prevent the burden of taxation from falling on the specific activity. These loopholes complicate the tax code and thereby raise compliance costs.

A high tax rate stimulates this loophole-writing process. At low tax rates, the harm and unfairness of tax provisions are more likely to be overlooked. Citizens are not so likely to become upset, and legislators are not so likely to be moved to sympathy, when the apparent injustice is slight. If tax rates are low, it makes less sense for a taxpayer, company, or industry to hire a lobbyist to persuade legislators to change the tax law.

The issue of retirement income illustrates how loopholes develop. One of the many harms that taxation inflicts on citizens is that it takes away funds that they would like to save for their retirement. When taxes were low, as they were in 1940, say, no one took much notice of this problem. As the tax rates went up, the problem was felt more keenly. More politicians came to see that the government was defeating, through taxation, the good intention it was fostering through its spending programs like Social Security. Exempting retirement savings from taxation seemed reasonable. From this sentiment came the array of retirement tax shelters—Keogh plans, IRAs, SEPs. And with these loopholes came a jump in compliance burdens: keeping records, gaining approval for employee plans, submitting appropriate documents to the tax authority and to employees. Naturally, this growth in compliance activities has produced an increase in enforcement burdens, as the tax authority seeks to prevent the abuse of the loophole, and has led to an increase in litigation, since the loophole creates additional points to dispute.

Governmental costs.   The changes in the tax system made to check growing tax evasion will also increase governmental costs. As the tax code gets more complicated, it becomes more expensive for tax officials to grapple with it. Audits take longer, for example, which means more auditors have to be hired. More penalties and more penalty disputes require more tax employees to handle them. More loopholes mean more work for the tax authority in supervising these exceptions to the tax code.

Through many indirect mechanisms, then, higher tax rates will cause even the seemingly fixed costs of a tax system—compliance costs, enforcement costs, and governmental costs—to increase. A tax system is a complex, interrelated whole, and the pressures generated by higher tax rates are eventually distributed in the form of higher costs throughout the system.

Policy Implications

Two important observations follow from the realization that tax system costs are a variable function of the tax rate. The first is that *tax system costs must be allocated to each and every spending program.* Policy makers might be tempted to ignore this point by supposing that tax system costs are fixed. The cost of running the tax system, they would say, is paid when the first federal dollar is raised, and therefore all the additional billions in taxes are collected free. This is clearly not the case. As tax rates are raised to pay for more and more spending programs, the costs of the tax system increase too.

As we said, the exact shape of this relationship is difficult to define. The two main tax system costs behave differently. The disincentive cost is clearly an exponential one. Compliance costs, as we just explained, are by no means fixed; but they probably increase less rapidly than tax rates. These two somewhat offsetting patterns suggest that the overall relationship may approximate proportionality: tax system costs are directly proportional to tax rates. This would seem to be a serviceable assumption to use, at least until comprehensive computations are available. This assumption means that the 65 percent figure we have found as the cost of the tax system should properly be added to the budgetary cost of each governmental expenditure. For example, the federal highway that appears to cost $100 million has a true social cost of $165 million when tax system costs are included.

A second policy implication of our finding is that *easing the compliance and enforcement burdens of the tax system is partly a matter of reducing taxes.* Since higher tax rates increase tax system costs, it follows that lowering tax rates is one way to bring about a decrease in these costs. This point seems to have been overlooked in Washington. In their approach to tax simplification, policy makers have taken it as axiomatic that all changes should be revenue-neutral, that is, that they should not lower the amount of taxes collected. This stance means that they have put one solution to the problem of tax complexity out of reach.

Management Failure

As we noted earlier, high tax rates are only part of the cause of high tax system costs. In the federal system, the overall tax extraction rate had risen to nearly its present level thirty years ago. (It went from 4.9 percent of the GNP in 1934 to 18.3 percent in 1960 and further increased to 19.2 percent by 1989.)[4] However, the great leap in tax law complexity and costs in the compliance and enforcement area seems to have occurred since the mid-1970s. Moreover, it appears that other countries, with higher levels of tax extraction than the United States, do not have such high tax system costs.[5]

These observations suggest that the escalating compliance and enforcement costs in the U.S. system are not so much the result of high tax rates as they are the consequence of poor management.

Notes

Introduction

1. Richard Bach, *The Bridge across Forever* (New York: Dell, 1989), p. 330.

Chapter 1

1. Charles Adams, *Fight, Flight, and Fraud: The Story of Taxation* (Curaçao: Euro-Dutch Publishers, 1982), p. 49.

2. Quoted in Paul Johnson, *A History of Christianity* (New York, Atheneum: 1976), p. 75.

3. Ibid.

4. AAFRC (American Association of Fund-Raising Counsel) Trust for Philanthropy, press release, June 7, 1991.

Chapter 2

1. Joel Slemrod, "Optimal Taxation and Optimal Tax Systems," National Bureau of Economic Research (NBER) working paper 3038 (July 1989), p. 1.

2. According to the 1988 *Money* magazine survey of tax preparers, national accounting firms charged an average of $1,567 to prepare the same return that H & R Block offices prepared for an average of $266. The report pointed out that the tax-planning tips the CPA firms included with their tax returns would have more than repaid the customer the extra cost of using these higher-priced preparers. Greg Anrig, Jr., "Even Seasoned Pros Are Confused This Year," *Money*, March 1988, p. 138.

3. These studies are reviewed in Joel Slemrod and Nikki Sorum, "The Compliance Cost of the U S. Individual Income Tax System," *National Tax Journal* 37 (December 1984), p. 462.

4. Arthur D. Little, Inc., *Development of Methodology for Estimating the Taxpayer Paperwork Burden* (Washington, D.C.: Internal Revenue Service, 1988), p. III–23.

5. John H. Wicks, "Taxpayer Compliance Costs from Personal Income Taxation," *Iowa Business Digest* (August 1966), pp. 16–21.

6. Slemrod and Sorum, p. 465.

7. The final report of this study, released in June 1988, is *Development of Methodology for Estimating the Taxpayer Paperwork Burden.*

8. Since the Little report was published, IRS officials have been reanalyzing and recomputing the figures and have come up with lower numbers. One of these figures is 5.004 billion hours for 1985, given in James T. Iocozzia and Garrick R. Shear, "Trends in Taxpayer Paperwork Burden," in Internal Revenue Service, *Trend Analyses and Related Statistics, 1989 Update* (Washington, D.C., 1989), p. 56. Another figure for the same year is 4.982 billion hours, given in a letter to the author from Elinor A. Convery, chief, modeling and special studies, IRS research division, September 8, 1989. Given the well-documented tendency for IRS officials to be both biased and careless in the manipulation of figures (see, for example, the section "Half of What We Do Are Errors" in Chapter 3), these "recomputations" would seem less trustworthy than the original figures supplied by the Little study.

9. Internal Revenue Service, *Annual Report 1990*, p. 13.

10. James L. Payne, *The Culture of Spending* (San Francisco: ICS Press, 1991), pp. 34–39.

11. *Development of Methodology*, pp. IV–24, VII–11.

12. Ibid., pp. IV–24, 25, 35, VII–14.

13. The original idea of the diary study was to have taxpayers keep diaries of the time they spent on their tax compliance activities and in this way to achieve a more accurate measurement. Unfortunately, the diary survey was flawed both in design and execution. In the first place, important components of tax compliance activity, such as record keeping and learning, take place on a year-round basis, and are therefore not accessible to a diary study focused only on the tax season, as this diary study was. In practice, the diary was inadvertently delivered too late to a "relatively high proportion of Diary Study respondents," who had already filled out their tax forms. In these cases, the interviewer read the questions to the respondents, "who had very little time to consider their responses." In other cases, it was apparent that respondents did not actually keep the diary but rushed to fill it in when the interviewer arrived to collect it (ibid., pp. IV–35, IV–37).

Although the Little authors had great doubts about the validity of this 739-respondent diary study, they did not set it aside, as it seems they should have done. Instead, they weighted its results *equally* with the results from the 3,831-respondent mail survey. Since the diary study yielded tax compliance times only 56 percent as large as the mail survey, the effect of averaging the two studies together is to reduce the survey results of the individual tax compliance burden by 22 percent (the business compliance burden did not involve a diary study).

14. Slemrod and Sorum, p. 465.

15. Julie H. Collins, Valerie C. Milliron, and Daniel R. Toy, "An Empirical Analysis of Household Demand for Tax Preparers" (Department of Accounting, University of North Carolina Business School, 1989, mimeo). The table of tax

preparation times supplied by Julie Collins gave the number of respondents in each time category. To compute total time, I first ascribed each respondent the time of the midpoint of the category and in this way computed an average time for the sample of 19.54 hours. This was multiplied by the number of individual returns filed in 1987 (103.46 million) to yield a total nationwide figure of 2.02 billion hours.

16. *Development of Methodology,* p. II–6.

17. Ibid., pp. IV–2, VI–2.

18. In 1985, total IRS costs were $3,617,376,000 (of which 73 percent were for labor and fringe benefits), and the average number of employees was 92,792. Given in Internal Revenue Service, *1985 Annual Report,* tables 23 and 25. The typical IRS work year, including allowances for holidays and vacations, is 1,844 hours.

The hourly cost per employee is therefore

$$\frac{\$3,617,376,000}{92,792 \times 1,844} = \$21.14.$$

19. C. Eugene Steuerle, *Who Should Pay for Collecting Taxes? Financing the IRS* (Washington, D.C.: American Enterprise Institute, 1986), p. 71.

20. In 1986 Arthur Andersen had U.S. revenues of $1.350 billion and 20,120 employees. Assuming a work year of 1,844 hours, these figures will yield a revenue per employee hour figure of $36.39 for 1986. Since 1985 figures were not available, I adjusted the 1986 figure for inflation back to 1985 by subtracting $0.92, the average yearly increase in this figure for the 1986–1988 period. This gives a 1985 revenue per employee hour cost of $35.47. Data on Arthur Andersen supplied courtesy of *Public Accounting Report,* March 15, 1988, and March 15, 1989.

21. An accounting firm probably has a higher proportion of professional personnel than an ordinary business tax compliance unit (76 percent of Arthur Andersen's employees are classified as professional staff). Hence, its average wage per employee would tend to be higher. Second, accounting firms have some advertising costs, whereas a tax compliance unit would have none. This is probably not a significant problem, since major accounting firms are not selling to the general public. One factor that might make this estimate too low is that it is based on U.S. revenue only, whereas some of the employees being counted have a role in helping generate international revenue.

22. The figure of 85 percent comes from *Development of Methodology,* p. II–5. The revenue per employee hour figure of $35.47 should not be confused with the hourly billing rate. The hourly billing rate for a professional employee must also pay for the the nonbillable working hours of that employee and for all other support staff not working on a billable basis (such as managers, clerks, or librarians).

23. Average annual total compensation in 1985 was $25,266, as given in U.S. Department of Commerce, *Statistical Abstract of the United States 1990,* p. 406, table 665. When this figure is divided by 1,844, the number of hours in the typical work year, the result is $13.70 per hour.

24. The study found that individual compliance costs were 6.8 percent of tax revenue if the nationwide average wage was used to value taxpayer time, and

10.8 percent of tax revenues if each taxpayer's own reported wage was used. See Jeff Pope and Richard Fayle, "The Compliance Costs of Personal Income Taxation in Australia 1986/87: Empirical Results," *Australian Tax Forum 7*, no. 1 (1990), pp. 85–126, cited in Marsha Blumenthal and Joel Slemrod, "The Compliance Cost of the U.S. Individual Income Tax System: A Second Look after Tax Reform" (University of Michigan, Office of Tax Policy Research, September 1991), p. 4.

25. In 1985, 1.5 million to 2 million returns were prepared by individuals on a personal computer, and there were over fifty vendors of tax preparation software. See Erik Puskar, "Home Computer Trends and Tax Preparation," in Internal Revenue Service, *Trend Analyses and Related Statistics: 1986 Update* (Washington, D.C., 1986), p. 153.

In 1989, 37 million calls were received by the toll-free telephone assistance service, and another 27.8 million calls were made to the Tele-Tax system, which gives recorded messages and automated responses about the status of refunds. Internal Revenue Service, *1989 Annual Report*, p. 10.

26. Since the taxpayer is engaged in a temporary, once-yearly job, it is likely that he uses overhead facilities less efficiently than full-time tax compliance workers. For example, if he buys a computer program for calculating taxes, he uses it only once instead of many times. This point suggests that the taxpayer's overhead costs might be higher than those of full-time tax compliance workers.

27. The best-known work on the valuation of individual tax compliance time in the United States is that of University of Michigan economist Joel Slemrod and his coworkers. Slenrod applied an econometric methodology in an attempt to establish the value of compliance time from a survey question covering tax years 1982 and 1989. A number of problems with this methodology seem to have undermined its validity. These include the following points:

1. The survey question on which the methodology was based was left unanswered by nearly half of the respondents (perhaps because, among other things, it contained a logical contradiction). In public opinion polling, a nonresponse rate over 20 percent generally indicates an invalid instrument.

2. The survey question, which was designed to elicit a hypothetical wage rate, did not mention that it was tax work that was being offered. Therefore, respondents who did answer it were answering in terms of the desirable jobs they would voluntarily accept, not tax work, the value of which Slemrod was attempting to establish.

3. The wage rate being sought by the question excluded all fringe benefits and labor costs understood to be paid by employers, and excluded all overhead facility costs. (In a separate question, respondents were asked to state their out-of-pocket costs in tax compliance, but these values were handled separately, not incorporated into the wage rate.)

4. After obtaining a wage rate from the survey question, Slemrod reduced this figure to an after-tax wage, using the individual's marginal tax rate. It is unclear why an after-tax wage should be used to reflect the social value of tax compliance work. It would seem that the general principle that should apply is that the social value of any service or good is reflected by its market-determined price, not its after-tax price. Slemrod appears to be the only tax compliance researcher to employ the after-marginal-tax wage to value individual compliance time.

Since these distortions lead to an to understatement of the value of tax compliance labor, it is not surprising that Slemrod's methodology produces an extremely low figure for the value of individual tax compliance work, $10.09 per hour in 1989. One indication of this figure's questionable validity is that it is way below even the nationwide average compensation figure for 1989, of $16.14 per hour. Another fact that throws doubt on the soundness of this methodology is the trend in the figures. In the 1982 study, Slemrod's method valued taxpayer compliance time at $13.68 per hour, compared with $10.09 in the 1989 study. This decline makes no sense in view of the fact that prices and wages increased 20–40 percent in the 1982–1989 period. See Blumenthal and Slemrod, "The Compliance Cost of the U.S. Individual Income Tax System," especially table 2.

28. The Little study is somewhat ambiguous on this point. Occasionally the authors allude to the calculation of "equivalent times" in connection with paid preparers (e.g., p. II–4). However, the report contains no discussion of the methodology of such a calculation, nor its results, and in presenting the final figures declares that the burden or time of paid preparers is excluded for individual taxpayers (e.g., pp. II–6, III–22). Officials in the Research Division of the IRS who were familiar with the study were of the belief that the burden of paid preparers are not included in the individual taxpayer burden (February 21, 1989, interview).

29. The Slemrod and Sorum survey of Minnesota taxpayers for the tax year 1982 found the average cost for paid assistance was $76 (p. 466). To adjust this figure for regional bias, it was multiplied by 1.34, which is the ratio of the unweighted national average tax preparation cost to the north-central costs (using the NSPA figures for an itemized form 1040 given in Table 3). To adjust for inflation to tax year 1985, the figure was increased by 25.5 percent, three times the 8.5 percent increase in average H & R Block charges per customers for 1984–1985 (H & R Block *1985 Annual Report*, p. 7). This figure is typical of the rapidly increasing tax compliance charges of the early 1980s.

30. Internal Revenue Service, *SOI Bulletin* 8, no. 3 (winter 1988–89), p. 124. This figure applies to the 1984 tax year.

31. For the tax year 1988, the total number of estimated tax returns filed is given as 35,488,541. Since five documents are involved for each filer (form 1040ES and four quarterly payments), the number of filers is approximately one-fifth this figure. Internal Revenue Service, *1988 Annual Report* (Washington, D.C., 1989), p. 46.

32. In 1988, the IRS assessed 3,114,574 penalties in connection with the administration of the individual estimated tax and abated 120,585. *1988 Annual Report*, p. 55.

33. For the British figures, see Cedric Sandford, Michael Godwin, and Peter Hardwick, *Administrative and Compliance Costs of Taxation* (Bath: Fiscal Publications, 1989), pp. 86–95.

34. Among the taxpayers tripped up by these rigorous depositing requirements was the State of West Virginia, which, for the 1988–89 fiscal year, owed over $500,000 in interest and penalties for missing federal depositing deadlines. *Insight*, September 4, 1989, p. 44.

35. Real or imagined irregularities by businesses in filing and paying employment taxes resulted in 10,611,031 assessed penalties in 1988. 1,942,847 of these

penalties were abated after protest (i.e., they were judged by the IRS itself to be unjustified). This is twice the rate of abatements as obtains for other penalties. *1988 Annual Report*, p. 55.

36. Letter of Philip L. Shriver, CPA, in *1988 Tax Return Filing Season* (Hearing before the Subcommittee on Oversight, Committee on Ways and Means, U.S. House of Representatives, 100th Cong., 2d Sess., February 23, 1988), p. 120. Shriver pointed out that the cost of complying with these rules for uniform capitalization of inventory "in many cases exceed the additional revenue to the Government."

37. For a review of the Information Collection Budget program, see General Accounting Office, *Paperwork Reduction: Little Real Burden Change in Recent Years* (Washington, D.C., June 1989).

Chapter 3

1. The statement appears on p. 22. See p. 19 of the *1988 Annual Report* for a similar declaration.

2. *Internal Revenue Service Operations* (Hearing before the Subcommittee on Oversight, Committee on Ways and Means, U.S. House of Representatives, 100th Cong., 1st Sess., February 6, 1987), p. 107.

3. See, for example, the discussion of Norm Fox, chief, operations research section, examinations, in Office of the Assistant Commissioner, Planning, Finance and Research, Internal Revenue Service, *Conference on Tax Administration Research January 1985* (Washington, D.C., 1985), vol. 2, pp. 58ff. It is remarkable that the supervisory-level official quoted above was misinformed about this elementary aspect of IRS procedure, a procedure described even in the IRS annual reports (see, for example, *1988 Annual Report*, p. 18).

4. Internal Revenue Service, *1990 Annual Report*, p. 36, t. 16.

5. Sidney Weinman, "Oh-oh . . . You're Being Audited," *Sylvia Porter's Personal Finance*, November 1988, p. 38.

In a 1987 survey of taxpayers in Oklahoma and Pennsylvania, respondents were asked "If the IRS sent you an audit notice, which statement would most accurately characterize your feelings?" The proportions of responses were as follows:

	Percentage
"I'd feel a great deal of anxiety"	9.6
"I'd feel some anxiety"	33.8
"I would not feel anxiety, but I would be annoyed"	44.3
"It wouldn't bother me"	9.1
"I'd look forward to the challenge"	3.2
Total ($N=219$)	100.0

See: Julie H. Collins, Valerie C. Milliron, and Daniel R. Toy, "An Empirical Analysis of Household Demand for Tax Preparers" (Department of Accounting, University of North Carolina Business School, 1989, mimeo), pp. 19, 30.

6. Sweden and Denmark are discussed in Nathan Boidman, "A Summary of What Can Be Learned from the Experience of Other Countries with Income Tax Compliance Problems," in American Bar Association, *Income Tax Compliance* (Reston, Va., 1983), p. 155.

7. IRS, *1990 Annual Report*, p. 28. In 1966, 3.1 million returns were examined out of a total of 69.7 individual income and fiduciary tax returns filed, for a coverage rate of 4.4 percent, IRS *1967 Annual Report*, pp. 16, 23.

8. In a 1985 study that attempted to learn if there was any relationship between the quality of an audit and the time spent, IRS researchers came up with the surprising result that the higher-quality examinations took less time: 3.1 hours, compared with 3.5 hours for the lower-quality examinations. Becky Knowles, "Time Required for Quality Examinations," research abstract in Internal Revenue Service, *Trend Analyses and Related Statistics: 1986 Update* (Washington, D.C.: 1986), p. 193.

9. There is a wide range of charges for representation in audits, covering a wide range of circumstances. For taxpayers whose returns they have prepared, H & R Block preparers will attend an audit without charge. Some CPAs also follow this practice. In these cases, there is still a representation cost, of course; it simply is borne in a different way. A survey of public accountants (noncertified accountants) in 1988 found that the average fixed fee for audit representation ranged from $89 in the north central region to $156 in the Northeast. National Society of Public Accountants, *Income and Fees of Accountants in Public Practice: A 1988 Survey Report*, p. 28, tables 6, 7. These practitioners are less specialized and tend to handle the simpler tax cases. The fees for CPAs and tax lawyers, who appear to do the bulk of the representation work, are many times this figure. In the tabulation that follows are given the reported fees from the different practitioners I interviewed. In making my final estimate from these reports, I have weighed them according to the apparent care the practitioner made in reporting the figures and the representativeness of the respondent's clientele. My overall distillation of these figures is that the average cost is $350 for office audit representation and $1,500 for field audit representation.

Reported Audit Representation Costs

	Office audit		Field audit	
	Minimum	Typical	Minimum	Typical
H & R Block		"Free"		
Noncertified accountants (NSPA)		$89–156		
CPA/tax lawyer, California		$1,000		
CPA/former IRS examiner, South Carolina	$270		$1,000	
CPA, Idaho		$250		

CPA, national firm, California			$6,000	$11,000
Tax lawyer, Michigan	$200		$2,000	
CPA, local firm, Ohio	$500		$2,000	
Tax lawyer, Texas		$3,000		
CPA, Tennessee	$175	$500	$500	

10. In the *1988 Annual Report*, the text on "Examinations" (p. 17) says that "IRS examined 1.03 million returns. . . ." In table 7 (p. 48), the number of returns examined is given as 1.14 million; the "percent coverage" was 1.03, and this seems to be the number the writer used and mislabeled.

A few sentences farther down, the text on p. 17 says that "through correspondence by service center tax examiners, 18 million returns were corrected. . . ." This absurdly high figure is contradicted in table 7, which reports that service centers examined 175,682 returns. (Possibly the error was caused by rounding this figure to 180,000 and then adding two more zeros.)

In table 7, on p. 49, we notice that the percentage of no-change returns for corporations in the category from $1 million to under $5 million is said to be "144." The number is impossible. Perhaps the intended figure was 14.4 percent.

For misleading claims, consider the table on IRS collections and costs (table 27, p. 39 in the *1990 Annual Report*). In order to exaggerate the success and efficiency of the IRS, this table uses the gross collection figure, a figure that runs about 10 percent higher than the net collection figure (taxes collected minus refunds made), which is the appropriate one. The gross collection figure is not honestly labeled as such but is called simply "collections," to lull unsuspecting readers into supposing they are seeing a valid collection figure. This error or deception has appeared from time immemorial in IRS annual reports. See note 11 for another example of a misleading claim.

11. This claim is misleading in suggesting that ACS is the backbone of the collection process, and it is also misleading in suggesting that the IRS is improving its control of the problem of overdue and delinquent accounts.

On the first point, a GAO survey of collection processes noted that about two-thirds of all collected overdue funds ($15.4 billion out of $23.3 collected) are collected at the notice stage, before accounts are transferred to collections. Within collections, fewer than half of ACS attempted levies are successful; and this system itself appears to collect only about 3 percent of all unpaid taxes: U.S. General Accounting Office, *Statistics on IRS' Use of Levies to Collect Delinquent Taxes* (Washington, D.C., July 1989), pp. 3, 10.

On the alleged improvement in collection of delinquent accounts, IRS figures show the total amount of uncollected tax obligations growing by 600 percent since 1977, to $59 billion in 1988: Doug Beazley and Rusty Geiman, "Selected Trends in Collection Inventory Revisited," in Internal Revenue Service, *Trend Analyses and Related Statistics: 1989 Update* (Washington, D.C., 1989), pp. 187, 189.

12. U.S. General Accounting Office, *Accessibility, Timeliness, and Accuracy of IRS' Telephone Assistance Program* (Washington, D.C., February 1989), p. 21.

13. Noted in C. Eugene Steuerle, *Who Should Pay for Collecting Taxes?* (Washington, D.C.: American Enterprise Institute, 1986), p. 15.

14. *The Effectiveness of IRS' Information Returns Program* (Hearing before a subcommittee of the Committee on Government Operations, U.S. House of Representatives, 99th Cong., 2d Sess., April 29, 1986), p. 25.

15. Statement of Robert M. Tobias, national president of the National Treasury Employees Union, in *Administration's Fiscal Year 1988 Budget Proposals Relating to the Internal Revenue Service* (Hearing before the Subcommittee on Oversight of the Committee on Ways and Means, U.S. House of Representatives, 100th Cong., 1st Sess., April 23, 1987), p. 208.

16. *The Effectiveness of IRS' Information Returns Program*, p. 25. The IRS *1990 Annual Report* declares (p. 8) that the error rate in payer reports to the IRS in its Information Returns Program is 5 percent.

17. *Insight*, May 21, 1990, p. 47.

18. See Jim Dumais and Carolyn Quinn, "A Look at the Individual Nonfiler Survey," in Internal Revenue Service, *Trend Analyses and Related Statistics: 1987 Update* (Washington, D.C., 1987), pp. 93, 98, 99. In this study of individuals identified by computer screening as potential nonfilers, only 2.2 percent were true nonfilers who owed significant tax. The rest of the cases involved pointless compliance burdens for the targeted citizens: 87.1 percent were not legally required to file; 2.9 percent were owed refunds; 2.2 percent owed trivial amounts of tax (less than $200), and 5.7 percent were individuals who actually had filed, but who—because the IRS had garbled its own data about them—came out as nonfilers. The size of this last group, projected to nationwide totals, was 1.7 million individuals. The misclassification of these taxpayers represented errors that, as the IRS researchers ruefully commented, "should not have occurred given the checks built into the Service's delinquency lead development system."

19. U.S. General Accounting Office, *IRS Could Reduce the Number of Unproductive Business Nonfiler Investigations* (Washington, D.C., May 1988), p. 13.

20. *Serious Problems Exist in the Quality of IRS Correspondence with Taxpayers* (Hearing before a subcommittee of the Committee on Government Operations, U.S. House of Representatives, 100th Cong., 2d Sess., July 13, 1988), pp. 11–12.

21. Joseph S. Coyle, "Four Basic Letters Can Help You to Win When the IRS Demands Extra Tax Money from You That It Doesn't Deserve," *Money*, April 1990, p. 86.

22. Internal Revenue Service, *1990 Annual Report*, p. 10.

23. U.S. General Accounting Office, *Administration of Selected Filing Penalty Cases at Austin Service Center* (September 1990), p. 15.

24. Internal Revenue Service, *1985 Annual Report*, table 14 (p. 67), shows a total of 22,035,067 penalties assessed (in all enforcement programs), and 4,529,165 penalties abated. It is worth noting that the larger penalties are more likely to be protested and abated. In 1985, $2.6 billion of penalties were abated out of $5.7 billion assessed. This is an abatement rate of 46 percent.

25. David Burnham, *A Law unto Itself* (New York: Random House, 1989), p. 121.

26. U.S. General Accounting Office, *Who's Not Filing Income Tax Returns? IRS Needs Better Ways to Find Them and Collect Their Taxes* (Washington, D.C., July 11, 1979), pp. 62–63. The sample was 400, and only 7 actual filings were produced. Some of these delinquent nonfilers either had no significant tax obligation or were owed a refund. Subtracting such cases would probably lower the number of productive "hits" for the program to less than 1 percent.

27. For 1975, The American Bankers Association estimated that the unit cost of preparing the 1099 and 1087 information forms was 19 cents, plus the (then) 13 cents for postage: Letter from Larry Banyas, The American Bankers Association, June 23, 1976, printed in *Oversight Hearings into the Operations of the IRS (Income Information Document Matching Program)* (Hearing before a subcommittee of the Committee on Government Operations, U.S. House of Representatives, 94th Cong., 2d Sess., April 12, 1976), p. 179.

To adjust these figures to 1985, the 19-cent cost rises to 38 cents (the consumer price index exactly doubled between 1975 and 1985), and the cost of a first class stamp rose to 20 cents. Hence the unit cost was 58 cents for the 850 million payer reports filed in 1985, or $493 million. This figure is a conservative accounting, since it ignores (a) start-up costs in establishing reporting systems, (b) costs of unravelling complaints and errors, and (c) higher costs for smaller, less efficient firms.

28. This was how Representative Byron L. Dorgan (D-N.D.), himself a former state tax commissioner, put it. Dorgan formed a "Dorgan Task Force," cochaired by former IRS commissioners and other luminaries of the culture of taxing, which urged closing the "tax gap" by expanding the number of IRS enforcement personnel. See *Administration's Fiscal Year 1988 Budget Proposals Relating to the Internal Revenue Service* (Hearing before the Subcommittee on Oversight of the Committee on Ways and Means, U.S. House of Representatives, 100th Cong., 1st Sess., April 23, 1987), pp. 6, 10–11, 20. In the 1986 congressional hearings on the IRP before a subcommittee of the House Government Operations Committee, both the subcommittee chairman, Representative Doug Bernard, and Johnny Finch, associate director of the General Accounting Office, uncritically repeated an IRS yield-cost statistic of $17 for the IRP, a figure that assumes zero taxpayer burden for this enforcement program. See *The Effectiveness of IRS' Information Returns Program*, pp. 2, 6.

29. Frank Malanga, "The Relationship between IRS Enforcement and Tax Yield," *National Tax Journal* 39 (September 1986), pp. 335–36. The figures and conclusions of this paper were cited approvingly by C. Eugene Steuerle, a former head of Treasury's economic staff analyzing domestic tax issues, in *Who Should Pay for Collecting Taxes?*, p. 24. Incidentally, the yield-to-cost figure of 11.8 is not the correct division of the reported yield and cost. The figure should be 12.0.

30. See, for example, the presentation and discussion in *The Effectiveness of IRS' Information Returns Program*, p. 5 and passim. All the participants, members of Congress and IRS officials, spoke of assessments as if these were the amounts actually collected. The fact that assessments are not yields was noted in one GAO report on the IRP. In presenting "yield" figures for the Information Returns Program in 1979, the GAO used "dollars assessed less refunds," and came up with a figure of $362 million. See *IRS' Administration of the Tax Laws (Income Information Document Matching)* (Hearing before a subcommittee of the Committee on

Government Operations, U.S. House of Representatives, 96th Cong., 2d Sess., October 1, 1980), p. 50. This compares with a figure of $601 million for "net tax assessed" from the IRP program in 1979, which IRS researchers treated as "revenues" from the program in declaring IRP to be "one of the most cost-effective Examination programs." See David Hill and Fred J. Riley, "Trends in IRP Underreporter Cases," in *Trend Analyses and Related Statistics: 1987 Update*, pp. 85–86.

Hence, even a preliminary effort by GAO to improve the validity of the yield figures resulted in a number that is only 60 percent of the figure the IRS uses for IRP program yield.

As the GAO report pointed out, its figure of $362 million was not a final collection figure either, but was merely a modified assessment figure. To obtain the true yield from an enforcement program like IRP one would have to track a sample of cases to see how each finally comes out. According to the IRS, this tracking process would involve following the cases for seven or eight years, as noted in U.S. General Accounting Office, *Difficulties in Accurately Estimating Tax Examination Yield* (Washington, D.C., August 1988), p. 22.

It is worth noting that the $2.3 billion yield figure for IRP in 1985 is contradicted even by subsequent IRS figures. In response to my Freedom of Information Act request, the IRS alleged (letter of February 22, 1990) a "net assessment" of $1,763,974,968 for IRP in 1985. This is a figure already 23 percent lower than the alleged $2.3 billion yield of the Malanga study and apparently reflects shrinkage owing to abatements from the initial assessment figure.

31. In one computer matching program, where the Social Security accounts were matched with IRS data, the IRS assessed some 500,000 employers with $2.7 billion of additional taxes, interest, and penalties in the period 1981–1984. Of this initial assessment, $1.4 was abated outright as involving some type of IRS error, $0.8 was still in dispute, or otherwise unpaid, and only $0.5 billion had been collected by September 1987, three to six years after the initial assessment. This $0.5 billion represents a true collection rate of 18.5 percent of the initial assessment of $2.7 billion. U.S. General Accounting Office, *1988 Annual Report on GAO's Tax-Related Work*, (Washington, D.C., September 1989), p. 36. Amazingly, GAO advised that IRS expand this enforcement program—ignoring, as GAO always ignores, the burden on taxpayers who must grapple with IRS accusations (over half of which, GAO's own figures show, were unjustified).

Another indication of the gap between initial assessments and yields comes from the data on penalties. Calculations made with the figures given in table 14 of the *1985 Annual Report* show that 21 percent of the initial penalties and 46 percent of the initial penalty *amounts* were already abated by the time the annual report went to press (see this chapter's note 23). As these percentages illustrate, the larger penalties are more likely to be contested (and abated). If these figures are correct and representative of IRP cases (which are included in them), this means that the yield of the IRP program can be no higher than 54 percent of the initial assessments.

32. The formula for calculating the social cost of a governmental expenditure is

$$\text{Social cost} = \text{budgetary cost} + (.65 \times \text{budgetary cost})$$

Hence, the social cost of the $192 million budgetary cost of the IRP is

$$192 + (.65 \times 192) = 317$$

33. The use of a higher yield figure would produce a somewhat higher ratio; but even using the most generous figure, the $1.763 billion "net assessment" claimed in the FOI response noted in note 30, the yield-to-cost ratio would rise to only 1.06. Another change, which would slightly increase the yield-to-cost figure, would be to allocate some of the cost of the payer reporting burden (of $493 million) to the nonfiling program, thus reducing this cost figure for the IRP calculations.

A lower yield-to-cost figure would be obtained if the "downstream costs" of the program were included. The IRP generates cases for collections, appeals, and tax litigation; and the costs of these, to both the government and the private sector, would have to be included. In addition, the true yield of the program could be smaller than the figure we have assumed. Finally, Malanga could have understated the true budgetary costs of the IRP program (by failing to include management overhead expenses, for example).

34. Hill and Riley, p. 85.

35. *Taxpayers' Bill of Rights* (Hearings before the Subcommittee on Private Retirement Plans and Oversight of the Internal Revenue Service of the Committee on Finance, U.S. Senate, 100th Cong., 1st Sess., April 10 and 21, 1987), part 1, pp. 177–78.

Chapter 4

1. Internal Revenue Service, *1985 Annual Report* p. 66, table 11. The number given is the number of separate taxpayers filing appeals. When these appeal petitions reach the IRS Chief Counsel Office, they are grouped into "cases," which may contain two or more taxpayers whose appeal involves the same issue. Hence, the chief counsel's statistics on administrative appeals show about half the number of cases as there are taxpayers involved in the appeals process. The statistics concerning Tax Court filings and administrative appeals docketed before the Tax Court have this same confusion, with the chief counsel's figures reflecting cases that involve a larger number of taxpayers.

Technically, the audit appeals registered in 1985 will not all pertain to audits performed in 1985, since some of the appeals are coming from prior years, and some of the 1985 audits will figure in the following years' appeals figures.

2. In 1985, the 91,134 administrative appeals represented 6.2 percent of the 1.5 million returns examined. In addition to these administrative appeals, 43,437 audit results were appealed directly to the Tax Court.

3. Compiled from data in IRS *1980 Annual Report*, pp. 66–67, 72, 74. In order to make the figures comparable, the total amount under appeals received given in table 15 ($3.831 billion) was divided by the number of taxpayers appealing, given as 84,849 in table 12, not by the number of cases given in table 15. See note 1 for an explanation of the discrepancy between "cases" and "taxpayers."

4. Internal Revenue Service, *Examination of Returns, Appeal Rights, and Claims for Refund* (Publication 556, revised December 1988), p. 3.

5. The respondents quoted a wide range of costs, reflecting differences in cases themselves as well as differences in their charges. At the low end, some respondents indicated that in a rare simple case, the charge could be in the $300 range. At the higher end, costs of $20,000 to $35,000 were quoted. One tax lawyer pointed out that the fees for an audit appeal could go as high as $150,000 if the attorney were working on a case that affected a group of companies. Another factor that can lead to very high costs is the need for expert appraisal—to establish the value of a mineral property, for example. The figures quoted by the different respondents are as follows (I have placed respondents with the greatest familiarity with audit appeals toward the top of the list):

Respondent	Estimated charge for audit appeal
Tax Lawyer, Michigan	$300 least possible charge, $35,000 typical very high charge
Tax Lawyer, New York	$2,500 to $10,000 typical range
Tax Lawyer, New York	$20,000 for typical major case
CPA, South Carolina	$270 least possible charge for individual, $540 least possible charge for corporation
CPA, Ohio	$5,000 typical low charge
CPA, California	$20,000 typical charge for client of national accounting firm
Tax Lawyer, Texas	$6,000 typical low charge, $20,000 typical high charge
Tax Lawyer, IRS	$2,500 typical charge
CPA, Idaho	$500 typical low charge
Tax Lawyer, Kansas	$5,000 typical charge

After evaluating the different estimates and trying to assess the frequency with which they apply, I estimate the average cost of audit appeal representation in 1988–89 at $7,000. The median, or typical, figure would be less, perhaps around $4,000. Ideally, this figure ought to be subject to some correction for inflation to be applied to 1985, our focus year; but in view of its imprecision, such a refinement seems moot.

6. One IRS survey of taxpayers in the appeals process claimed to have found that "over two-thirds of the taxpayers did not have a representative. . . ." This finding seems implausible. James Iocozzia, "Appeals Taxpayer Attitude Study," in Internal Revenue Service, *Trend Analyses and Related Statistics: 1987 Update* (Washington, D.C., 1987), p. 174.

7. For a background survey of the Tax Court system, see the report of the IRS chief counsel in *Administration's Fiscal Year 1989 Budget Proposals Relating to the Internal Revenue Service and the U.S. Tax Court* (Hearing before the Committee on Oversight of the Committee on Ways and Means, U.S. House of Representatives, 100th Cong., 2d Sess., April 13, 1988), pp. 113–38.

8. George Hansen, *To Harass Our People: The IRS and Government Abuse of Power* (Washington, D.C.: Positive Publications, 1984), p. 106.

9. Most of the respondents were selected at random from the American Bar Association's directory of tax section committee members. Three respondents contacted declined to make any estimate of tax litigation costs. The estimates obtained are listed below, with the more experienced practitioners listed toward the top of the list.

Respondent	Estimate for Tax Court representation costs
Tax Lawyer, Michigan	$30,000–$35,000 average cost, $75,000 for large case
Tax Lawyer, New York	$25,000–$35,000 average cost, $75,000–$125,000 for major case
Tax Lawyer, New York	$2,000 smallest possible cost, $100,000–$200,000 for major case
Tax Lawyer, California	$10,000 for simplest case
Tax Lawyer, Washington, D.C.	$10,000–$20,000 for simplest case; $300,000 for major case
Tax Lawyer, IRS	$10,000 minimum cost; $200,000 for major case
CPA, California, national firm	$50,000 typical cost
Tax Lawyer, Kansas	$10,000–$15,000 minimum
Tax Lawyer, Texas	$5,000 cost above cost of audit appeal, for small case
Tax Lawyer, Texas	$10,000 minimum cost

10. Since this figure is based on reports made in the 1988–1989 period, it probably reflects some inflation relative to 1985, the year we focus upon in this study. A correction for this aspect seems an unnecessary refinement given the roughness of the estimate.

11. Internal Revenue Service, *1985 Annual Report*, p. 39. This 34,258 figure is the result of subtracting the "small" cases (14,884) from the total number of cases received (49,142). A footnote reports that some 1986 cases are included in the total, but an inspection of the 1986 cases received (48,787) indicates no unusual displacement of cases.

The figures being used are those from the IRS chief counsel. As already noted, these figures can group several taxpayers into one case. Hence, the number of actual taxpayer litigants is higher than the 34,258 figure. It is not clear, however, that each separate taxpayer litigant would have a separate attorney.

12. *Administration's Fiscal Year 1989 Budget Proposals Relating to the Internal Revenue Service and the U.S. Tax Court*, p. 120.

13. *Oversight of IRS and Justice Department Prosecution of Several Tax Cases* (Hearings before the Subcommittee on Oversight of the Internal Revenue Service, Committee on Finance, U.S. Senate, 99th Cong., 2d Sess., 1986), part 1, p. 127.

14. A survey by Louis Harris and Associates found 22 percent admitting to understating income or overstating deductions (or both). Internal Revenue Service, *1987 Taxpayer Opinion Survey*, conducted by Louis Harris and Associates, July–August 1987 (Washington, D.C., 1988), p. 76. A confidential survey of 100 taxpayers in the Boston area in 1988 found that 50 percent admitted to omitting some income within the previous three years. See John Carroll, "Tax Law Changes and Taxpayer Decision Making," in Internal Revenue Service, *Change and Complexity as Barriers to Taxpayer Compliance: Conference Report* (Washington, D.C., November 17–18, 1988), p. 30.

15. David Burnham, *A Law unto Itself* (New York: Random House, 1989), pp. 83–84.

16. U.S. General Accounting Office, *Investigating Illegal Income: Success Uncertain, Improvements Needed* (Washington, D.C., April 1988), p. 19.

17. Suzanne Scotchmer and Joel Slemrod, "Randomness in Tax Enforcement," National Bureau of Economic Research (NBER), working paper 2512, (February 1988), p. 1.

18. According to the IRS *1990 Annual Report* (p. 38) there were 1,073,443 exempt organizations on file at the end of 1990.

19. U.S. Treasury Department, *Annual Report of the Commissioner of Internal Revenue, Fiscal Year Ended June 30, 1950*, p. 55.

20. *1975 Annual Report*, p. 53, and *1990 Annual Report*, p. 42. In both figures, the cases of the national office are excluded and advisory opinions are included.

21. Chief counsel, Internal Revenue Service, *1977 Annual Report*, p. 21.

22. Ibid., p. 22; IRS *1990 Annual Report*, p. 42.

Chapter 5

1. *Insight*, July 10, 1989, p. 42, and August 7, 1989, p. 47.

2. *Taxpayers' Bill of Rights* (Hearings before the Subcommittee on Private Retirement Plans and Oversight of the Internal Revenue Service of the Committee

on Finance, U.S. Senate, 100th Cong., 1st Sess., April 10 and 21, 1987), part 1, p. 237.

3. *IRS Summary Collection Policy Impact on Small Business* (Hearings before the Subcommittee on Oversight of Government Management of the Committee on Governmental Affairs, U.S. Senate, 96th Cong., 2d Sess., July 31, 1980), pp. 40–47.

4. *Taxpayers' Bill of Rights*, part 1, p. 164.

5. Ibid., part 2, p. 93. In 1988, the head of the IRS employees' union complained about the "counterproductive" pressure that IRS managers were putting on collection officers to make case closures instead of allowing them to make settlements that are "fair to the taxpayer and fair to the government." *Administration's Fiscal Year 1989 Budget Proposals Relating to the Internal Revenue Service and the U.S. Tax Court* (Hearing before the Subcommittee on Oversight of the Committee on Ways and Means, U.S. House of Representatives, 100th Cong., 2d Sess., April 13, 1988), p. 231.

6. *Taxpayers' Bill of Rights*, part 1, pp. 221–22.

7. Ibid., part 1, p. 37. A case was cited where the IRS seized a $40,000 home and sold it for $1,725, the amount of the tax debt. Thus, the taxpayer was penalized $40,000 for a tax debt of $1,725. When the case was taken to court, the IRS claimed "that it was under no duty to sell seized property at fair or reasonable market value. . . ." In another hearing, an IRS collections officer testified that seizures typically recover less than 15 percent of the tax debt owed. *IRS Summary Collection Policy Impact on Small Business*, p. 37.

8. Ibid., pp. 64–68.

9. Ibid., pp. 60–103; *Taxpayers' Bill of Rights*, part 1, p. 154.

10. George Hansen, *To Harass Our People: The IRS and Government Abuse of Power* (Washington, D.C.: Positive Publications, 1984), pp. 65–66.

11. *Taxpayers' Bill of Rights*, part 1, p. 177.

12. Ibid., part 2, p. 96.

13. Ibid., part 2, p. 118.

14. U.S. General Accounting Office, *Extent and Causes of Erroneous Levies* (Washington, D.C., December 1990), p. 6.

15. Asked by Senator Pryor if there were other cases like Treadway's, tax specialist and former IRS agent Joseph B. Smith, Jr., said "I travel all over the United States helping people. The answer to the question is yes. There are a lot of Treadways in the United States." *Taxpayers' Bill of Rights*, part 1, p. 111.

16. See the discussion of the Kilpatrick case in Chapter 9, note 19.

17. *IRS Summary Collection Policy Impact on Small Business*, p. 67.

18. Barbara W. Rothacher, *Deer Graze on My Roof* (1983), pp. 105–6.

19. *Bonner County Daily Bee*, August 1, 1989, p. 1; August 11, 1989, p. 1; August 12, 1989, p. 10; January 20, 1990, p. 1.

20. A 1990 survey of IRS top managers produced an interesting mix of responses to a question about the nice versus the nasty approach to tax administration. To the statement, "There should be more emphasis on treating taxpayers as customers and less hard-line enforcement tactics," the responses were as follows:

	Percentage
Strongly agree	14
Agree	44
Disagree	31
Strongly disagree	6
Other, no answer	5
Total	100 (N = 858?)

The managers, incidentally, were drawn from all branches of the IRS; 10 percent were from the collections division. The survey was conducted by the Joseph & Edna Josephson Institute of Ethics and published as *Internal Revenue Service Survey of Managers Opinions, Values and Behaviors* (Marina del Rey, Calif.: January 1991), p. 40.

21. Many clauses in the Taxpayers' Bill of Rights that attempt to regulate IRS abuses have escape hatches that nullify them. The clause prohibiting evaluation of IRS collection employees on the basis of "production quotas," sec. 6231, part (a), is contradicted by part (b) which says, in effect, that what the IRS already is doing is fine. The clause addressing garbled and incoherent notices (sec. 7521, part a) concludes that these notices are always valid, no matter how incoherent. The clause encouraging IRS adherence to installment payment plans (sec. 6159) gives IRS officials many ways to arbitrarily and subjectively abrogate them, including simply announcing a jeopardy assessment, which can be made for no reason (see the discussion of the Treadway case in the text). The attempt to protect personal residences from seizure (sec. 6236 [13]) is nullified by clause (e) which defines two methods whereby IRS officials may, on an entirely subjective, arbitrary basis, seize homes.

The original Taxpayers' Bill of Rights legislation aimed at genuine taxpayer protections, but it appears that its teeth were pulled by the culture of taxing legislators in Congress before its final passage. As explained in Chapter 11, this group of senior tax committee congressmen, who control tax enforcement policy, have adopted the IRS perspective and generally enact its wishes into law. The IRS was opposed to the definition of any significant taxpayer rights.

22. Another activity, investigations of delinquent returns, will not be treated separately, since the cost of these will fall under categories already mentioned, especially compliance costs and collection costs.

23. This Taxpayers' Bill of Rights provision went into effect on July 1, 1989; but many banks ignored it and continued to send levied funds to the IRS without delay. *Insight*, October 30, 1989, p. 44.

24. Internal Revenue Service, *1980 Annual Report*, p. 72, table 13, and *1990 Annual Report*, p. 37, table 19.

25. Ibid.

26. The total number of levies issued in 1985 is given as 1,418,000 in the IRS *1985 Annual Report*, p. 66, table 13. A General Accounting Office study of the Automated Collection System determined that 1.9 notices of levy are issued per taxpayer. *Statistics on IRS' Use of Levies to Collect Delinquent Taxes* (Washington, D.C., July 1989), p. 10. If we use this conversion, the 1,418,000 levy notices issued in 1985 pertained to 746,000 intended taxpayers.

In practice, not all levy notices affect taxpayers. Some insight into this issue comes from the GAO survey just mentioned. The results showed that only 47.3 percent of the levies issued were productive. The GAO did not look into what happened with the other 53 percent of cases. It seems that many of these involved erroneous notices—that is, as in the Information Returns Program, taxpayers incorrectly acted against on the basis of garbled information or simply through clerical inattention. In some cases, however, the error in the intended levy notice means that the levy misses the taxpayer altogether: the IRS has incorrect name or account information (or the account has been closed). In these cases, which I will estimate at 10 percent of intended taxpayers subjected to the levy process, there would be no burden for the taxpayer. Applying this correction to the previous figure gives us an estimate of 671,000 as the number of taxpayers actually affected by the levy process in 1985.

27. IRS reply to author's Freedom of Information Act request, December 20, 1989. The number of taxpayers on installment agreements increased to 904,235 in 1991. *Wall Street Journal,* April 17, 1991, p. 1.

28. *Taxpayers' Bill of Rights,* part 1, p. 345.

29. The total number of tax liens filed in 1985 was 705,000. To arrive at the number of taxpayers affected, we must reduce this figure to adjust for cases where more than one lien was filed against the same taxpayer, and also for cases where the taxpayer was also subjected to a levy (and has therefore already been included in our tabulations). In the absence of data on what these overlaps might be, I estimate that half of the liens involve double counting. Therefore, I estimate that an additional 352,000 taxpayers were affected by liens.

Hence, in 1985 a total of 1,023,000 taxpayers were subject to levies or liens, or both.

30. One of the many complications of attempting such calculations is the possibility that the asset deprivation cost should have already been included in the accounting of the disincentive cost if the levy is a correct one and made carefully. That is, some businesses are economically unprofitable when the cost of taxes is included. A tax foreclosure merely demonstrates what calculations of the disincentive cost of taxation (otherwise known as marginal excess burden) should have already estimated, namely, that the business should not have been attempted given the burden of taxation. Of course this point would not hold true for levies made in error or incompetently administered.

31. The source for the number of levies, liens, and seizures is Internal Revenue Service, *1985 Annual Report,* p. 66, table 13, modified as explained in notes 26 and 29.

The computations underlying the respective figures are as follows:

levies, resistance cost, taxpayer time: 120 hrs × 28.31 $/hr × 671,000 = $2,280,000,000

levies, resistance cost, representation: $500 × 671,000 = $336,000,000

liens, resistance cost, taxpayer time 120 hrs × 28.31 $/hr × 352,000 = $1,196,000,000

liens, resistance cost, representation: $500 × 352,000 = $176,000,000

32. Doug Beazley and Rusty Geiman, "Selected Trends in Collection Inventory Revisited," in Internal Revenue Service, *Trend Analyses and Related Statistics: 1989 Update* (Washington, D.C., 1989), p. 189.

33. Joel Friedman and Rusty Geiman, "Characteristics of Statute Expired Cases," in Internal Revenue Service, *Trend Analyses and Related Statistics: 1986 Update* (Washington, D.C., 1986), pp. 73–75. I added the numbers indicated in fig. 1 to arrive at the 1975 figure.

34. IRS response to author's Freedom of Information Act Request, December 20, 1989.

Chapter 6

1. For a survey of this literature, see David G. Davies, *United States Taxes and Tax Policy* (Cambridge: Cambridge University Press, 1986), pp. 58–76.

2. Charles E. Stuart, "Swedish Tax Rates, Labor Supply, and Tax Revenues," *Journal of Political Economy* 89 (October 1981), pp. 1020–38.

3. "More Nations Warm to Tax Reform," *Insight*, May 16, 1988, p. 45. In Sweden, top tax rates have gone down from 80 percent in the early 1980s to 62 percent in 1990, going to 50 percent in 1991. Tony Horwitz, "Sweden Faces Chill as Economy Stagnates," *Wall Street Journal*, April 5, 1990, p. A19.

4. The sources used for Table 11 are as follows: Edgar K. Browning, "On the Marginal Welfare Cost of Taxation," *The American Economic Review* 77 (March 1987), p. 21; Jerry A. Hausman, "Labor Supply," in Henry J. Aaron and Joseph A. Pechman, eds., *How Taxes Affect Economic Behavior* (Washington, D.C.: The Brookings Institution, 1981), p. 61; Charles Stuart, "Welfare Costs per Dollar of Additional Tax Revenue in the United States," *The American Economic Review* 74 (June 1984), p. 358; Roger H. Gordon and Burton G. Malkiel, "Corporation Finance," in Aaron and Pechman, eds., *How Taxes Affect Economic Behavior*, p. 178 (the disincentive cost as a percentage of revenue collected is calculated from the figures given in table 6 by dividing the efficiency gains by the revenue loss [sign reversed]); Jane G. Gravelle and Laurence J. Kotlikoff, "The Incidence and Efficiency Costs of Corporate Taxation When Corporate and Noncorporate Firms Produce the Same Good," *Journal of Political Economy* 97 (August 1989), p. 774, table 6; Charles L. Ballard, John B. Shoven, and John Whalley, "General Equilibrium Computations of the Marginal Welfare Costs of Taxes in the United States," *The American Economic Review* (March 1985), p. 135, table 3; Dale W. Jorgenson and Kun-Young Yun, "The Excess Burden of Taxation in the U.S. (Paper prepared for presentation at the Coopers & Lybrand Foundation symposium, U.S. Tax Policy for the 1990s, New York, November 7–8, 1990), p. 18.

5. Michael J. Boskin, "Efficiency Aspects of the Differential Tax Treatment of Market and Household Economic Activity," *Journal of Public Economics* 4 (1975), p. 12.

6. Edgar K. Browning, "The Marginal Cost of Public Funds," *Journal of Political Economy* 84 (April 1976), pp. 283–98.

7. Jerry A. Hausman, "Labor Supply," in Henry J. Aaron and Joseph A. Pechman, eds., *How Taxes Affect Economic Behavior* (Washington, D.C.: The Brookings Institution, 1981), pp. 54, 57, 64.

8. Martin Feldstein and Joel Slemrod, "Inflation and the Excess Taxation of Capital Gains on Corporate Stock," *National Tax Journal* 31 (1978), pp. 107–18.

9. "Making Us Poorer," *Wall Street Journal*, May 8, 1978, p. 20.

10. Ibid.

11. Michael J. Boskin, "Taxation, Saving, and the Rate of Interest," *Journal of Political Economy* 86, (1978), pp. S3–S27. Based on his review of the literature, economist J. Gregory Ballentine commented (in 1981), concerning the corporation tax, "Previous analysis of the welfare loss associated with the misallocation of capital and the distortion in the timing of consumption suggests that the combined loss may be on the order of 1 percent of GNP." For 1988, this would be a loss of $50 billion, or 46 percent of corporation taxes collected. This 46 percent figure is an average cost figure. See "Comments," in Aaron and Pechman, p. 192.

12. Martin Feldstein, "Tax Rules and Business Investment," in Martin Feldstein, ed., *Taxes and Capital Formation* (Chicago: University of Chicago Press, 1987), pp. 63–72; Lester C. Thurow, *The Impact of Taxes on the American Economy* (New York: Praeger, 1971), p. 33.

13. Roger H. Gordon and Joel Slemrod, "Do We Collect Any Revenue from Taxing Capital Income?" in Lawrence H. Summers, ed., *Tax Policy and the Economy* 2 (Cambridge, Mass.: MIT Press, 1988), p. 120.

14. These two approaches are called differential analysis and balanced-budget analysis, respectively. In differential analysis, tax revenues are held constant and tax effects are compared to an ideal lump-sum tax. In balanced-budget analysis, revenue and spending are allowed to vary. The differences between these two approaches has been discussed by the following authors: Charles Stuart, "Welfare Costs per Dollar of Additional Tax Revenue in the United States," *American Economic Review* 74 (June 1984), pp. 358–59; Charles L. Ballard, "Marginal Welfare Cost Calculations; Differential Analysis vs. Balanced-Budget Analysis," *Journal of Public Economics* 41 (1990), pp. 263–76, and "Marginal Efficiency Cost Calculations for Different Types of Government Expenditure: A Review," (Paper presented at the Australian Conference in Applied General Equilibrium, Melbourne, May 27–28, 1991); Don Fullerton, "If Labor Is Inelastic, Are Taxes Still Distorting?" National Bureau of Economic Research (NBER) working paper 2810 (January 1989).

15. Hausman, "Labor Supply," p. 27.

16. Ballard, Shoven, and Whalley, p. 128. It appears the authors meant benefit-cost instead of cost-benefit.

17. Alan J. Auerbach and James R. Hines, Jr., "Investment Tax Incentives and Frequent Tax Reforms," *American Economic Review* 78 (May 1988), p. 211.

18. Jonathan Skinner, "The Welfare Cost of Uncertain Tax Policy," NBER working paper 1947 (June 1986), p. 19.

19. Ibid., p. 21. Skinner notes (p. 20) that his model does not include government expenditures in the utility function and that to some extent this may have produced an overestimate of the welfare cost of uncertain tax policy.

20. David Collard, "Compliance Costs and Efficiency Costs of Taxation," in Cedric Sandford, Michael Godwin, and Peter Hardwick, *Administrative and Compliance Costs of Taxation* (Bath: Fiscal Publications, 1989), app. E, p. 276. This point is also noted by Edgar K. Browning in his unpublished 1990 paper, "Tax and Nontax Labor Supply Distortions."

Chapter 7

1. For similar quotations, from both Learned Hand and Justice Felix Frankfurter endorsing tax avoidance, see Robert Chappell, *Secrets of Offshore Tax Havens* (ABM Publishing Company, 1985), pp. 90–91.

2. Vito Tanzi, ed., *The Underground Economy in the United States and Abroad* (Lexington, Mass.: D. C. Heath, 1982), p. 4.

3. Ibid., p. 18. See also Carl P. Simon and Ann D. Witte, *Beating the System: The Underground Economy* (Boston: Auburn House, 1982), p. xiv.

4. *Internal Revenue Service's 1988 Report on the "Tax Gap"* (Hearing before the Subcommittee on Oversight of the Committee on Ways and Means, U.S. House of Representatives, 100th Cong., 2d Sess., March 17, 1988), pp. 20, 21, 23. The $406.4 billion figure is reached by adding the unreported income of non-filers to the underreported income of filers. For the unpaid tax figure, I have used the more conservative estimate of assessments after appeals.

5. Even some tax collectors realize that tax evasion can be economically constructive. When the head of Britain's Board of Inland Revenue was asked what he proposed to do to combat the underground economy, he replied, "Do about it? Why, it's the only efficient sector of the economy." Quoted in American Bar Association, *Income Tax Compliance* (Reston, Va., 1983), p. 442.

6. The GAO report is *Who's Not Filing Income Tax Returns? IRS Needs Better Ways to Find Them and Collect Their Taxes* (Washington, D.C., July 11, 1979). This is a comprehensive effort to identify nonfilers by matching government files, especially Social Security files and IRS files, which involved a number of adjustments to correct for spurious and misleading aspects of the tally. The study came up with a figure of from 4.1 million to 5.3 million nonfilers in 1972 (p. 78). For our purposes, I take the midpoint of this range, 4.7 million. This figure would seem to have two, offsetting, biases: (1) It misses workers who have left no paper trail and who therefore are invisible to the matching process. (2) It includes "ghosts," apparent nonfilers that are the result of garbled information and flaws in the matching procedure.

Data on the income levels of these nonfilers (see, for example, *Who's Not Filing?* p. 87, table 3) indicate that about 20 percent fall in the low-income category (defined as less than $3,000 gross income). Although these individuals may have had a legal obligation to file, it seems probable that their tax debts were quite small. They should be seen as simply not bothering to comply with the tax system rather than energetically evading it. Subtracting this 20 percent gives 3.7 million "significant" nonfilers. This figure is then increased by 15 percent to adjust for the population increase in the period 1972–1985, to give a total of 4.3 million significant nonfilers in 1985. (This adjustment makes the conservative assumption that the proportion of nonfilers in the population did not increase over this period.)

7. This estimate is supported by the figures advanced by Simon and Witte in *Beating the System*, p. xiv. Their estimates place the tax evasion fraction of the underground economy at between 43 percent and 57 percent of the entire underground economy.

8. Obviously, this 10 percent figure is an important part of the overall estimate, but it can be justified only roughly, as follows. The upper bound for this figure could not be much more than about 40 percent. Under assumptions

of economic rationality, workers would not go underground if the cost of doing so exceeded their tax burden plus their compliance cost. This break-even point would be around 40 percent of the worker's income under current conditions. The lower bound is a figure greater than zero if we assume the worker inconveniences himself to remain underground.

9. David Burnham, *A Law unto Itself* (New York: Random House, 1989), pp. 208–16.

10. Just how expensive it can be for a tax shelter promoter to counter government challenges is illustrated by the case of William Kilpatrick, a promoter who specialized in coal leases. He reports that he underwent two FBI investigations, four SEC investigations, and "hundreds" of IRS actions, as well as two grand jury proceedings. In an attempt to get him, the IRS undertook criminal proceedings in which they, and Justice Department officials, committed a large number of violations and abuses. These government efforts failed, but Kilpatrick reports he spent $6 million in legal fees to counter them. William A. Kilpatrick, *The Big Tax Lie* (New York: Simon and Schuster, 1986), pp. 126–27, 213ff.

11. The charges for investment tax shelters vary, depending partly on the size of the potential tax saving (and hence upon the risk that promoters will encounter problems with the IRS). One accountant knowledgeable in this field reported that the typical cost to buy into a limited partnership tax shelter arrangement was 30 percent of the capital invested, made up of a 5 percent charge for accounting and legal services, a 7 percent sales commission, and an 18 percent overpayment for the underlying investment being purchased. Another accountant put the purchase overhead at 10 to 15 percent of the investment with, in some cases, additional charges (or deductions from earnings) during the life of the arrangement. These observations suggest an estimate of 20 percent for overhead costs for an investment tax shelter.

In prepared testimony in 1988, the president of the National Treasury Employees Union made the following declaration, based on IRS figures: "As of December, 1985, the Examination Division had a record inventory of 413,665 tax shelter cases—a number that had grown steadily since IRS began examinations of abusive tax shelters in 1981. This backlog emerged despite closure of 505,000 cases during 1981–1985 with assessments totaling $8.2 billion. . . ." (Quoted in *Administration's Fiscal Year 1989 Budget Proposals Relating to the Internal Revenue Service and the U.S. Tax Court* [Hearing before the Subcommittee on Oversight of the Committee on Ways and Means, U.S. House of Representatives, 100th Cong., 2d Sess., April 13, 1988], p. 233.) Thus, the IRS examined a total of 918,665 "abusive" shelters, covering, I judge, the six-year period 1979–1984. In this accounting, I am assuming one taxpayer per shelter case. Of course, the IRS did not audit all such arrangements. Since it was making a special effort to target these arrangements, however, we will assume a rather high audit coverage rate of 50 percent (this would be comparable to the audit rate for the largest corporations). Under this assumption, then, there were 2 × 918,665, or 1,837,330, taxpayers entering into investment shelter arrangements in this six-year period, or 306,000 per year. Making the assumption that the average investment was $75,000, the yearly overhead cost of tax shelters was 306,000 × $75,000 × .20 = $4.6 billion.

Another way to estimate this cost is to work from IRS assessments of taxes owed, as revealed from its findings in examinations of "abusive" tax shelters. Our assumption is that the overhead cost of shelters would be less than the tax evaded (otherwise, it would not be rational for the taxpayer to enter into these arrangements). IRS audits found that for the tax shelter cases closed during the 1981–1985 period, the tax evaded per taxpayer averaged $16,238. This figure is calculated by dividing the $8.2 billion in assessed taxes by the 505,000 cases to which they apply, given in the source just cited. Correcting this figure for inflation to 1985 gives an average figure of $19,300.

Taking this $19,300 figure as an average for taxes avoided, we then say that the avoidance costs for this amount must have been between this figure and zero. The midpoint of this range, $9,650, suggests itself as a plausible estimate of this cost. Multiplying this figure times the 306,000 taxpayers entering shelters each year gives $3.0 billion.

For an overall figure, I average the two estimates, $4.6 and $3.0 billion, which yields $3.8 billion.

12. *Insight,* July 10, 1989, p. 43.

13. See the discussion of the Kilpatrick case, in note 10.

14. George Cooper, *A Voluntary Tax? New Perspectives on Sophisticated Estate Tax Avoidance* (Washington, D.C.: The Brookings Institution, 1979), p. 1.

15. Ibid., p. 39.

16. Interview with M. Sharon Green, American Bar Association librarian, December 29, 1989.

17. This figure was quoted in *Ohio Lawyer,* September/October 1988, p. 18. The figure applies to 1987.

18. The calculation is $30,093 \times \$178,707 \times .30 = \$1,613,000,000$.

19. *The Fidelity Master Plan for Savings and Investments: Plan Summary* (Fidelity Investments, n.d.).

20. Interview with Jennifer L. Davis, research analyst, Employee Benefit Research Institute (Washington, D.C.), January 2, 1990. This figure is based on data collected from IRS form 5500 submissions and does not include IRA, SEP, and Keogh plans; however, it would include some pension plans not motivated by tax sheltering.

21. Internal Revenue Service, *SOI Bulletin* 6 (winter 1986–87), p. 8. This figure is for 1985.

22. *Tax Havens and Their Use by United States Taxpayers: An Overview,* Report to the commissioner of internal revenue submitted by Richard A. Gordon, special counsel for international taxation (Washington, D.C., January 12, 1981), p. 52.

23. Ibid., pp. 32–39; Berdj Kenadjian, "Levels and Significance of Tax Haven Use by Controlled Foreign Corporations," in Internal Revenue Service, *Trend Analyses and Related Statistics: 1986 Update* (Washington, D.C., 1986), pp. 135–43.

24. Chappell, *Secrets of Offshore Tax Havens,* p. 142.

25. *Federal Express International Newsletter,* November 1989, pp. 4, 11.

26. James R. Hines, Jr., and R. Glenn Hubbard, "Coming Home to America: Dividend Repatriations by U.S. Multinationals," National Bureau of Economic Research (NBER) working paper 2931 (April 1989), p. 34.

27. *Tax Havens and Their Use by United States Taxpayers* (p. 41, table 4) shows international deposits in tax havens going from $10.6 billion in 1968 to $384.9 billion in 1978. Table 1 (p. 38) shows that in the period 1968–1978, U.S. direct investment in tax haven areas grew twice as fast as U.S. investment in other foreign countries.

28. Ibid., p. 41.

29. This extrapolation was produced by calculating the linear regression for the five years 1974–1978 and then using this equation to estimate the 1985 value.

30. One problem with this deposit figure is that it is a year-end figure. The actual amount of money that passed through the tax haven banking system each year would be higher than the amount on deposit at any one time. Second, not all U.S. tax avoidance money goes to the specific tax havens involved in the calculation. Every country in the world is probably the recipient of some U.S. tax-avoiding money. These two considerations suggest that the total amount of tax-avoiding money flowing from U.S. taxpayers, including corporations, could be considerably understated.

It is true, however, that not all of the international deposits in the Western Hemisphere tax havens reflect a tax avoidance effort. Some of these funds represent normal commercial activity. Second, some of the funds in tax havens represent drug income that has been driven underground by the illegal status of the drug trade, not by the tax system. Therefore, as already noted, overhead costs connected with this realm should not be included in our tabulations. These two considerations suggest that the bank deposit figure would overstate the real value of offshore banking induced by the tax system.

The $344 billion figure therefore represents only a rough approximation of the number we would like to have, for it incorporates a number of (one hopes, offsetting) distortions. It is somewhat encouraging to note that several other crude estimates of the volume of international tax avoidance money seem to fall in the same general range. An IRS study of tax havens in the Caribbean determined that "the excess holdings (defined as those holdings beyond the requirements needed to finance foreign trade) of foreign assets in the Bahamas, the Cayman Islands and Panama together amounted to over $300 billion in 1982." Berdj Kenadjian, "Levels of Caribbean Tax Haven Use," in Internal Revenue Service, *Trend Analyses and Related Statistics: 1985 Update,* IRS document 6011 (Washington, D.C., 1985), pp. 162–63. In its survey of international money laundering, *Time* (December 18, 1989, p. 52) estimated that the total "grey money" (funds from noncriminal sources) passing through international financial institutions is "$1 trillion or more each year." It is reasonable to suppose that about a third of these funds would be of U.S. origin.

31. For an investor setting up a contractual company (see text) with $10,000, the set-up cost would amount to 28 percent of the funds invested, and the yearly management fees would be 2.5 percent (Chappell, p. 142). If larger amounts were invested, these fractions would go down, of course. With a $1 million investment, the set-up cost would be about 1.4 percent of the amount invested. Of course, with a larger sum at risk, the taxpayer would probably spend more time and money investigating and monitoring the arrangement. One source notes that to set up a simple fiduciary account that guards the anonymity of the depositor, Swiss banks

charge between 1/8 and 1/2 percent of the amount deposited (*Tax Havens and Their Use by United States Taxpayers*, p. 37).

Comprehensive IRS investigations into Caribbean tax avoidance arrangements found that the standard commission for the salesmen and managers of these shelters was 10 percent of the amount invested. *Tax Evasion, Drug Trafficking and Money Laundering As They Involve Financial Institutions* (Hearings before the Subcommittee on Financial Institutions Supervision, Regulation and Insurance of the Committee on Banking, Finance and Urban Affairs, U.S. House of Representatives, 99th Cong., 2d Sess., April 16, 17, 23 and May 14, 1986), pp. 161–94, 201.

Money-laundering operations are said to charge a 4 percent fee for recycling ordinary grey (tax avoidance) money and 7 to 10 percent for drug money (*Time*, December 18, 1989, p. 50). In one laundering operation of $50,000 (drug-related), a Cayman Islands firm charged 6 percent to handle their part of the operation (*Tax Havens and Their Use by United States Taxpayers*, p. 126).

Since most of the money devoted to tax avoidance in offshore havens is relatively legitimate and in rather large amounts, it would seem appropriate to use a somewhat lower handling charge for an average figure. The figure I have chosen is 2.0 percent.

32. Martin Feldstein and Shlomo Yitzhaki, "The Effects of the Capital Gains Tax on the Selling and Switching of Common Stock," *Journal of Public Economics* 9 (1978), pp. 17–36; Joseph J. Minarik, "Capital Gains," in Henry J. Aaron and Joseph A. Pechman, *How Taxes Affect Economic Behavior* (Washington, D.C.: The Brookings Institution, 1981), pp. 241–77.

Chapter 8

1. On a work-load basis, in 1985, 276,001 cases were filed in federal district courts (this figure includes an adjustment factor for trivial cases). In addition, a total of 33,506 cases were filed in the twelve regional courts of appeal. This makes for a total (work-load basis) case load of 309,507. See *Departments of Commerce, Justice, and State, the Judiciary, and Related Agencies Appropriations for 1987* (Hearings before a subcommittee of the Committee on Appropriations, U.S. House of Representatives, 99th Cong., 2d Sess.), part 3, pp. 8, 46.

The total number of 1985 tax litigation cases received, not counting the 49,142 cases filed with the Tax Court, was 37,634. See Internal Revenue Service, *1985 Annual Report*, p. 33.

Using these figures, the fraction of all federal court cases that are tax cases is 37,634/309,507 = 0.12.

2. The IRS *1985 Annual Report*, p. 18, reports that 64 percent of the 2,091 sentenced defendants received prison terms.

3. The number of federal prisoners who are tax offenders can be calculated by multiplying the yearly number of new sentences by the average length of sentence. One source gives the average prison term for those sentenced as 29 months. See Office of the Assistant Commissioner for Planning, Finance and Research, Internal Revenue Service, *Conference on Tax Administration Research January 1985* (Washington, D.C., 1985), vol. 2, p. 88. Using this figure and the figure of 1,338 sentenced offenders gives a total tax offender prison population

of 3,233 (1,338 × 29/12). Since the total federal prison population in 1985 was 32,580, the fraction of tax offenders to the total would be 10 percent (3,233/32,580). Another source gives the average prison term for tax offenders as thirty-eight months. See *Taxpayers' Bill of Rights* (Hearings before the Subcommittee on Private Retirement Plans and Oversight of the Internal Revenue Service of the Committee on Finance, U.S. Senate, 100th Cong., 1st Sess., April 10 and 21, 1987), part 1, p. 290. Use of this thirty-eight-month figure would put the proportion of federal tax offenders at 13 percent of federal prison population.

4. Total payments made by the Financial Management Service in 1985 were $703 billion, of which $78 billion were IRS refund checks. See *Treasury, Postal Service, and General Government Appropriations for Fiscal Year 1986* (Hearing before a subcommittee of the Committee on Appropriations, U.S. House of Representatives, 99th Cong., 1st Sess.), part 1, p. 206.

5. This point is noted in C. Eugene Steuerle, *Who Should Pay for Collecting Taxes? Financing the IRS* (Washington, D.C.: American Enterprise Institute, 1986), pp. 26–27.

6. The misleading gross collection figure is used each year in the table of the IRS annual report that presents the "cost of collecting $100." See, for example, *1990 Annual Report*, p. 39, table 27. The gross collection figure of $1056.4 billion was used (and misleadingly labeled "collections" in table 27), when the net collection figure that should have been used was $956.7 billion. C. Eugene Steuerle, former head of Treasury's economic staff analyzing domestic tax issues, relies on this misleading IRS presentation to report that IRS costs were 0.48 percent of collections in 1985. See *Who Should Pay for Collecting Taxes?* p. 3.

7. Internal Revenue Service, *1961 Annual Report*, p. 66; *1990 Annual Report*, p. 41.

8. The current dollar figures for IRS expenses are $363.7 million for 1960 and $5440.4 million for 1990, see *Annual Report 1989*, p. 55, table 22, and *Annual Report 1990*, p. 39, table 27. To adjust these figures for inflation, I have used the consumer price index figures of 3.373 for 1960 and 0.78 for 1990.

The IRS total budget authority was $5.195 billion in 1989 and $6.135 billion proposed for 1991, as compiled from *Budget of the United States Government, Fiscal Year 1991*, p. A-242.

9. See *1990 Annual Report*, p. 39, table 27. As previously noted, this table is flawed in using gross tax collections instead of net collections and in failing to subtract IRS costs from receipts to obtain an "available revenue" figure. It also slightly understates IRS costs by excluding interagency reimbursements. These errors produce an understatement of relative governmental costs. Since this understatement tends to be consistent from year to year, the series can be used to indicate rough trends.

10. *Administration's Fiscal Year 1989 Budget Proposals Relating to the Internal Revenue Service and the U.S. Tax Court* (Hearing before the Subcommittee on Oversight of the Committee on Ways and Means, U.S. House of Representatives, 100th Cong., 2d Sess., April 13, 1988), p. 173.

11. Hilary Stout, "Deep Problems at IRS Cause the U.S. to Miss Billions in Revenue," *Wall Street Journal*, January 2, 1990, p. A1.

12. Ibid.

13. Ibid. The 11.3 percent turnover figure, which applies to 1984, was noted in *Administration's Fiscal Year 1989 Budget Proposals*, p. 238.

14. Bud Roper, "The Environment in Which the IRS Must Operate," in *Conference on Tax Administration Research January 1985*, vol. 2, p. 138.

15. Some survey questions indirectly indicate this trend. Asked to estimate the proportion of taxpayers who cheat on their taxes, respondents in 1966 gave an average estimate of 25.3 percent; in 1984 the figure was 40.5. On another question, in 1984, 51 percent of respondents thought tax cheating was becoming more common, and only 5 percent thought it was becoming less common. The expectation of punishment also seems to be declining. In 1966, 31 percent of respondents believed there was more than a fifty-fifty chance of being caught for tax cheating by "small amounts." In 1984, this figure had fallen to 15 percent. Yankelovich, Skelly and White, Inc., "Taxpayer Attitudes Study Final Report," Prepared for the Internal Revenue Service (December 1984, mimeo), pp. 42, 43, 157.

16. U.S. General Accounting Office, *ADP Modernization: IRS' Automated Examination System—Troubled Past, Uncertain Future* (Washington, D.C., June 1989), pp. 1–2.

17. Internal Revenue Service, *1985 Annual Report*, p. 5.

Chapter 9

1. *Administration's Fiscal Year 1989 Budget Proposals Relating to the Internal Revenue Service and the U.S. Tax Court* (Hearing before the Subcommittee on Oversight of the Committee on Ways and Means, U.S. House of Representatives, 100th Cong., 2d Sess., April 13, 1988), p. 231. This figure appears in the prepared statement of the president of the National Treasury Employees Union.

2. Ibid., p. 232.

3. *Public Accounting Report* 11, no. 11 (June 1, 1988), p. 4.

4. A well-documented recent suicide caused by the IRS was that of Alex Council, in June of 1988. Council's suicide note explained that he was taking his life so that his wife could use the insurance money to fight an IRS lien on his property. She did just that and won the case in court. The federal judge concluded that the IRS had made a mistake and the Councils owed nothing. See "Horribly Out of Control," *Money*, June 1990, pp. 6–8.

5. Although some IRS agents may get sadistic pleasure in "leaning on" taxpayers, many are distressed by their role and begin to realize that they are serving as cats-paws for none-too-competent politicians in charge of the system. One collections officer, testifying before a congressional committee in 1980, was struck by the paradox that while politicians were lamenting the recession and worrying about its effect on businesses, he, as a collections officer, was ordered to ignore the fact that businesses were in an economic squeeze: "Don't you believe it unfair for one agency of the Government to take action against citizens who cannot secure funds because of the economic conditions [the ongoing recession], when the Government itself is more than partially responsible for these very same economic conditions?" Statement of Warren J. Ingersoll, Jr., in *IRS Summary Collection Policy Impact on Small Business* (Hearings before the Subcommittee on

Oversight of Government Management of the Committee on Governmental Affairs, U.S. Senate, 96th Cong., 2d Sess., July 31, 1980), p. 34.

6. *Taxpayers' Bill of Rights,* part 1, p. 307.

7. Ibid., p. 309.

8. One of the escape hatches in provisions designed to safeguard taxpayers is the jeopardy clause, which states that the safeguard in question can be over-ridden if the official believes the collection of the tax is in jeopardy. Since the official can make this jeopardy assessment on subjective and even counterfactual grounds (see, for example, the Treadway case discussed in Chapter 5), many of the safeguards boil down to saying that "the agent is not supposed to do *x*, unless he wants to."

9. IRS prepared comments on the Taxpayers' Bill of Rights, in *Taxpayers' Bill of Rights* (Hearings before the Subcommittee on Private Retirement Plans and Oversight of the Internal Revenue Service of the Committee on Finance, U.S. Senate, 100th Cong., 1st Sess., April 10 and 21, 1987), part 1, p. 243.

10. Ibid.

11. Internal Revenue Service, *1961 Annual Report,* p. 43. The average payment to informers was $777.

12. *Wall Street Journal,* August 22, 1990.

13. Nathan Boidman, "A Summary of What Can Be Learned from the Experience of Other Countries with Income Tax Compliance Problems," in American Bar Association, *Income Tax Compliance* (Washington, D.C., 1983), p. 154.

14. *Insight,* December 4, 1989, pp. 42–43. (This story covers the IRS's forcing lawyers to report cash payments of over $10,000 by their clients.)

15. *The Effectiveness of IRS' Information Returns Program* (Hearing before a subcommittee of the Committee on Government Operations, U.S. House of Representatives, 99th Cong., 2d Sess., April 29, 1986), pp. 124–27.

16. George Cooper, *A Voluntary Tax? New Perspectives on Sophisticated Estate Tax Avoidance* (Washington, D.C.: Brookings Institution, 1979), p. 52.

17. Charles Adams, *Fight, Flight, Fraud: The Story of Taxation* (Curaçao: Euro-Dutch Publishers, 1982), p. 222.

18. Hilary Stout, "Investigators Say the IRS Ignored Wrongdoing Data," *Wall Street Journal,* July 26, 1989, p. B7.

19. Ibid. Even when IRS abuses of power are judicially criticized, the culprits seem to go unpunished. In the Kilpatrick case, for example, IRS and Justice Department officials committed numerous abuses in their efforts to "get" an innocent taxpayer. A federal district judge dismissed the case because of these abuses, which included, in his words, "knowing presentation of misinformation to the grand jury and mistreatment of witnesses." Nevertheless, the guilty agents were not prosecuted, nor even placed on administrative leave. The pattern was the same in the Omni case. See *Oversight of IRS and Justice Department Prosecution of Several Tax Cases* (Hearings before the Subcommittee on Oversight of the Internal Revenue Service of the Committee on Finance, U.S. Senate, 99th Cong., 2d Sess., June 19 and 20, 1986), part 1, pp. 11, 222.

20. David Burnham, *A Law unto Itself: Power, Politics and the IRS* (New York: Random House, 1989), pp. 261ff; Carlton Sherwood, *Inquisition: The Persecution and Prosecution of the Reverend Sun Myung Moon* (Washington: Regnery Gateway,

1991). In the Moon case, one of the instigators of the political persecution by the IRS was Republican Senator Robert Dole.

21. George Hansen, *To Harass Our People: The IRS and Government Abuse of Power* (Washington, D.C.: Positive Publications, 1984), pp. 32–33, 130–38.

22. *How to Use the FOIA (Freedom of Information Act) Effectively against the IRS* (Sunnyvale, Calif.: Falcon Press, 1982), p. 24.

23. Burnham, pp. 70–72.

24. Hansen, pp. 93, 100–104.

25. Burnham, pp. 296–99.

26. Hansen, pp. 71–81.

27. Barbara W. Rothacher, *Deer Graze on My Roof* (1983), p. 106

28. Internal Revenue Service, *1965 Annual Report*, p. 33. From time to time, the IRS offers a quantitative estimate of the amount of "voluntary" compliance. In the *1961 Annual Report* (p. 25) the claim was: "Approximately 97 percent of all revenue collected in fiscal year 1961 was collected through voluntary compliance with tax laws." In the *Annual Report 1988* (p. 16) the claim was: "Over 83 percent of taxpayers voluntarily report their tax without any enforcement effort." Like so many IRS figures claiming virtues for the system, these numbers reflect a painful lack of intellectual sophistication. The figures are (roughly) referring to the proportion of taxpayers not subject to actual enforcement actions like audits and forced collections and have nothing to do with "voluntary" motivation. Consider a robbery in progress, with the thief pointing a gun at his victim's head and saying, "Your money or your life." Following IRS terminology, if the victim then gives up his wallet, compliance is "voluntary." Only if shots are fired does the transaction cease to be voluntary.

29. Randolph E. Paul, *Taxation in the United States* (Boston: Little, Brown, 1954), p. 82.

Chapter 10

1. There are two ways of representing tax system burdens. One approach is to focus on the cost of raising one additional dollar of tax revenue. This is the marginal cost. The other approach is to ask, How much does the entire tax system cost? In other words, if the tax system were done away with altogether, how much would be saved? The answer to this question reflects average cost.

Ideally, we would like to have separate measurements of the marginal cost and of the average cost for each burden. As a practical matter, it is virtually impossible to measure marginal cost for most of the burdens of a tax system. We measure total cost and (dividing total cost by the amount of revenue collected) average cost. The only available measure of marginal cost is this average cost figure. The assumption that marginal cost approximates average cost is a rough one, but, as I explain in the Appendix, "Tax Rates and Tax System Costs," not without justification.

In discussing tax system costs in this book, therefore, I have generally treated average cost figures as marginal costs. The one exception to this practice is with the disincentive effect. This effect has been calculated with a mathematical model that yields distinct values for marginal cost and for average cost. In general, the marginal cost figure of 33.2 percent of tax revenues is the one we are most interested in; it is incorporated in the finding that each additional dollar raised costs 65 cents—as presented in the second column of Table 15.

The corresponding average cost figure from the Ballard, Shoven, and Whalley study is 23.8 percent of tax revenues. This is the figure that should be multiplied by the tax revenue figure to calculate how much would be saved if the entire tax system were done away with. Since available tax revenue was $652.557 billion in 1985 (see Chapter 8), the total cost of the disincentive effect was $155.3 billion, as given in the first column of Table 15.

For all the other burdens, the total cost given in the first column of Table 15 has been derived as explained in the chapter on the respective burden. Then this total cost figure has been divided by the available revenue figure ($652.557 billion) to yield an average cost figure (also treated as a marginal cost figure) given in the second column of Table 15.

Thus, Table 15 incorporates both perspectives on tax system burdens, marginal cost and total cost. For this reason, it is not internally consistent, in the sense that multiplying the marginal cost figure (65 percent of tax revenues) times tax revenues will not produce the total cost figure shown in the table.

2. These unestimated costs include the following: the private sector costs of criminal investigations, correspondence sweeps, refund correspondence, and representation for computer notices and penalties; the asset deprivation costs, asset replacement costs, credit impairment cost of levies and liens, and all costs of seizures; the disincentive cost of compliance costs; the costs of investment lock-in and churning, tax exemption lobbying costs; direct and indirect legislative costs. The largest of these would be the disincentive cost of compliance costs.

3. *Evaluation of the Economic Impact of the Job Corps Program,* Third Follow-up Report (Princeton, N.J.: Mathematica Policy Research, September 1982).

4. Ibid, p. 248. For purposes of presentation, I am slightly simplifying. The actual budgetary costs were $4,143 with additional nonbudget costs of $927, for a total cost of $5,070. Strictly speaking, only the $4,143 should be considered a budgetary cost subject to the 1.65 correction factor. Applying this refinement makes no difference to the ultimate conclusion: the benefit-cost ratio of the Job Corps program still comes out as less than one.

5. Ibid., p. 276.

6. A. Allan Schmid, *Benefit-Cost Analysis: A Political Economy Approach* (Boulder, Colo.: Westview Press, 1989), p. 169.

7. The IRS has an interest in understating the size and growth of the compliance burden, since this reflects unfavorably on the organization. The Arthur D. Little methodology permits the computation of the compliance burden if sophisticated rules for evaluating the burden of each form and worksheet are carefully applied, and if *all* forms and worksheets (along with their correct usage counts) are enumerated. It is a methodology in which any omission, made through carelessness or bias, will produce an underestimate of the compliance burden.

It would be of some help in verifying the calculations if the IRS officials in charge of this system would produce a printout of the form values and form counts going into the total figure. I asked them about this in a visit to IRS headquarters in February 1989. I was told that no such tabulation is available and that there is no intention to produce one.

8. *Wall Street Journal*, February 8, 1990, p. A2.

9. The 1977 average H & R Block fee is mentioned in *Tax Simplification Proposals* (Field hearings before the Subcommittee on Oversight of the Committee on Ways and Means, U.S. House of Representatives, 95th Cong., 1st and 2d Sess., December 13, 1977), p. 113; for 1985 and 1988 figures, see Table 3 in Chapter 2. The 1990 figure was reported to be "near $50" in the *Wall Street Journal*, April 11, 1990, p. 1.

10. Letter of Philip L. Shriver, CPA, to Robert J. Leonard, chief counsel, Committee on Ways and Means, U.S. House of Representatives, April 16, 1990.

11. Robert T. Bonafide, "A View from the Trenches," *National Tax Journal* 40 (September 1987), p. 467.

12. *Wall Street Journal*, May 3, 1982, p. 33, and April 11, 1990, p. 1.

13. Marsha Blumenthal and Joel Slemrod, "The Compliance Cost of the U.S. Individual Income Tax System: A Second Look after Tax Reform" (Office of Tax Policy Research, University of Michigan, Ann Arbor, September 1991), p. 8. A 1989 survey of tax practitioners by the Syracuse University Center for Tax Studies also supports the conclusion that the tax compliance burden has increased: "The compliance burden significantly increased due to the increased complexity brought about by changes in the law, principally as a result of the Tax Reform Act of 1986." See Judyth A. Swingen and Susan B. Long, "The Impact of the Tax Reform Act of 1986 on Compliance Burdens: National Survey Results," (Center for Tax Studies, Syracuse University, n.d., mimeo), p. 18.

14. To illustrate the trend, the average time per return for office examinations was 3.8 hours in 1985 and 4.6 hours in 1988 (IRS, letter in response to Freedom of Information Act request, January 9, 1990).

15. The figures on abatements reflect a number of factors. To some extent, they indicate penalties that IRS officials acknowledge to be erroneous or unjustified. Used in this way, the abatement figure greatly understates the actual number of such unjustified or erroneous actions, since, in order to have a penalty abated, the taxpayer has to (a) initiate an attempt to have his incorrect penalty abated, (b) succeed in reaching an appropriate decision maker in the IRS bureaucracy, and (c) get an IRS official naturally biased against taxpayers to repudiate what his agency has done and forgo the revenues implied in the assessment. It should be noted, however, that abatement figures seem to contain some misleading statistical "static," and thus may exaggerate the number of genuine abatements. This issue is raised in the General Accounting Office report *Erroneous Penalties for Failure to File Returns or Pay Taxes Can Be Reduced* (April 1990), p. 12.

16. Jane G. Gravelle and Laurence J. Kotlikoff, "Corporate Taxation and the Efficiency Gains of the 1986 Tax Reform Act," National Bureau of Economic Research (NBER) working paper 3142 (October 1989), p. 33.

17. Don Fullerton and James B. Mackie, "Economic Efficiency in Recent Tax Reform History: Policy Reversals or Consistent Improvements?" *National Tax Journal* 42 (March 1989), pp. 1–13; Roger H. Gordon and Joel Slemrod, "Do We Collect any Revenue from Taxing Capital Income?" in Lawrence H. Summers, ed., *Tax Policy and the Economy* 2 (Cambridge, Mass.: MIT Press, 1988), pp. 89–130; Del Bradshaw and Richard McKenzie, "How the 1986 Tax Reform Act Affects People's Taxes" (Center for the Study of American Business, Washington University, St. Louis, April 1989, mimeo).

18. Dale W. Jorgenson and Kun-Young Yun, "The Excess Burden of Taxation in the U.S." (Paper prepared for presentation at the Coopers & Lybrand Foundation symposium, U.S. Tax Policy for the 1990s, New York, November 7–8, 1990). In their model, the marginal excess burden of the tax system in 1985 was 46 percent of revenue raised; under the post-1986 tax act conditions, this fell to 38.3 percent.

One study that contradicts the generally positive conclusions about the 1986 tax act is by Lawrence H. Goulder and Philippe Thalmann, "Approaches to Efficient Capital Taxation: Leveling the Playing Field vs. Living by the Golden Rule," NBER working paper 3559 (December 1990).

19. This finding came from an ABC–*Washington Post* poll taken in May 1988, cited by Fred Barnes in "Mr. President, Read Our Lips: No New Taxes," *Imprimis* 19, no. 9 (September 1990), p. 3.

20. Herbert Stein, "Congress's Amazing Budget Tricks," *Wall Street Journal*, June 27, 1989, p. A 14.

21. Irving Freilich, "H.U.D.—No Big Surprise," *New York Times*, August 13, 1989, p. 23.

22. Richard L. Doernberg, "The Market for Tax Reform: Public Pain for Private Gain," in *Tax Notes*, November 28, 1988, pp. 965–69. This article was originally prepared as the keynote speech for an IRS conference on tax complexity. After IRS officials reviewed it, Doernberg was disinvited, not because they objected to the theory that Congress was corrupt, but because Doernberg refused to omit the names of the senior tax committee members who he felt were the worst offenders, especially Senators Packwood, Dole, and Bentsen and Representative Rostenkowski, see ibid., p. 905.

23. John F. Witte, "The Income Tax Mess: Deviant Process or Institutional Failure?" (Paper prepared for presentation at the 1985 Annual Meeting of the American Political Science Association), p. 19.

24. Henry J. Aaron and Harvey Galper, *Assessing Tax Reform* (Washington, D.C.: Brookings Institution, 1985), p. 1, cited in Witte, p. 1.

25. Teresa Tritch and Deborah Lohse, "The Pros Flub Our Tax Test (Again!)," *Money*, March 1991, p. 96.

26. The method, suggested by Charles Clotfelter, consists of subtracting the percentage who have overstated their taxes from the percentage who have understated them. The logic is that the overstaters are all caused by unintentional errors, and that the size of the unintentional errors in the tax understating group is the same. Hence, the size of the cheating group—deliberate tax understaters—can be estimated by subtracting overstaters from the larger group of tax understaters.

The data for the 1949 audit showed that only 25 percent of the returns had errors of $2 or more, and these ran 91 percent against the government and 9 percent for the government. Hence:

	Percentage
No change	75.00
Tax overstaters	2.25
Tax understaters	22.75

Proportion intentionally understating = 22.75 − 2.25 = 20.5.

Although not specifically a TCMP audit, this 1949 audit corresponded to it in form and purposes. It was a test sample of 162,000 1948 returns to evaluate the bureau's audit control program. See U.S. Treasury Department, *Annual Report of the Commissioner of Internal Revenue, Fiscal Year Ended June 30, 1950,* p. 8.

The data for the 1985 TCMP audit were supplied under the Freedom of Information Act (letter of June 12, 1990) and show the following breakdown:

	Percentage
No change	44.01
Tax overstaters	9.37
Tax understaters	46.62

Hence, proportion intentionally understating = 46.62 − 9.37 = 37.25.

Chapter 11

1. James L. Payne, *The Culture of Spending* (San Francisco: ICS Press, 1991).

2. U.S. General Accounting Office, *1988 Annual Report on GAO's Tax-related Work,* pp. 20, 23, 24, 26, 28, 34, 35, 55, 56, 59, 73.

3. The GAO does urge the IRS to reduce the high error rate in its enforcement programs. This stance, indirectly, would tend to reduce taxpayer burdens because the IRS would harass fewer innocent taxpayers if it made fewer mistakes. However, even in these cases, the GAO emphasis is not on reducing the burden on taxpayers but on reducing the costs to the IRS. For example, in urging the IRS to reduce the error rate in the Information Returns Program, the closest the GAO ever got to noting the burden on taxpayers was the comment that errors "confuse and frustrate taxpayers, increasing the [IRS] correspondence work load as taxpayers write again trying to resolve the same issue." Ibid., p. 61. Thus, the GAO position was not that confusing and frustrating taxpayers is wrong in and of itself, but only that this confusion adds to IRS costs in having to deal with them.

4. Prepared statement of Donald C. Alexander, *Internal Revenue Service Operations* (Hearing before the Subcommittee on Oversight of the Committee on Ways and Means, U.S. House of Representatives, 100th Cong., 1st Sess., February 6, 1987), p. 104.

5. Ibid., p. 105. Data on IRS penalties given in U.S. General Accounting Office, *Options for Civil Penalty Reform* (Washington, D.C., September 1989), p. 2, and David Burnham, *A Law unto Itself: Power, Politics and the IRS* (New York: Random House, 1989), p. 58.

6. *Administration's Fiscal Year 1988 Budget Proposals Relating to the Internal Revenue Service* (Hearing before the Subcommittee on Oversight of the Committee on Ways and Means, U.S. House of Representatives, 100th Cong., 1st Sess., April 23, 1987), pp. 184–99.

7. Quoted in Burnham, p. 306.

8. Interview of December 19, 1991.

9. *Taxpayers' Bill of Rights* (Hearings before the Subcommittee on Private Retirement Plans and Oversight of the Internal Revenue Service of the Committee on Finance, U.S. Senate, 100th Cong., 1st Sess., April 10 and 21, 1987), part 1, pp. 227, 229.

10. In a major statement to Congress in 1980, the Director of the GAO's General Government Division, William J. Anderson, discussed the possible "enhancement" of tax revenues from interest and dividends and urged Congress "to establish withholding on interest, dividends, and independent contractors; and to increase the penalties for failure to file information returns." *IRS' Administration of the Tax Laws (Income Information Document Matching)* (Hearing before a subcommittee of the Committee on Government Operations, U.S. House of Representatives, 96th Cong., 2d Sess., October 1, 1980), p. 47. Even as far back as 1962, IRS officials had been pushing for the adoption of interest and dividend withholding, see Thomas J. Reese, *The Politics of Taxation* (Westport, Conn.: Quorum Books, 1980), p. 46.

11. The vote in the Senate for repeal was 91 to 5; in the House, 382 to 41. In my account, I have relied on narratives and roll call data given in Congressional Quarterly, *Almanac 1982*, pp. 29–39, 84-H, 85-H, and *Almanac 1983*, pp. 261–64, 15-S, 40-H.

12. Congressional Quarterly, *Almanac 1985*, p. 479. On the 1984 votes approving the 1984 Deficit Reduction Act (which contained the auto log provision), the vote was 318 to 97 in the House and 76 to 5 in the Senate. See Congressional Quarterly, *Almanac 1984*, p. 150. CQ's comprehensive review of the provisions of this bill did not mention auto logs.

13. "Public Comments on Proposed Regulations," *Tax Analysts' Daily Tax Highlights and Documents,* May 10, 1989, p. 1319.

14. D. Alden Newland and Max E. Klinger, "Section 89: How Smaller Businesses Can Cope," *The Practical Accountant,* May 1989, pp. 16–32.

15. Jeanne Saddler, "Small Business Celebrates Blow to Tax Code Section 89," *Wall Street Journal,* September 18, 1989, p. B2.

16. *Wall Street Journal,* September 29, 1989, p. A14. The vote in the House to repeal Section 89 was 390 to 96.

17. To be usable, the roll call votes bearing on the issue of compliance and enforcement must not be too lopsided (I use 80 percent to 20 percent as the criterion). On highly lopsided votes, one is confusing the substance of the vote with the congressman's desire to posture or to go along with others on a forgone conclusion. The four Senate votes that are suitable for revealing a pro-IRS/ antitaxpayer dimension on the tax administration issue are the following (I rely on Congressional Quarterly's numbering and data):

1. Vote 247, July 22, 1982. An attempt to weaken the interest-withholding provision. The Reagan administration was strongly committed to this and the other revenue enhancement tax administration provisions. Out of party loyalty, Republicans were thus more pro-IRS than they would normally be.

2. Vote 252, July 22, 1982. A proposal (which passed 70 to 25) to drop a proposed requirement in the 1982 tax act that forced employers to estimate

employee tips. This provision would have added compliance burdens and also would have been a source of employee-employer friction and suspicion. The supporters of retaining this provision included die-hard Republican supporters of the Reagan revenue enhancement package.

3. Vote 23, April 3, 1985. A proposal (which passed) to drop the tax and record-keeping requirements for employee's minor personal use of a business vehicle.

4. Vote 115, June 5, 1986. This was a vote aimed at directing the IRS not to elaborate regulations that would involve auto logs. Though the log idea had been roundly defeated in 1985, the IRS was still going ahead with regulations that tended to amount to auto record-keeping requirements.

18. This test is to some degree complicated by the fact that the two 1982 votes used in the tabulation were more a measure of partisan loyalties than a measure of pro- or antitaxpayer sentiment. Since it was a package proposed by President Reagan and supported by the Senate Republican leadership, a number of senators reversed their usual positions. Senior Democrats, especially Long and Bentsen, whose normal stance is pro-IRS, took the protaxpayer side in order to go on record against Reagan; certain junior Republicans, like Wallop, Armstrong, and Symms—fairly consistent protaxpayer senators—voted against the taxpayer position in order to uphold Reagan. Without this distorting partisan effect, the trend shown in Table 20 would be even clearer.

19. The chairman of the Senate Finance Committee from 1965 to 1980, Russell B. Long (D-La.), typified this irresponsible approach. During a 1975 committee session, one committee member complained he did not understand an amendment Long was pressing the committee to vote on. Long brushed his objection aside saying, "If we waited until everyone knew what they were voting on we would never get anything done." Quoted in Reese, p. 161.

Chapter 12

1. U.S. General Accounting Office, *IRS Can Improve Its Program to Find Taxpayers Who Underreport Their Income* (March 1991), p. 2.

2. Ibid., p. 3. The GAO does disapprove of errors in IRS enforcement programs but mainly because errors add to IRS budgetary costs. Since the GAO has never made a study of the burden of the underreporter program on taxpayers, its allegation that the program is cost-effective is a pseudoscientific claim that implicitly ascribes zero cost to the entire private sector burden of the program.

3. U.S. General Accounting Office, *Federal Tax Deposit Requirements Should Be Simplified* (July 1990), p. 14.

4. *Business Community's Compliance with Federal Money Laundering Statutes* (Hearing before the Subcommittee on Oversight of the Committee on Ways and Means, U.S. House of Representatives, 100th Cong., 2d Sess., September 20, 1990), p. 3.

Appendix, "The Burden of Initial Enforcement Contacts"

1. IRS Tables supplied under the Freedom of Information Act, January 9, 1990.

2. In one congressional hearing, a Minneapolis truck driver appeared to protest a system that had put him through an office audit ten times in the past twelve years. "Each time I have been audited, it is a day off work. That is 2 weeks [of work] I have lost." *Tax Simplification Proposals* (Field hearings before the Subcommittee on Oversight of the Committee on Ways and Means, U.S. House of Representatives, 95th Cong., 1st and 2d Sess., December 13 and 14, 1977, and January 16, 1978), p. 228. In one of his audits, the examiner demanded that he go to a bank to obtain documentary proof of a transaction. Frustrated at losing time on the audit process the taxpayer replied, "You are on the payroll of the Government, you go do it."

3. In a published article on participating in a represented office audit, the author reported that he spent "about 20 hours of anxious preparation." This is twice the figure we are assuming. He also reported that the tax preparer's fee was $350, the same figure we assume for this cost. Joe Anthony, "How I Survived a Tax Audit," *Reader's Digest*, April 1991, p. 108.

4. IRS Tables supplied under the Freedom of Information Act, January 9, 1990.

5. Some useful information on penalties is found in data from the St. Louis district published in *Tax Simplification Proposals*, p. 19. Out of 123 penalty appeals acted on, 29 were abated, and 94 penalties were not abated. Thus the number of penalties appealed was 4.24 times the number actually abated.

It was also stated that in a set of 117 appeals there were 144 separate penalties involved. Hence, this indicates that the number of affected taxpayers is .8125 for each penalty assessed.

6. Joseph S. Coyle, "Four Basic Letters Can Help You to Win When the IRS Demands Extra Tax Money from You That It Doesn't Deserve," *Money*, April 1990, pp. 86, 91.

7. David Burnham, *A Law unto Itself* (New York: Random House, 1989), p. 121.

8. For handling IRS penalties and other assessments, a California tax lawyer reported a typical charge of $1,200–$1,500; a California CPA reported a typical charge of $200–$300; an Ohio CPA specified $400–$500; a South Carolina CPA said his typical charge for a simple CP-2000 case was $90. Some tax practitioners communicated that sometimes they deal with these notices at no additional charge to their established clients. This does not mean that their services are "free" in a social cost sense, but that the cost is billed in other ways. Putting these different figures together, I estimate the average cost at $250.

9. U.S. General Accounting Office, *Who's Not Filing Income Tax Returns? IRS Needs Better Ways to Find Them and Collect Their Taxes* (Washington, D.C., July 11, 1979), pp. 29, 31. The estimate for zero and insignificant tax (less than $75) is mine, based on the income profile of nonfilers given on p. 87 of the GAO publication.

10. Table 14 in the IRS *1985 Annual Report* gives a tabulation of "Civil Penalties Assessed and Abated," showing a total of 22,035,067 for 1985. Two IRS officials I questioned were of the opinion that these penalties were in addition to those

assessed by examinations, IRP, and the nonfiling program; however, a response to my Freedom of Information letter (February 22, 1990) declared that this figure does include penalties from other enforcement programs. I judge this latter interpretation to be the more plausible.

11. To arrive at this figure, I first multiplied the total number of penalties assessed, 22,035,067, by .8125 to adjust for the fact that some taxpayers receive more than one penalty (see note 5 in this section). This gives 17,903,000 *taxpayers* affected by penalties. From this number are subtracted the 9,118,000 taxpayers affected by examinations, service center corrections, IRP, and nonfiling notices (as given in Table 6). (The criminal investigation cases do not involve penalties.)

12. *Serious Problems Exist in the Quality of IRS Correspondence with Taxpayers* (Hearing before a subcommittee of the Committee on Government Operations, U.S. House of Representatives, 100th Cong., 2d Sess., July 13, 1988), p. 148. In the same hearing, Abraham Schneier of the National Federation of Independent Business stated that tax practitioners typically charge $500 or more to contest an unjustified penalty (p. 164).

13. Coyle, p. 91.

Appendix, "Tax Rates and Tax System Costs"

1. In the models currently employed by economists, ". . . excess burden roughly rises with the square of the tax rate. . . ." Jane G. Gravelle and Laurence J. Kotlikoff, "The Incidence and Efficiency Costs of Corporate Taxation When Corporate and Noncorporate Firms Produce the Same Good," *Journal of Political Economy* 97 (August 1989), p. 775.

2. Charles T. Clotfelter, "Tax Evasion and Tax Rates: An Analysis of Individual Returns," *The Review of Economics and Statistics* 65 (August 1983), p. 368. Richard K. Vedder reports finding a relationship between marginal tax rates and the disposition to evade taxes by not filing a return. See "Do's and Don'ts of Tax Reform," in *Increasing Productivity and Administrability of the Tax Code* (Hearing before the Subcommittee on Oversight of the Internal Revenue Service of the Committee on Finance, U.S. Senate, 98th Cong., 2d Sess., September 17, 1984), p. 132. A survey of Oregon taxpayers found that the main explanation for tax cheating was "high taxation." See Robert Mason and Lyle D. Calvin, "Public Confidence and Admitted Tax Evasion," *National Tax Journal* 37 (December 1984), p. 490.

3. An elementary model of the tax evasion decision makes the pressure to evade taxes a positive function of the taxes to be saved and a negative function of the inhibitions against evasions. These inhibitions include both moral feelings against evasion and fears of being punished. Since this inhibition factor is constant and the taxes to be saved are a direct function of tax rates, the pressure to evade will increase faster than tax rates.

The equation for this model would have this form:

$$E = aT - I$$

where:

E = effort devoted to tax evasion/avoidance. This can be expressed in monetary terms, for example, the amount of money one is willing to pay a tax shelter promoter to arrange a tax avoidance scheme.

T = tax liability. This is a direct function of the tax rate, (R); that is, $T = kR$.

I = the inhibitions against tax avoidance/evasion, whether moral, patriotic, or fear-inspired.

With this expression, if tax rates double, the resources devoted to tax evasion/avoidance will more than double.

4. Office of Management and Budget, *Budget of the United States Government, Fiscal Year 1991* (Washington, D.C., 1990), p. A-287, table 2.3. The figure given is the overall federal extraction rate expressed as a fraction of GNP. The actual effective tax rates on capital and labor income, including state and local taxes, are much higher. One calculation puts the effective tax rate for capital income at 37.2 percent and for labor income at 37.1 percent in 1980, see Jonathan Skinner, "The Welfare Cost of Uncertain Tax Policy," National Bureau of Economic Research (NBER) working paper 1947 (June 1986), p. 14.

5. A study of governmental and compliance costs in the British tax system found that they amounted to only 3.68 percent of revenue collected. Cedric Sandford, Michael Godwin, and Peter Hardwick, *Administrative and Compliance Costs of Taxation* (Bath: Fiscal Publications, 1989), p. 192. Although this study involved some serious understatements (for example, labor overhead costs of tax compliance were omitted), even after allowing for these it appears that the British tax compliance cost is well below the U.S. figure. Another clue to the lower compliance burden in the United Kingdom is the fact that only 10.5 percent of the taxpaying population use paid advisers (p. 68). In the United States, the corresponding figure is 49 percent.

A study of tax compliance costs in Canada found that these amounted to 6.9 percent of the taxes collected. François Vaillancourt, *The Administrative and Compliance Costs of the Personal Income Tax and Payroll Tax System in Canada, 1986* (Toronto: Canadian Tax Foundation, 1989), p. 83.

Index

Aaron, Henry, 160
ACS. *See* Automated Collection System (ACS)
Adams, Charles, 13, 139
Alexander, Donald C., 166
Altman and Weil survey, 110
American Bar Association
Real Property, Estates, and Trust Law section, 110
Tax Section, 167
American Institute of Certified Public Accountants, 167
Anker, Kurt, 42
Anxiety, 130–31, 185
Arthur D. Little study. *See* Little study
Audit
effect of, on taxpayer, 38–40
selection for, 36
of Tax Compliance Measurement Program, 161
Audit insurance, 131
Audit system, IRS, 36, 38–39
appeals in, 54–56
burdens of, 199–203

costs of examination participation under, 39–40
See also Discriminant function (DIF) formulas
Auerbach, Alan, 96
Auto log requirement, 173–74
Automated Collection System (ACS), 43, 73–74
Automated Examination System, 125–26

Bach, Richard, 1, 2
Ballard, Charles L., 93, 94, 95
Banking system, 105–6
Bankruptcy cases, 62
Barter, 105–6, 107
Benefit-cost analysis, 151–53
Bentsen, Lloyd, 170
Blumenthal, Marsha, 155
Bonafide, Robert T., 155
Boskin, Michael, 91, 92
Browning, Edgar, 91
Burnham, David, 204
Business growth limits, 105, 106

Capital
  disincentives in taxation of, 91–93
  in underground economy, 106
Caplin, Mortimer, 168
Cash, Adam, 106
Chase Econometrics Associates, 92
Citizen resistance
  effect of, on efficiency, 125
  to forcible seizure, 129–30
Civil service system, 124
Collard, David, 99
Collection agents, 68
Collection costs, government, 122
Collection process, forced, 67–68
  burdens of, 70–73
  dilemma of, 83–85
  emotional burden of, 69
  error rate in IRS, 73–74, 78
  extension of collection period
    in, 169
  levies, liens, and seizures
    under, 81–83
  monetary costs of, 81–83
  policies of, 74–79
  private sector costs under,
    83–85
  See also Automated Collection
    System (ACS); Levies;
    Liens; Seizures
Collins, Julie H., 23
Compensation principle
  objections to, 188–90
  in present tax law, 184–85
  proposed, 183–84, 186, 188
Compliance
  activities for taxpayer in, 15–16
  burden of, 8–9, 29
  components of taxpayer
    burden in, 16–18
  costs of, 4, 96, 98, 149–51, 158,
    213–14
  costs of interest and dividend
    withholding in, 171

  cost of, to economic activity, 9,
    98–99
  criminal investigation aspect of,
    40
  inequality of, 30
  Little study of burden of, 19–23
  tax reform effects on costs of,
    154–55
  underground workers avoid
    costs of, 107
  value of time spent in, 23–29
  voluntary, 70
  See also Deterrence policy;
    Enforcement system, IRS;
    Little study
Compliance time methodology,
  222–23n27
Computer systems, IRS
  enforcement using, 41–42, 85
  mishandling of, 73, 74
  as monitoring device, 11
  See also Automated Collection
    System (ACS)
Congress
  costs of, related to taxes, 121
  perspective of, toward IRS, 50
  tax matters and legislative
    work of, 121
Corporations
  disincentives in taxation of,
    92–93, 100
  tax compliance costs for small,
    33–34, 97
Correspondence sweeps, 48–49
Cost of credit impairment, 69
Costs
  of asset deprivation and
    replacement, 69
  of compliance and enforce-
    ment, 96–98
  of resistance in forced collec-
    tion, 68–69
Criminal investigation costs, 40–41

Data collection
  as cost of tax compliance, 17
  flawed system of, 73
Decision making
  components of congressional,
    165–70
  tax collectors dominate, 10–11
Deficit Reduction Act (1984),
  173–74
Democratic theory, 172, 191–92
Demyanick, Dale, 209
Denmark, 38
Deterrence policy
  of tax system, 35–36, 130
  in voluntary compliance
    concept, 70–72
Diary study, 23, 220n13
  See also Auto log requirement
Discriminant function (DIF)
  formulas, 36
Disincentive effect
  in cost of compliance, 98–100,
    149
  on economic activity, 9, 98–99
  estimates and calculation of
    costs, 89–93, 99
  estimates of combined federal
    tax, 93–95
  examples of tax system, 87–89
  for labor, 97–98
  trend toward lower costs of,
    158
Dividend withholding debate,
  171–73
Doernberg, Richard, 160

Economic planning, 96–97
Employee benefit status, 64
Employee Retirement Income
  Security Act (1974), 111
Enforcement costs, 5–36, 53
  categories of, 37–38
  factors creating increased, 96

trend in, 156–58
  See also Collection process,
    forced; Tax litigation
Enforcement system, IRS
  computer systems for, 41–49
  errors of, 43–49, 185–86
  See also Information Returns
    Program (IRP); Levies;
    Liens; Penalties; Problem
    Resolution Program; Tax
    litigation
Equal value assumption, 196–97

Foreign sales corporations
  (FSCs), 114–15
Freedom of speech, 140–42
Frustration, 185
Fund-raising, voluntary, 13–14
  See also Philanthropy

Galper, Harvey, 160
General Accounting Office
  (GAO)
  perspective of, toward IRS, 46,
    50, 228–29nn30, 31
  studies of IRS nonfilers (1979,
    1988), 44–45, 107, 239n6
  study of Automated Collection
    System (1989), 235–36n26
  study of mail-out (1975), 48–49
  study of error rate of ACS, 74
  study of IRS filing penalties
    (1989), 47
  survey of collection processes
    (1989), 226n11
  survey of IRS correspondence
    (1987), 45–46
  survey of nonfilers (1979), 207
  tax studies of, 165–66
Gibb, Charles, 70
Gibbs, Lawrence, 73, 170
Gladstone, William, 147
Goldberg, Fred T., 124

Gordon and Malkiel estimate, 92
Gordon, Richard A., 61
Gordon, Roger, 93
Gramm-Rudman-Hollings Act,
    135
Gravelle, Jane, 93

Hand, Learned, 103
Hansen, George, 80, 142
Harberger, Arnold, 91
Harris, Art, 68
Hausman study, 91
Herbert, Auberon, 128, 129
Hines, James, 96, 115
Holmes, Oliver Wendell, 147–48
House Ways and Means Com-
    mittee, 97, 121, 175
H & R Block, 28
Hubbard, R. Glenn, 115

Informants
    forced by IRS, 137
    paid tax, 136–37
    recorded message for, 136
    rewards to, 11, 61
Information Returns Program
    (IRP)
    arguments to scale back, 52
    assessing burden of, 203–6
    cost and yield of, 50–52
    effectiveness of, 52
    error rate in, 46
    as IRS enforcement technique,
        42, 44, 48, 49
    yield-to-cost ratio in, 51
Information use, 142
    See also Data collection; Infor-
        mation Returns Program (IRP)
Ingersoll, Warren J., Jr., 72, 75
Interest-withholding debate,
    171–73
Internal Revenue Service (IRS)
    cost to operate, 119

criminal investigations by,
    40–41
groups that reinforce position
    of, 164–70
increased inefficiency of,
    124–25
Problem Resolution Program
    of, 46, 124
public perceptions of, 52
question of future of, 161
response to erroneous
    correspondence, 47
See also Collection process,
    forced; Compliance; Enforce-
    ment system, IRS
Intimidation of lawmakers, 143
Investment as tax avoidance,
    116–17
IRAs, 216
IRP program. *See* Information
    Returns Program (IRP)

Jorgenson, Dale W., 158

Keogh plans, 216
Klein, Mike, 68
Kotlikoff, Lawrence, 93

Levies
    as action of IRS collections
        division, 81
    calculating burden of, 81–83
    number of, 3–4
    rise in rate of, 157–58
Levin, Carl, 143
Liens
    as action of IRS collections
        division, 81
    calculating cost of, 83
    rise in rate of, 157–58
Little study, 19–23, 34,
    219–20n4, 223n28
    See also Diary study

Long, Edward V., 142
Loopholes, 94, 215–16

McCarthy, James D., 47, 52
Mack, Eric, 129
Malkiel, Burton, 92
Mansfield, Harry K., 41
Metzenbaum, Howard, 69
Money laundering, 114
Morality of taxation, 129
Morella, Constance A., 168

Negligence cases, 62–63
Nonfiler program
  burdens of, 207–8
  computer matching for, 42

Office of Management and
  Budget, 34, 121
Omnibus Budget Reconciliation
  Act (1990), 169
Ottinger, Richard, 172

Paperwork Reduction Act (1980),
  19, 34, 181–82
Payment-reporting requirements,
  49
Payroll deposit regulations, 187
Penalties
  for payment, 47–48
  in tax enforcement, 157
  volume of, 208
Pension plans, 111–12
Philanthropy, 13–14
Pickel, J. J., 191
Policy makers
  and mismanagement of tax
    system, 10–11
  position of, on tax burden,
    29–34
  role of, in tax-making process,
    96
Poll tax, 100–101, 130–31

Power abuse, 139–40
Prison system, federal, 120–21
Privacy, 137–38
Private letter rulings, 63
Problem Resolution Program, 46,
  124
Property, taxpayer, 75
Pryor, David, 73, 143, 170
Public opinion, 161
  See also Citizen resistance

Raby, William L., 146
Rangel, Charles, 36
Refund interest provision,
  184–85
Retirement income plans, 111
Retirement savings, 111
Revenues
  distortions in figures for,
    122–23
  gross collection figures as, 122
  from subsidized citizens, 12
Rogers, Will, 147
Rostenkowski, Dan, 97, 175
Rule of law principle, 61, 138–39
  See also Uniformity principle

Sandford, Cedric, 33
Schriebman, Robert S., 74
Seizures
  as action of IRS collections
    division, 81
  estimating cost of, 83
  no equity and sacrifice, 71
  of taxpayer property, 75
Self-employed individuals, 30–33
SEPs, 216
Shays, Christopher, 45
Sherwood, Carleton, 141
Shoven, John B., 93, 94, 95
Skinner, Jonathan, 98
Slemrod, Joel, 16, 19, 20, 23, 29,
  93, 155

Smith, Joseph B., Jr., 72, 132
Social cost
  of forced collections, 68–69
  of nonfiler actions, 107
  of penalty–penalty abatement
    system, 48
  to run tax system, 152
  of tax avoidance and evasion,
    104–18
  of tax enforcement burden, 37
  of tax shelters, 108–16
  of underground economy,
    105–7
Social cost analysis
  aims of, 195, 197
  equal value assumption in,
    196–97
  inclusion of taxpayer in, 197–98
  taxpayer guilt not relevant in,
    36–37
Socialization process, 174–76
Sorum, Nikki, 19, 20, 23, 29
Spending programs, government
  allocation of tax system costs
    to, 216
  proposed taxpayer compensa-
    tion plan as, 188–89
  self-subsidies in, 11–12
Stein, Herbert, 159
Strassels, Paul N., 130
Stress, 131–33
Stuart, Charles, 89
Summons enforcement cases,
  62, 65–66
Surveillance system, federal,
  10–11, 85, 141–42
  See also Informants
Sweden, 38, 89

Tax Act (1982)
  effect of campaign against, 173
  enforcement and penalty
    requirements in, 171

hearings before passage of, 172
Tax administration policy
  decisions for, 170–71
  focus of, on revenue cash flow,
    186–88
Tax administrators
  perspective of, on collection, 72
  perspective of, on forced
    collections, 72–73
  position of, on tax burden,
    29–34, 50
Tax avoidance, 103–4
  costs of devices for, 9
  estimating costs of, 103–18
  methods for, 105
  motivation for, 213–14
  through foreign tax havens,
    113–16
  See also Tax havens
Tax code
  frequent revision of, 96
  increased complexity of, 65
  lobbying to change, 117
  Section 89 of, 174–75, 183
  threats motivating compliance
    with, 35
Tax Compliance Measurement
  Program, 161
Tax evasion, 103–4
  case against Sun Myung
    Moon, 141
  as crime, 60–61
  estate taxes and, 109–10
  estimating costs of, 103–18
  motivation for, 213–14
  prosecution for, 135
  social cost of, 197
  through foreign tax havens,
    113–16
  See also Retirement income
    plans; Tax havens; Tax
    shelters; Underground
    economy

Tax-exempt status requests,
63–64
Tax havens
deposits in international,
242nn27, 28, 30
estimates of social cost of,
113–16
Tax law changes, 96–97
See also Tax Reform Act (1976);
Tax Reform Act (1986)
Tax litigation
audit appeals as, 54–56
costs of, to private sector,
55–56, 64–66
criminal, 59–62, 119–20
federal handling of, 119
IRS selection of criminal cases
in, 60–62
for refunds, 59
See also U.S. Department of
Justice; U.S. Tax Court
Taxpayer
burden of enforcement on,
49–52
burden of responding to
penalty, 208
calculating cost of compliance
time to, 23–29
compliance activities of, 15–23
inequalities in tax compliance
burden of, 30–32
motivation of, 145–47
proposed compensation to,
182–83
time as cost in tax litigation, 58
Taxpayer Compliance Measurement Program (TCMP), 104
Taxpayer impact statement
proposal, 181
Taxpayers' Bill of Rights law
escape hatches in, 235n21,
246n8
passed (1988), 80

provisions for taxpayer participation under, 181
Senate hearings on (1987–88),
74, 142, 246nn9, 10
Taxpayer time, 55–56, 58
Tax preparer
cost to taxpayer of paid, 27–29
fees of, 155
taxpayer seeks assistance of,
155
Tax protest organizations, 142
Tax rates
effect of, on costs of tax
system, 216–17
effect of, on loopholes, 215–16
effect of, on tax avoidance and
evasion, 213–14
relation of, to tax system costs,
212–13
Tax Reform Act (1976), 65–66
Tax Reform Act (1986)
effect of, on compliance
burden, 154–55
investment tax shelter changes
of, 109
passive loss regulations of, 214
reduction of disincentive cost
by, 158
and Section 89 regulations of
tax code, 174–75, 183
Tax refunds, 49
Tax requirements, 21–22
Tax returns, 156
Tax shelters
charges for investment,
240–41n11
costs of retirement, 111–12
estate, 109–10
social cost of investment, 108
Tax system
based on force, 145
burden of, 1–5, 8–10
changes in, 4

Tax system (*continued*)
  changing attitudes toward,
    158–62
  complexity of, 124–25, 138
  cost of citizen restraint in, 65–66
  costs related to tax rates,
    212–13, 216
  deterrence philosophy of, 70–73
  disincentives in U.S., 87–89
  economist evaluation of, 160
  estimated costs of, 119–23,
    149–51, 179
  factors increasing cost of, 216–17
  forced collection process in,
    67–68
  general litigation cases in, 62–63
  mismanagement of, 10
  moral and emotional costs of,
    9, 69
  operation outside due process
    principle, 75
  overhead cost to operate, 51
  protests against, 142–44
  rulings and determinations by,
    63–64
  selfish attitude toward, 146
  trends in costs of, 123, 154–58
  use of force by, 127–30
Tax yield-to-cost ratio, 50–51
Tidwell, Victor H., 146
Transfer system, government
  costs in, 7–8
  self-subsidy in, 12–13
Treadway, Thomas L., case,
  74–76, 81

Uncertainty, tax policy, 96–98
Underground economy
  estimates of social costs of,
    106–18
  tax avoidance and evasion in,
    104–7
  See also Banking system; Barter;
    Business growth limits

Underreporter program. *See*
  Information Returns Program
  (IRP)
Uniformity principle, 139
U.S. Department of Justice, Tax
  Department, 119–20
U.S. Department of the
  Treasury
  Financial Management Service,
    121
  Offices of Tax Analysis and
    Tax Legislative Counsel, 121
U.S. Senate Finance Committee,
  175–76
U.S. Tax Court
  appealed decisions of, 62
  bargaining system of, 138–39
  cost of, 119
  cost of taxpayer's time for case
    in, 58
  enforcement actions of, 156–57
  increased number of cases in,
    65
  legal costs for cases in, 57
  small cases in system of, 58–59
U.S. Tax Court cases
  audit appeals as, 55
  estimates of costs for, 57–58
  settlement through negotiation
    in, 57
University of Michigan Panel
  Survey on Income Dynamics,
  91

Vedder, Richard, 160
Voluntarism, 144–45

Wealth redistribution, 7
Weil, David, 110
Whalley, John, 93, 94, 95
Wicks, John, 18–19
Witte, John, 160

Yun Kun-Young, 93, 158

About the Author

James L. Payne holds a Ph.D. in political science from the University of California, Berkeley, and has taught at Yale, Wesleyan, Johns Hopkins, and Texas A & M. In 1985 he resigned his professorship at Texas A & M to become an independent scholar and consultant. He is now director of Lytton Research and Analysis in Sandpoint, Idaho. Payne is the author of a pathbreaking study of congressional spending habits, *The Culture of Spending: Why Congress Lives beyond Our Means* (ICS Press, 1991) and has published nine other books and many scholarly and popular articles. His commentary on political issues has appeared in the *Wall Street Journal, Fortune, National Review,* and *Reader's Digest.*